T. J. Crowen

Mrs. Crowen's American Lady's Cookery Book

T. J. Crowen

Mrs. Crowen's American Lady's Cookery Book

ISBN/EAN: 9783744794435

Printed in Europe, USA, Canada, Australia, Japan

Cover: Foto ©Lupo / pixelio.de

More available books at **www.hansebooks.com**

MRS. CROWEN'S
AMERICAN
LADY'S COOKERY BOOK,

COMPRISING EVERY VARIETY OF INFORMATION FOR

ORDINARY AND HOLIDAY OCCASIONS,

AND CONTAINING OVER

1200 ORIGINAL RECEIPTS

FOR PREPARING AND COOKING

SOUPS AND BROTHS, FISH AND OYSTERS, CLAMS, MUSCLES AND SCOL-
LOPS, LOBSTERS, CRABS AND TERRAPINS, MEATS OF ALL KINDS,
POULTRY AND GAME, EGGS AND CHEESE, VEGETABLES AND
SALADS, SAUCES OF ALL KINDS, FANCY DESSERTS, PUD-
DINGS AND CUSTARDS, PIES AND TARTS, BREAD
AND BISCUIT, ROLLS AND CAKES, PRESERVES
AND JELLIES, PICKLES AND CATSUPS,
POTTED MEATS, etc., etc.,

TOGETHER WITH

VALUABLE AND IMPORTANT HINTS, ON CHOOSING AND PURCHASING ALL KINDS OF
PROVISIONS, AND PREPARING RIPE FRUITS FOR TABLE, BILLS OF FARE
FOR THE RELIEF OF YOUNG HOUSEKEEPERS, ARRANGEMENT OF
THE TABLE FOR EVERY VARIETY OF DINNER PARTIES, ETI-
QUETTE OF THE DINNER TABLE, COOKERY FOR
INVALIDS, CARVING MADE EASY, etc.

The whole being a Complete System of American Cookery,

BY MRS. T. J. CROWEN.

ILLUSTRATED WITH SEVERAL DIAGRAMS.

NEW YORK:
DICK & FITZGERALD, PUBLISHERS.

Entered according to Act of Congress, in the year 1847, by

T. J. CROWEN,

in the Clerk's Office of the District Court for the Southern District of New York.

Entered according to Act of Congress, in the year 1866, by

DICK & FITZGERALD,

in the Clerk's Office of the District Court for the Southern District of New York.

For a Complete Index to this work, see page 453.

PREFACE.

The AMERICAN LADY'S COOK BOOK, which was first published under the title of the "American System of Cookery," is now presented with numerous additions and thorough revision. To its already acknowledged practical value, are added a great number of excellent original receipts, enhancing it materially, placing the uninitiated on a par with the most experienced, and offering to the experienced something *new* for every day uses.

The System of Cookery studied and adopted in the preparation of this volume of receipts, is strictly hygenic in its effects, and although particularly adapted to our own country, it is not the less useful for other countries.

Simplicity, that is, adherence to *first principles*, even in the preparation of food, will generally be found to produce the most healthful results. It may not be generally understood, but it is most certainly true, that to prepare simple food is as much a work of art as the mystifications and elaborations of the cuisine, and many persons in this country possessing unlimited means prefer the less luxurious preparations. This book of receipts is recommended particularly to foreign cooks, as it instructs them in many things peculiar to this country, in which books merely compiled from, or imitations of, foreign books, are deficient.

It is hoped that both natives and foreigners will give the present edition a fair trial, and the author trusts it will return them daily satisfaction.

THE

AMERICAN SYSTEM OF COOKERY.

SOUPS.

Soup.—In soup making the greatest care is necessary that the vessel for it be perfectly clean, and free from any grease or sand.

An iron soup-pot must be washed with a teaspoonful of potash or bit of soda the size of a small nutmeg, dissolved in hot water, immediately after using; this will remove all greasiness and taste of onion, or any peculiar taste which might injure the next soup to be made.

An iron pot or well tinned or porcelain kettle is best for soup making.

Soup must have a sufficient time to make;—boil gently, that the meat be tender, and give out its juices.

The pot must not be uncovered more frequently than is necessary for skimming it clear.

The required quantity of salt put in with the meat will cause the scum to rise, and therefore make the soup clearer.

Allow a quart of water and a teaspoonful of salt for each pound of meat.

Soup may be made of any sort of fish, flesh or fowl inferior pieces of meat, such as the neck or scrag, knuckle bone, etc.

Remains of cooked meats of several kinds together make a good soup; for this purpose, the meat should be chopped or cut small, and seasoned with pepper and salt, and hot water, (not boiling,) a quart to each pound of meat put to it; then let it simmer gently for half an hour before putting in the vegetables.

Care should be taken that no one seasoning predominates; for this reason the exact quantity of each sort is specified in the following receipts.

Take off every particle of scum as it rises, and before the vegetables are put in.

The greens and vegetables for soup must be carefully prepared, that is, picked clean and washed.

Where fat soup is not liked, the grease must be skimmed off before putting in the vegetables; it will then be fit for other uses.

Soup meat must be put down in cold water and boiled very gently.

The water in which meat or fowls have been boiled, will make good broth; it is not rich enough for soup without the addition of other meat.

The meat from which soup has been made, is good to serve cold thus: take out all the bones, season with pepper, and salt, and catsup, if liked, then chop it small, tie it in a cloth, and lay it between two plates, with a weight on the upper one: slice it thin for luncheon or supper; or make sandwiches of it; or make a hash for breakfast; or make it in balls, with the addition of a little wheat flour and an egg, and serve them fried in fat, or boiled in the soup.

The vegetables used in soups are carrots, leeks, parsley, turnip, celery, tomatoes, ochras, cabbage, cauliflower, green beans, peas, and potatoes.

One leek, one large carrot, one bunch of parsley, and two turnips for a pot of soup.

One head of celery, one leek, two small turnips, and five or six small potatoes, another.

Five or six tomatoes skinned and the seeds

squeezed out, one leek, a bunch of parsley, and five or six potatoes cut small, another.

Carrot, cabbage, turnip tomatoes, and potatoes, another.

Ochras alone are sufficient vegetable for a dish of soup.

Green peas and new potatoes are enough for lamb soup.

Vermicelli or maccaroni are enough with the usual seasoning for chicken, lamb, or veal soup.

It is well to begin to prepare the vegetables as soon as the meat is put down.

Trim and scrape carrots clean, and cut them across in slices quarter of an inch thick, and notch the edge of each slice neatly, or cut each slice in stars or rings ; or grate it on a coarse grater—grated, it gives a fine amber color to the soup.

Wash parsley and cut it small. Pare turnips and cut them in slices quarter of an inch thick, then divide each slice in halves or quarters. Cut leeks in slices as thick as a dollar piece.

Cut celery in half inch lengths ; the delicate green leaves impart a fine flavor to the soup.

Take the skins from tomatoes, and squeeze out some of the seeds.

Shave cabbage in thin slices.

Slice ochras ; boil cauliflower in water, then cut it small.

Pare potatoes if old, or scrape, if young ones. Slice old potatoes an inch thick, and put them into soup fifteen minutes before it is done.

If the soup is too rich by boiling a long time, make it less so by the addition of boiling water.

Peas, sweet corn cut from the cob, green beans stringed and cut small, or lima beans may be used in soups.

Pearl barley or rice are used as thickening.

Grated carrot gives a fine amber color to soup; it must be put in as soon as the soup is free from scum.

To color soup brown; use browned flour or a little burnt brown sugar in the thickening.

Pounded spinach leaves, give a fine green color to soup. Parsley, or the green leaves of celery put in soup will serve instead of spinach.

Pound a large handful of spinach in a mortar, then tie it in a cloth and wring out all the juice; put this to the soup you wish to color green, five minutes before taking it up.

Mock turtle, and sometimes veal or lamb soups are liked this color.

Ochras give a green color to soups.

To color soup red, skin six red tomatoes, squeeze out the seeds and put them into the soup with the other vegetables—or take the juice only as directed for spinach.

For white soups, which are of veal, lamb or chicken, none but white vegetables are used; rice, pearl barley, vermicelli, or maccaroni for thickening.

To make Portable Soup.—Take about twenty-five pounds of the leg of beef, take off all the skin and fat as well as you can; then take all the meat and sinews clear from bones; put it in a large pot, and put to it four gallons and a half of water, and put it over a gentle fire; then put ten ounces of salt and two and a half of pepper to it; let it boil gently; take off the scum as it rises; peel six onions or as many leeks, and add them to it, with a small bundle of thyme, and a dry hard crust of bread; stir it well together, cover the pot close, and let it simmer gently for four or five hours, then uncover it and stir it together again, after which cover it close; and let it boil until it is a rich strong jelly, which you will know by taking a little now and then in a saucer to cool; when you find it so, take it off and strain it through a coarse muslin bag; press it hard, then strain it through a coarse hair sieve into a large earthen pan, and when it is quite cold take off the scum and fat, and take the jelly clear from settlings at the bottom, then put it in a large well-tinned stew-pan; and set it on a stove with a slow fire; keep stirring it often, and take care that it neither sticks to the pan or burns.

When you find the jelly very stiff and thick, as it will be, in lumps about the pan, take it out and put it in large deep earthenware cups; set the cups in a pan, and fill it with boiling water nearly to the top of the cups, taking care that no water gets into them; keep it boiling very gently all the time, add more boiling water as it wastes away, until you find the jelly like a stiff glue; take out the cups, and when they are cool, turn out the glue on a coarse new flannel; let it lay eight or nine hours, then put in the sun until it is quite hard and dry. Put it in boxes of tin, with writing paper between the pieces, and keep them in a dry cool place; let the boxes be covered with a close fitting cover.

When wanted for use, pour boiling water on to it, and stir it all the time until it is melted. A piece the size of a hickory nut will make a pint of water very rich. Boil celery or any vegetable you like in the water before putting in the glue; when it is dissolved let it boil up once.

A small bit dissolved in boiling water makes a fine broth.

OYSTER SOUP.—Take of water and milk, each three pints; set it on the fire to boil; roll half a pound of butter crackers, or soda biscuit fine, and add to the milk and water with a pint of oysters chopped fine; let it boil until the flavor of the oyster is given to the soup, and the crackers are well swelled, then add salt and pepper to taste, and three pints more of the oysters, with a quarter of a pound of sweet butter; cover it for ten minutes more, then serve it in a tureen. A small saltspoonful of cayenne pepper added to it when the oysters are put in, is by most persons considered an improvement.

ANOTHER OYSTER SOUP.—Take a knuckle of veal or a leg of lamb; allow a quart of water and a teaspoonful of salt to each pound; set it over a gentle fire and let it simmer (after having come to a boil) for at least two hours; skim it clear, then put to it half a pound of rolled crackers, pepper and salt to taste, and a quart of oysters. Let it boil up once, then add a bit of butter the size of a large egg, and serve without the meat. Vermicelli or maccaroni may be used instead of crackers for this soup if preferred.

LOBSTER SOUP.—After having boiled a lobster, take it from the shell, roll two or three crackers, and put them to the meat, which must be cut small—put of milk and water, each a quart, into a stewpan, with a tablespoonful of salt and a teaspoonful of pepper; when it is boiling hot, add the lobster, cut small, and the green inside if liked, and a quarter of a pound of sweet butter; let it boil closely covered for half an hour; break a dozen butter crackers, or six or seven soda biscuit, into a tureen, pour the soup over and serve.

CABBAGE AND MILK SOUP.—Cut a large white-heart cabbage in quarters, first taking off the outside leaves, put it in two quarts of boiling water, cover it, and set it over a fire for half an hour; then take out half of the water, add three pints of boiling milk, quarter of a pound of sweet butter, and pepper and salt to taste; cover it for ten minutes; cut slices of delicately toasted bread, in squares or lozenges, (first taking off the crust,) put them in a tureen and pour the soup over—or, instead of toast, use broken soda biscuit.

Ox-head Soup.—Take the skin and eyes from an ox head; put half of it in cold water over night, then break the bones and wash it in warm water; put it in a soup-kettle with water more than to cover it, let it boil gently; salt it and skim it clear, and when the meat is tender, add two turnips sliced, a grated or sliced carrot, one leek or one or two sliced white onions, five or six potatoes cut small, and salt and pepper to taste; then cover and stew gently until the meat parts from the bones; then take out the meat and bones, and serve the soup in a tureen. If the soup is richer than is liked, add boiling water.

Pick all the meat from the bones, season with pepper, salt, and made mustard, chop it small, tie it in a cloth and press it between two plates. When cold, it is fine for supper or sandwich, sliced thin.

Green Pea Soup.—Wash a small quarter of lamb in cold water, and put it into a soup-pot with six quarts of cold water; add to it two tablespoonfuls of salt, and set it over a moderate fire—let it boil gently for two hours, then skim it clear; add a quart of shelled peas, and a teaspoonful of pepper; cover it, and let it boil for half an hour, then having scraped the skins from a quart of small young potatoes, add them to the soup; cover the

2

pot, and let it boil for half an hour longer; work quarter of a pound of butter, and a dessert spoonful of flour together, and add them to the soup ten or twelve minutes before taking it off the fire.

Serve the meat on a dish with parsley sauce over, and the soup in a tureen.

ANOTHER GREEN PEA SOUP.—Put two-pounds of veal, or lamb cutlets or steaks, and quarter of a pound of salt fat pork, sliced thin, into two quarts of water, set it over a moderate fire; when it boils, skim it clear, add a quart of shelled peas and a dozen small new potatoes (their skins scraped off), cover it close for nearly an hour, or until the peas are tender, then add half a teacup of sweet butter, with a heaping teaspoonful of wheat flour worked into it, and pepper to taste; if the pork is not sufficient, add more salt.

Serve in a tureen, without the meat. Shelled Lima beans may be used in their season instead of peas.

TURTLE SOUP.—Cut the head off the turtle the day before you dress it, and place the body so as to drain it well from blood; then cut it up in the following manner: divide the back, belly, head and fins, from the intestines and lean parts; take care to cut the gall clean out without breaking—scald in boiling water the first named parts so as to take off the skin and shell; cut them in neat square pieces and throw them into cold water; boil the back and belly in a little water long enough to extract the bones easily, then make a good stock of a leg of veal, a slice of ham, and the flesh of the inside of the turtle; let it do away until it is browned, then fill it up with water, and the liquor and bones of the boiled turtle. Season with sliced lemon, whole pepper, a bunch of parsley, a leek sliced, and salt to taste. Let it boil slowly for four hours, then strain it to the pieces of back, belly, head and fins of the turtle (take the bones from the fins); add to it half a pint of Madeira wine and quarter of a pound of fresh sweet butter, with a tablespoonful of flour worked into it, and a lemon sliced thin; let it boil gently for two hours, then serve.

In cutting up the turtle, the fat should be taken great care of; it should be separated and cut in neat pieces, and stewed tender in a little of the soup, and put into the tureen when ready to serve.

CATFISH OR BULLHEAD SOUP.—Cut the heads from two pounds of fish, skin and clean them, and wash them well; cut them in pieces, and put with them one pound of fat ham or salt pork, some pepper, and two quarts of water; let it boil until the fish is tender; beat two fresh eggs with two teaspoonfuls of flour and a gill of milk, stir it into the soup, add a tablespoonful of butter, let it boil together for a few minutes, then take out the ham or pork, and serve in a tureen.

Eel soup may be made in the same manner, or like lobster soup.

SOUP WITHOUT MEAT.—Put two quarts of water in a stew-pan with a penny roll cut up, add a teaspoonful of salt and a white onion or two, cut small, cover it close and let it boil for half an hour; then add the white part of a bunch of celery, cut small, and quarter of a pound of sweet butter—add pepper to taste; cover it, and let it boil for half an hour longer; break half a pound of crackers into a tureen, pour the soup over, and serve.

Soup Maigre.—Melt half a pound of butter in a stew-pan, slice six onions into it, add two heads of celery, cut small, one small cabbage, and a bunch of parsley, cut small; shake these together over the fire for fifteen minutes, then stir in three rolled crackers; add further, two quarts of boiling milk or water, and pepper and salt to taste; let it boil gently for three quarters of an hour, then take it from the fire, stir into it two well beaten eggs, and serve.

Mock Turtle Soup.—Clean and wash a calf's head, split it in two, save the brains, boil the head until tender in plenty of water; put a slice of fat ham, a bunch of parsley cut small, a sprig of thyme, two leeks cut small, six cloves, a teaspoonful of pepper, and three ounces of butter, into a stew-pan, and fry them a nice brown; then add the water in which the head was boiled, cut the meat from the head in neat square pieces, and put them to the soup; add a pint of Madeira and one lemon sliced thin, add cayenne pepper and salt to taste; let it simmer gently for two hours, then skim it clear and serve.

Make a forcemeat of the brains as follows: put them in a stew-pan, pour hot water over, and set it over the fire for a few minutes, then take them up, chop them small, with a sprig of parsley, a saltspoonful of salt and pepper each, a tablespoonful of wheat flour, the same of butter, and one well-beaten egg; make it in small balls, and drop them in the soup fifteen minutes before it is taken from the fire; in making the balls, a little more flour may be necessary. Egg balls may also be added.

Green Bean Soup.—String half a peck or less of young green beans, cut them in pieces an inch long, and finish the same as directed for green pea soup.

SPLIT PEAS SOUP.—Put a quart of split peas in water to cover them, at night, with half a teaspoonful of saleratus; next day take them from the water in which they were soaked, and put to them two quarts of water and a pound of salt pork, with a bone of beef; let it boil gently until the peas are tender, then add five or six potatoes, and pepper to taste.; cover it for fifteen minutes, then add a tablespoonful of butter and flour each, worked together—cover it until the potatoes are done, which will be about fifteen minutes: serve in a tureen.

DRIED BEAN SOUP.—Make the same as split peas soup.

FISH SOUP.—Take different sorts of small fish, steam them until tender; them add some veal broth, cut two turnips in slices, also one leek and one head of celery; let it boil for half an hour, then strain it, or take out the bones; season with pepper and salt, work a table-spoonful of wheat flour, with quarter of a pound of butter, add egg balls.; cover for ten minutes and serve.

CHICKEN SOUP, (*Yellow.*)—Take two pounds of veal or lamb, and one small chicken cut up; boil these in three quarts of water, skim it clear; slice a leek, or two white onions, grate two small or one large carrot, and put to the soup; add two tablespoonsful of salt and one of pepper; let it boil gently for nearly two hours, then add a table-spoonful of butter, and the same of flour worked together, cover it for fifteen minutes and serve it in a tureen.

Take the chicken into a deep dish. add butter

and pepper to it, and serve garnished with sprigs of parsley. The meat may be made in balls and put in the soup; chop it fine; add a tablespoonful of butter and flour each, and a saltspoonful of pepper, with one beaten egg; dip your hands in flour, and make the preparation in balls, drop them into soup with the butter and flour.

CHICKEN SOUP, *(White.)*—Make as directed for yellow soup, without the carrot; season with pepper and salt only; put a cup of well washed rice or pearl barley as soon as it is clear from scum; when nearly done add a tablespoonful of butter and flour, each worked together; let it boil for ten minutes longer, then serve.

ONION SOUP.—Put a quarter of a pound of butter in a stew-pan, with six large white onions cut in slices, let them fry a nice brown, then add six crackers rolled, pepper to taste, and a quart of boiling water; let it simmer for fifteen minutes, and serve.

ANOTHER ONION SOUP.—Put half a pound of butter into a stew-pan and let it boil; have ready ten or twelve large onions, peeled and cut in slices, put them into the butter and fry to a nice brown, sprinkle in a tablespoonful of flour, shake the pan often, and keep it over the fire for ten minutes, then add three pints of boiling milk, stir it well. cut some pie paste in slips and drop them in; add salt to taste; let it boil for ten minutes, stirring it frequently, then take it from the fire, work the yolks of two hard boiled eggs with a tablespoonful of vinegar, first mix a little of the soup with this, then stir it into the remainder.

SHIN OF BEEF SOUP. 23

HARE SOUP.—Skin and clean a hare, then cut it up; season with salt and pepper, and fry a nice brown with lard or butter; then put it in a soup-pot, with two onions sliced and fried, a bunch of parsley fried, and enough hot water to cover it; let it simmer gently for half an hour, then add two or three blades of mace, a glass or two of Maderia or port wine, a tablespoonful of browned flour worked into a small teacup of butter; let it simmer for half an hour, and serve.

The bones of poultry added to this soup while boiling, and taken out before serving, will improve it. A teaspoonful of made mustard may be added.

A chicken, or old fowl, or duck soup, may be made in the same manner.

SHIN OF BEEF SOUP.—Get a shin bone of beef weighing four or five pounds; let the butcher saw it in pieces about two inches long, that the marrow may become the better incorporated with the soup, and so give it greater richness.

Wash the meat in cold water; mix together of salt and pepper each a tablespoonful, rub this well into the meat, then put into a soup-pot; put to it as many quarts of water as there are pounds of meat, and set it over a moderate fire, until it comes to a boil, then take off whatever scum may have risen, after which cover it close; and set it where it will boil very gently for two hours longer; then skim it again, and add to it the proper vegetables which are these—one large carrot grated, one large turnip cut in slices, (the yellow or ruta baga is best) one leek cut in slices, one bunch of parsley cut small, six small potatoes peeled and cut in half, and a teacupful of pearl barley well washed; then cover it and let it boil gently for one hour, at which time add another tablespoonful of salt and a thickening made of a tablespoonful of wheat flour and a gill of water stir it in by the spoonful; cover it for fifteen minutes and it is done.

Three hours and a half is required to make this soup: it is best for cold weather. Should any remain over the first day, it may be heated with the addition of a little boiling water, and served again.

Take the meat from the soup, and if to be served with it, take out the bones, and lay it closely and neatly on a dish, and garnish with sprigs of parsley; serve made mustard and catsup with it. It is very nice pressed and eaten with mustard and vinegar or catsup.

In making this soup there may be this variation: instead of the last thickening, make a batter of two well-beaten eggs, half a pint of milk, and as much wheat flour as will make a smooth batter, about as thick as pound cake; drop it by the spoonful into the boiling soup, until all is used, then cover it for fifteen minutes. This is called egg dumplings.

BEEF SOUP.—Take four pounds of beef, for four quarts of water, and finish with any vegetables you like, the same as shin-of-beef soup, or as follows—

Take two tablespoonsful of salt, and one of pepper, (fine black) rub it well into the meat, then put it over a moderate fire, with one quart of water; let it boil very gently for one hour, then add three quarts of boiling water, cover it close, skim it clear and let it boil very gently for another hour, in which time prepare the vegetables as follows—One large carrot scraped and cut in thin slices, one large or two small turnips cut in the same manner, six small potatoes of equal size cut in halves, and one head of celery, leaves and white part cut small; the carrots and turnips should be sliced about one-third of an inch thick.

When the first hour is up, put in the carrots, fifteen minutes after add the turnips and celery; after another fifteen minutes, put in the potatoes and a thickening made of two tablespoonsful of flour and as much cold water as will make a smooth thin batter; stir it in by the spoonful; cover the pot for fifteen minutes; let it boil, and as soon as the potatoes are tender it is done. Soup should not be taken off the fire whilst making.

BEEF BROTH.—Take four pounds of beef, crack the bone in two or three places, wash it in cold water, and put it with a gallon of water over a moderate fire; add to it a heaping tablespoonful of salt, and a teaspoonful of pepper; let it boil slowly, take off the scum as it rises; in two hours add a bunch of parsley cut small, or a head of celery, let it simmer for an hour longer.

Toast some slices of bread a delicate brown, cut it in squares or lozenges, put them in a tureen, and pour the soup over.

A cup of pearl barley, well washed, and put in with the meat will be liked by invalids; or vermicelli or maccaroni stewed tender in it, is both healthful and palateable.

A leek, or two or three tomatoes may be added to the broth.

VEAL OR LAMB SOUP.—The scrag or neck of veal or lamb, or the leg, is best for making soup. A slice of corned pork or ham is an improvement to veal or lamb soup.

For four pounds of meat allow four quarts of water; wash the meat in cold water, trim off the rough ends, and shape it neatly, then put it and the odd bits into a soup pot with a quart of cold water, a heaping tablespoonful of salt and a tea-

B

spoonful of fine pepper; cover it close, and let it simmer gently for one hour, then skim it clear; add three quarts of boiling water, and let it boil gently for one hour longer; then skim it again, and add sliced ochras, or any other vegetables which may be preferred—a leek sliced, a bunch of parsley cut small, and a carrot grated or cut in slices and the edges neatly notched; or a bunch of asparagus, the tops and green parts cut the size of peas or a little larger. These vegetables should be put in half an hour before the soup is done. Three hours will be required for making the soup; if asparagus is used, toast some thin slices of bread, butter them freely, cut them small, and put them in the tureen before putting in the soup.

For suitable combinations of vegetables, see introductory remarks.

Take up the meat by itself, and serve with drawn butter sauce and mashed potatoes.

The bones of poultry or cold roast beef put in with the meat to make the soup, and taken out before serving, improves the flavor of veal or lamb soup; cold fried or broiled steaks, whether of beef or lamb, may be added to the soup and improve it.

Vermicelli, maccaroni, green peas, ochras or tomatoes, may be used in these soups; a tablespoonful of sweet butter, with a heaping teaspoonful of flour worked into it, should be stirred into the soup, ten minutes before taking it from the fire.

Calf's Head Soup.—Get a cleaned calf's head, split it open, and save the brains to make forcemeat balls; put it in a soup-pot with five quarts of water, add to it a heaping tablespoonful of salt and a teaspoonful of pepper, set it over a moderate fire and take off the scum as it rises. After three hours, take out the head, take the bones from it, cut the best of it in square pieces, skin the tongue and cut it in slices, and return it to the soup; now add the vegetables, which are these: one head of celery cut small, one leek sliced thin, one large, or two small carrots sliced thin and the edges neatly notched, and six equal sized small potatoes, pared and cut in halves; cover the pot for half an hour; then work two tablespoonfuls of butter with the same of flour and stir it into the soup. Make forcemeat balls of the brains, thus: scald them and chop them small, add a teaspoonful of butter and the same of wheat flour, season with pepper and salt, and make it in small balls; flour the outside of each, and drop them into the boiling soup about fifteen minutes before it is done.

The soup may be served without the meat, except the tongue and balls—the meat may, in such case, be chopped and seasoned with pepper and salt to taste; then tie it in a muslin bag and press it between two plates until cold; serve sliced thin for sandwiches or supper—or make it a hash for breakfast.

CHICKEN BROTH.—Cut up a full grown chicken, put to it three pints of cold water, a tablespoonful of salt, and half a teacup of pearl barley (or rice if preferred); cover it close and let it simmer for an hour, then skim it clear, add pepper to taste; take the chicken into a dish, put bits of sweet butter over, shake some pepper over, and serve with mashed potatoes—serve the soup in a tureen.

The barley or rice may be omitted, and five or six rolled crackers, with a tablespoonful of butter, substituted when the broth is nearly done.

VEAL BROTH.—Boil gently a knuckle of veal in five pints of water; put to it a tablespoonful of salt, and half a teacup of well-washed rice or pearl barley; let it simmer gently for nearly three hours, taking off the scum as it rises; add pepper to taste.

Instead of pearl barley or rice, vermicelli or rolled cracker may be used, or bread toasted and cut small and put in the tureen.

VERMICELLI SOUP.—Swell quarter of a pound of vermicelli in a quart of warm water, then add it to a good beef, veal, lamb or chicken soup or broth with quarter of a pound of sweet butter; let the soup boil for fifteen minutes after it is added.

TO MAKE EGG DUMPLINGS FOR SOUP.—To half a pint of milk put two well-beaten eggs, and as much wheat flour as will make a smooth, rather thick batter free from lumps; drop this batter, a tablespoonful at a time, into boiling soup.

EGG BALLS FOR SOUP.—Take the yolks of six hard boiled eggs and half a tablespoonful of wheat flour, rub them smooth with the yolks of two raw eggs and a teaspoonful of salt; mix all well together, make it in balls and drop them into the boiling soup a few minutes before taking it up.

MACCARONI SOUP.—To a rich beef or other soup, in which there is no seasoning other than pepper or salt, take half a pound of small pipe maccaroni, boil it in clear water until it is tender, then drain it and cut it in pieces of an inch length, boil it for fifteen minutes in the soup and serve.

MUTTON BROTH.—Take a scrag of mutton, cut it in thick slices, and rub each with pepper and salt; then put them into a soup-pot; allow a quart of water to each pound of meat, and cover the pot close; take off the fat and scum as it rises; after one hour add half a teacup of rice or pearl barley, one leek sliced thin, one turnip sliced, and any other vegetable which may be liked; let it boil slowly for nearly an hour longer, then serve.

CLAM SOUP.—Take fifty large or one hundred small sand clams, and their liquor from the shells; strain the liquor; add to it a quart of milk and water each; if the clams are large, cut each in two and put them into it; set them over a moderate fire until the clams are tender; (about one hour,) skim it clear; put to it half a pound of soda crackers broken small, or half a pound of butter crackers rolled fine; cover the pot for ten minutes, then add quarter of a pound of sweet butter, and serve hot.

SAVOY SOUP.—Remove the outside leaves, cut in quarters and boil in clear water two small heads of Savoy cabbage; when tender drain off, and press all the water from them; then put them to as much beef broth as will cover them: put it into a closely covered stew-pan or soup-pot over a moderate fire for one hour; set on the fire a large frying-pan with a quarter of a pound of sweet butter; let it become hot; shake flour from a dredging box over it, until the whole surface is white, then stir it until it becomes brown, taking care not to burn it; cut two large white onions into it, and fry them; as soon as they are nicely colored, add it to the soup; soak some crackers or sliced rolls in a quart of boiling milk or water and add it to the soup.

Veal or chicken broth may be used for this soup.

STOCK FOR GRAVY SOUP OR GRAVY.—Cut the

meat from a knuckle of veal, and put it with a pound of lean beef, into two quarts of water; add one tablespoonful of salt, and a teaspoonful of pepper; cover it close and let it stew until very tender, then strain it and use for soup or gravy.

CABBAGE SOUP.—Boil five pounds of corned or salt beef in five quarts of water, very gently for one hour, and skim it clear, then add two small heads of cabbage cut in quarters and well washed, (examine carefully, as insects are sometimes concealed between the leaves;) when it is done tender, which it will be in about forty minutes, take out the largest pieces, and drain them in a cullender, put them in a covered dish, over a pot of boiling water to keep it hot; as soon as the meat is tender, take that up also, (try it by sticking a fork into it, if when you twist the fork the meat breaks, it is enough,) put it between two plates to press, and set it over a pot of hot water to keep hot; add to the soup two or three turnips peeled and sliced; one large or two small carrots sliced or grated, and an onion or leek sliced also; six or eight equal sized potatoes peeled neatly; let it boil for half an hour when the vegetables will be done; stir into it a batter made of a tablespoonful of wheat flour and cold water; cover it for ten minutes and it is done.

Then take the potatoes into a dish and serve the soup in a tureen.

Thus you have a dish of meat, a tureen of soup, and potatoes and cabbage accompanying vegetables. These constitute, with some simple dessert, a good family dinner.

VEGETABLE SOUP, *(Summer.)*—Take three or four young carrots, three young turnips, and one leek scrape the carrots and peel the turnips, and cut them in thin slices; cut each slice of turnip in four; put them in two quarts of broth seasoned with salt and pepper to taste; cover it, and let them boil for fifteen minutes, then add a head of white lettuce cut small, and a bunch of parsley broken up; cover it and let them boil for fifteen minutes longer, and it is done.

SOUP IN HASTE.—Chop some cold cooked meat very fine, and put a pint of it with some gravy or a bit of butter into a stew-pan; season with pepper and salt; dredge over an even tablespoonful of flour, then add a quart or more of boiling water; cover it close, and set it over a moderate fire for half an hour; then strain it through a coarse cloth, toast some thin slices of bread delicately brown, cut them in small squares or diamonds, put them into a tureen and pour the soup over. This soup may be made of uncooked meat in the same manner; a quart of water to a pound of meat makes a rich soup.

Maccaroni or vermicelli boiled tender may be put to the soup ten or twelve minutes before taking it up; carrots sliced thin and cut in stars, with turnips and new potatoes, boiled tender in clear water and added to the soup fifteen minutes before taking it up. Also a few stalks of celery with the delicate green leaves cut small, or a bunch of parsley put in at the same time, make a fine delicate soup.

BROWNING FOR SOUPS AND GRAVIES.—Put two or three tablespoonfuls of brown sugar into a frying-pan, set it on the fire to brown, stirring with a spoon that it may not burn; when sufficiently dark colored, stir into it about a pint of boiling water; when it is thoroughly incorporated, put it into a bottle, and when cold, cork it close. Use a tablespoonful or more as may be wanted to give color to gravies or soup. Or put wheat flour into a frying pan and brown it carefully without burning. Keep it dry in a box.

FISH.

INTRODUCTORY REMARKS.—There are general rules for choosing fish of most sorts.

If the gills are red and full, and the whole fish firm and stiff, it is good.

If on the contrary, the gills are brownish, the eyes sunk, and the flesh flabby, they are stale.

One who is not a judge of fish, had better not trust to their own choice, but deal with those on whose word they can rely. Let such choose for you, it will be to their interest to serve you honestly.

Great care must be taken to see that the fish be properly cleaned before dressing; that is, they must be perfectly free from scales, and every particle of the inside scraped from the backbone; but not washed beyond what is really necessary, as that diminishes the flavor of most fish.

To boil fish, put it on the drainer of a fish-kettle and cover it with water just hot; let it boil gently, otherwise the skin will break before the inside is done.

Allow ten minutes for each pound of fish, unless it is very thick, then allow a few minutes longer. Small fish weighing a pound and a half or so will require about fifteen minutes. To try it, pass a knife blade next the bone; if the flesh parts easily, and looks white, it is done.

If fish is not taken from the water as soon as done it will become woolly; if it is done before it is wanted, take it up, set the drainer crosswise of the kettle, and lay a folded napkin over the fish.

A suitable kettle for boiling or stewing fish is very necessary, and may be had from any of the hardware or furnishing stores. In the absence of a fish kettle, put the fish in a circle on a dinner plate, and tie a napkin over it, then put in a large kettle. When done take it up carefully by the cloth, drain off all the water, take off the napkin and slide the fish on a white napkin, neatly folded on a large dish; garnish with sprigs of parsley, and serve.

Fresh shad, haddock, and whiting are considered by some persons better for salting a night before cooking.

Fresh water fish have often a muddy taste and smell, which may be got rid of by soaking in strong salt and water.

To FRY OR BROIL FISH PROPERLY.—After the fish is well cleansed, lay it on a folded towel and dry out all the water. When well wiped and dry, roll it in wheat flour, rolled crackers, grated stale bread, or Indian meal, whichever may be preferred; wheat flour will generally be liked.

Have a thick-bottomed frying-pan or spider, with plenty of sweet lard salted; (a tablespoonful of salt to each pound of lard,) for fresh fish which have not been previously salted; let it become boiling hot, then lay the fish in and let it fry gently, until one side is a fine delicate brown, then turn the other; when both are done, take it up carefully and serve quickly, or keep it covered with a tin cover, and set the dish where it will keep hot.

To BROIL.—Have a clean gridiron, and a clear but not fierce fire of coals; rub the bars with a bit of beef suet, that the fish may not stick; fish must be broiled gently and thoroughly; there are few things more offensive than underdone fish.

For the broil, have ready a dish with a good bit of butter in which is worked a little salt and pepper, enough for the fish. Lay the fish upon it, when both sides are nicely done, and with a knife blade put the butter over every part; fish should be turned with a broad blade knife, or a pancake turner.

All salt fish require to be soaked in cold water before cooking, according to the time it has been in salt. When it is hard and dry, it will require thirty-six hours soaking, before dressing; the water must be changed three or four times. When fish is not very salt or hard, twenty-four hours will be sufficient.

For frying fish, beef suet or dripping or sweet oil may be used instead of lard; butter is not good, it spoils the color and tastes strong.

Fish have a fine appearance prepared in the following manner: clean and wash them, and wipe them dry with a nice soft towel; then wet them over with beaten egg, and dip them in bread crumbs or rolled crackers. If done twice over with the egg and cracker or crumbs, it will have a finer appearance.

The largest sized pan fish, weighing nearly or quite a pound each, should be scored or cut across each side from the head to the tail, nearly to the bone, and about an inch apart, that it may be well done. Garnish with sprigs of parsley. Have ready a thick bottomed frying pan, with plenty of lard salted; let it become boiling hot; lay the fish carefully in, and let them fry gently, until one side is a rich yellow brown, then turn the other and do likewise: when both are done take them carefully up on a hot dish, and serve. Garnish with fried parsley.

DRIED CODFISH.—This should always be laid in soak, at least one night before it is wanted; then take off the skin and put it in plenty of cold water; boil it gently, (skimming it meanwhile) for one hour, or tie it in a cloth and boil it.

Serve with egg sauce; garnish with hard boiled eggs cut in slices, and sprigs of parsley. Serve plain boiled or mashed potatoes with it.

STEWED SALT COD.—Scald some soaked cod by putting it over the fire in boiling water for ten minutes; then scrape it white, pick it in flakes, and put it in a stew-pan, with a tablespoonful of butter worked into the same of flour, and as much milk as will moisten it; let it stew gently for ten minutes; add pepper to taste, and serve hot; put it in a deep dish, slice hard boiled eggs over, and sprigs of parsley around the edge.

This is a nice relish for breakfast, with coffee and tea, and rolls or toast.

CODFISH CAKES.—First boil soaked cod, then chop it fine, put to it an equal quantity of potatoes boiled and mashed; moisten it with beaten eggs or milk, and a bit of butter and a little pepper; form it in small, round cakes, rather more than half an inch thick; flour the outside, and fry in hot lard or beef drippings until they are a delicate brown: like fish, these must be fried gently, the lard being boiling hot when they are put in; when one side is done turn the other. Serve for breakfast.

TO MAKE A DISH OF COLD BOILED COD.—Chop fine some cold boiled cod, put to it an equal quantity or more of boiled potatoes chopped or mashed; add a good bit of butter and milk to make it moist, and put it in a stew-pan over a gentle fire; cover it, and stir it frequently until it is thoroughly heated; taking care that it does not burn; then take it up, make it in a roll or any other form, mark the surface, take a pinch of ground pepper between your finger and thumb, and put spots at equal distances over it; or wet it over with melted butter, and brown it in an oven before the fire.

Fresh Cod.—Fresh cod when good, are firm, and the gills red, and the eyes are full; if at all soft or flabby it is not good. A fine fish is thick at the back; the shoulder or piece near the head of a large cod is better for boiling than a small fish.

To Boil Fresh Cod.—If you have not a fish kettle, after cleaning the fish carefully, lay it on a plate in a circle, and tie a clean towel about it; to a gallon of hot water put a tablespoonful of salt and a gill of vinegar; put in the fish and boil according to its weight.

Serve with plain boiled potatoes and drawn butter, parsley, or egg sauce.

Garnish with sprigs of parsley; lay a folded napkin on the dish under the fish.

Broiled Fresh Cod.—Split a fresh codfish from head to tail by the backbone; cut each side into pieces about three inches wide; dip each piece in flour and broil it over a clear brisk fire of coals; lay the inside to the fire first. Have ready a steak dish, with a quarter of a pound of butter, in which is worked of salt and pepper each a teaspoonful; lay the pieces of fish on as they are done; turn them two or three times in the butter and serve. Or let the fish be cut across in steaks, of an inch in thickness, and finish in the same manner.

Fried Codfish Steaks.—Cut the fish in steaks of about one inch thickness: or it may be, split as for broiling; dip each piece in wheat flour, or rolled cracker, or Indian meal; have some lard, (which is salted in proportion, a tablespoonful of salt to a pound,) let it become boiling hot in a frying-pan; lay in the steaks; let them fry gently, without stirring them, until one side is a fine brown, then turn each steak carefully with a broad knife; when both sides are done, serve hot, with sprigs of parsley over it.

BAKED COD.—Clean a good sized fish, weighing four or five pounds; wash it and dry it well in a cloth; rub it inside and out with a mixture of pepper and salt; cut a slice from a loaf of bread, spread it thickly with butter; moisten it with hot water, and fill the body of the fish; tie a thread around it to keep the dressing in, then put bits of butter, the size of a hickory nut, all over the surface; dredge flour over it until it looks white; then lay a trivet or some muffin rings in a dripping-pan, and lay the fish on; put in a pint of water to baste with, then put it in a hot oven and baste frequently; in one hour it will be done. Take it up on a hot dish, add a gill of vinegar to the gravy, or a lemon cut in very thin slices; dredge in a little flour; let it boil up once; stir it well; add a very little hot water if necessary, then strain it into a gravy boat, lay the sliced lemon over the fish, and serve.

HADDOCK.—These are chosen and dressed the same as cod.

SHAD.—These are in season from the last of March until May; they are chosen by the same rules as other fish.

These fish may be fried, baked, boiled, or salted.

FRIED SHAD.—Scale the fish, and cut off the head, then split it open down the back, at the side of the backbone; take out the entrails; keep the roe or eggs to be fried with the fish; then cut it in two from head to tail, and cut each side in pieces, two or three inches wide; rinse them in cold water, wipe them dry, and dip each in wheat flour, and fry in salted lard; when the inside, which must always be cooked first, (of any fish) is done a fine brown, turn the other; the fat must be boiling hot when the fish is put in, and then fried gently, that it may not be too dark colored.

The soft roe is much liked by some; fry it in the same manner, as also the eggs; these last must be well done.

BROILED SHAD.—Cut the fish the same as for frying, or merely split it in two; lay it on a gridiron over a bright steady fire of coals; let it broil gently; put the inside to the fire first, that it may be done through; have ready a steak dish with nearly a quarter of a pound of sweet butter, and a teaspoonful of salt and pepper each, worked into it: when both sides of the fish are done, lay it on the dish, turn it several times in the butter, cover it with a tin cover, and set the dish where it will keep hot, until ready to serve.

BAKED SHAD.—Scale the shad clean, cut off the head, and split the fish half way down the back; scrape the inside perfectly clean; make a stuffing thus: cut two slices of a baker's loaf of wheat bread, spread each thickly with butter; sprinkle with pepper and salt, and a little pounded sage if liked; moisten it with hot water; fill the belly with this; wind a cord around it to keep in the stuffing; dredge the outside well with flour; stick bits of butter, the size of a hickory nut all over the outside; mix a teaspoonful each of salt and pepper together, and sprinkle it over the whole surface; then lay the fish on a trivet or muffin rings in a dripping pan; put in a pint of water to baste with, and keep the gravy from burning; if this all wastes before the fish is done, add more hot water; bake for one hour in a quick oven; baste frequently. When done take the fish on a steak dish; if there is not enough gravy in the pan, (there should be at least half a pint,) add more hot water; dredge in a heaping teaspoonful of flour, then put to it a bit of butter, and, if liked, a lemon sliced thin, and the seeds taken out. Stir it smooth with a spoon, and pour it through a gravy strainer into a gravy boat; lay the slices of lemon over the fish, and serve with mashed potatoes.

SEA BASS.—These fish may be fried or boiled. If fried, garnish with fried parsley. The largest of them for frying, weighing nearly a pound each, must be scored as directed in introduction to this chapter.

For boiling, serve with plain boiled potatoes, and drawn butter, or parsley, or lemon sauce.

BLACK FISH.—These fish may be boiled, fried, stewed, or broiled.

To FRY BLACK FISH.—Scale the fish, and scrape the inside clean to the back bone; wash it in water, with a little vinegar; wipe it dry with a clean towel; then dip it in wheat flour, or rolled crackers. Have in a thick-bottomed frying-pan plenty of lard salted, (a large tablespoon of salt to a pound of lard); let it become boiling hot; then lay in the fish, and fry it gently, until one side is a fine brown; then turn it carefully. When both sides are done, take it up and serve.

Fried fish may be garnished or ornamented with

sprigs of green or fried parsley, or thin slices of lemon, fried.

Stewed Black Fish.—Put a fish weighing about five pounds on a fish-drainer; after having properly cleansed it, put it into the fish-kettle with hot water to cover it; add to it a few blades of mace, a large teaspoonful of salt, and a wineglass of port wine; let it simmer or boil gently for half an hour; then skim it clear; work into a smooth mass quarter of a pound of sweet butter, and a heaping tablespoonful of wheat flour; take from the fish part of the water in which it was boiled, leaving it scarcely covered; then add the flour and butter, with a teaspoonful of pepper; dip a bunch of parsley into boiling water, cut it small, and add it to the stew; cover it close for twenty minutes, and let it simmer gently; then take the fish up on a dish, and serve with the gravy or sauce over. A sliced lemon without the pits may be added with the parsley by those who like it. Serve with plain boiled or mashed potatoes.

Black-fish dressed in this manner is very delicious.

To stew smaller fish, lay them in a dripping-pan with enough hot water to cover them; add a teaspoonful of salt, and two or three blades of mace, and half a wineglass of vinegar or Madeira wine; set it in an oven, or over a fire; cover the pan, and let them boil gently for fifteen minutes; then add, for four or five pounds of fish, quarter of a pound of butter, with a tablespoonful of flour worked into it, or rolled crackers, a bunch of parsley, scalded and cut small, and a teaspoonful of pure fine pepper; let them simmer for ten minutes after the seasoning is added, and they are done. Serve with the sauce over, and plain boiled or mashed potatoes.

To Boil Black Fish.—See directions for fresh codfish. Serve with drawn butter, or parsley sauce.

Perch.—Clean these fish well, wash, and wipe them dry, then fry them as directed. See p. 33-34.

Striped Bass.—These fish are best fried or boiled. See directions for boiling or frying fish.

Halibut.—This fish is fine, whether cut in steaks, and broiled, or fried; or the thick part boiled. Fry or broil as directed for codfish. Steaks or fillets cut from the tail part are very fine, and may be fried or broiled more nicely than any other.

To Boil Halibut.—Take a piece weighing four or five pounds, scrape the skin clean, dredge flour over it, and boil according to its weight,—ten minutes to a pound. Serve with plain boiled potatoes, and drawn butter, or egg, or parsley sauce. Cold boiled halibut may be served the same as codfish; any of the sauce which may remain may be put with the cold fish.

Salmon.—When salmon is fresh and good, the gills and flesh are of a bright red, the scales clear, and the fish stiff. When first caught there is a whiteness between the flakes, which, by keeping, melts down, and the fish becomes richer.

Salmon requires to be well boiled. When underdone it is unwholesome.

Boiled Salmon.—Run a long needle with a packthread through the tail, centre, and head of a fish, to bring it in the form of a letter S. Put it in a fish-kettle, with hot water to cover it, and a small teaspoonful of salt (cut three or four slanting gashes in each side of the fish before making it into the form, otherwise the skin will break and disfigure it); allow ten minutes gentle boiling for each pound of fish. Or a piece of a large fish may be boiled.

Serve with lobster, or anchovy, or drawn butter sauce, and plain boiled or mashed potatoes.

BROILED SALMON.—Cut some slices about an inch thick, and broil them over a gentle, bright fire of coals, for ten or twelve minutes. When both sides are done, take them on to a hot dish; butter each slice well with sweet butter; strew over each a very little salt and pepper to taste, and serve.

BAKED SALMON.—Clean the fish, rinse it, and wipe it dry; rub it well outside and in, with a mixture of pepper and salt, and fill it with a stuffing made of slices of bread, buttered freely, and moistened with hot milk or water (add sage or thyme to the seasoning if liked); tie a thread around the fish, so as to keep the stuffing in (take off the thread before serving); lay muffin rings, or a trivet in a dripping-pan, lay bits of butter over the fish, dredge flour over, and put it on the rings; put a pint of hot water in the pan, to baste with; bake one hour if a large fish, in a quick oven; baste frequently. When the fish is taken up, having cut a lemon in very thin slices, put them in the pan, and let them fry a little; then dredge in a teaspoonful of wheat flour; add a small bit of butter; stir it about, and let it brown without burning, for a little while; then add half a teacup or more of boiling water, stir it smooth, take the slices of lemon into the gravy-boat, and strain the gravy over. Serve with boiled potatoes. The lemon may be omitted if preferred, although generally it will be liked.

SALMON TROUT.—Dressed the same as salmon.

SPICED SALMON (PICKLED).—Boil a salmon, and after wiping it dry, set it to cool; take of the water in which it was boiled, and good vinegar each equal parts, enough to cover it; add to it one dozen cloves, as many small blades of mace, or sliced nutmeg, one teaspoonful of whole pepper, and the same of alspice; make it boiling hot, skim it clear, add a small bit of butter, (the size of a small egg,) and pour it over the fish; set it in a cool place. When cold, it is fit for use, and will keep for a long time, covered close, in a cool place. Serve instead of pickled oysters for supper.

A fresh cod is very nice, done in the same manner; as is also a striped sea bass.

DRIED OR SMOKED SALMON.—Cut the fish down the back, take out the entrails, and roe, scale it, and rub the outside and in with common salt, and hang it to drain for twenty-four hours.

Pound three ounces of salt-petre, two ounces of coarse salt, and two of coarse brown sugar: mix these well together, and rub the salmon over every part with it; then lay it on a large dish for two days; then rub it over with common salt, and in twenty-four hours it will be fit to dry. Wipe it well, stretch it open with two sticks, and hang it in a chimney, with a smothered wood-fire, or in a smoke-house, or in a dry, cool place.

Shad done in this manner are very fine.

SMOKED OR DRIED SALMON, BROILED.—Rinse some smoked salmon in cold water, wipe it dry, and lay it on a clean gridiron, over a bright fire of coals. Turn it, and when it is thoroughly heated through, take it on a dish, butter it well with sweet butter, add pepper to taste, and serve hot.

This is a fine relish for breakfast or supper. Broil smoked shad in the same manner. The inside of any fish must be put to the fire first.

A Dish of Salt Salmon.—Salmon is often put down in brine. It is to be soaked and boiled, as directed for salt codfish, or it may be boiled for breakfast. Or pull off the skin, and pick in flakes the thick side of a salmon; pour scalding hot water over it, let it stand for a few minutes; then pour it off; add to it enough milk or hot water to moisten it; put it over the fire, and let it simmer for five minutes; then add a tablespoonful of butter, shake over a little wheat flour and pepper to taste, stir it for a few minutes, and it is done. A fine relish for breakfast or supper.

Eels.—Eels to be good, must be as fresh caught as possible; skin them, cut off the heads, cut them open and scrape them clean to the back bone.

For frying or broiling, the middle sized fat ones are best; those caught in fresh water have a muddy taste, and should be put in salted water for a short time before cooking. Eels may be boiled and served with drawn butter or parsley sauce, and boiled potatoes.

Baked Eels.—After skinning and cleaning eels, take a shallow pan, cut them in lengths the depth of the pan, and stand them upright into it. The pan must be filled; put in water nearly an inch deep; strew salt and pepper over; put bits of butter the size of a hickory nut over the whole surface; dredge flour over until they look white, also a bunch of parsley cut small, and an onion chopped if liked; set them in a moderate oven to bake for nearly an hour; when done, take them from the pan, add a wine-glass of vinegar, or a lemon sliced thin; to the gravy dredge in a little flour, add a bit of butter; stir it smooth; give it one boil, then turn it over the fish; if lemon is used, a little water may be necessary.

FRICASEED EELS.—After skinning, cleaning, and cutting five or six eels in pieces of two inches in length, boil them in water nearly to cover them, until tender; then add a good sized bit of butter, with a teaspoonful of wheat flour or rolled cracker worked into it, and a little scalded and chopped parsley; add salt and pepper to taste, and a wine-glass of vinegar if liked; let them simmer for ten minutes and serve hot.

FRIED EELS.—After cleaning the eels well, cut them in pieces two inches long; wash them and wipe them dry; roll them in wheat flour or rolled cracker, and fry as directed for other fish, in hot lard or beef dripping, salted. They should be browned all over and thoroughly done.

Eels may be prepared in the same manner and broiled.

FRESH MACKEREL.—These fish to be good must be cooked as soon as possible after they are caught.

They may be broiled, fried, or baked the same as shad—also salted.

DRIED MACKEREL.—Take fresh caught mackerel, scale them and cut them down the back to the tail, leave the heads on; then hang them by the tail in a cool place to drain; strew some salt on the bottom of a pan; sprinkle the fish plentifully with it, and lay them two by two, the insides together in the pan; let them lie twelve hours, then rinse off the salt, and hang them to drain for half an hour, after which pepper the insides a little, and lay them on stones, aslant toward the sun, to dry; take care never to put them out when the sun is not hot on them, nor until the stones are heated and dry; lay the insides to the sun—they will be perfectly cured in one week; stretch them open with two sticks. Or instead of drying, after having prepared them in this manner, smoke them.

Salt Mackerel.—Split fresh caught mackerel down the back, scrape the insides clean, spread them open on a board, and strew them plentifully with salt; then strew salt over the bottom of a tub; lay the fish two by two, the insides together, and lay them in the tub; strew salt between each layer; half coarse and half fine salt; then cover them close—put plenty of salt above the last layer of fish.

To dress Salt Mackerel.—Take mackerel from the salt, and lay them inside downwards in a pan of cold water for two or three days change the water once or twice, and scrape the fish clean without breaking it. When fresh enough, wipe one dry and hang it in a cool place; then fry or broil, or lay one in a shallow pan, the inside of the fish down; cover it with hot water, and set it over a gentle fire, or in an oven for twelve or fifteen minutes; then pour off the water, turn the fish; put bits of butter in the pan, and over the fish; sprinkle with pepper, and let it fry for five minutes, then dish it.

Trout.—These may be stewed, fried, broiled or baked.

PIKE OR PICKREL.—These may be stewed, fried, or broiled.

There are many more fine fish not mentioned herein, but as the process of stewing, boiling, broiling, and frying is very nearly the same for all sorts of fish, it does not seem necessary to mention more.

HERRINGS.—These are eaten in three varieties—fresh, salted, and smoked or red herrings.

Salted herrings are to be soaked in clear water before boiling, the same as mackerel.

Red herring are to be skinned, split in two, and the insides and backbone taken out; or they may first be broiled, then skinned.

To cook fresh herrings, scale and prepare them the same as any other fish.

TO BOIL FRESH HERRING.—Dry them well; rub them over with a little salt and vinegar, and skewer their tails in their mouths; lay them on a fish plate and boil for ten or twelve minutes in water slightly salted. Serve with plain boiled potatoes and drawn butter.

CHOWDER.—Slice some fat salt pork very thin; strew it over with onions chopped small, and some fine pepper; then cut a haddock, fresh cod, or any other firm fish, in thin steaks; take out the bones; lay some of the sliced pork at the bottom of the kettle, with some of the seasoning; then put a layer of fish, then put over some soaked crackers or biscuit; then another layer of the seasoned pork, after which fish and crackers, and a few bits of butter, and so on alternately pork, fish and crackers, until the kettle is two-thirds full, then put in about a pint of water and cover the pot with a thick iron cover with a rim; set it over a gentle fire; put coals and ashes on the cover, and bake two or three hours or more, if the pot is large. When done, turn it out on a dish and serve with pickles. It may be baked in an oven.

SHELL FISH.

To Choose Lobsters.—These are chosen more by weight than size, the heaviest are best; a good small sized one will not unfrequently be found to weigh as heavily as one much larger. If fresh, a lobster will be lively and the claws have a strong motion when the eyes are pressed with the finger.

The male is best for boiling; the flesh is firmer, and the shell a brighter red; it may readily be distinguished from the female; the tail is narrower, and the two uppermost fins within the tail are stiff and hard. Those of the hen lobster are not so, and the tail is broader.

Hen lobsters are preferred for sauce or salad, on account of their coral. The head and small claws are never used.

To Boil Lobster.—Put into a large kettle water enough to cover the lobster, and salt, a dessert spoonful to a quart of water; when it boils fast, put in the lobster, head first, which kills it instantly; keep it boiling briskly for half an hour, then take it from the water with the tongs, and lay it to drain; wipe off all the scum from it, and rub it over with a bit of butter tied in a cloth, or some sweet oil; break off the large claws, and crack each shell without shattering, but so that they may come easily to pieces; lay a napkin on a large steak dish; with a sharp knife split the body from head to tail, and lay it open on the napkin; put a large claw at either end, and serve with melted butter sauce.

Or else take out all the meat from the shells, and lay it neatly on a dish, and serve with melted butter, or a sauce made thus—

Sour Sauce for Boiled Lobster.—Put of water and vinegar each a gill into a stew-pan, and set it over the fire; when it is boiling hot take it off, put to it quarter of a pound of sweet butter and a teaspoonful of made mustard, and, if liked, the green inside of the lobster; add a saltspoonful of ground pepper; stir it until thoroughly blended, and serve in a gravy boat; serve lettuce with lobster.

BROILED LOBSTER.—After having boiled the lobster, split it from head to tail; take out what is called the lady; lay it open; put bits of butter over the meat; sprinkle a little pepper over it, and set the shells on a gridiron over bright coals, until nicely heated through—fifteen or twenty minutes does them. Serve in the shells.

BUTTERED LOBSTER.—Boil a lobster, then take the meat from the shell, and mince or chop it small; put the coral and green inside if liked, (leave out what is called the lady,) to a wine-glass of vinegar or hot water, and a quarter of a pound of fresh butter; add a saltspoonful of cayenne pepper, and made mustard, if liked; and put it with the lobster in a stew-pan over a gentle fire; stir it until it is thoroughly heated throughout. Serve hot—serve with it lettuce in a salad bowl; garnish with hard boiled egg; serve rolls with it.—For supper or a second course dinner dish.

LOBSTER SALAD.—Break apart one or two heads of white heart lettuce, lay the leaves in cold water, rinse them well, then shake the water from each leaf, and lay them, the largest first, in a salad bowl, the stalk inwards. Lay the delicate small leaves around the edge; or cut it all small before putting it in the bowl.

Having boiled a hen lobster, take the meat from the shell and cut it small; rub the coral to a smooth paste, with the green inside if liked, and a tablespoonful of oil or melted butter; add to it a teaspoonful of made mustard, and a saltspoonful of black pepper; add a gill of sharp vinegar; stir it smooth, then mix it with the minced lobster and salad, and serve with cold butter and crackers or rolls. The lobster and dressing must not be put with the lettuce until ready to serve.

To Choose Crabs.—If fresh, the joints of the claws will be stiff, and the inside have an agreeable smell; the heaviest for their size are best,—light ones are watery. Crabs are stale when the eyes look dull.

To Boil Crabs.—Have a pot of boiling water in which is salt, (a tablespoonful to the quart) throw the crabs in, and keep them boiling briskly for twelve minutes, if large; then take them out, wipe the shell clean, and rub them over with a bit of butter; break off the small claws; spread a napkin on a large dish, and lay the crabs on it in regular rows, beginning at the outside. Serve with cold butter and rolls.

To Boil Scollops.—Wash them clean, then put them in a pot, the edges downwards. When all are in, put to them a pint of water, cover it close, and set it over a hot fire; when the shells are wide open and the inside loosens, they are done; then take them out and trim them clean; add pepper and salt, and a good sized bit of butter, and some of the liquor in which they were boiled; dredge over a little flour, and put the whole into a stew-pan, over the fire for ten minutes. Have some thin slices of bread nicely toasted, cut it small, put it in a deep dish, and pour the scollops over.

Soft Shelled Clams.—These are very fine if properly prepared. They are good only during cold weather and must be perfectly fresh.

Soft shelled clams may be boiled from the shells, and served with butter, pepper, and salt over.

To Boil Soft Shell Clams.—Wash the shells clean, and put the clams, the edges downwards, in a kettle; then pour about a quart of boiling water over them; cover the pot and set it over a brisk fire for three quarters of an hour; pouring boiling water on them causes the shells to open quickly and let out the sand which may be in them.

Take them up when done; take off the black skin which covers the hard part, trim them clean, and put them into a stew-pan; put to them some of the liquor in which they were boiled; put to it a good bit of butter and pepper and salt to taste; make them hot; serve with cold butter and rolls.

STEWED SOFT SHELL CLAMS.—Get fifty clams taken from their shells, and freed from the black skin; wash them well in clear water and put them in a stew-pan with very little water; cover and set it over a gentle fire for half an hour; then add to them a bit of butter the size of a large egg or larger; dredge in a tablespoonful of flour, and salt and pepper to taste; stir it in them; cover the stewpan for ten minutes, then serve hot. Many persons like the addition of a wine-glass of vinegar.

TO FRY SOFT CLAMS.—Get them taken from the shell, as they are very troublesome to clean. Wash them in plenty of water, and lay them on a thickly folded napkin to dry out the water; then roll a few at a time in wheat flour, until they will take up no more. Have a thick-bottomed frying pan one third full of boiling hot lard, and salted; (in proportion, a tablespoonful of salt to a pound of lard,) lay the clams in with a fork, one at a time; lay them close together and fry gently, until one side is a delicate brown, then turn carefully and brown the other; then take them off on a hot dish. When fried properly, these clams are very excellent.

HARD SHELL CLAMS.—Hard shell clams may

be prepared for table in a variety of ways. The sand clams, either large or small, are preferable to any other, being whiter and more tender. Those called Quahogs are least delicate eating of all.

To Boil Hard Shell Clams.—Wash the shells until they are perfectly clean, then put them into a kettle, with the edges downwards; add a pint of water, cover the pot and set it over a brisk fire; when the shells open wide they are done. Half an hour is generally enough for them; if a strong taste to the juice is not liked, put more than a pint of water to them. When done, take the clams from the shells into a deep dish; put to them some of the juice, a good bit of butter, and some pepper; or toast some thin slices of bread, butter them and cut them small, and put them in the dish before putting in the clams and juice.

Stewed Clams.—Take fifty large sand clams from their shells, and put to them their own liquor and water in equal parts, nearly to cover them; put them in a stew-pan over a gentle fire for half an hour; take off any scum as it rises, then add to them a teacup of butter, in which is worked a tablespoonful of wheat flour, and pepper to taste; cover the stew-pan, and let them simmer for fifteen minutes longer, then serve. Pour it over toast if preferred.

Substituting milk for water makes them more delicate and white.

Any other than sand clams, require one hour to stew; that is, three quarters of an hour before putting in the seasoning.

Fried Hard Shell Clams.—Get the large sand clams; wash them in their own liquor; dip them in wheat flour or rolled crackers as may be preferred, and fry in hot lard or beef dripping, without salt; or dip each one in batter made as for clam fritters.

CLAM FRITTERS.—Take fifty small or twenty-five large sand clams from their shells; if large, cut each in two, lay them on a thickly folded napkin; put a pint bowl of wheat flour into a basin, add to it two well-beaten eggs, half a pint of sweet milk, and nearly as much of their own liquor; beat the batter until it is smooth and perfectly free from lumps; then stir in the clams. Put plenty of lard or beef fat into a thick-bottomed frying pan, let it become boiling hot; put in the batter by the spoonful; let them fry gently; when one side is a delicate brown, turn the other.

OMLET OF HARD SHELL CLAMS.—Make a batter of two well-beaten eggs, to a pint of milk and a gill of the liquor from the clams, with a pint bowl of wheat flour; beat it until it is smooth and perfectly free from lumps; then stir into it fifty small sand clams, or twenty-five large ones, chopped small; have a small frying-pan, put into it a teacup of lard or beef fat; make it boiling hot; put in the batter half an inch deep, and set the pan over a gentle heat until one side is a fine brown; pass a knife blade around the edges and under it occasionally to loosen it from the pan; then turn the other side. When both are done turn it into a dish. This quantity of batter will make several omlets.

CLAM PIE.—Make a paste as follows: Rub half a pound of sweet lard into a pound of wheat flour, with a teaspoonful of salt, until it is all incorporated, then add enough cold water to wet it into a paste or dough, and work it smooth. Dip your hands in flour to prevent its sticking to them; flour a paste-board and cut the crust to nearly half an inch thickness. Take a deep tin basin, and having rubbed the inside over with butter, line the bottom and sides with the paste; (first line the bottom, then the sides, pressing it together at the bottom,) put into it twenty-five large or fifty small clams, nicely taken from their shells; dredge in wheat flour until the whole looks white; add bits of butter the size of a hickory nut over the whole surface; sprinkle over nearly a teaspoonful of fine pepper, then nearly fill the basin with clam juice and water in equal parts; lay skewers across the basin to support the top crust; roll out the paste, cut several small slits each side of the centre, and lay it carefully over the pie; trim it off at the edges neatly with a knife, dip your fingers in flour, and pinch the side and upper crust together. Bake one hour in a quick oven.

The top crust may be made of puff paste. Instead of lard or beef dripping, the same quantity of finely chopped beef suet may be used.

CLAM POT PIE.—Make a crust as for clam pie, or thus: Put two pounds of wheat flour into a bowl; make a hollow in the centre of it; put into it a teaspoonful of salt, and a pint of butter-milk or sour milk; measure a small teaspoonful of dry saleratus with it, a little hot water, when all is dissolved and a little cooled, put it to the sour milk or buttermilk, then proceed to make it into a soft dough with as much cold water as may be necessary; dip your hands in dry flour to prevent the dough sticking to them. Rub over the sides of an iron dinner pot with a bit of butter, and line the sides only; with the paste made in the hands not more than half an inch thick, press it closely against the pot, then put into the bottom fifty large clams, quarter of a pound of sweet butter cut small, a small teaspoonful of ground pepper strewed over, and half a small nutmeg, grated, if liked; dredge wheat flour over until it looks white; put of clam juice and water enough to nearly reach the top of the paste; lay skewers across; roll out a crust for the top, and whatever paste remains, cut it in small squares, and drop it in before putting on the crust; cut a slit in the centre, cover the pot close and set it over a gentle fire for one hour; then take it up and serve as soon as done. The crust becomes heavy by standing.

This is a dish much liked by those who are fond of clams. The paste directed in this receipt is delicate and far more healthful than any other.

PICKLED CLAMS.—Boil them from the shells, then take them with a skimmer into a basin or stone pot, take of their own liquor half enough to cover cover them, and the same quantity of strong vinegar; whole pepper, alspice and mace each a teaspoonful; make this hot and pour it over the clams. After twenty-four hours they are fit for eating, and will keep good for a long time.

SEA CLAMS.—These are cooked the same as soft shell clams.

CLAM CHOWDER.—Butter a deep tin basin, strew it thickly with grated bread crumbs, or soaked cracker; sprinkle some pepper over and bits of butter the size of a hickory nut, and, if liked, some finely chopped parsley; then put a double layer of clams, season with pepper, put bits of butter over, then another layer of soaked cracker; after that clams and bits of butter; sprinkle pepper over; add a cup of milk or water, and lastly a layer of soaked crackers. Turn a plate over the basin, and bake in a hot oven for three quarters of an hour; use half a pound of soda biscuit, and quarter of a pound of butter with fifty clams.

SCOLLOPED CLAMS.—Put six rolled crackers to twenty-five small clams, and a piece of butter the size of a large egg; add a small teacup of water; cut the butter small; and mix all together with a saltspoonful of ground pepper; butter a scolloped tin plate, put the mixture in, and bake for one hour in a hot oven. When done turn it out on a dish.

OYSTERS.—Oysters must be fresh and fat to be good. They are in season from September to May.

The small ones, such as are sold by the quart, are good for pies, fritters, or stews; the largest of this sort are nice for frying or pickling for family use.

The largest oysters are bought for broiling, frying, stewing, or pickling. These have a finer appearance, but are no better to the taste.

TO FEED OYSTERS.—Put oysters in water and wash them with a broom until they are perfectly clean; then lay them, the largest shell downwards, in a tub; sprinkle well with flour or oat-meal; wet them with water: repeat this operation daily, and they will fatten.

OYSTER FRITTERS.—Take a quart of oysters from their own liquor, strain it and add to it half a pint of milk and two well beaten eggs; stir in by degrees flour enough to make a smooth but rather thin batter; when perfectly free from lumps put the oysters to it, have some lard or beef dripping made hot in a frying pan, salt it a little, and when it is boiling hot put in the batter with a large spoon, having one or more oysters in each; hold it over a gentle fire until one side is a delicate brown—turn each fritter separately. When both sides are done, take them on a hot dish, and serve for breakfast or supper.

FRIED OYSTERS.—Take large oysters from their own liquor onto a thickly folded napkin to dry them off; then make a tablespoonful of lard or beef fat hot, in a thick-bottomed frying pan, add to it half a saltspoonful of salt; dip each oyster in wheat flour, or cracker rolled fine, until it will take up no more, then lay them in the pan, hold it over a gentle fire until one side is a delicate brown; turn the other by sliding a fork under it; five minutes will fry them after they are in the pan. Oysters may be fried in butter, but it is not so good; lard and butter half and half is very nice for frying. Some persons like a very little of the oyster liquor poured in the pan after the oysters are done, let it boil up, then put it in the dish with the oysters; when wanted for breakfast, this should be done.

Oysters to be fried, after drying as directed, may be dipped into beaten egg first, then into rolled cracker.

FRIED OYSTERS (*in batter.*) —— Take two well beaten eggs, half a pint of milk, and as much wheat flour, or rolled cracker, as will make a nice batter; dry the oysters on a napkin, put a fork through the ear or hard part, and dip each oyster into the batter, then fry as before directed.

Oysters fried in butter are apt to be too dark colored, and taste strong.

BROILED OYSTERS.—Take the largest oysters from their own liquor, lay them on a folded napkin to dry off the moisture, then dip each one in wheat flour or rolled cracker, or first into beaten egg and then into rolled cracker; have a gridiron made of coarse wire, put it over a bright but not fierce fire of coals, lay the oysters carefully on, when one side is done turn the other, put some sweet butter on a hot plate, sprinkle a little pepper over, lay the oysters on, and serve with crackers.

TO FRY SMALL OYSTERS.—Take them singly from their own liquor, by the ear with a fork, dip each one in wheat flour or rolled cracker, and fry in hot lard or beef dripping as before directed; when all are cooked, pour a little of the liquor or oyster juice into the pan, let it boil up once, then put it in the dish with the oysters; this is not generally done, but will be much liked.

OYSTERS ROASTED.—Wash the shells perfectly clean, wipe them dry, and lay them on a gridiron, the largest side to the fire; set it over a bright bed of coals, when the shells open wide and the oyster looks white, they are done; fold a napkin on a large dish or tray, lay the oysters on in their shells, taking care not to lose the juice: serve hot.

When oysters are served roasted at supper, there must be a small tub between each two chairs, to receive the shells, and large coarse napkins called oyster napkins. Serve cold butter and rolls or crackers with roasted oysters.

BOILED OYSTERS.—Wash the shells nicely, and put them into a pot or pan, with the edges downwards; put a pint or little less of water to them, and put them over a brisk fire. As soon as the shells open wide, take them off and take out the shells; then take up the oysters with a skimmer into a deep dish; put to them some of the liquor which boiled from them, add to it butter and pepper to taste, and serve with rolls, crackers or toast.

For persons in delicate health, this manner of preparing oysters is both light and healthful.

FRICASEED OYSTERS.—Wash fifty large oysters in their own liquor, then strain it over them, and put them into a stewpan over a gentle fire. Work a heaping teaspoonful of wheat flour or rolled cracker into a teacup of sweet butter, add a saltspoonful of pepper and the same of ground mace if liked; when the oysters are hot, skim them clear, add the seasoning, and cover close for five minutes, or until the oysters are plump and white.

Serve with dressed celery, and bread and butter sandwich or crackers.

OYSTERS STEWED WITH MILK.—Take a pint of fine oysters, put them with their own liquor, and a gill of milk into a stew-pan, and if liked, a blade of mace; set it over the fire, take off any scum which may rise; when they are plump and white turn them into a deep plate; add a bit of butter, and pepper to taste.

Serve crackers and dressed celery with them. Oysters may be stewed in their own liquor without milk.

PICKLED OYSTERS, No. 1.—Take fine large oysters, put them over a gentle fire with their own liquor; add to them a small bit of butter the size of a hickory nut, to one hundred, let them simmer gently, stir them carefully that they may not burn. When they are plump and white, take them from their liquor with a skimmer, into a flat dish; have a large table covered with a thickly folded cloth, then spread out and nicely smooth each oyster, and lay them on; let them remain until they are cold and firm.

Take of their own liquor half enough to cover them, add to it as much good vinegar, make it hot; have ready a stone pot or tureen, put into it a layer of oysters, over them strew a saltspoonful of ground mace, and a dozen cloves, alspice, and whole pepper. Then another layer of oysters, and spice and oysters alternately, until all are used; then pour over the vinegar and juice, and set them in a cold place. They will be fit for use the next day, and will remain good for months in a cold place. They may be put in glass jars or bottles: a little sweet oil put in the top of each and stopped and sealed tight, they will keep good for a year. A bit of cotton applied to the top of a bottle after drawing the cork, will absorb the oil.

There can be no better mode of pickling oysters. Pickled in this manner they have been eaten by epicures and pronounced delicious!

To Pickle Oysters, No. 2.—Take one hundred large oysters from their own liquor, rinse them in clear water, then put them into a stew-pan, add a quart of water and a tablespoonful of salt, and set it over a gentle fire until they are plump and white; then take them from the water with a skimmer into a large dish, and set them in the cold. Put to the liquor in which they were boiled, an equal quantity of good vinegar, a tablespoonful of whole pepper, and the same of cloves, alspice, and mace. When the oysters are perfectly cold pour the pickle over.

This receipt was obtained from a professor of the

art of pickling, and otherwise rendering oysters irresistible, as was also receipt number 1, which is unquestionably the best. In number 2, the oyster is more agreeable to the eye, being whiter, and the liquor more clear.

To SERVE PICKLED OYSTERS.—Take them from the liquor into a glass dish, ornament the edge with a wreath of the most delicate leaves of celery or parsley, and serve with bread and butter sandwich.

To PICKLE SMALL OYSTERS.—Put them over the fire in their own liquor until they are plump and white; take off the scum; then take them up with a skimmer, spread them on flat dishes and set them in the cold; put to their own liquor an equal quantity of vinegar; alspice, cloves, whole pepper, and mace, mixed—a tablespoonful to a quart of the pickle; when the oysters are firm and cold, pour it over them whilst it is warm. Set them in a cold place, and they will be fit for use the next day; if you wish to keep them, put them in glass jars or wide mouthed bottles, and cork and seal them.

OYSTER CHOWDER.—Butter a two quart tin basin; cover it with soaked crackers, strew bits of butter, the size of a nutmeg, over, then put in a double layer of oysters, sprinkle a little fine pepper over, and a little finely chopped parsley, if liked; then put a layer of soaked crackers and bits of butter as before; then another layer of oysters and seasoning, and lastly soaked crackers and butter, and a pint of the oyster liquor, and milk or water.
Bake forty minutes in a hot oven; when done, turn it out on a dish. A quarter of a pound of sweet butter, and half a pound of crackers soaked

nearly soft in milk or water, to three pints of oysters and pepper to taste.

This is a Native American receipt, and will be found none the less delicious on that account. Small sand clams may be done in the same manner. Most persons would prefer this to oyster pie.

OYSTER PIE.—For the paste see clam pie, or use puff paste. .Butter a deep tin two quart basin, line the bottom and sides with the paste, rolled to about half an inch thickness; take a quart or three pints of oysters from their own liquor and put them into the pie; cut a quarter of a pound of sweet butter in bits the size of a hickory nut, strew these over the oysters; sprinkle over a teaspoonful of ground pepper, and dredge them white with wheat flour, then strain the oyster liquor over; add to it enough milk or water very nearly to reach the top of the paste; lay some skewers across; roll some of the paste to nearly half an inch thickness, make an aperture in the centre to allow the steam to escape, or several small incisions with a knife on either side of the centre; cover the pie; dip your fingers in flour, and pinch the top and side paste neatly together. Bake nearly an hour in a quick oven; draw out the skewers before sending to the table.

The edge of an oyster or meat pie may be ornamented with a wreath of leaves cut with a tin cutter from a sheet of paste rolled thin, on a well-floured slab. Wet the under surface as you put them on, to make them stick; the slit in the centre may be ornamented in the same manner, or with a paste flower. The ornament for the edge may be varied as the taste of the artist may direct. Strips of paste braided, or made a chain of, or a row of shells cut of the paste and moulded like wax, are a neat ornament.

The upper crust may be wet over with a feather dipped lightly in the yolk of an egg, beaten with a little milk. This is called gilding.

To Serve Oyster, Meat or Chicken Pies.—When ready to serve, lay a fringed doyle or small napkin on a plate, larger than the basin in which the pie is baked; set the pie on it, then turn the edges of the napkin up against the basin, and put sprigs of parsley, or green leaves of celery or delicate vine leaves on the edge of the plate, under the napkin so as to keep it in its place;—or any other tasteful arrangement which may render the dish ornamental.

Oysters Stewed with Wine.—(Receipt one hundred years old.) Rub over the bottom and sides of a silver or any other chafing dish; lay some oysters in it, strew over them a little pepper and minced parsley; then put to them half a glass of Champagne wine, cover them with slivers of butter, cut very thin; strew grated bread or rolled crackers over; put a cover over the dish, and set them cooking, with fire over and under, until they are a fine brown; then take off all the fat, wipe the rim of the dish, and serve hot. This may be done in an oven instead.

Oysters au Parmesan.—Instead of grated bread or crackers, as in the foregoing receipt, use grated parmesan or English cheese.

Scolloped Oysters —Butter some small scolloped tin pans; strew grated bread or rolled crackers over, and strew thin slices of butter over; then put in oysters nearly to fill the pans; strew them thickly with rolled crackers or bread crumbs; sprinkle pepper over and bits of butter; add a little of the oyster liquor; put bits of butter over the whole surface, and bake in a quick oven for three quarters of an hour; then turn them out on a dish and serve. They should be nicely browned.

Muscles.—Wash the shells clean, and put them in a kettle with a little water; set them over the fire until the shells are all open; then take them up, take out the beard from each one; put them in a deep dish, put butter, pepper, and salt over, and serve with catsup, and vinegar in a castor.

Stewed Muscles.—Having boiled them from the shells, take the beard out and put them in a stew-pan, with a little of the liquor in which they were boiled; strain it to them; add some cream or milk, and a bit of butter, and pepper and salt to taste; dredge flour over; stir them with a spoon, and let them simmer gently for ten minutes. Serve hot with toast.

MEATS.

DIRECTIONS FOR BUYING AND DRESSING BUTCHERS' MEAT.

Any but experienced judges of meat are recommended to buy of none but such butchers as neither kill or sell inferior stock.

Buy of some one particular butcher, and let him choose for you, only telling him what you want; take such as he recommends, and his own interest will cause him to deal honestly, if he has no higher motive; none will be likely to risk losing a good customer by selling inferior pieces; you will find a uniformity of prices for the same cuts of the best stock, go where you will in the same city.

To CHOOSE BEEF.—When beef is good it may be known by its texture and color; the lean will have a fine open grain of a deep coral or bright carnation red; the fat rather inclining to white than yellow; and the suet firm and white. Very yellow fat is generally considered sufficient proof of inferior beef.

If you wish to keep beef two or three days in hot weather, do not salt it, but dry it well in a clean cloth, rub ground pepper plentifully over every part of it first, then flour it well, and hang it in a cool dry place where the air will come to it; be sure always that there is no damp place about it; when you find any, dry it with a cloth; pepper will secure meat from flies.

The best roasting pieces of beef are the Prime ribs, sirloin, and what is known as porter-house piece; it may be recognised by the bone.

The best steaks are cut from the sirloin and porter-house. The last mentioned cut probably took its name from having been the most highly esteemed steak, and so dished for the palate of the epicure at porter-houses, which were formerly the only eating houses. Fine steaks may be cut from between the ribs.

The round of tender, fat beef, cuts very good steaks, as does also the cross-ribs, but these are juiceless compared with the other pieces. The lean of fat beef is the most juicy and tender.

The neck, shin, or marrow bone, leg or head, make good soups.

Beef skirts are good for sausage meat, stewing, hashes, or for mince pie meat; or they may be broiled or fried.

To keep beef, take out the kernels from the neck pieces where the clod is taken off, two from each round of beef, one in the middle, the other in the flap, and one in the thick flank, in the middle of the fat; if these are not taken out, particularly in summer, it cannot be kept sweet, even for salting; there is also another kernel between the rump and edge bone.

BEEF SALTED OR CORNED, RED, *to keep for years.*—Cut up a quarter of beef. For each hundred weight take half a peck of coarse salt, quarter of a pound of saltpetre, the same weight of saleratus, and a quart of molasses, or two pounds of coarse brown sugar. Mace, cloves and alspice may be added for spiced beef.

Strew some of the salt in the bottom of a pickle tub or barrel; then put in a layer of meat, strew this with salt, then add another layer of meat, and salt and meat alternately, until all is used. Let it remain one night. Dissolve the saleratus and saltpetre in a little warm water, and put it to the molasses or sugar; then put it over the meat, add water enough to cover the meat, lay a board on it to keep it under the brine. The meat is fit for use after ten days. This receipt is for winter beef.—Rather more salt may be used in warm weather.

Towards spring take the brine from the meat, make it boiling hot, skim it clear, and when it is cooled, return it to the meat.

Beef tongues and smoking pieces are fine pickled in this brine. Beef liver put in this brine for ten days, and then wiped dry and smoked, is very fine. Cut it in slices, and fry or broil it. The brisket of beef, after being corned, may be smoked, and is very fine for boiling.

Lean pieces of beef, cut properly from the hind quarter, are the proper pieces for being smoked. There may be some fine pieces cut from the fore quarter.

After the beef has been in brine ten days or more, wipe it dry, and hang it in a chimney where wood is burnt, or make a smothered fire of sawdust or chips, and keep it smoking for ten days; then rub fine black pepper over every part, to keep the flies from it, and hang it in a dry, dark, cool place. After a week it is fit for use. A strong, coarse brown paper, folded around beef, and fastened with paste, keeps it nicely.

Tongues are smoked in the same manner. Hang them by a string put through the root end. Spiced brine for smoked beef or tongues will be generally liked.

For convenience make a pickle as mentioned for beef, keep it in the cellar, ready for pickling beef at any time. Beef may remain in three or four or more days.

BEEF SALTED. *for immediate use.*—Take a piece

of beef weighing five or six pounds (it should not weigh more); mix together a gill of fine salt, the same of coarse brown sugar, and a teaspoonful of powdered saleratus. Rub this mixture well over the meat; then take a thick, coarse cloth, flour it well, put the meat into it, and fold it close; pin it or tie it securely, put it into a pot of hot water, and keep it boiling gently, allowing fifteen minutes for each pound of meat.

This very nearly resembles corned beef. Beef tongues may be boiled in the same manner.

Pickled Beef.—Take a piece of beef weighing five or six pounds; rub it well over with pepper and salt, stick it full of cloves, cover it with vinegar, and turn it every day for a fortnight. As the vinegar wastes, add more; then put it down in a stew-pot, with vinegar and water, equal parts; cover it close, add a few blades of mace, and when it is tender put in a pound of butter, cut small, dredge in a teacupful of browned flour; put to it a leek, and a bunch of parsley, cut small, and let it continue to stew slowly for half an hour, until the gravy is brown and rich. Take it up, and serve with the gravy over, the same as a-la-mode beef.

Or take it up when it is boiled tender, before the seasoning is put in; slice it thin for supper or sandwiches. Beef tongue may be done in the same manner.

Beef Tripe.—Beef tripe may be dressed in a variety of ways, by which to recommend it to the palate. It may be fried, stewed, or broiled. It is to be cleaned and boiled tender before dressing in any other manner.

To Clean Tripe.—Empty it, and rinse it clean

in cold water; then sprinkle fine lime all over it, put it in a tub, and cover with warm water; let it remain three or four hours, then scrape it clean with a knife, and if the dark does not all come off easily, sprinkle more lime on, and let it lay an hour longer; then scrape it again, take it out, and wash it well in clean cold water, and put it in weak salt and water for one night and day; then change the water and let it lay another night. Keep it for three or four days in salt and water, changing it every day; it will then be white and clean. Take it out, cut it in pieces about twelve inches long, and six wide, and if you please lay it in buttermilk, or sour milk, part of a day, to whiten it; then rinse it in clear water, boil it tender. When cold, dress it as you like; keep it in weak vinegar, or vinegar and water.

In New-York markets, tripe may be bought cleaned and boiled.

To Fry Tripe.—Take prepared tripe, lay it in water, with a little salt, over night; in the morning scrape the rough side clean, wipe it dry; then dip it in wheat flour or rolled crackers.

Have a thick-bottomed frying-pan, put into it a cup of lard or beef dripping, let it become boiling hot; then lay the tripe in, the rough side down first, let it fry gently; when this side is a delicate brown turn the other and do likewise; then take it from the pan, add to the fat in which it was fried a wine-glass of vinegar, let it boil up once, then pour it in the dish with the tripe, or you may use water instead of vinegar.

Rolla-Cheese.—Take the skirts of beef, cut it in narrow strips, and lay it, fat and lean, on pieces of prepared tripe, the rough side in, season with pepper and salt (put about a large teaspoonful of salt, and half of a small one of fine pepper to each pound of meat); roll each piece of tripe up, with a portion of the meat in it; do not fill it quite full; draw the edges together, and sew them with a strong thread, making them in rolls; sew up the ends; after all are made, drop them into a pot of hot water, and let them boil gently, until a straw will easily penetrate them; then take them from the water, and lay them in a vessel or tub side by side, lay a board and weight over them, to press them flat; when cold keep them in vinegar and water. Cut them in thin slices, for breakfast, supper, or luncheon.

FRICASEED TRIPE.—Cut a pound of tripe in narrow strips, put a small cup of water or milk to it, add a bit of butter the size of an egg, dredge in a large teaspoonful of flour, or work it with the butter; season with pepper and salt, let it simmer gently for half an hour, serve hot. A bunch of parsley cut small and put with it is an improvement.

BROILED TRIPE.—Prepare tripe as for frying, lay it on a gridiron over a clear fire of coals, let it broil gently; when one side is a fine brown, turn the other side (it must be nearly done through before turning); take it up on a hot dish, butter it, and if liked, add a little catsup or vinegar to the gravy.

BEEF LIVER.—Cut the liver in thin slices, dip each slice in wheat flour or rolled crackers, and fry in hot lard or beef dripping; season with pepper and salt. It must be thoroughly cooked, and a fine brown.

Some persons prefer liver fried with onions,—if

so, peel and cut in slices a sufficient number of onions; fry them in hot lard or beef dripping, to a nice brown; season with pepper and salt. Serve in a dish with the liver.

BEEF STEAK WITH ONIONS.—Take an inferior beef steak from the round or cross-rib; fry it with beef fat; season with pepper and salt; fry some onions also, and serve in the dish with the steak.

BEEF HEAD-CHEESE.—Split a beef head in two, take out the eyes, crack the side bones, and lay it in water for one night, to draw out the blood, then put it in a kettle with sufficient water to cover it, let it boil gently, skimming it often; when the meat loosens from the bones, take it from the water with a skimmer into a bowl or tray; take out every particle of bone; season with a small teacupful of fine salt, and half as much pepper; chop it fine; add a tablespoonful of powdered thyme or sage, tie it in a cloth, and press it by laying a gentle weight on it. When cold, it may be cut in slices for luncheon or supper.

POTTED HEAD.—Thoroughly clean an ox head, split it in two, take out the eyes and brains, then boil it gently, in sufficient water to cover it; skim it clear, when the bones loosen it is done enough then take it up, take out every particle of bone strain the liquor in which it was boiled, add pepper and salt to taste, and put it with the meat in a stew-pan or dinner-pot over a gentle fire, and let it simmer until the water is nearly all done away, then put it in a stone pot, press it down and let it become cold.

To be eaten sliced for luncheon or supper.

Beef Skirts.—This part of beef may be broiled and well buttered, made in a pie or stewed with onions and potatoes.

Beef Stewed *(ragoo.)*—Cut two pounds of beef in neat square pieces, season with a tablespoonful of salt and a teaspoonful of pepper, and put it in a stew-pan, with water scarcely to cover it; set it where it will simmer slowly; cut two small carrots quarter of an inch thick, cut the edge of each slice in notches, and put them in hot water over the fire for ten minutes, then add to them five or six small potatoes, pared and sliced in the same manner; then cover the stew-pan for ten minutes longer, when these vegetables will be done enough. Dip a bunch of parsley into boiling water and cut it small; cut a leek or white onion very small,—now skim the meat; take a piece of butter, the size of a large egg, work a tablespoonful of wheat flour with it and stir it with the meat; then put in the prepared vegetables; cover the stew-pan, and set it where it will simmer for fifteen minutes; then take it from the fire; put the meat in the centre of the steak dish, put the sliced carrots and potatoes around it and turn the gravy over. A tablespoonful of tomato catsup may be added to the gravy, or serve catsup with it.

To Stew a Round of Beef.—Boil the beef until it is rather more than half done; gash it with a sharp knife, then rub it over with salt and pepper and sweet herbs chopped small; one sliced carrot; also a leek or onion cut small; dredge it white with flour; strew bits of butter over, and put it into a dinner pot with a pint or more of the water in which it was boiled; cover it close, and let it bake or stew slowly for two hours; add a little hot water when it may be necessary to keep it from burning; turn it once; when it is nicely browned, take it up, add a little boiling water to the gravy, stir it well together, let it boil up once, and then pour it over the meat.

BEEF BOUILLI.—Take a round of beef or a part of one, take out the bone and tie it together in a neat form with a strong cord; put with it any odd bits of butchers' meat, whether beef, veal, or lamb, or the giblets of game or poultry; put it in a dinner-pot, with water to cover it, over a moderate fire, when it boils skim it clear; when it is tender, (allow fifteen minutes to each pound of meat,) put in some salt and pepper; add one or two carrots sliced and an onion or leek cut small, also a bunch of parsley; then put in a teacup of browned flour and the same of butter; cover it for twenty minutes, then take up the meat, add a wine-glass of wine, or catsup to the gravy, then strain it over the meat.

BEEF HEART BAKED OR ROASTED.—Cut a beef heart in two, take out the strings from the inside; wash it with warm water, rub the inside with pepper and salt, and fill it with a stuffing made of bread and butter moistened with water, and seasoned with pepper and salt, and, if liked, a sprig of thyme made fine; put it together and tie a string around it, rub the outside with pepper and salt; stick bits of butter on, then dredge flour over, and set it on a trivet, or muffin rings, in a dripping pan; put a pint of water in to baste with, then roast it before a hot fire, or in a hot oven; turn it around and baste frequently. One hour will roast or bake it; when done, take it up, cut a lemon in thin slices, and put it in the pan with a bit of butter; dredge in a teaspoonful of flour; let it brown; add a small teacup of boiling water, stir it smooth, and serve in a gravy tureen.

Beef Heart Stewed.—Wash a beef heart in warm water; take the strings from the inside, and fill it with a stuffing made of bread buttered, and sprinkled with pepper and salt, and moistened with hot water. An onion finely minced, or a sprig of thyme may be added, if liked; then put it in an iron dinner-pot or bake-pan, with three pints of hot water; cover it and let it boil slowly, until it is tender; skim it clear; then if the water is not nearly boiled away, take out all but about half a pint; add to it a quarter of a pound of butter; cut small, dredge in a heaping tablespoonful of wheat flour, sprinkle over a small teaspoonful of fine pepper, and a large one of salt; cover the pot, and set it over a moderate fire to finish. When the lower side begins to brown turn the other, and brown that also—take care not to let it burn. Then take it up, add a cup of hot water or wine to the gravy; let it boil up once, stir smooth, then pour it over the heart, and serve with plain boiled or mashed potatoes. Tomato catsup may be put in the gravy, instead of wine—or served with it.

Beef Kidneys.—These may be split and fried, or broiled, or they may be chopped small, and made a hash or stew. Cut them in half, or mince them, and put them in a stew-pan, with enough hot water to moisten them; then cover them close, and let them simmer gently until tender; add a good bit of butter, pepper and salt to taste, and some browned flour; a wine-glass of wine or catsup may be added, if liked. Let them simmer for ten minutes longer. Toast some thin slices of bread delicately brown, take off the crust, and lay them in a dish, and put the stew or hash over. A finely chopped onion or leek may be added to it, if liked.

Smoked Beef.—After the beef has been in the brine ten days or more, hang it in a chimney over a wood or sawdust fire—it must be a smothered fire if made of wood. Keep it smoking for ten days or a fortnight; then rub the outside over every part with black pepper, and hang it in a cool dry place. To serve it, cut off some of the outside, and chip it thin with a sharp knife for tea. After it is cut, keep a thick paper folded about it.

Hashed Beef.—Take some very rare done or uncooked beef, chop it small, one-fourth as much fat as lean, and moisten it with water or gravy; if with water, add a bit of butter rolled in flour; put it in a closely covered stew-pan, over a gentle fire, for half an hour; then dredge in a little browned flour, add salt and pepper to taste, and cover it for fifteen minutes, and serve. Or cut some thin slices of toast in neat squares, put them in the dish, and put the hash on it; or serve it on boiled rice.

Some persons like a teaspoonful of made mustard or catsup put to it before dishing it.

Potato and Beef Hash.—Mince some cold beef, a little fat with the lean, put to it as much cold boiled potatoes chopped as you like, (the quantity as of meat or twice as much,) season with pepper and salt; add as much gravy or hot water as will make it moist, then put in a stew-pan over a gentle fire; dredge in a small quantity of wheat flour; stir it about with a spoon, cover the stew-pan, and let it simmer for half an hour—take care that it does not burn. Dish it with or without a slice of toast under it; for breakfast. This hash may be made without potatoes; if water is used instead of gravy, a bit of butter may be added, more or less, according to the proportion of fat with the lean meat.

Beef Cakes.—Chop fine some underdone beef, lean, with such a proportion of fat as you like, add to it a chopped leek or onion, if liked, season with pepper and salt; a small teaspoonful of salt and a salt-spoonful of pepper, mix well; flour your hands and make the mince in small cakes of about half an inch thickness, and fry them in hot beef dripping or lard; if you like, fry a few sprigs of parsley with them.

These cakes may be made with boiled potatoes, mashed with one-third (or more) as much finely minced beef, season as before, moisten slightly with water or gravy, and finish as before directed.

Beef Steaks.—Sirloin, and what is known in New-York markets as porter-house steaks, are the choicest cuts. If the beef is not very tender and young, it may be improved by beating gently with a rolling pin or potato beetle before cooking, the steaks should be nearly the thickness of an inch: beef steaks must on no account be washed. By keeping beef as long as possible without tainting, it may be improved in flavor, and will eat more tender; broiling is by far the best manner of cooking beef steaks.

Broiled Beef Steak.—Have a bright clear fire of coals, rub the gridiron bars with a bit of suet, lay on the steak, and let it broil gently until one side is done, then take the steak over the steak-dish to catch the blood before turning it, then lay the upper side to the fire. For a fine steak, (weighing about two pounds and a half,) take quarter of a pound of sweet butter on the dish, work a small teaspoonful of fine pepper and a large one of salt into it; when the steak is done, put it on the butter, when it melts a little turn the steak; repeat the turning once or twice, then put a tin cover over and serve quickly; the dish must be hot.

Beef steaks are generally preferred broiled so that the middle will be slightly red. Tomato catsup to be served with beef steak.

BEEF STEAKS FRIED, *to taste like a broil.*—Have ready a bright quick fire, put a bit of butter in a pan, and when it is hot, lay the steak evenly in, let it fry quickly, turn it once or twice to retain the juice; work some butter, pepper, and salt together as for a broiled steak, make a steak dish hot, and when the steak is done to taste, lay it on the dish, then put the butter on it, turn it once or twice on the dish and serve hot. Steaks done in this manner are pronounced by epicures as fine as broiled.

FRIED BEEF STEAKS.—Cut some of the fat from the steak, and put it in a frying pan and set it over the fire; if the steaks are not very tender, beat them with a rolling pin, and when the fat is boiling hot, put the steak evenly in, cover the pan and let it fry briskly until one side is done, sprinkle a little pepper and salt over, and turn the other; let it be rare or well-done as may be liked; take the steak on a hot dish, add a wineglass or less of boiling water or catsup to the gravy; let it boil up once, and pour it in the dish with the steak.

BEEF STEAK PIE.—Take some fine tender steaks, beat them a little, season with a salt-spoonful of pepper and a teaspoonful of salt to a two pound steak; put bits of butter, the size of a hickory nut, over the whole surface, dredge a tablespoonful of flour over, then roll it up and cut it in pieces two inches long; put a rich pie paste around the sides and bottom of a tin basin; put in the pieces of steak, nearly fill the basin with water, add a piece of butter the size of a large egg, cut small, dredge in a teaspoonful of flour, add a little pepper and salt, lay skewers across the basin, roll a top crust to half an inch thickness, cut a slit in the centre; dip your fingers in flour and neatly pinch the top and side crust together all around the edge. Bake one hour in a quick oven.

BEEF STEAK PUDDING.—Beat a beef steak well, make a paste in this manner; take two pounds of flour and a teaspoonful of salt, rub into it a teacup of lard or beef dripping to half a pint of sour milk; put the same quantity of water; dissolve a small teaspoonful of saleratus in it, and make a paste of the flour with it; use as much as may be necessary to make a nice dough; then flour a cake board and rolling-pin, and roll the paste to less than half an inch thickness; lay on the steak, let the paste be two inches larger every way than the steak; then roll it up; flour a pudding cloth and wrap the pudding in it; secure the ends, and put it into a pot of boiling water, and set it over the fire; let it boil two hours; then take it from the cloth and serve with melted butter. To be cut in slices across.

BEEF AND ONION STEW.—Cut two pounds of meat in pieces the size of an egg, and put it in a stew-pan with enough warm water nearly to cover it; cover the stew-pan, and let it simmer slowly for half an hour; then skim it clear, peel five or six small onions and cut them in thick slices; pare half a dozen large potatoes and cut them in half, or quarters; add a small tablespoonful of salt, and a small teaspoonful of pepper to the stewed meat; then put in the potatoes and onions. If the meat is lean, (it is best to have a small proportion of fat,) add a bit of butter the size of a large egg; shake over it a tablespoonful of wheat flour, or work it into the butter; cover the stew-pan close, and let it stew gently that it may brown without burning; one hour is required for making this stew. If the potatoes are cut smaller than halves, they should be put in twenty minutes before it is done; half an hour will be required to cook them if cut in two.

FRIED BEEF STEAKS, WITH GRAVY.—Take a round or cross rib steak; if it is not tender, beat it with a rolling pin; cut off some of the fat, and put it in a frying-pan: add to it for each pound of meat a small teaspoonful of salt, and a salt-spoonful of pepper; then put in the steak; cut it so that it will lay flat; cover the pan, and let it fry as quick as possible without burning; when one side is done, or browned, turn the other, and when that is done, more or less rare according to taste, take the pan from the fire; take the steak on a hot dish; then dredge in to the pan a tablespoonful of wheat flour, stir it around, and when it is brown, (unless there is plenty of fat,) add a bit of butter and a teacup of boiling water; stir it smooth, taste it, and if it is not seasoned to taste, add a little more of salt and pepper; then pour it through a gravy strainer over the steak, and serve with catsup in the castor. This gravy does not require to be fat, but well seasoned and a fine brown.

MINCED BEEF.—Chop some cold under-done beef very fine; put to each pound of meat a small teaspoonful of salt, and an even filled saltspoon of pepper; add to it enough hot water or gravy scarcely to moisten it, and put it into a stew-pan; cover it close, and set it over a gentle fire for half an hour; stir the mince occasionally; toast one or two thin slices of bread a fine brown; cut off the crust and lay it on a dish, and put the mince over. Or instead of toast, boil some rice as follows:—To a small teacup of well washed rice, put a quart of hot water, and a teaspoonful of salt; put it in a stewpan; cover it, and set it over a gentle heat for three-quarters of an hour; do not stir the rice; then take it from the fire; take off the cover and set it before the fire for five minutes to grain; then put it on a flat dish, and put the mince on it—if you please, reserve part of the rice, to be eaten with butter and sugar, or wine sauce. This may be served for breakfast, or a side dish at dinner.

TO ROAST BEEF.—Have a bright clear fire before putting down the roast; if it is large, have a fire according; let it be a clear steady fire, with a bed of coals at the bottom—this is for a wood fire; for a coal fire, make one large enough to last the length of time required for the roast, (fifteen minutes for each pound of meat;) make the front of the fire clear from ashes, and brush up the hearth; rinse the meat in cold water, wipe it dry, mix salt and pepper, a teaspoonful of salt, and a salt-spoonful of pepper, for each pound of meat; rub it over every part, then put it evenly on the spit, taking care not to run it through the best parts, or if it is done in a reflector, set it on a trivet or muffin rings, and turn the pan about as occasion may require;) then put it down at a little distance from the fire, that the outside may not be too much done before the inside is cooked; put at least a pint of water in the dripping-pan, with which to baste; replenish with boiling water, so that there shall not be less than a pint of gravy, when the meat is done, for a piece weighing five or six pounds; when about half done, clear the front of the fire, and set it a little nearer; turn the meat so that all sides may be done evenly; fifteen minutes before it is done, if you please, dredge with the fat of the meat wheat flour until it looks white; baste it freely, and set it to finish; when done, take it on to a large dish, and cover with a tin cover; set the dripping over the fire, dredge in a small tablespoon of flour, stir it smooth; when it is a fine brown, add a teacup of boiling water; let it boil up, stirring it meanwhile; then pour it through a gravy strainer into a tureen; if there is much fat, skim nearly all of it off: or, instead of dredging in flour, make a thin smooth batter of a tablespoonful of flour, and a small cup of cold water; let the gravy in the pan become boiling hot before stirring it in; then stir it smooth, and when it is a fine rich brown, strain it into the tureen, and serve with the meat.

The vegetables most proper with roast beef are, plain boiled or mashed potatoes, with boiled spinach, beets or dressed celery, and turnips mashed, or squash. If you please, pickles, or grated horseradish, may also be served with roast beef instead of spinach or celery, with made mustard and catsup in the castor.

In roasting meat it should be so placed as to bring the largest, or thickest part, nearest the fire. In roasting beef its juiciness depends on the frequency of basting it, after it has fairly begun to roast.

BAKED BEEF.—A fine roasting piece of beef

may, if properly managed, be baked in a stove oven, so nearly to resemble a roast, as to be mistaken for it :—

Prepare the meat as for roasting ; lay some muffin rings or a trivet in a dripping-pan, set the meat on, and put a pint or more of hot water in the dripping-pan to baste with ; make the oven hot—then put in the meat: close the oven, and when it begins to roast or bake, baste freely, (do not draw out the pan, but use a long-handled spoon,) every fifteen minutes until it is done. Should the meat seem like to burn, leave open the oven door; add hot water to the pan as it wastes, that the gravy may not burn ; allow fifteen minutes for each pound of meat to cook, unless you wish to have it very rare ; about fifteen minutes before it is done, dredge wheat flour over until it is white ; then baste it freely and finish. If there is much fat in the pan, take some out; take out the rings or trivet, shake from the dredging-box a tablespoonful of flour, stir it thoroughly into the gravy ; then add a teacup of boiling water; let it boil up once, then strain it through a gravy strainer into the tureen. Serve the same vegetables as with roast beef.

BEEF A-LA-MODE.—Take a piece of the round or any lean piece of beef; take out the bone, and fill it with a stuffing made of bread, made moist with hot water, and seasoned with pepper and salt and a bit of butter or chopped suet ; make a mixture of a tablespoonful of pepper, same of salt, and of sweet herbs finely powdered ; rub the seasoning well into the meat; stick cloves over the whole surface ; tie a tape around it to keep it in shape ; then put it in a bake-pan or dinner-pot, with water nearly to cover it, over a gentle fire ; cover the pot as closely as possible, let it simmer, or boil gently, according to its weight, allowing fifteen minutes for each pound of meat. When the meat is tender, and the water nearly out, dredge flour over until it is white, then turn it over, add a teacup of butter, and a minced onion or leek ; cover the pot, and set it nearer the fire, to brown the meat ; scrape a carrot and cut it in slices a quarter of an inch thick ; notch the edge of the slices neatly, and put them in a stew-pan with boiling water, and set it over the fire ; when it is tender, take it up with a skimmer; dip a bunch of parsley into boiling water, cut it small and add it and the sliced carrot to the meat : after having turned them again, let them stew for a few minutes ; then take the meat on a dish, take off the tape, dredge a little flour to the gravy, add a small teacup of boiling water, stir it smooth ; then pour it over the meat, and serve. A glass of wine or vinegar may be put to the gravy instead of the water, or a large tablespoonful of tomato catsup.

ROUND OF BEEF—(*French Receipt.*)—Parboil a round of beef, in a little water, for half an hour; then take it up and put it into a deep dish ; cut gashes into the sides of the meat, that the gravy may come out ; put salt and pepper into every gash ; put it into a deep dish ; fill up the dish with claret wine ; set it over a chafing dish of coals ; add two or three blades of mace ; cover it, and let it stew for an hour and a half; turn the meat several times ; add a handful of pickled capers or nasturtion buds, with two or three white onions or leeks, cut small, and a bunch of parsley minced fine ; stew all together until the meat is very tender; toast some slices of bread nicely, cut it small, put the meat on them and pour the gravy over.

A NICE WAY TO SERVE COLD BEEF.—Cut cold roast beef in slices, put gravy enough to cover them, and a wineglass of catsup or wine, or a lemon sliced thin; if you have not gravy, put hot water and a good bit of butter, with a teaspoonful or more of browned flour; put it in a closely covered stew-pan, and let it simmer gently for half an hour. If you choose, when the meat is down, cut a leek in thin slices, and chop a bunch of parsley small, and add it; serve boiled or mashed potatoes with it. This is equal to beef a-la-mode.

Or, cold beef may be served cut in neat slices, garnished with sprigs of parsley, and made mustard, and tomato catsup in the castor; serve mashed, if not new potatoes, with it, and ripe fruit, or pie, or both, for dessert, for a small family dinner.

VEAL.—Veal should not be kept long before dressing, as it by no means improves by keeping. The loin is apt to taint under the kidney. When soft and slimy it is stale; it will be cool and firm and have an agreeable smell when fresh.

In the shoulder, if the vein is a clear red, it is good. When there are any yellow or dark spots it is stale. The breast and neck when good look white and clear. Veal must always be well cooked.

Such as are not judges of butchers' meat, had better buy of one person on whose judgment and honesty one may rely. Be willing to pay a fair price.—You will soon find that the best articles of marketing have a uniform price, according to the season of it. That is, the same cuts of the best stock will be found to sell at the same price at the same season. The prices of poultry, lamb and veal varies according to the earliness of the season.

The leg of veal is generally boiled or made soup of. The loin also may be boiled, but is best roasted, or cut in chops and broiled or fried. The shoulder may be roasted,—it may be boned and stuffed and then roasted, or it may be split, after having been boned, and fried or broiled.

The breast may be roasted, stewed or broiled, or made a pie.

Steaks are cut from leg or shoulder. The neck or scrag may be cut in chops or fried, broiled or stewed; or a dish of soup may be made of it.

Calf's liver is cut in steaks, and fried like beef liver, or it may be broiled and buttered.

Veal sweet-breads are roasted with the breast, or they may be fried or stewed.

Calf's head may be boiled and served with a sauce, and a soup made of the liquor in which it is boiled.

The head and feet are used for making jellies.

To BOIL VEAL.—Put it in hot water, (not boiling,) to cover it, put to it a tablespoonful of salt, cover the pot, and let it boil very gently, taking off the scum as it rises; allow fifteen minutes for each pound of meat; four pounds of meat will require one hour gentle boiling. Serve boiled veal with drawn butter, or oyster, or lemon, or parsley sauce, and plain boiled potatoes, with pickles, or lettuce, or celery. Boil the loin and serve with egg sauce.

CALF'S HEAD.—Clean it very nicely, and soak it in salt and water, that it may look white, (clean as directed for beef tripe,) take out the eyes, take out the tongue to salt, and the brains to make a little dish; boil the head very tender, and serve with a sauce, or take it up, put bits of butter all over it, dredge with flour, and season with pepper and finely sifted sweet herbs, if liked; set it in a hot oven or before the fire; baste with some of the water in which it was boiled, or squeeze the juice of a lemon over; roast it a fine brown; then take it on a hot dish and put a tin cover over; add a piece of butter, the size of an egg, to the gravy; cut a small lemon in thin slices, and make the gravy boiling hot; add them to it; let them fry brown, then put a teaspoonful of browned flour, and a teacup of boiling water to the gravy, and serve, with the meat. The lemon may be dispensed with if preferred—it will generally be liked.

To Make a Dish of Calf's Brains.—Wash them in salt and water, then boil them tender, and take them in a dish; put butter and pepper over, and serve.

Or, after washing the brains in salt and water, wipe them dry, and dip them in wheat flour, or into beaten egg, and then into bread crumbs, and fry in hot lard or beef dripping; season with pepper and salt, and slices of lemon fried, if liked.

Calf's Head Cheese.—Boil a calf's head in water enough to cover it, until the meat leaves the bones, then take it with a skimmer into a wooden bowl or tray; take from it every particle of bone; chop it small; season with pepper and salt, a heaping tablespoonful of salt, and a teaspoonful of pepper will be sufficient; if liked, add a tablespoonful of finely chopped sweet herbs; lay a cloth in a cullender, put the minced meat into it, then fold the cloth closely over it, lay a plate over, and on it a gentle weight. When cold it may be sliced thin for supper or sandwiches. Spread each slice with made mustard.

Calf's Head *(a fine Dish.)*—Boil a calf's head, (after having cleaned it,) until tender, then split it in two, and keep the best half; (bone it if you like) cut the meat from the other in uniform pieces, the size of an oyster; put bits of butter, the size of a nutmeg, all over the best half of the head; sprinkle pepper over, and dredge on flour until it looks white, then set it on a trivet or muffin rings in a dripping pan; put a cup of water into the pan and set it in a hot oven or before a hot fire; turn it that it may brown evenly; baste once or twice. Whilst this is doing, dip the prepared pieces of the head in wheat flour or batter, and fry in hot lard or beef dripping, a delicate brown; season with pepper and salt and slices of lemon, if liked. When the roast is done put it on a hot dish, lay the fried pieces around it and cover it with a tin cover; put the gravy from the dripping pan into the pan in which the pieces were fried, with the slices of lemon, and a teaspoonful of browned flour, and, if necessary a little hot water. Let it boil up once, then strain it into a gravy boat and serve with the meat.

The water in which the head was boiled, will make a dish of soup, by adding seasoning and vegetables.

VEAL SAUSAGES.—Take equal quantities of veal and fat salt pork, chop it small, season with pepper and finely chopped herbs if liked; mix the seasoning well together with the meat, tie it in a cloth, and hang it in a cool dry place. When wanted for use flour your hands, make the preparation in small cakes, and fry in a little hot lard. Serve with boiled vegetables.

VEAL SWEETBREADS.—Wash them in warm water, then put them in a stew-pan with a little salt and pepper, and pour boiling water over to cover them; let them boil for five minutes, then take them up, wipe them dry, and dip them in rolled cracker, or egg batter, or wheat flour, and fry them in hot lard or beef dripping. Or, instead, wet them over with beaten egg, then dip them in rolled cracker until they will take up no more, then fry them or broil on an oyster gridiron, (made of coarse wire.)

VEAL CHOPS.—Cut veal chops about an inch thick; beat them flat with a rolling-pin, put them in a pan, pour boiling water over them, and set them over the fire for five minutes; then take them up and wipe them dry; mix a tablespoonful of salt and a teaspoonful of pepper for each pound of meat; rub each chop over with this, then dip them, first into beaten egg, then into rolled crackers as much as they will take up; then finish by frying in hot lard or beef dripping; or broil them. For the broil have some sweet butter on a steak dish; broil the chops until well done, over a bright clear fire of coals; (let them do gently that they may be well done,) then take them on to the butter, turn them carefully once or twice in it, and serve. Or dip the chops into a batter, made of one egg beaten with half a teacup of milk, and as much wheat flour as may be necessary. Or simply dip the chops without parboiling into wheat flour; make some lard or beef fat hot in a frying-pan; lay the chops in, and when one side is a fine delicate brown, turn the other. When all are done, take them up, put a very little hot water into the pan, then put it in the dish with the chops.

Or make a flour gravy thus: After frying them as last directed, add a tablespoonful more of fat to that in the pan, let it become boiling hot; make a thin batter, of a small tablespoonful of wheat flour and cold water; add a little more salt and pepper to the gravy, then gradually stir in the batter, stir it until it is cooked and a nice brown; then put it over the meat, or in the dish with it; if it is thicker than is liked, add a little boiling water.

Veal Chops Stewed.—Rinse the chops in cold water, and rub them over with a seasoning of salt and pepper, then put them into a stew-pan with hot water nearly to cover them; cover the pan, and set it over a gentle fire for fifteen minutes, then take off any scum which may have risen; add to the stew a piece of butter with flour worked into it—in proportion, a tablespoonful of flour, and a quarter of a pound of butter to three pounds of meat. Dip a bunch of parsley into boiling water; cut it small, then add it to the stew; stir it, in cover it and let it simmer for half an hour and it is done. The breast of veal cut small with a bone in each piece, may be stewed in this way.

Veal Stewed Brown.—Cut three pounds of neck, or scrag, or loin, into pieces with a bone in each; or leave it whole. Rub each over with a mixture of pepper and salt, and put them into a dinner pot or stew-pan, with nearly enough water to cover them; set it over the fire, and let it boil gently until the meat is tender; then skim it clear, add to it quarter of a pound of butter cut small; dredge in a tablespoonful of browned flour, and set it over a fire; let it brown nicely without burning; stir it occasionally. When it is so, add a teacup of boiling water; let it boil up once, then serve with the gravy. About one hour will be required to make this stew.

Veal Stewed with Vegetables, (*Ragout.*)— Wash three pounds of veal in cold water, then cut it small and put it in a stew-pan, with water nearly to cover it; add a tablespoonful of salt and a teaspoonful of pepper; cover the stew-pan and let it simmer for twenty minutes, then skim it clear. Whilst the meat is stewing, scrape one large or two small carrots and cut them in thin slices, quarter of an inch thick, notch the edges and put them in a stew-pan with boiling water to cover them and set it over the fire until they are tender; dip a bunch of parsley into boiling water, and mince it fine; cut a leek in thin slices; pare and cut six small potatoes in halves or quarters, then take the carrot from the water with a skimmer; put quarter of a pound of sweet butter to the meat; dredge over it a tablespoonful of browned flour and add the vegetables; cover the stew-pan and let it stew gently for half an hour; then take the meat on a dish, put the vegetables around it, pour the gravy over, and serve.

To Roast Veal.—Rinse the meat in cold water, if any part is bloody, wash it off; make a mixture of pepper and salt, allowing a large teaspoonful of salt and a saltspoonful of pepper for each pound of meat; wipe the meat dry; then rub the seasoning into every part, shape it neatly, and fasten it with skewers, and put it on a spit, or set it on a trivet or muffin rings, in a pan; stick bits of butter over the whole upper surface; dredge a little flour over, put a pint of water in the pan to baste with, and roast it before the fire in a Dutch oven or reflector, or put it into a hot oven; baste it occasionally, turn it if necessary that every part may be done; if the water wastes add more, that the gravy may not burn; allow fifteen minutes for each pound of meat; a piece weighing four or five pounds will then require one hour, or an hour and a quarter.

When it is nicely browned and done, take it up; add a bit of butter the size of a large egg to the gravy, dredge in a tablespoonful of flour, stir it smooth, let it brown, add a cup of boiling water to it ; then strain it into a gravy-boat, and serve with the meat; serve plain boiled or mashed potatoes with the meat, with such green vegetables as may be liked.

VEAL ROASTED, *to look like a duck.*—Bone a fine shoulder of veal, rinse it in cold water, and rub it all over, inside and out, with a mixture of salt and pepper ; then make a stuffing as follows : cut some slices of wheat bread, and butter them freely ; sprinkle salt and pepper over, and make them moist with hot water ; with this fill the place of the bone, then draw the edges of the meat together under, so as to form it in the shape of a duck or fowl, and secure it with skewers. Then set it on a trivet or muffin rings, in the dripping-pan, put bits of butter all over the surface, put a pint of boiling water in the pan, to baste with, and make the gravy. Then put it in a Dutch-oven, or a reflector, before the fire, or in a hot stove oven. Baste frequently, that it may not burn ; turn it about, that all sides may be nicely browned. Just before it is done, dredge a little wheat flour over, put a tablespoonful of butter into the pan, and baste freely with it to finish. Then take it on a dish, cover it with a tin cover. Dredge a tablespoonful of flour to the gravy, stir it smooth ; then add a teacup of boiling water, let it boil up once, stirring it. Then strain it into a tureen and serve with the meat. A lemon sliced thin, and fried in the pan after the meat before making the gravy, may be served in the dish with the meat or gravy.

Plain boiled or mashed potatoes, with any other

vegetable which may be liked, may be served with roast veal: also, pickles of any kind.

VEAL HASHED.—Cut a pound of cold veal small, season it to taste with pepper and salt, dredge a large teaspoonful of wheat flour over it, add a bit of butter the size of an egg, put it in a stew-pan, put water enough to make it moist; then cover it close and set it over a gentle fire for half an hour; stir it occasionally; if liked, a bunch of parsley may be cut small and added to it; when half done, toast some thin slices of bread delicately brown, cut it in small squares or diamonds, and serve the hash on it; for breakfast. A glass of wine may be added.

VEAL MINCED WITH POTATOES.—Chop some cold veal very fine, put to it an equal quantity, or more if you choose, of cold boiled potatoes, chopped; also season with pepper and salt to taste; add to it veal gravy or hot water to moisten it, and a good bit of butter; dredge a little flour over, stir it all together, and put it in a stew-pan, over a moderate fire, cover it close for half an hour, stirring it occasionally; when thoroughly heated it is done.

VEAL PIE.—Cut a breast of veal small, and put it in a stew-pan, with hot water to cover it; add to it a tablespoonful of salt, and set it over the fire; take off the scum as it rises; when the meat is tender, turn it into a dish to cool: take out all the small bones, butter a tin or earthern basin or pudding-pan, line it with a pie paste, (see clam pie,) lay some of the parboiled meat in to half fill it; put bits of butter the size of a hickory nut, all over the meat; shake pepper over, dredge wheat flour over until it looks white; then fill it nearly to the top with some of the water in which the meat was boiled; roll a cover for the top of the crust, puff paste it, giving it two or three turns, and roll it to nearly half an inch thickness; cut a slit in the centre, and make several small incisions on either side of it; lay some skewers across the pie, put the crust on, trim the edges neatly with a knife; bake one hour in a quick oven. A breast of veal will make two two quart basin pies; half a pound of nice corned pork, cut in thin slices and parboiled with the meat, will make it very nice, and very little, if any butter, will be required for the pie; when pork is used, no other salt will be necessary.

POTATO AND VEAL PIE.—Peel and cut small some cold boiled potatoes; cut some cold veal small; put some of the meat in the bottom of a baking-dish or tin basin; put on it a layer of potatoes, sprinkle pepper and salt over and bits of butter; then another layer of meat, and potatoes, and seasoning, and so continue until the pan is nearly full; then add to it water or gravy to moisten it; cover it with a pie crust, and bake in a quick oven for three quarters of an hour.

VEAL POT PIE.—Cut a breast or scrag of veal in chops or small pieces and put it in a dinner-pot with water to cover it; add half a pound of salt pork, cut in thin slices, or a tablespoonful of salt; let it boil gently, taking off the scum as it rises, until the meat is tender, then take it, and the water in which it was boiled, into a dish to cool; then make a common pie-crust, or a more healthful one as follows:—Put two pounds of wheat flour into a deep dish, make a hollow in the centre, put into it a teaspoonful of salt, and the same of saleratus, powdered fine and dissolved in a cup of water; then make it into a soft dough with buttermilk or sour milk; use as much as may be necessary; wipe the dinner-pot dry; make the dough half an inch thick, and line the sides only, of the pot, with the crust;. press it close against the sides of the pot; put the parboiled meat in the bottom; roll out the paste, reserve enough to cover the top of the pot pie, and cut the remainder in small squares; strain the water in which the meat was boiled, and put it in the pot; if there is not enough nearly to reach the top of the side crust, add water; drop in the bits of paste or dough, dredge in a tablespoonful of wheat flour; add quarter of a pound of butter, cut small, unless pork is stewed with the meat, when half as much butter is enough; put in a large teaspoonful of pepper; then lay some skewers across, from one side crust to the other, and put on the top crust; make a slit in the centre to let out the steam; cover the pot close, and set it over a moderate fire; three quarters of an hour will bake it; take care that the fire is not so great as to burn it. Half a dozen small potatoes, nicely peeled, may be put into the pie with the meat.

In dishing the pot-pie, take the top crust up first, then take up the meat and gravy on another dish, and lastly, the brown crust from the sides, on a dish with some of the gravy over. Or, take the meat into the centre of the dish, put the crust around it, and turn the gravy over.

CALF'S FEET ROASTED.—Clean calf's feet, and boil them just tender, then let them cool. When cold, rub them over with a mixture of salt and pepper, and tie them on a spit; baste with a cup of hot water, in which is melted two ounces of butter, when nearly done dredge them white with flour baste freely, and let them finish. When nicely brown, take them up, add a cup of water to the gravy in the dripping-pan, put to it a tablespoonful of browned flour and a piece of butter the size of an egg; stir it smooth, then strain it and serve in a tureen; or instead of water, use port wine in the gravy.

CALF'S FEET STEWED.—Clean the feet; divide each one in two, cover with water and boil till tender, then finish as directed for veal stew.

PORK, HAMS, &c.

To CHOOSE PORK.—If the rind of pork is tough, and thick, and cannot easily be impressed with the finger, it is old.

If fresh, the flesh will look cool and smooth; when moist or clammy it is stale. The knuckle is the first to become tainted.

Pork is often what is called measly, and is then almost poisonous; measly pork may easily be detected; the fat being full of small kernels. Swill or still-fed pork is not fit for curing; either dairy or corn fed is good.

Fresh pork is in season from October to April.

In cutting up a large hog, it is first cut in two down the back and belly. The chine or backbone should be cut out from each side the whole length, and is either boiled or roasted. The chine is considered the prime part. The sides of the hog are made into bacon, and the inside or ribs is cut with very little meat; this is the spare rib.

There is a large spare-rib on either side, which is generally divided in two, called a sweet-bone and a blade-bone, these are served broiled.

The bacon is one whole side, and contains a fore-leg, and a ham, which is the hind leg, and if left with the bacon, is called a gammon.

Hogs' lard is made of the inner fat of the bacon hog.

Pickled pork is generally made of the flesh of hogs, as is also bacon; porkers are not as old as hogs, their flesh is whiter and less gross, but not equally tender.

A porker is usually divided into quarters; the fore-quarter consists of the spring or fore-leg. The fore-loin or neck, the spare-rib, and griskin.

The hind quarter consists of the leg and loin. The feet and ears may be used in a variety of ways, and should be cut off before the legs are cured. The head may also be made use of to advantage, either pickled for boiling or smoking, or roasted, or baked, or made head-cheese of.

The bacon hog is sometimes scalded to take off the hair, and sometimes singed. The porker and roasting pig is always scalded, and the hair scraped off.

Fresh pork must always be well cooked, it is unpalatable otherwise.

SPARE-RIB.—Broil the blade-bone and spare-rib nicely over a bright clear fire of coals; let it be well done. It is best to cover it whilst on the grid-iron, as by so doing it is sooner done and the sweetness is kept in. Put the inside to the fire first, and let it be done nearly through before turning it; when done, take it on a hot dish, butter it well, season with pepper and salt, and serve hot.

Head Cheese.—Having thoroughly cleaned a hog's head or pig's head, split it in two with a sharp knife, take out the eyes, take out the brains, cut off the ears, and pour scalding water over them and the head, and scrape them clean. Cut off any part of the nose which may be discolored so as not to be scraped clean; then rinse all in cold water, and put it into a large kettle with hot, (not boiling) water to cover it, and set the kettle (having covered it) over the fire; let it boil gently taking off the scum as it rises; when boiled so that the bones leave the meat readily, take it from the water with a skimmer into a large wooden bowl or tray, take from it every particle of bone; chop the meat small and season to taste with salt and pepper, and if liked, a little chopped sage or thyme; spread a cloth in a cullender or sieve; set it in a deep dish, and put the meat in, then fold the cloth closely over it, lay a weight on which which may press equally the whole surface, (a sufficiently large plate will serve.) Let the weight be more or less heavy, according as you may wish the cheese to be fat or lean; a heavy weight by pressing out the fat, will of course leave the cheese lean.

When cold, take the weight off; take it from the cullender or sieve, scrape off whatever fat may be found on the outside of the cloth, and keep the cheese in the cloth in a cool place, to be eaten sliced thin, with or without mustard, and vinegar, or catsup.

After the water is cold in which the head was boiled, take off the fat from it, and whatever may have drained from the sieve, or cullender, and cloth; put it together in some clean water, give it one boil; then strain it through a cloth, and set it to become cold; then take off the cake of fat. It is fit for any use.

Pork Cheese, Soused.—Clean and split a pig's head and boil it, till the bones are loose; then take it up, take the bones carefully from it, make a seasoning of salt, pepper, chopped sage, and a little ground alspice, and mace, if liked; cut the boned meat in slices, sprinkle each with the seasoning, and lay them together in a cloth. When all are in, fold the cloth closely around the meat and lay it under a gentle weight.

Take of the water in which the head was boiled and vinegar, equal parts. Mix them together, and put it over the meat, to cover it. This will keep good for months. It is best to keep the cloth folded about it. Slice it thin, for breakfast, luncheon, or supper.

Farmer's way of Salting Pork.—Cut up the pork, strew salt on the bottom of the pork barrel; then put in a layer of pork, edgeways down, strew it plentifully with salt; then another layer of pork, salt it plentifully, and so continue until all is in, strewing the top plentifully with salt; let it lie three or four days; then make a salt and water brine, strong enough to float an egg, and pour it over the meat, and lay a weight on it, to keep it under the brine.

To Cure Hams.—Take one ounce of saltpetre for a fourteen pound ham; make it fine, and dissolve it in a little molasses; rub it well over the cut side of the meat, and around the bone, and over the whole ham. Then pack them, the small end down, into a barrel with fine salt sprinkled between and over them; let them remain for two or three days; then make a cold brine of salt and water, which will bear an egg, and cover the hams with it. After three weeks they are fit to smoke, or they may remain in the brine three months without injury.

Hams cured in this way are delicious, and keep well, and have a fine red color when cooked.

Any part of pork may be salted in this manner. The cheeks or head split in two, or any other pieces for boiling or smoking, are much finer in this than any other way of curing. Beef tongues may also be done in this manner. This pickle will keep pork good for two years if necessary.

To Smoke Hams or Tongues.—Hang hams by a string through the small end, in a smoke-house, or chimney where wood is burnt, or over a smothered fire of sawdust or chips. Let them hang for ten days.

Hams, Dry Salted.—For each small ham of seven pounds' weight, take a large tablespoonful of finely pounded saltpetre, and a tablespoonful of molasses. Mix these well together; then rub it well over the cut or inside of the ham, and around the bone; make a place with your finger, and insert as much as you can of the mixture; then rub the ham well over with fine dry salt; repeat the salt every fine day, until it has been done four times; then rinse it in cold water, and smoke it for ten days. Then rub black pepper around the bone, and all over the cut side, to keep the flies from it, and hang the hams in the smoke-house, or cover them with coarse canvass; sew it tightly, and whitewash them. Let them dry; then hang them in a cool, dark place.

An Excellent Pickle for Pork.—Nine pounds of salt, coarse and fine equal parts, to six gallons of water, two pounds of brown sugar, or a quart of molasses, two ounces of saltpetre, and one ounce of saleratus. Dissolve the saltpetre and saleratus in the water; then add the salt, and put it in a kettle, and boil and skim it clear; then put it in your pickle tub; when cold it is fit for use.

Always keep the meat under the brine, by means of a suitable bit of board, and a weight.

Pork for boiling should be laid in this brine for a few days.

Beef may be put in the brine in which pork has been, but it will not do to put pork in beef brine; the blood from the beef will cause the pork to spoil.

Hog's Head, Pickled.—Put a head in the pickle above mentioned, for three or four days; then take it out, wash and scrape it; then boil it, and finish as directed for head-cheese, without the salt, or like soused head.

Sausage Meat.—Take of pork three-quarters, and one of beef, chop it fine, put four ounces of fine salt, and one of pepper, to every ten pounds of meat: mix the seasoning well into the meat; then put it in small muslin bags, tie them close, and hang them in a dry, cool cellar. When wanted for use, cut it in slices, or form it in small cakes, flour the outside of each, and fry in hot lard. Let them be nicely browned. Serve with boiled vegetables. Fine hominy may be boiled, and served with them for breakfast.

Pork Sausages.—Take such a proportion of fat and lean pork as you like; chop it quite fine, and for every ten pounds of meat take four ounces of fine salt, and one of fine pepper; dried sage, or lemon thyme, finely powdered, may be added if liked; a teaspoonful of sage, and the same of ground alspice and cloves, to each ten pounds of meat. Mix the seasoning through the meat; pack it down in stone pots, or put it in muslin bags. Or fill the hog's or ox's guts, having first made them perfectly clean, thus. empty them, cut them in lengths, and lay them three or four days in salt and water, or weak lime water; turn them inside out once or twice, scrape them; then rinse them, and fill with the meat.

If you do not use the skins or guts, make the sausage meat up the size and shape of sausages, dip them in beaten egg, and then into wheat flour, or rolled crackers, or simply into wheat flour, and fry in hot lard. Turn them, that every side may be a fine color. Serve hot, with boiled potatoes or hominy; either taken from the gravy, or after they are fried, pour a little boiling water into the gravy in the pan, and pour it over them; or first dredge in a teaspoonful of wheat flour, stir it until it is smooth and brown; then add a little boiling water, let it boil up once, then put it in the dish with the sausages.

Chopped onion and green parsley may be added to the sausage meat, when making ready to fry.

Or sausage meat may be tied in a muslin bag, and boiled, and served with vegetables; or let it become cold, and cut in slices.

PORK SAUSAGE (*to eat cold.*)—Take of fat and lean equal quantities, and put them in a pickle or brine, for six days. Then take it up, chop it fine, have some leek or onion chopped fine, and put it to the meat, with one ounce of fine pepper to ten pounds, and alspice to taste. Have ready an ox gut, cleaned as directed (they may be kept in salt and water until wanted, when they must be soaked), fill it with the meat, tie both ends, wrap it in a fold of muslin, and hang it to smoke, the same as a ham, for ten days or a fortnight. It is eaten sliced thin, with or without first having boiled it. Rub ground ginger or pepper over the outside of them, and hang in a cool, dry place.

To Make Bologna Sausage.—Take of lean beef and pork, each three pounds, two pounds of fat pork or bacon, and a pound and a half of beef suet; put hot water to the lean meat, and set it over the fire for half an hour; then cut it small, each sort by itself, shred the suet, and pork or bacon, each by itself. Season with fine pepper thyme, and ground mace; fill ox skins with it, tie them in eight inches lengths, and put them in a beef brine for ten days; then smoke them the same as ham or tongue. Rub ground ginger or pepper over the outside, after they are smoked, and keep them in a cool, dry place.

Or rub them over with sweet oil, and the ashes of vine twigs.

To Prepare a Pig's Head for Baking.— Clean the head, and split it open; take out the brains and eyes, wash it, and rub it outside and in with a mixture of salt and pepper, and lay it on a trivet or muffin rings (the cut side of the head down), in a dripping-pan; put a pint of water with a teaspoonful of salt, and a saltspoonful of pepper, and set it in a hot oven. When it begins to bake, baste it with the water, which must be replenished according as it wastes. When nearly done, baste with butter, and finish (about one hour will be required for it). Take it up, dredge a tablespoonful of flour to the gravy, let it boil up once, then strain it, and serve with the meat. Serve plain boiled or mashed potatoes, and pickles, and stewed apples, or cranberries with it. Or if baked in a brick oven, put bits of butter over, and dredge it quite white with flour, before putting it in; have plenty of water in the pan; let it remain in the oven one hour; then make the gravy, and serve.

To ROAST A PIG.—Thoroughly clean the pig, then rinse it in cold water, wipe it dry; then rub the inside with a mixture of salt and pepper, and if liked, a little pounded and sifted sage; make a stuffing thus: cut some wheat bread in slices half an inch thick, spread butter on to half its thickness, sprinkled with pepper and salt, and if liked, a little pounded sage and minced onion; pour enough hot water over the bread to make it moist or soft, then fill the body with it and sew it together, or tie a cord around it to keep the dressing in, then spit it; put a pint of water in the dripping-pan, put into it a tablespoonful of salt, and a teaspoonful of pepper, let the fire be hotter at each end than in the middle, put the pig down at a little distance from the fire, baste it as it begins to roast, and gradually draw it nearer, continue to baste occasionally, turn it that it may be evenly cooked; when the eyes drop out it is done; or a better rule is to judge by the weight, fifteen minutes for each pound of meat, if the fire is right.

Have a bright clear fire, with a bed of coals at the bottom, first put the roast at a little distance, and gradually draw it nearer; when the pig is done stir up the fire, take a coarse cloth with a good bit of butter in it, and wet the pig all over with it, and when the crackling is crisp take it up; dredge a little flour into the gravy, let it boil up once, and having boiled the heart, liver, &c., tender, and chopped it fine, add it to the gravy, give it one boil then serve.

To Bake a Pig.—Prepare a pig, as for roasting, and lay it on a trivet or on muffin rings in a dripping pan, stick bits of butter all over it, sprinkle pepper and salt over, and dredge some flour over; put a pint or more of water in the pan, then set it in a quick or hot oven, baste frequently, when nearly done baste with a spoonful of butter, and close the oven to finish; then take it up, dredge a tablespoonful of flour to the gravy, set it over the fire to brown, stir it smooth and if necessary, add a little hot water, let it boil up once then strain it and serve with the pig.

Pig to roast or bake may be stuffed with boiled potatoes, seasoned with butter, pepper and salt, and made soft with a cup of milk.

To make a dish of the Harslet.—Having boiled the heart, liver, &c., in water, with a little salt till tender chop them small, add a good bit of butter or the gravy from the pan, put it in a stewpan over a gentle fire, season high with pepper and salt, dredge in a large teaspoonful of flour, stir it and let it simmer gently until it is hot, then serve in a side dish with the pig.

Roast or baked pig may be served whole if small, or lay it on a dish, cut of the head, and before drawing out the spit, split the body in two from head to tail, lay the two halves together on the dish, split the head and lay a half on either side of the body with the ears. A quarter of a large pig may be roasted in the same manner.

Sauces to serve with roast Pig or Pork.—
Mashed potatoes, boiled onions, turnips mashed, pickled beets, mangoes or cucumbers, or dressed celery and cranberry sauce, stewed apples, or currant jelly.

To Roast Pig like Lamb.—Take the forequarter of a large roasting pig, skin it, rub it well over with a seasoning of salt and pepper, and chopped mint if liked, then roast or bake it, dredge a little flour over, and baste with a little butter about fifteen minutes before taking it up—served with mashed potatoes, etc., as for roast pig.

To Roast a Loin.—Take a sharp pen-knife and cut the skin across, then cut over it in the opposite direction so as to form small squares or diamonds; rub every part of it with a mixture of salt and pepper, put bits of butter the size of a hickory nut over the skin side, and roast or bake it—serve with the gravy, boiled potatoes mashed, turnips mashed, and dressed celery or pickles, and tart apples stewed without sugar.

Leg of Pork.—Prepare it the same as a loin, and roast or bake it.

Pork Tender Loin.—This part of pork is the most delicate; it may be got where pork is cut up for packing or salting. It may be fried or broiled, if it is too thick, split it in two. Steaks cut from the tender-loin are nice, but not equal to the tender-loin, which is cut with the grain; steaks are cut across it. The chine of pork may be roasted?

To Stew Fresh Pork.—Cut the spare-rib or any other lean part in chops, and put them in a stew-pan with water nearly to cover them; season with pepper and salt; let them simmer gently for half an hour, then skim them, dredge in a tablespoonful of flour to about two pounds of meat; add a teaspoonful of salt and a small one of pepper, with a bit of butter the size of an egg; stir the seasoning well into the stew, cover it, and let it simmer for fifteen minutes, or until the meat is very tender. Serve with plain boiled potatoes, and pickles or dressed celery.

Or potatoes may be pared and cut in quarters, and stewed with the meat; put them in with the seasoning, and cover for twenty minutes.

Pigs' Feet Soused.—Scald and scrape clean the feet; if the covering of the toes will not come off without, singe them in hot embers, until they are loose, then take them off. Many persons lay them in weak lime water to whiten them. Having scraped them clean and white, wash them and put them in a pot of hot (not boiling) water, with a little salt and let them boil gently, until by turning a fork in the flesh it will easily break, and the bones are loosened. Take off the scum as it rises. When done, take them from the hot water into cold vinegar, enough to cover them; add to it one-third as much of the water in which they were boiled; add whole pepper and alspice, with cloves and mace if liked, put a cloth and a tight fitting cover over the pot or jar.

Soused feet may be eaten cold from the vinegar, split in two from top to toe, or having split them, dip them in wheat flour and fry in hot lard, or broil and butter them. In either case, let them be nicely browned.

Pigs' Feet Pie.—Boil the feet then take out all the large bones, cut the flesh in half, line a buttered tin basin with pie-crust, and put it half or one-third full of the meat; season with salt and pepper, and bits of butter the size of a hickory nut over the whole surface; dredge flour over, until it looks white, and fill nearly to the top with water; cover with a pie or puff paste crust; cut a slit in the middle;

pinch the top and side crust neatly together at the edge, and bake one hour in a hot oven.

Serve pickles and mashed potatoes with this pie. A fine pot-pie may be made of pigs' feet in the same manner

To Choose Hams.—Run a knife or skewer in at the knuckle, and at the thickest part of the ham next the bone, if it comes out clean and smells sweet, the ham is good. If, on the contrary, the blade of the knife is smeared and smells rank or strong, it is not good.

To Boil Ham.—Wash the ham in cold water two or three times, and put it in a kettle of hot (not boiling) water to cover it; let it boil gently, according to its weight (fifteen minutes to each pound) it must be kept slowly boiling all the time; keep the pot covered except to take off the scum as it rises; if it is like to boil over, take the lid partly off.

Putting meat down to boil in cold water draws out its juices. Hard or fast boiling makes it tough and hard.

When it is done, take off the skin, trim off the under side neatly, and put spots of pepper and stick cloves at regular intervals over the whole upper surface. Or dredge it well with wheat flour or rolled crackers, and brown it in a hot oven, or before a hot fire. Serve hot with the gravy from it, and boiled vegetables; or it may be served cold. Trim the bone with parsley, or the delicate leaves of celery, and put sprigs of the same around it on the dish; lemon sliced and dipped in flour, or butter and fried, may be laid over the ham and on the dish. Mashed potatoes, stewed apple, or cranberry, dressed celery, or boiled spinach, or cauliflower and mashed turnips are served with hot ham

With cold ham serve pickles or dressed celery, or both, and bread and butter sandwich.

To Boil a Leg of Pork.—Take a leg of pork which has been in pickle for three or four days, soak it for half an hour in cold water to make it look white, then tie it in a nicely floured cloth, and put it in hot water to cover it. Boil the same as ham. When done, take a small sharp knife, and cut through the skin in a straight line about a quarter of an inch apart; put spots of pepper over and serve with the same vegetables as for ham; or with mashed potatoes, turnips mashed, and pickles or tart apples stewed without sugar. Currant jelly or cranberries may be served with ham or leg of pork.

Pig's Cheek—Is smoked and boiled like ham with vegetables; boiled cabbage or fried parsnips may be served with it.

To Make a Stew of Smoked Meat.—Cut slices from the thin part of a smoked shoulder, or from the cheek—and having washed them in cold water, put them in a dinner-pot, with water nearly to cover it; scrape two parsnips and cut them in slices an inch thick; pare some potatoes and cut them in two, then put parsnips and potatoes with the meat, and add pepper to taste; cover the pot, and set it over a moderate fire, that it may brown nicely without burning; when done take up the meat and vegetables, dredge in a little wheat flour, stir it about until it is brown, then add a little hot water; stir it smooth, and serve with the meat and vegetables.

Corned or pickled pork may be stewed in the same manner.

PORK CHOPS, STEAKS AND CUTLETS.—Fry or stew pork chops, after taking off the rind or skin, the same as for veal.

Cutlets and steaks are also fried, broiled, or stewed, the same as veal.

TO FRY OR BROIL SALT PORK AND BACON.—Cut some slices from corned pork, or streaked bacon, (fat and lean,) put them in a pan, pour boiling water over, set it over the fire, and let it boil up once; then pour the water off, and fry them in their own fat; sprinkle with pepper, and if liked, a little dried sage, or thyme, pounded fine; when both sides are nicely browned, take them up, put a little hot water or some vinegar in the pan, let it boil up once, and put it in the dish with the meat. Or, having fried the meat, dredge a teaspoonful of flour into the gravy; while it is hot, stir it about; then add a little hot water, stir it smooth, and pour it into the dish with the meat.

TO BROIL.—After having parboiled the slices with plenty of water in the pan, lay them on a gridiron, over a bright fire of coals; sprinkle a little pepper over; when both sides are done, put them on a hot dish, put a little butter over and serve. Or, whilst broiling, dip the slices several times into a dish of hot water.

Salt pork is very nice fried thus:—Cut it in thin slices, put them in the frying-pan, with hot water to cover them, set it over the fire, let it boil up once, then pour off the water, shake a little pepper over the meat, and fry it nicely, in its own fat, both sides; then take it up, add to the gravy a large teaspoonful of flour, stir it smooth; then put to it a cup of milk, stir over the fire for a few minutes, shake pepper over, then put it in the dish with the meat.

Cold boiled potatoes, sliced thin, may be fried in the pan, after pork or bacon, and served with it; parsnips boiled, cut in thin slices and fried, may also be served with fried salt meat.

Or, having boiled some cabbage or spinach, and pressed all the water from it, cut it small, put it on a steak dish, lay the fried meat on it, and pour the gravy over. Vinegar is generally eaten with the vegetable.

To Fry Ham.—Cut some fine slices from the large end of the ham, take off the skin, put them in a frying-pan, and pour hot water over; set it over the fire, and let it boil up once, then pour the water off, take the slices up, put a spoonful of lard in the frying-pan, and let it become hot; dip the slices in rolled cracker, or wheat flour, and fry them a nice brown; when one side is done, turn the other, then take them on a dish, put a very little water in the pan, let it boil up once, put it over the meat.— Or, if a flour gravy is wanted, make a thin batter with a teaspoonful of flour, and cold water, and stir it into the gravy in the pan; let it brown, and if too thick, put a little hot water to it; stir it smooth and serve with the meat.

To Broil Ham.—Cut some slices of ham, quarter of an inch thick, lay them in hot water for half an hour, or give them a scalding in a pan over the fire; then take them up, and lay them on a gridiron, over bright coals; when the outside is browned, turn the other; then take the slices on a hot dish, butter them freely, sprinkle pepper over and serve.

Or, after scalding them, wipe them dry, dip each

slice in beaten egg, and then into rolled crackers, and fry or broil.

HAM GRAVY.—When a ham is almost done with, cut off what meat remains on the bone, break or saw the bone small, and put it in a sauce-pan with hot water to cover it; set the stew-pan over the fire, and let it simmer gently; then strain it, add a little pepper, and fine sage if liked, dredge in a tablespoonful of browned flour, and add a bit of butter, stir it over the fire for a few minutes; then having toasted some slices of bread, a nice brown, lay them in a dish, and serve the gravy over.

Or, serve ham gravy with boiled vegetables.

TO MAKE LARD.—Take the leaf fat from the inside of a bacon hog, cut it small, and put it in an iron kettle, which must be perfectly free from any musty taste, set it over a steady, moderate fire, until nothing but scraps remain of the meat; the heat must be kept up, but gentle, that it may not burn the lard; spread a coarse cloth in a wire sieve, and strain the liquid into tin basins, which will hold two or three quarts; squeeze out all the fat from the scraps.

When the lard in the pans is cold, press a piece of new muslin close upon it, trim it off at the edge of the pan, and keep it in a cold place. Or it may be kept in wooden kegs with close covers.

Lard made with one-third as much beef suet as fat, is supposed by many persons, to keep better; it is better, made in this way, cooking.

DIRECTIONS.

For Boiling and Serving Meat with Vegetables, for Making Succatash, Sour Kraut, Cooking Pork and Beans, &c. &c.

SALT CODFISH AND POTATOES.—Take soaked dried codfish, a quarter of a fish; take off the skin and hang it to dry—pare a dozen or more fine large potatoes, wash them two or three times in cold water, and put them into a dinner pot, lay such a portion of the codfish as you wish, on them, with or without first trying it in a cloth, put hot water enough to cover all; cover the pot close, and let it boil for three quarters of an hour; take the potatoes with a skimmer into a covered dish, take the fish on to a steak dish, and garnish with hard boiled eggs cut in slices, and sprigs of green parsley; serve with parsley or egg sauce over the fish and in a tureen—serve with potatoes and pickles. Or the dish may be served in this manner: mash the potatoes, make them very moist with hot milk and a large bit of butter; pick all the bones from the fish and chop it fine, then put them together, and pepper to taste; make it in a roll or any other form, put spots of black pepper over, lay slices of hard boiled eggs over, and sprigs of parsley around it on the dish, and serve with pickles.—Or wet the surface over with a little butter melted in hot milk, and brown it in an oven or before the fire.

TO MAKE SOUR KRAUT.—Have ready a vinegar or white wine cask, about four inches from the bottom have a vent peg. Take a number of the best white cabbages, strip off all the outside leaves and slice the heads transversely or across, as thin as possible, until you have as much as you require, then lay over the bottom of the cask vine twigs, to the height of the peg; on these put a layer of sliced cabbage three inches deep, strew it plentifully with fine salt, use one pound of salt to fifty of the cabbage; then put another layer of cabbage, and salt and cabbage alternately until the cask is two-thirds full; let the last layer be of salt, put cabbage leaves all over, cover them with a cloth and a piece of wood which will fit the inside of the cask, and place a heavy stone upon it.

After four or five days, draw out the peg, and let the brine run off, rinse the cloth, wash the board and stone, add more salt over the top, and replace cloth, board and weight.

Repeat this operation at intervals of not more than a month, so that what flows from the cask is clear and free from smell.

Keep the cask in a moderate temperature during the whole year. Take it from the cask with a wooden spoon or fork.

TO SERVE SOUR KRAUT.—Take out as much sour kraut as you wish from the cask, and soak it for at least two hours in cold water, then take it into a cullender to drain; put it into a large stew-pan or dinner-pot, put on it a piece of corned pork or bacon, and put hot water over nearly to cover it; cover the pot and set it over a moderate fire for an hour or more until the pork is done—serve with the meat on it. Or cut the bacon or pork in slices, strew pepper over them, lay the sour kraut on, put hot water nearly to cover it, cover the pot close and set it over a moderate fire for an hour and a half. Or it may be boiled with water, and fried sausages put over it and served; or the sausages may be boiled with it, and the skins taken off, before serving.

HAM AND EGGS FRIED.—Cut some nice slices of ham, put them in a frying pan, cover them with hot water, and set the pan over the fire, let it boil up once or twice, then take out the slices and throw out the water, put a bit of lard in the pan, dip the slices in wheat flour or finely rolled crackers, and when the fat is hot put them into the pan, sprinkle a little pepper over; when both sides are a fine brown take them on a steak dish, put a little boiling water into the pan, and put it in the dish with the meat.

Now put a bit of lard the size of a large egg into the pan, add a saltspoonful to it, let it become hot; break six or eight eggs carefully into a bowl, then slip them into the hot lard, set the pan over a gentle fire; when the white begins to set, pass a knife blade so as to divide an equal quantity of white to each yolk, cut it entirely through to the pan that they may cook the more quickly; when done take each one up with a skimmer spoon, and lay them in a chain around the edge of the meat on the dish. Fried eggs should not be turned in the pan.

Spinach boiled and pressed free from water and chopped small, may be put on the centre of a steak dish, lay the fried ham on it, pour the gravy over, place the fried eggs around it. Vinegar may be eaten with the spinach.

POACHED EGGS WITH FRIED HAM.—Fry the ham as above directed, take a clean frying or omlet-pan, nearly fill it with boiling water, set it over a gentle fire, break the eggs singly into a cup and slip each into the boiling water, cover the pan for four or five minutes—when done, take them up with a skimmer on to a dish, sprinkle a little pepper and salt over, add a small bit of butter, and serve in a dish or over the ham.

Pork and Beans.—Take two quarts of dried white beans, (the small ones are best,) pick out any imperfections, and put them to soak in cold water, more than to cover them, let them remain one night; the next day, about two hours before dinner time, throw off the water; have a pound of nicely corned pork, a rib piece is best; put the beans in an iron dinner-pot; score the rind or skin of the pork, in squares or diamonds, and lay it on the beans, put in hot (not boiling) water to cover them, add a small dried red pepper, or a saltspoonful of cayenne; cover the pot close, and set it over a gentle fire for one hour; then take a tin basin, or earthen pudding-pan, rub the inside over with a bit of butter, and nearly fill it with the boiled beans, lay the pork in the centre, pressing it down a little; put small bits of butter over the beans, dredge a little flour over them, and the pork, and set it in a moderately hot oven, for nearly one hour.

Serve in the dish in which it was baked, thus:— Lay a nicely fringed small napkin on a dinner plate; set the basin or pan on that, turn the corners of the napkin up against it, and keep it in place by sprigs of green parsley or celery leaves on the plate under it, and so continue a wreath around the dish, concealing the pan entirely. Serve pickles and mashed potatoes with it.

If liked, the beans and pork may be boiled for half an hour longer, and served without baking; if there remains any over, they may be baked another day, or they may be served cold.

Ham with Vegetables—(*a family dinner.*)— After boiling a small ham, or part of a large one, take it up, skin it and set it in a dripping-pan, or dish; sprinkle pepper over, dredge flour over, and brown it in a hot oven, or before a fire. Boil such vegetables as you wish to serve with it, in the liquor in which it was boiled, first skimming off the fat if there is much, as it will then be fit for frying potatoes, parsnips, or other vegetables; if cabbage or turnips are served with boiled meat, they may be boiled together in the water; if spinach or parsnips are served, it is best to boil the potatoes in fair water separately; parsnips give out their flavor too much, and spinach discolors.

If parsnips are used, after boiling them tender, take off the skins, cut them in thin slices, across or lengthwise, and fry them in hot fat to a nice brown; when one side is done, turn the other; the potatoes also, may be fried; or, having been boiled done, put them in the pan with the meat, and brown them whole; or mash them with milk and butter; make them in a neat form, and brown the outside before the fire, or in an oven.

Potatoes to serve with ham or tongue, may be boiled, and fried in slices, or whole, thus:—Put some fat in the pan, and let it become hot, or fry some slices of fat pork, put in small sized boiled potatoes, sprinkle a little pepper over; cover the pan, and let them fry rather quickly, turn them when one side is done, or cut them in slices before frying. Serve them around the meat, on the same dish, or separately.

The appearance of a boiled dinner may be greatly improved, by the manner of serving up the vegetables.

SUCCATASH.—Take of dried sweet corn and white beans—one quart of dried sweet corn, to one or two of beans.

Put the beans to soak in a basin, with water to cover them; rinse the corn in cold water, and put them in a basin with water to cover it, let them remain until the next day; within two hours of dinner time, pour the water from the beans, pick out any imperfections, and put them with the corn, with the water in which it is soaked, into a dinner-pot; cut a pound of nicely corned pork in thin slices, put it to the corn and beans, and put over them hot water, rather more than to cover them; add a very small red pepper, or a saltspoonful of cayenne, and cover the pot close; set it where it will boil very gently, for an hour and a half, then put it in a deep dish; add a bit of butter to it and serve.

The pork may be scored, and not cut up, if preferred, and served in a separate dish.

Dried corn and beans may be soaked and cooked in this manner, without the pork; when taken up, add plenty of sweet butter, season with salt and pepper, and serve. Lima beans are the best. The small white kidney bean next.

FRIED SAUSAGES, *or sausage-meat, spinach, or other vegetable.*—Make hot some fat salt pork slices, or lard, in a frying pan, and fry the sausages, or meat, a nice brown; have some nicely boiled spinach or cabbage, pressed free from water, chop it fine, and lay it on a steak dish; lay the fried sausages in it, put a very little hot vinegar to the gravy in the pan, and pour it over.

Water may be used instead of vinegar; the vegetable is most generally eaten with vinegar.

Or, serve with mashed potatoes, instead of spinach or cabbage. Sausage-meat may be fried, and served in the same manner as sausages.

Hominy boiled, (see p. 192.) may be served with fried sausages. This is a favorite Southern dish.

TO BOIL CORNED PORK WITH VEGETABLES.— Take a side or rib piece of corned pork, put it in a kettle of hot (not boiling) water, and boil it gently, according to its weight, fifteen minutes to each pound; cover the pot. Cut a large white heart cabbage in four, take off the outside leaves, and cut the stalk close down to the head; wash the quarters in cold water; examine between the leaves that there are no insects secreted; half an hour before the meat is done, take off the cover, skim it clear, and put the cabbage in, with a small red pepper, or a saltspoonful of cayenne; press the cabbage down; pare a dozen fine potatoes of equal size, and wash them in two or three waters, and put them in the pot; cover it and let it boil for half an hour, then take out the meat, cut the skin across in squares or diamonds, and set it where it will keep hot; or dredge flour over it and set it before the fire, or in an oven to brown. Let the vegetables boil for quarter of an hour longer; when they are done, take the potatoes in a deep covered dish, put the cabbage into a cullender and press out all the water, and lay it on a large dish, making a platform, and lay the pork on it; or serve it on a deep dish, and the pork on an oval dish.

If the pork is very salt, put it to soak in cold water one night before boiling. Savoy cabbage or spinach may be used instead of white cabbage; fifteen minutes fast boiling will be enough for either of these.

Potatoes should not be boiled with spinach, as it colors them green; it requires so short time boiling that the potatoes may be boiled before it is put in.

Bacon or smoked chops or shoulder may be boiled in the same manner.

A pickled or corned tongue may be boiled in this manner. Skin it when done; sprinkle pepper over it; dredge flour over; put bits of butter over, and set it in an oven for half an hour.

To Boil Salted or Corned Beef.—Wash the brine from a piece of corned beef, and put it into a pot of hot (not boiling) water; take off the scum as it rises; allow fifteen minutes for each pound of meat; then try if it is tender; let it boil gently. When it is done, take it up and press it between two plates.

Cabbage, or spinach, or some other greens, are generally boiled with salt beef; put down the beef in time that it may be done before it is time to boil the vegetables, and set it to press whilst the vegetables are boiling.

To Prepare the Cabbage.—Take off the discolored outside leaves, and cut each head in four; look well between the leaves to see that no insects are secreted; wash the quarters, and put them in the water in which the meat was boiled; set it over the fire and let it boil fast for three quarters of an hour; if you wish the potatoes boiled with it, choose large equal sized ones, and put them in with the cabbage; when they are done take the potatoes into a covered dish; put the cabbage into a cullender; press out all the water. If you wish to have the meat hot, after pressing it, put it into the pot ten minutes before taking up the vegetables. Serve the cabbage and potatoes in covered dishes, and the meat on an oval dish.

The Yellow or ruta-baga turnip is much liked instead of cabbage; pare off the thick outside, cut them in halves, or if very large, quarter them. Boil same length of time as for cabbage. Take them up and serve as directed for cabbage; or mash them fine, and smooth with a bit of butter and a little pepper; mash the potatoes with a gill of hot milk, and a bit of butter the size of an egg. Put potatoes and turnips in covered dishes; heap them high in the centre; smooth over the surface in flutes with a knife blade meeting in the centre, as a common point. Take a pinch of fine pepper in the fingers and put it over the whole surface in spots. Put the meat on an oval dish, and vinegar and made mustard in the castor.

Thus you have a nicely served family dinner, to which may be added some simple dessert.

A boiled Indian pudding is both appropriate and healthful.

Take a quart of sweet yellow cornmeal, stir it into boiling water, and a teaspoonful of lard, with a teaspoonful of salt, to make it so as to mould in the hands. Make it in balls the size of a teacup, drop them in the pot, and let them boil fast for half an hour. Serve with butter and sugar, or syrup.

Or, put to the meal as much of the boiling water as will make a thick batter; add a large teaspoonful of salt; stir it smooth, and tie it loosely in a pudding bag, put it in the pot with the meat, or in fair water and boil for one hour. Serve with a sauce or syrup.

PARSNIP STEW.—Cut half a pound of fat salt pork in slices, and a pound of beef or veal in bits; put them in a dinner pot, with very little water. Scrape some parsnips, and cut them in slices an inch thick; wash and put them to the meat; pare and cut six small sized potatoes in halves. Cover the pot close and set it over a bright fire for half an hour; then dredge in a tablespoonful of wheat flour, add a small bit of butter, and a small teaspoonful of pepper, stir it in, and set it over the fire to brown for fifteen minutes. Take the stew into a dish and serve.

LAMB.

To Choose Lamb.—The vein in the neck of a fore-quarter of lamb will be a fine blue, if it is fresh; if it is of a green or yellowish color, it is stale.

The hind-quarter becomes first tainted under the kidney. It is best to buy of a respectable butcher; let him choose for you, and you secure the best article, at his recommendation.

A fore-quarter includes the shoulder, neck, and breast.

A hind-quarter is the leg and loin.

The pluck is sold with the head, liver, heart and lights. The melt is not used with us.

The fry contains the sweet-breads, skirts, and some of the liver.

Lamb may be hashed, stewed, roasted, fried, or broiled, or made in a pie, the same as veal.

Harslet Hashed.—Skin the head and boil it with the liver, heart, &c. When tender, cut the meat from the head, and chop it fine with the other; season with salt and pepper to taste; dredge it white with flour, and put it to a cup of water, to keep it from burning; put it over a moderate fire, and stir it with a spoon until thoroughly heated; then serve in a deep dish with boiled rice or hominy. A bit of butter may be added before taking it up.

To Broil a Breast of Lamb.—Have a clear bright fire of coals; when the gridiron is hot, rub it over with a bit of suet, then lay on the meat, the inside to the fire first; let it broil gently; when it is nearly cooked through, turn the other side; let it brown nicely; put a good bit butter on a steak dish; work a large teaspoonful of salt, and a small one of pepper into it; lay the meat upon it; turn it once or twice, and serve hot.

The shoulder may be broiled in the same manner. Let the fire be clear and bright, but not scorching.

Lamb Stewed with Peas.—Cut the scrag or breast of lamb in pieces, and put it in a stew pan with water enough to cover it. Cover the stew-pan close, and let it simmer or stew for fifteen or twenty minutes; take off the scum, then add a tablespoonful of salt and a quart of shelled peas; cover the stew-pan and let them stew for half an hour; work a small tablespoonful of wheat flour with a quarter of a pound of butter, and stir it into the stew; add a small teaspoonful of pepper; let it simmer together for ten minutes. Serve with new potatoes, boiled. A blade of mace may be added, if liked.

Lamb Chop, *like a Crown.*—Cut a loin of lamb in chops; rub them over with a mixture of pepper and salt, and, if liked, a very little grated nutmeg. Dip them in the beaten yolk of an egg, and then dip them in rolled cracker, and fry them in hot lard or beef dripping. When done, place them like a crown; put a bit of butter in the pan; add a little pepper, and a bunch of parsley cut small, or a lemon sliced thin; let it fry for a few minutes, then dredge in a tablespoonful of wheat flour; stir it about; then put to it a cup of boiling water; stir it over the fire for five or six minutes; then pour it inside of the crown and serve.

Lamb Steaks with Wine or Currant Jelly.—Rub lamb steaks or cutlets over with a mixture of salt and pepper, then dip them into beaten egg, and afterwards into rolled crackers or wheat flour; put of lard and butter each a tablespoonful into a frying-pan; when it is boiling hot, lay in the steaks or cutlets, and fry them gently to a nice brown. When one side is done, turn the other; when done, take them up, add to the gravy in the pan a wine-glass of Port or Madeira wine, or a tablespoonful of currant jelly and a little hot water; let it boil up once, then pour it over the steaks or cutlets and serve. Or the steaks may be broiled and the wine or jelly made hot, with a bit of butter, and put over them.

QUARTER OF LAMB ROASTED.—Wash a quarter of lamb with cold water; mix a large tablespoonful of salt, and a heaping teaspoonful of pepper, and rub it well over every part of the meat; then spit it or lay it on muffin rings or a trivet in a dripping-pan; put a pint of water in the pan to baste with; set it before the fire in a dutch oven, or reflector, or in a hot stove oven; baste very often after it begins to roast; lay it so that the thickest part may be nearest the fire; allow fifteen minutes for each pound of meat; baste with the water in the pan until nearly done; add more as it wastes; then put to it quarter of a pound of butter; baste the meat with it; dredge it white with flour; stir up the fire to brown it.

In roasting a piece of meat, set it at a little distance from the fire at first, gradually drawing it nearer to finish; take care not to scorch it. When done, take it out on a hot dish, and cover it with a tin cover. Set the dripping-pan over the fire, dredge a tablespoonful of wheat flour to it; stir it smooth, add a little boiling water if necessary; stir the gravy over the fire for a few minutes, then strain it into the gravy tureen, and serve with boiled new potatoes, stewed peas and lettuce.

In making the gravy, a glass of Port or Madeira wine, or a large spoonful of red jelly dissolved in water may be substituted for the water and flour.

Lemon sliced thin and put in the dripping-pan, fifteen or twenty minutes before the meat is done, and served as a garnish for the meat, is much liked—the leaves of a bunch of green mint finely minced and moistened with vinegar, with the addition of a spoonful of sugar, is sometimes served with the lamb.

Lamb may be baked in a hot oven nearly to equal a roast. Have the oven as hot as possible without burning, and baste frequently.

To Prepare a Quarter of Lamb for Boiling.—Wash a quarter of lamb in cold water; then rub it all over with a mixture of salt and pepper; dredge well with wheat flour, and put it in a pot of hot (not boiling) water; cover the pot and let it boil gently, allowing fifteen minutes for each pound of meat; take off the scum as it rises. Serve with boiled potatoes and parsley, or drawn butter sauce; and mint sauce, and lettuce dressed. Break the leaves from some fine white heart lettuce and rinse each one in cold water; then cut them small; put a teaspoonful of made mustard with a teaspoonful of sugar, and the same of oil, beat them together in a cup; then add enough vinegar to fill a cup, and pour it over the lettuce.

MUTTON.

OBSERVATIONS ON MUTTON.—The pipe which runs along the bone inside of a chine or saddle of mutton, must be taken out. If it is to be kept any length of time, wipe the meat perfectly dry, and rub pepper over it, in every part. Whenever you find any moisture, wipe it dry, rub it with pepper, and dredge flour over. The kernels should be taken out by the butcher.

Mutton for roasting or steaks should hang as long as it will keep without tainting. Let it hang in the air in a cool dry place. Pepper will keep flies from it. The chine or rib bones should be wiped every day. The bloody part of the neck must be cut off. In the breast the brisket changes first. In the hind quarter, the part under and about the kidneys, is first to taint.

Mutton for stewing or boiling should not be so long kept. It will not be so fine a color if it is.

The lean of mutton should be a clear red, fine, close grain, and tender to the touch. The fat should be firm and white.

Skewer a piece of letter paper over the fat of mutton whilst roasting. When nearly done, take it off.

Steaks are cut from the leg. Chops and cutlets are cut from the shoulder, breast, loin, and neck or scrag.

The leg, loin, scrag, or breast, may be stewed.

If the leg of mutton is roasted, serve with its own gravy, with a spoonful of currant jelly, or red wine, made hot in it.

If boiled, serve drawn butter, parsley, or mock caper sauce, with tomatoes stewed, and plain boiled potatoes. A leg of mutton is better for boiling, it laid in a beef pickle, three or four days before it is wanted.

To make Mutton taste like Venison.—Take a fat hind quarter of mutton, let it hang several days—to ten pounds of meat, take a quarter of a pound of brown sugar, rub it well into the meat, then pour over it half a pint of port wine, the same of vinegar; let it lie in this four or five days, turning it every day; then wash it in cold water, and wipe it dry, and roast it; or, cut it in steaks, or chops, and fry, or boil them, or make it a pie.

Sugar gives a finer flavor to the meat, than does salt, which hardens the lean; sugar is a great preservative.

Mutton Pasty to eat like Venison.—Prepare the mutton as above directed; take a loin, and after boning it, beat it well with a rolling-pin, then wash it, season with pepper and salt, and lay it in a deep dish. To ten pounds of meat, take one pound of sweet butter, spread it in small bits over the meat; put a paste crust around the edge of the dish, put in with the meat a gill of water, and cover with a pie paste, an inch thick; cut a slit in the middle, and bake in a quick oven, two hours and a half; cover the paste with writing paper, that it may not be scorched.

Put the bones of the meat in two quarts of water, with a little salt, a few blades of mace, and whole pepper, let it boil slowly until it is half reduced, then add to it a tablespoonful of browned flour; let it boil up once, then strain it; when the pie is done, raise the crust and put the gravy in.

To make Mock Venison.—When the sheep is

killed, save the blood; keep stirring it all the time until it is cold, that it may not congeal; cut the sheep in two, take one side, cut the leg like a haunch, cut off the shoulder, loin, and neck, and breast, and steep them all in the blood, as long as the weather will permit; then take the haunch, hang it in a cool dry place, as long as it will keep sweet, then roast it like venison.

This is said to be very fine, if the weather is so that it may be kept several days. Take off the suet before putting it in the blood. Take the other parts, and lay them in a large deep pan, or tray; lay the fat side downwards, mix half a pound of brown sugar, and a quart of vinegar, with a quart of red wine, pour it over, and let it lie twelve hours; then take the neck, breast, and loin out of the pickle, cut them in chops, and broil or roast them, or make a pasty of them.

If it will keep, let the shoulder remain in the wine, etc., for a week, then put it in a beef pickle, or brine, for ten days, and smoke it like beef. To be eaten chipped fine. The leg or haunch may be done in the same manner, and very nearly resembles venison hams.

MUTTON HAMS.—These are cut, corned, smoked and eaten, the same as smoked beef, or venison hams.

SHEEP HARSLET HASHED.—When you cut up the sheep, take the heart, liver, and lights, wash them in cold water, then boil them tender, in plenty of water, and a tablespoonful of salt; take off the scum as it rises; then chop them fine, season with pepper, and sweet herbs, if liked, to taste; add quarter of a pound of butter, cut small, and enough hot water to moisten the hash; dredge in a tablespoonful of browned flour, and put the whole into a stew-pan, over a gentle fire, stir it frequently, and when it is thoroughly heated, take it up; three-quarters of an hour is about the time required for it. Serve with boiled vegetables and pickles.

HAUNCH OF MUTTON.—Keep the haunch as long as you can, and have it sweet, wash it with a little vinegar and water, before dressing it. Before putting the meat to the fire, rub it all over with a mixture of pepper and salt; make a stiff paste of wheat flour and water, roll it thin, and put it over the meat; have a large, bright fire, and set the meat at a little distance from it, (allow fifteen minutes to each pound of meat;) when half done take off the paste, draw it nearer the fire, and baste freely, with water from the pan; turn it so that every part may be done; half an hour before taking it up, stir up the fire, put quarter of a pound of butter in the pan, baste with it, dredge the meat white with flour, baste again, turn the meat over, baste freely, and dredge more flour over, and baste again; the fire must be bright for finishing. When done, take it up, put the dripping-pan over the fire, cut a lemon in thin slices into it, dredge in a large tablespoonful of browned flour, stir it smooth for ten minutes, then strain into a gravy tureen, and serve with the slices of lemon. Or, instead of a lemon, put a wineglass of port wine to the gravy.

Boiled potatoes, asparagus, or spinach, dressed celery, and currant jelly, is served with roast mutton.

Putting the paste over the meat, keeps in its juices, and therefore makes it sweeter. A gravy may be made of a pound of the loin of mutton, cut small and simmered in a pint of water, till reduced to half; salt it a little, stir in a teaspoonful of browned flour, and a little pepper; let it boil up once, then strain it, and serve with the meat, and currant jelly.

Mutton Currie.—Take a fine loin of mutton, take off all the fat, cut the meat small, cut some onions small, and fry them in hot lard; when nearly done, put in the meat; add a tablespoonful of curry powder, to each pound of meat, and a small teaspoonful of salt, fry gently; when nicely browned, put to it half a pint of hot water, and put it into a stew-pan; cover it close, and let it simmer for an hour; then serve with rice, boiled dry, in the dish under it, or in a separate dish.

A curry may be made the same as a stew, adding a tablespoonful of the powder for each pound of meat, or less, if preferred.

A Shoulder of Mutton.—Broil a shoulder of mutton over a clear bright fire of coals, let it broil gently, putting the inside to the fire first, cover it with a tin; when nearly done through, turn it; let it brown nicely; when it is done, take it on to a hot steak dish, sprinkle a small tablespoonful of salt, and a teaspoonful of pepper over; butter it freely, turn it once or twice in the seasoning, turn the inside down, cover it with a tin cover, and serve hot, with boiled hominy, or potatoes, for breakfast. The shoulder may be boned, before broiling.

To Broil a Breast of Mutton.—Parboil a breast of mutton, then wipe it dry, and broil it as directed for shoulder.

Mutton Chop Fried.—Cut some fine mutton chops without much fat, rub over both sides with a mixture of salt and pepper, dip them in wheat flour or rolled crackers, and fry in hot lard or beef drippings, when both sides are a fine brown, take them on a hot dish, put a wine-glass of hot water in the pan, let it become hot, stir in a teaspoonful of browned flour, let it boil up once, and serve in the pan with the meat. A tablespoonful of currant jelly may be stirred into the gravy, or a wine-glass of port wine instead of water. Or cut a lemon in thin slices, take out the pits, and fry them brown with a bit of butter in the pan, dredge in a teaspoonful of browned flour, add a wine-glass of hot water, stir it for a few minutes over the fire, then serve in the dish with the meat.

To Broil Mutton Chop or Steak.—Rub each over with a mixture of pepper and salt, lay them on a hot gridiron over a bright fire of coals; when done, and both sides a fine brown, take them on a dish, butter them freely, turn them once or twice on the dish, and serve hot. Or before putting the chops or steaks to the fire, dip them first into beaten eggs, then into rolled cracker; broil very gently; put pepper and salt with some butter on a dish, lay the broil on, turn it once or twice in the butter, and serve.

Leg of Mutton Boiled.—Wash a leg of mutton, dredge it well with flour, and wrap it in a cloth, then put it in a pot of hot water, and boil according to its weight. Serve with drawn butter or parsley sauce, with boiled vegetables and pickles.

VENISON.

The choice of venison is regulated by the fat, which when young is thick, clear and close. As it always begins to taint first towards the haunches, run a knife into that part, if it is tainted you will perceive a rank smell, and it will have a greenish appearance. If you wish, you may keep it a long time by careful management—wash it well in milk and water, wipe it perfectly dry, till there is not the least damp remaining on it, then rub ground pepper or ginger over every part, and hang it in a dry, airy, cool place; pepper or ginger is a good preservative against the fly.

When to be dressed, wash venison, thus kept in lukewarm water, and wipe it dry. The longer venison is kept without tainting, the sweeter it is.

VENISON STEAKS FRIED.—Cut venison steaks from the leg or loin, half an inch thick, dip them in rolled crackers or wheat flour; make of lard and sweet butter equal parts, or beef drippings, half the size of an egg, hot in a frying-pan, rub the steaks over with a mixture of pepper and salt, cover the pan and let them fry quickly, until one side is a fine brown, then turn the other, and finish frying without the cover; take care that they are not over done, then add to the gravy a glass of red wine, or a wine-glass of hot water, with a tablespoonful of currant jelly, stir it over the fire for a few minutes, then put it in the dish with the meat, and serve as hot as possible. Steak dishes of block tin, with heaters, are used for beef or venison. Lean steaks of fat beef cooked in this way, are equal to venison, for which the beef should be kept till ready to taint, then rinse them in cold water, wipe them dry, and finish as directed; the steaks should be cut small like venison.

To Broil Venison Steaks.—Let the gridiron become hot, rub the bars with a bit of suet, then lay on the steaks, having dipped them in rolled crackers or wheat flour, and set it over a bright, clear, but not fierce fire of coals; when one side is done, take the steak carefully over the steak dish, and hold it so that the blood may fall into the dish, then turn them on the gridiron, let it broil nicely; set a steak dish where it will become hot, put on it a bit of butter the size of an egg for each pound of venison, put to it a saltspoon of salt, and the same of black pepper, put to it a tablespoonful of current jelly, made liquid with a tablespoonful of hot water or wine, lay the steaks on, turn them once or twice in the gravy, and serve hot. Or they may be simply broiled, and served with butter, pepper, and salt; or having broiled one side, and turned the steaks, lay thin slices of lemon over, and serve in the dish with the steaks.

To Stew Venison.—Cut the venison in steaks, put some bits of butter in a chafing dish or tin pan, over hot coals or a lamp; when it is hot lay the steaks in season with a little pepper and salt, strew rolled cracker or bread crumbs over, add to it a wine-glass of port wine, cut a tablespoonful of current jelly in bits, and lay it over the steaks, cover it with a tin plate, put fire on it; when the steaks are nicely browned, take off the cover and serve. This may be done at table.

Venison Roasted.—To dress a haunch; chop off the shank, take off the skin, but none of the fat, then put it evenly on a spit, make a paste of flour and water, roll it thin, and fold it around the venison, put letter paper over it, and secure it with a packthread ; have a bright steady fire, and set the roast at a little distance from it ; put a pint of water in the pan, and baste occasionally, (allow fifteen minutes for each pound of meat,) turn it so that the fire may act with equal force on every part, put the largest part nearest the fire ; when half done take off the paste and paper, draw it nearer tne fire, put quarter of a pound of butter in the pan, with a glass of port or claret wine, add pepper and salt, and baste the meat freely, turn it that every part may be well done ; when nearly done, dredge it with wheat flour, baste and dredge again ; baste it and finish roasting ; when done, add currant jelly to the gravy, and serve with the meat.

Venison may be roasted, and served the same as beef, or with a spoonful of jelly in the gravy.

VENISON PASTY.—Bone a neck and breast of venison, season with pepper and salt, cut the breast in two or three pieces, lay the breast and neck end first ; then the best end on the top ; make a good puff paste, line the edge of a baking-dish, lay the meat in, put in half a pound of butter, cut small, and half a pint of water ; then put an inch thick paste crust over, cut a slit in the centre, lay a sheet of letter paper over, and bake two hours in a quick oven ; whilst the pie is baking, put the bones in a stew-pan, with two quarts of water, and let it boil gently down to half that quantity, season with a blade of mace, and whole pepper ; when nearly done, add a large tablespoonful of browned flour, stir it together for a few minutes, then strain it ; half an hour before the pie is done, take it out raise the crust, put the gravy in, and replace the crust; cut some leaves of paste rolled thin, ornament the edge and slit in the centre, with a wreath of these, or put a paste flower in the centre, and finish baking. Serve currant jelly with it.

Venison pie may be made the same as directed for veal, and baked in the same manner.

A Pretty Dish of Venison.—Cut a breast of venison in steaks, make quarter of a pound of butter hot, in a pan, rub the steaks over with a mixture of a little salt and pepper, dip them in wheat flour, or rolled crackers, and fry a rich brown; when both sides are done, take them up on a dish, and put a tin cover over; dredge a heaping teaspoonful of flour into the butter in the pan, stir it with a spoon until it is brown, without burning, put to it a small teacup of boiling water, with a tablespoonful of currant jelly dissolved into it, stir it for a few minutes, then strain it over the meat and serve.

A glass of wine, with a tablespoonful of white sugar dissolved in it, may be used for the gravy, instead of the jelly and water.

Venison may be boiled, and served with boiled vegetables, pickled beets, etc., and sauce.

Venison Sauce.—Half a pint of port wine made hot, with a tablespoonful of white sugar, the same of currant jelly, and a bit of butter, the size of a large egg.

POULTRY, GAME, &c.

In choosing poultry, the best way to determine whether it is young, is to try the skin under the leg or wing; if it is easily broken, it is young; or, turn the wing backwards; if the joint yields readily, it is tender; a fat fowl is best for any purpose.

After a chicken or fowl is killed, plunge it into a pot of scalding hot water; then pluck off the feathers, taking care not to tear the skin; when it is picked clean, roll up a sheet of white wrapping paper, set fire to it, and singe off all the hairs.— Poultry should be carefully picked, and nicely singed.

If a fowl is fresh killed, the vent will be close, and the flesh have a pleasant smell.

For Roasting.—Bruise the bone of the leg close to the foot, and draw out the string from the hips; cut a slit in the back of the neck, pass your finger around the front, and draw out the crop, turn back the skin, and cut off some of the neck, leave skin enough to turn over and fasten at the back. Cut off the vent, cut a slit from the end of the breast bone to it, and draw out the entrails, taking care not to break the gall; no washing will take off the bitter where it has touched; cut the entrail at the vent loose; break the back bone that it may lay flat on the dish when served; rinse the chicken inside with cold water, and wipe it dry, then rub it over with a mixture of salt and pepper. Prepare the stuffing as follows:

Cut two or three slices of wheat bread, spread it thickly with butter, season with pepper and salt, and if liked, a little powdered thyme, make it wet with milk or water, and fill with it; take two or three stitches with a coarse thread and needle to draw the slit together and keep the dressing in, turn the legs close to the sides and run a wire skewer through; run another skewer through the joint of the wing, and through the body to the other wing, and after taking the gall from the liver, and the inside from the gizzard, wash them and put them between the pinions and body; or parboil them and chop them fine for the gravy. The chicken or fowl is now trussed for roasting. Black footed poultry should never be chosen for boiling; for roasting they are as good.

For Boiling.—The apron or lower part of the body must be slit at the sides, and the legs put through; cut a slit across to take out the entrails and take out the crop, take care that it does not break, and so part of it remain in, to your lasting disgrace; turn the wings over against the back. To the stuffing of a fowl for boiling, may be added half a pint of small oysters; season well with butter, pepper and salt; or a bunch of parsley chopped may be put to the dressing. A full grown fowl is best for boiling.

Boiled Fowl or Chicken.—Having trussed and stuffed a fowl, dredge it well with wheat flour, then put it into a pot of hot water, cover it close, and let it boil gently, according to its weight and age; an old fowl may boil twice as long as a young one; allow fifteen minutes to the pound for a full grown fowl; take off the scum as it rises. Serve with plain boiled or mashed potatoes, and drawn butter, parsley or oyster sauce.

Pickles and dressed celery are served with boiled fowls; also mashed turnips, boiled asparagus, and cauliflower. Boiled ham or tongue, or corned beef, is generally served with boiled fowls.

An old fowl is fit for nothing but soup.

To Roast a Fowl or Chicken.—Have a bright, clear, and steady fire for roasting poultry; prepare it as directed; spit it, put a pint of hot water in the dripping pan, add to it a small tablespoonful of salt, and a small teaspoonful of pepper; baste frequently, and let it roast quickly, without scorching; when nearly done, put a piece of butter the size of a large egg to the water in the pan, when it melts, baste with it, dredge a little flour over, baste again, and let it finish; half an hour will roast a full grown chicken, if the fire is right. When done take it up, let the giblets (heart, liver, and gizzard,) boil tender, and chop them very fine, and put them in the gravy, add a tablespoonful of browned flour, and a bit of butter, stir it over the fire for a few minutes, then serve in a gravy tureen. Or put the giblets in the pan and let them roast.

Mashed potatoes, tomatoes stewed, mashed turnips, (ruta-baga or yellow are best,) dressed celery, or lettuce, and pickles and mangoes, are served with roast fowls. Also currant jelly, stewed apples, or cranberry jam.

A fowl may be roasted in a hot-stove oven, so as to be nearly as fine as before the fire; baste freely and often, and finish as directed for roasting before the fire; put muffin rings on a trivet in the dripping pan, and lay the fowl on, rub the outside over with pepper and salt, put bits of butter over, dust it lightly with flour; have a pint of water in the pan, let the oven be well heated, and baste often; make the gravy as before directed, be sure to have enough water in the pan, that the gravy may not burn; add hot water as it wastes.

To Stew or Fricassee Chickens.—Cut off the feet, cut off the legs at the hip, cut off the wings close to the body, take out the entrails; pass the knife close to the breast bone, up the sides to the wings, dividing the body in two, cut the back in two, (flatten each piece with a heavy stroke of the rolling pin or potato beetle,) make another incision close to the top of the breast bone, taking off what is called the wish bone, with the meat attached. This is for a full grown chicken, and is the proper way to carve a roast fowl.

Rinse the pieces in cold water, take the giblets (heart, liver, and gizzard,) from the entrails, with the fat, split the gizzard, peel it from the gravel bag, and cut it in halves, wash them all, and put them with the chicken into a stew-pan, with hot water nearly to cover them; add to it a small tablespoonful of salt, and a saltspoonful of pepper, cover it close, and set it to boil very gently, take off any scum as it rises; when tender, for a full grown chicken, take a teacup of butter, (or two ounces,) work into it a small tablespoonful of wheat flour, then add it to the stew, with a bunch of parsley washed and cut small, cover the stew-pan for fifteen minutes, let it simmer gently, and serve.

Lay nicely toasted thin slices of bread on a steak dish, put the back and breast of the chicken on first, and the other parts around it, and put the gravy over; egg balls may be added to the stew.

Half a pound of nicely corned pork cut in thin slices, and stewed with the chicken, is liked by many persons; in that case no other salt will be required, and only half as much butter. A blade of mace may be added to the seasoning, if liked. Half an hour or three quarters will be required for stewing chickens, an hour for a large fowl.

Mashed potatoes, or boiled new potatoes and lettuce, or dressed celery and pickles, to be served with this stew.

CHICKEN CURRIE.—Stew the chicken as directed above, adding to the seasoning a tablespoonful of currie powder for a small chicken.

Have some nice boiled chicken dry, put it on a dish, and serve with the currie over. (See currie powder page 198.)

TO BROIL CHICKENS OR FOWLS, (*Like a Steak.*) —Cut off the vent, cut a slit in the apron, (below the breast bone,) and draw out the entrails; take out the crop; cut the neck short; take off the wings, and split the chicken nearly in two, passing the knife from the vent up each side to the wing joints, but do not cut it apart; then spread it out flat, break the back and breast bone with a stroke of the potato beetle, or rolling-pin, and lay it on a hot gridiron over a bright fire of coals; put the inside to the fire first; put a tin cover over it, and let it broil rather quickly, until nearly cooked through; then turn it, stir up the coals, and let it finish without the cover. When it is nicely browned, take it on a steak dish, butter it freely; season with pepper and salt, (a teaspoonful of salt and the same of pepper) turn it once or twice in the gravy; serve it hot, with the inside down; having also broiled the wings, lay them on either side of the body. Or a chicken may be carved as for table, or as described for a stew.

Small young chickens are sometimes split up the back and spread out, or cut in two at the breast and back.

There is a way of preparing a chicken for broiling called a spread eagle. Cut the chicken open at the back, take out the entrails and crop, and flatten the breast bone, and turn the wings outward. Let it broil slowly with a cover, until thoroughly done, then brown the outside, and put it on a hot dish with butter, pepper and salt.

Covering it whilst broiling keeps the steam in, which makes it more juicy, and cooks it.

To Fry Chicken or Fowl.—Cut up the chicken as for stewing or fricassee; make some lard or beef dripping hot in a frying pan, rub each piece over with a mixture of pepper and salt; dip them in wheat flour or finely rolled cracker, and put them in the pan, (the cut side down) cover them and let them fry rather quickly until it is a fine brown, then turn the other side; leave off the cover and brown it nicely; when done take them up, add a bit of butter to the pan, with a very little hot water, and put it in the dish with the chicken.

Chickens may be fried with butter only; but it is apt to make them too dark colored; lemon sliced thin, and browned in the pan after the chickens, may be served in the gravy if liked; or dredge a little wheat flour into the hot fat; stir it about with a spoon, then add a wineglass of hot water; stir it for a few minutes, and pour it in the dish.

Chicken Pie.—Cut off the legs and vent, cut a slit and take out the entrails; cut off the hips, and cut it in two at the leg-joint, cut off the wings with as much flesh attached as possible; split the body up the sides, cut the back in two and flatten the bone; cut the small bone from the upper part of the breast, with some of the meat, rinse in cold water, and, unless the chickens are very young, put them in a stew-pan with water to cover them; add a large teaspoonful of salt, or half a pound of corned pork; cut in thin slices; add a saltspoonful of pepper; cover the stew-pan and let them boil slowly, until tender; skim it clear.

Make a paste crust, or as directed for pot-pie; rub butter over the sides of a pudding-pan or tin basin, and line it with the paste rolled to quarter of an inch thickness; put in the pieces of chicken, and pork, if it is used; put in butter the size of a small egg; cut it small. If pork is not used, take twice as much butter; dredge flour over until it is white; then put in the water from the stew-pan; if there is not enough to fill nearly to the top of the pie, add more water; roll out a paste or puff paste crust; cut a slit in the centre; make three or four small incisions on either side of it; lay skewers across the pie; lay the crust over; trim off the edges and bake for three quarters of an hour in a moderately hot oven; ten or fifteen minutes before it is done, brush the top of the pie with the yolk of egg beaten with a little milk, and finish baking. Serve mashed potatoes and pickles, with meat or chicken pies.

The edge of the pie may be ornamented with leaves cut with a tin cutter, from sheets of paste; put them on twenty minutes before it is done baking. One full-grown chicken will make two, two quart basin pies.

CHICKEN POT-PIE.—Take a full grown chicken or fowl; cut it as for stewing or pie; rinse it in cold water, and put it in a stew-pan with hot water to cover it; add half a pound of salt pork, cut in thin slices, if liked, or a large teaspoonful of salt; let it boil gently for half an hour, (unless it is a young chicken, when it need not be parboiled,) take off the scum; make a pie or pot-pie crust; make it rather more than half an inch thick; line the sides only of a dinner-pot; (if it extends too low down it will burn;) put the meat in the bottom, take a piece of butter, the size of a large egg, and cut it in small bits, put it over the meat; not half as much butter will be required if pork is used; dredge it white with flour; put in the water from the stew-pan, and if it does not reach nearly to the top of the crust, add more hot water; lay skewers across the top; roll out the paste; reserve enough to cover the pie; cut the remainder in small squares and drop them in the pie; then put on the top crust; cut a slit in the centre, and cover the pot. Set it over a moderate fire, to boil gently for three-quarters of an hour; then take a fork and try the top crust; if it is done take the pie up.

The side crust should be about four or five inches wide, and if a large pie, reach nearly to the top of the pot, that there may be plenty of gravy.

To Dish a Pot Pie.—Take up the top crust, with some of the gravy, take the brown crust from the sides on to a steak dish, then take the chicken on it, put gravy over it and serve. Pickles and mashed potatoes, are served with pot pie.

Chickens Scolloped.—Mince some cold chicken, without the skin; make it wet with gravy, or hot water, season with salt and pepper; to the minced meat of one chicken, put two ounces of butter, cut small.

Rub tin scolloped pans over with butter, strew rolled crackers over, put the minced chicken in, strew rolled crackers over, and bake in a hot oven for half an hour; when done, turn it out on a dish. Serve with dressed celery or pickles.

Chicken Patties.—Prepare a cold roast, or boiled fowl, as for scolloped chicken; line a buttered tin plate with a rich pie paste, put the mince in, and cover with a puff paste crust, cut a slit in the middle, and bake three-quarters of an hour in a moderately hot oven; or make it in small patty-pans, and bake half an hour. Serve with pickles.

Cold lamb or veal may be minced and done in the same manner.

A few minutes before they are done, brush them over with the yolk of an egg, beaten with a little milk, and finish; this is called gilding.

A CHICKEN SALAD.—Take a fine white bunch of celery (four or five heads), scrape and wash it white; reserve the delicate green leaves; shred the white part like straws, lay this in a glass, or white china dish, in the form of a nest. Mince all the white meat of a boiled, or white stewed fowl, without the skin, and put it in the nest.

Make a salad dressing thus:—Rub the yolks of two hard-boiled eggs to a smooth paste, with a dessert spoonful of salad oil, or melted butter; add to it two teaspoonsful of made mustard, and a small teaspoonful of fine white sugar, and put to it gradually (stirring it in), a large cup of strong vinegar.

Make a wreath of the most delicate leaves of the celery around the edge of the nest, between it and the chicken; pour the dressing over the chicken, when ready to serve; if the dressing is poured over too soon, it will discolor the celery.

White heart lettuce may be used for the nest instead of celery.

TURKEYS.—To choose a turkey, follow the directions for choosing chickens; a hen turkey is more plump and round, and is best for boiling.

A turkey should be young, full grown and fat.

The most highly esteemed mode of dressing, is roast or boil.

Turkeys may be stewed, and if young, fried or broiled, the same as chickens.

Roast and boiled turkeys are favorite holiday dishes; turkeys are roasted or boiled the same as fowls.

ROAST TURKEY.—Get a fine plump turkey, cut off the vent, cut a slit from the end of the breast bone to it, take out the entrails, take care not to break the gall on the liver: should the gall break on the liver, it must be thrown away, no washing will take off the bitter; take off the feet, and bruise the bone close to the foot, and draw out the string from the leg; cut a slit in the back of the neck, pass your finger around in front, and draw out the crop; cut the neck short, leave skin enough to fasten over against the back; wash the inside with cold water, wipe it dry; mix a tablespoonful of salt with a teaspoonful of pepper, rub the inside well with this, and also the place of the crop; make a stuffing as follows:—

Cut slices of wheat bread, pour hot water or milk over, to wet them; to half a sixpenny loaf, put a quarter of a pound of butter, a teaspoonful of pepper, and a teaspoonful of chopped sage, or thyme, if liked; fill the body with some of this; sew up the slit with a strong thread, and coarse needle; put enough of the dressing in the crop to make it look full, then draw the skin of the neck over the back, and fasten it with a skewer, turn the legs close to the body, and run skewers through each hip joint, and with a strong thread, tie the ends of the legs together; rub the outside over with pepper and salt, and put it evenly on the spit; put a pint of hot water in the pan to baste with, (add more, according as it wastes,) roast it according to its weight, allowing fifteen minutes to each pound of meat.

The fire must be bright and clear, and strong, though not fierce; if the turkey is large, set it at a little distance from the fire at first, let one side be put to the fire first, then turn the other, basting it freely with the water in the pan; the hips require the longest time to cook; gradually turn the turkey and baste, so that every part may be evenly done. When about two-thirds done, stir up the fire, add quarter of a pound of butter to the pan, and baste the turkey with it; dredge a little flour over, and turn it so that it may be nicely browned; take care not to scorch the breast bone; if necessary, skewer a piece of paper over it.

While roasting, take the heart and liver (carefully cut off the gall bag,) and boil them tender, in water nearly to cover them; chop them fine, season with salt and pepper. When the turkey is done, strain the gravy in the pan, and put it to the chopped giblets in a stew-pan, dredge in a tablespoonful of browned flour, and strain to it some of the water in which the liver and heart were boiled; let it simmer for a few minutes, then put it in a tureen, and serve with the turkey. Or if this gravy is not liked, dredge a little flour into the gravy in the pan, and set it over the fire, stir it for a few minutes, and if necessary, add a little hot water, then strain it through a gravy strainer into the tureen.

Take up the roast, draw the skewers out, and take out the threads, lay it on a dish, on its back, and serve with mashed potatoes, turnips mashed, dressed celery and pickles, stewed apples; cold boiled ham or tongue for a large dinner.

Mince pies for Christmas; pumpkin and apple pies for Thanksgiving.

A turkey may be stuffed with boiled potatoes mashed or chopped, and seasoned as directed for bread stuffing. Or for ordinary occasions, fat salt pork chopped small, may be used instead of butter.

To Boil a Turkey.—Prepare a turkey as for roasting; press the hips upward towards the wings, and turn the leg bones towards the back, tie them with a string passing over the back, secure the hips close to the body, by running skewers in at the joint, twist the wings over against the back, fill the body with a stuffing as follows: pour boiling water or milk on wheat bread or mashed potatoes, season high with pepper and salt, and if liked, a teaspoonful of fine sage or thyme, or a bunch of finely chopped parsley, fill the crop until it looks full, and turn the skin of the neck over against the back, and fasten it with a small skewer.

Dredge flour over the outside, tie it in a cloth, and put it in a pot of hot (not boiling) water, cover the pot, and let it boil gently, according to its weight, (fifteen minutes to the pound,) take off the scum, serve with drawn butter, celery or parsley sauce.

Mashed potatoes, turnips or squash, celery, pickles, and stewed apples, or cranberry jam, and cold ham or tongue, are served with boiled turkey.

Oyster stuffing is made as above directed, adding a pint of fine oysters to it. Serve with oyster sauce poured over, or in a tureen.

Roast or boiled turkey may be served cold for supper, or cold collation, with boiled ham cold, currant or cranberry jelly, and pickles and dressed celery.

Garnish with fresh water-cresses, parsley, or the delicate green leaves of celery.

Fragments of cold turkey may be advantageously used in the following manner: cut all the meat from the bones, chop it small; if there remains any of the stuffing, put it to the meat, if not, use bread crumbs, twice as much as of minced turkey; moisten it with gravy or hot water, and a bit of butter, season with pepper and salt to taste, and make it in small patties or pies, or butter tin pie plates, put the mince in, and bake in a hot oven; when done turn it out. Or put it into a frying pan, set it over a gentle fire, and stir it with a spoon until it is thoroughly heated.

The remains of boiled turkey may be made a salad, like chicken. The feet of chicken or turkey may be dished with a stew or fricassee; dip them in boiling water until the skin will peel off, cut off the claws, boil them tender, and put them in the stew.

FRICASSEED TURKEY, (White.)—Cut up a small young turkey, rinse it in cold water; put it in a stew-pan, with water to cover it; cover the stew-pan and set it over a gentle fire; take off the scum as it rises; add a large teaspoonful of salt when it is tender and white; add a small teaspoonful of pepper; work a tablespoon of flour with quarter of a pound of sweet butter; stir it into the fricassee by the spoonful. Dip a bunch of parsley in hot water, chop it small, and put it in the stew-pan; cover it, and let it simmer gently for fifteen or twenty minutes; then serve with boiled rice or mashed potatoes for breakfast or dinner.

BROWN FRICASSEE.—Cut up the turkey quite small; put it in a stew-pan with but little water to keep it from burning; if it boils out before the flesh is tender, add more hot water; cover it closely, and let it boil gently until tender; take off the scum;

put to the meat quarter of a pound of butter, a large teaspoonful of salt and a teaspoonful of pepper; set it over the fire, when the butter is hot, dredge in a tablespoonful of wheat flour or rolled crackers, and let it brown nicely; turning the pieces that each may have a fine color, then take it up, put a cup of boiling water to the stew-pan, stir it with a silver spoon, scraping the brown from the bottom; let it remain over the fire until it is smooth, and brown; then pour it through a gravy strainer over the meat.

Serve with mashed or plain boiled potatoes for breakfast, or with the addition of dressed celery for dinner.

To Choose a Goose.—Be careful in choosing a goose that it is young; an old goose is very poor fare. If the skin and joints are tender, and easily broken with the finger, it is young; a fat goose is best.

The feet and bill of a young goose are yellow; in an old one they are red.

When fresh killed the feet are pliable; if stale, they will be dry and stiff.

The loose fat from the inside of a goose should be taken out, and the fat from the lower part of the back. Goose grease may be used medicinally, but not for eating.

Some persons use it for making pie crust and for common molasses cake instead of other shortening.

To Roast a Goose.—Pick it perfectly clean, cut off the legs at the joints, and singe it nicely; cut off the vent; cut a slit from the breast bone to it, or across, below the breast bone; draw out the entrails; take off that leading to the vent; take out all the loose fat, save the heart and liver; cut a slit at the back of the neck, and draw out the crop; cut off a part of the neck, leaving enough of the skin to fasten over against the back; wash the inside of the body with cold water; wipe it dry, and rub it well with a mixture of salt and pepper; prepare the stuffing.

Cut a six penny loaf of wheat bread in slices, pour hot water over to wet them; then add a teaspoonful of salt and the same of ground pepper, and quarter of a pound of sweet butter, with a tablespoonful of finely powdered sage or thyme if liked. Fill the body, then sew up the slit; tie the ends of the legs together, or cut a place and put them in the body; pass a skewer through the hips, put the heart and liver between the wings and the body, and fasten close to it with a skewer; spit it, put a pint of water in the pan, to baste with; have a bright, steady and clear fire, with a bed of coals at the bottom, and set the goose at a little distance at first until it is heated through; put a teaspoonful of salt to the water in the pan and baste freely with it, after it has begun to roast; put one side to the fire first, then the other; after that the back, and lastly the breast, that it may be evenly done; gradually draw it nearer the fire; when nearly done, stir up the fire, put quarter of a pound of butter in the pan, and baste with it; dredge a little flour over it; turn it that every part may be browned; allow fifteen minutes for each pound of meat; it must be well done, which will depend on the state and management of the fire.

If the gravy is very fat take some of it off; put the pan over the fire; let it become hot, then stir into it a thin batter made of a tablespoonful of wheat flour and cold water, stir it until it is brown and smooth; if it is thicker than is liked, add a little boiling water, stir it in, and pour it through a gravy strainer into a tureen.

A goose may be equally well dressed in a hot oven or stove.

Prepare it as directed for roasting; set a trivet or muffin rings in a dripping-pan and place the goose with its back upon the trivet or rings; put a pint of hot water in the pan; put bits of butter the size of a large hickory nut over the body; dredge wheat flour over, and set it in a thoroughly heated brick or stove oven; baste it freely and often; when done take it from the pan, cover it, and set it before the fire to keep hot; put the pan over the fire, take out the rings or trivet; add a bit of butter the size of an egg, and when it is hot stir into it a thin batter made of a tablespoonful of wheat flour and cold water; if too thick, add hot water to thin it; stir it smooth and pour through a gravy strainer into a tureen. A lemon sliced thin and fried in the gravy before putting in the batter and served over the goose, or put in the tureen with the gravy, is liked by some persons.

The stuffing may be made of boiled potatoes, chopped or mashed, instead of bread, and moistened with milk. An onion or leek finely minced may be added to the gravy if liked.

Half a pound of fat corned pork chopped small, may be put with the stuffing instead of butter for ordinary occasions, if preferred.

A young goose may be cut up and made in a pie or pot-pie.

An old goose may be rendered eatable thus:— Empty it and put it in hot water to cover it, and let it boil until tender, then roast it or make a fricassee.

The vegetables to be served with roast goose are as follows:

Plain boiled or mashed potatoes, mashed yellow turnips, or winter squash, apples stewed without sugar; or cranberry jam, boiled onions, pickles, and dressed celery.

Dessert—Apple, pumpkin, custard or mince pies.

TO BROWN-STEW A GOOSE WHOLE.—Pick a goose clean, singe and empty it, flatten the breast bone with the side of a cleaver or rolling pin; wash it in cold water and take out the inside fat, rub it well outside and in with a mixture of salt and pepper, cut off the neck, leaving enough of the skin to fasten over the back; boil some potatoes and chop them small, season with pepper and salt, and if liked, a bunch of parsley or a leek cut fine, or a tablespoonful of sage or thyme; add quarter of a pound of butter and a cup of milk; fill the body and sew it up; put it in a dinner pot or iron bake kettle with the back downwards, put in hot (not boiling) water to half cover it, cover the pot or kettle and set it over a moderate fire, let it boil till tender; try it, by sticking a fork in the most fleshy part; the water will be nearly out, then add a quarter of a pound of sweet butter, cut small, or half a pound of fat salt pork cut in thin slices; dredge in a tablespoonful of wheat flour, turn the goose over, the breast downwards, and cover the pot close; set it down in front of the fire with a bed of coals under the pot and let it brown without burning. When done take it up, add a cup of hot water and dredge in a little flour, stir it smooth; when it is nicely browned, turn it over the goose and serve, with plain boiled or mashed potatoes, mashed turnips and pickles, etc.

TO MAKE A RAGOUT OF THE PRECEDING RECEIPT.—Whilst the goose is stewing, scrape a carrot and cut it in thin slices, notch the edges neatly and boil them in a little water until tender, cut a leek in slices, dip a bunch of parsley into hot water and cut it small; when the breast side of the goose is done a fine brown turn the other down; add the vegetables, cover it, and in fifteen minutes take up the goose; add a small cup of hot water to the gravy, stir into it a tablespoonful of browned flour, let it boil up once, then put it over the goose and serve. A head of celery parboiled and cut small may be used in place of the leek.

To Choose Ducks.—Ducks must be fat and plump and thick on the breast. If a duck is young the skin can be easily broken with the finger, and the feet are pliable.

Tame ducks are prepared for the table the same as young geese.

For roasting, have a hot fire and baste freely and often; half an hour will be sufficient for the smallest, the larger in proportion.

Wild ducks should be fat, the claws small, reddish and supple; if they are not fresh, on opening the beak, there will be a disagreeable smell; the flesh of the hen is the most delicate.

Pick them clean without scalding, cut the wings close to the body and empty it, cut off a part of the neck and singe them nicely.

Having drawn wild ducks, wipe them well inside with a cloth, rub each outside and in with a mixture of pepper and salt; cut a slice of wheat bread, dip it in hot water, spread it thick with butter, sprinkle pepper over, and put it in the body, sew it up, truss the legs close to the body, and fasten them with skewers; then split them or lay them on a trivet in the dripping pan; have a bright, clear fire, that they may roast quickly; put half a pint of water in the pan, put to it a teaspoonful of salt and an onion sliced thin, baste with this for ten or twelve minutes (to take off the fishy taste peculiar to wild ducks) throw it away, put half a pint of hot water in its place, put in a little pepper, baste the ducks with butter, dredge a little flour over and baste with the water in the pan; turn them that every part may be done. Half an hour, with a hot fire and frequent basting will roast them nicely. Serve the ducks as hot as possible.

Whilst the ducks are roasting, boil the giblets tender in a little water; chop or mince them fine; add to the mince pepper and salt, a small bit of butter and a teaspoonful of browned flour; when the ducks are done put it in the pan with the gravy, set it over the fire, stir it for a few minutes, then serve in a tureen. Make a glass of wine hot, put to it a tablespoonful of currant jelly and white sugar each, and serve with wild ducks, or put a wineglass of port in the pan; a few minutes before taking them up baste the ducks once or twice with it; add a tablespoonful of jelly and the gravy.

Or, half roast wild ducks without seasoning. When they are brought to the table, slice the breast, strew over pepper and salt, pour a little port wine over, or squeeze the juice of an orange or lemon over; add a bit of butter, the size of an egg, sprinkle over a teaspoonful of fine white sugar; cut up the bird, and set it over a chafing dish, turn it that it may be nicely done; or prepare it in this manner and set it on coals before a hot fire.

CANVAS BACK DUCKS.—Canvas back ducks are served in the same manner as wild ducks, without the onion in the basting; as there is no disagreeable taste to destroy, that is not necessary.

G*

Canvas back ducks may be served the same as goose or tame duck. Roast them according to their size.

To Roast Ducks in a Pot.—Draw a pair of fat ducks, rinse the inside with cold water, wipe it dry; dip a slice of bread in hot water, spread butter thickly over it, sprinkle pepper and a little salt over and put one in the body of each; sew up the slit; skewer the legs and wings close to the body, rub pepper and salt over the outside of each, and lay them with the backs down, in an iron dinner pot or bake kettle; put in a pint of hot water, cut quarter of a pound of butter in slices and put it over the breast of the ducks, cover the pot close and set it over a moderate fire for half an hour, then dredge a tablespoonful of wheat flour, turn the ducks over and cover the pot, stir up the fire and let them brown nicely without burning; about fifteen minutes will do them; when done take them up; add a teacup of boiling water to the gravy, stir it smooth and pour it over the ducks and serve.

If the ducks are done in an iron bake kettle, with coals and ashes on the lid, they will not require to be turned.

A lemon sliced thin, and put in the gravy before the water, or a glass of wine, and a spoonful of jelly, instead of water, may be considered an improvement.

Ducks may be cut up, and stewed, or roasted, in this way, or they may be fried like chickens.

Wild duck requires less time to cook than tame.

Pigeons.—Pigeons should be fresh killed; when in good order, they are plump on the breast, and fat at the vent, and the feet are pliable. When stale, the vent is loose and open, and has a greenish withered appearance.

Wild pigeons, when fat, are preferred to tame.

Empty, and truss pigeons, the same as chickens or ducks; roast, broil, fry, or stew them, according to the following several directions.

To Broil Pigeons.—Split young pigeons down the back, take out the entrails; broil the heart; take out the breast bone, or flatten it, and lay them on a hot gridiron (the inside to the fire,) over a fire of bright coals; put a tin cover over, and let them broil briskly; when nearly cooked through, take off the cover, stir up the coals, and turn the pigeons, and let them brown nicely; if necessary, add fresh coals; for half a dozen young pigeons, put a quarter of a pound of butter on a plate, add to it a small tablespoonful of salt, and a teaspoonful of pepper; work them together, put the broil on, turn each piece once or twice in the gravy, and serve hot.

Large tame pigeons are cut in two at the back, and breast, for broiling, or frying.

To Fry Pigeons.—Pick pigeons clean, split them open down the back, and take out the entrails, and if large, cut them in two at the breast; rub each piece over, with salt and pepper, mixed; make some beef dripping, or lard and butter, (equal parts) hot, in a frying-pan, dip each piece of pigeon in wheat flour, or rolled cracker, put them in the pan, with the inside down; cover the pan, and let them fry quickly, until one side is a fine brown, and nearly cooked through; then take off the cover, and turn the other side; when both are done, take them on a hot steak dish, put a small bit of butter on each, sprinkle a little pepper over, put a table spoonful of hot water in the pan, let it boil up once, and put it in the dish; serve hot.

A few thin slices of fat corned pork, may be broiled, or fried, and served with the pigeons; no other salt will be required.

Slices of bread nicely toasted, with the outside crust cut off, may be put in the dish under a fry or broil.

PIGEONS STEWED, (white.)—Cut off the vent, cut a slit from the breast bone to it, take out the entrails; rinse the inside, and rub the pigeons outside and in, with a mixture of salt and pepper; make stuffing as for chickens; fasten the legs close to the body, and twist the wings against the back, and put them in a dinner-pot on their backs, with the necks in the centre of the pot; put in hot water nearly to cover them, cover the pot close, and set it over a moderate fire for half an hour, skim it, then add quarter of a pound of butter, with a tablespoonful of wheat flour worked into it, a small tablespoonful of salt, (for half a dozen pigeons,) and a teaspoonful of pepper, with a bunch of green parsly cut small, cover it, and let them simmer for twenty minutes, then serve them in their gravy.

Serve dressed celery and pickles with them.

Pigeons may be cut up and stewed in the same manner in less time.

The feet may be left on; hold them in boiling water until the skin will easily peel off, cut off the toes at the first joint, cross them, and fasten them together below the breast.

Pigeons may be stuffed and trussed in this way, for roasting.

TO MAKE A BIRD'S NEST.—Boil some yellow macaroni gently, until it is quite swelled out and tender, then cut it in pieces, the length of a finger, and lay them on a dish like a straw nest.

Truss pigeons with the heads on, (having scalded and picked them clean,) turned under the left wing, leave the feet on, and having stewed them, arrange them as in a nest; pour the gravy over and serve.

The nest may be made of boiled rice, or bread cut in pieces, the length and thickness of a finger, and fried a nice brown in hot lard, seasoned with pepper and salt. Or, make it of bread, toasted a yellow brown. Any small birds may be stewed or roasted, and served in this way.

To Stew Pigeons Brown.—Pick the pigeons, and take out the entrails; into a bit of butter the size of a small egg, work a small teaspoonful of pepper, and a very little salt; having rinsed the inside of each pigeon with cold water, and wiped it dry, put in the butter, sew up the slit, draw the legs together below the breast bone, tie them with a thread; rub salt and pepper over the outside of each, and put them the backs downward and necks in the centre, into an iron dinner pot or baking kettle, with a pint of hot water; cover them close, set the pot or kettle over a moderate fire for half an hour for young pigeons, or until tender for old ones, then skim them, dredge in a tablespoonful of wheat flour, and to half a dozen of pigeons, put quarter of a pound of butter, and a small teaspoonful of pepper, cover the pot, and set it over a bright fire to brown, turn them that they may brown nicely on the breast; when done take them up, add a cup of boiling water to the gravy, dredge a teaspoonful of browned flour into it, stir it smooth, and let it boil up once, then pour it through a gravy strainer over the stew, and serve.

Thin slices of bread toasted delicately brown,

may be laid on the dish under the stew. Any small birds may be stewed in this manner, requiring less time in proportion to their size.

Pigeons may be cut in halves and stewed brown.

A brown stew may be made in the following manner: take half a pound of nicely corned fat pork, cut it in thin slices, and put it down in the pot under the birds; when the water is nearly out, and the meat begins to brown, dredge in a little flour, and turn them so as to brown the birds, add a bit of butter the size of an egg, and a teaspoonful of pepper; when they are nicely browned, take them up, add a little hot water to the gravy, stir it smooth; strain it over the birds, and serve.

A few slices of lemon may be put in the pot with the pepper and butter, and served in the gravy, if liked

PIGEON PIE.—Clean and truss three or four pigeons, rub the outside and in with a mixture of pepper and salt; rub the inside with a bit of butter, and fill it with a bread and butter stuffing, or mashed potatoes; sew up the slit, butter the sides of a tin basin or pudding dish, and line (the sides only,) with pie paste, rolled to quarter of an inch thickness; lay the birds in; for three large tame pigeons, cut quarter of a pound of sweet butter and put it over them; strew over a large teaspoonful of salt, and a small teaspoonful of pepper, with a bunch of finely cut parsley, if liked; dredge a large tablespoonful of wheat flour over; put in water to nearly fill the pie; lay skewers across the top, cover with a puff paste crust; cut a slit in the middle, ornament the edge with leaves, braids, or shells of paste, and put it in a moderately hot or quick oven, for one hour; when nearly done, brush the top over with the yolk of an egg beaten with a little milk, and finish.

The pigeons for this pie may be cut in two or more pieces, if preferred.

Any small birds may be done in this manner.

Pigeon Pot-pie.—Clean the pigeons, cut each in two, and finish, the same as chicken pot-pie.

Roast Pigeons.—Clean the pigeons, and stuff them the same as chickens; leave the feet on, dip them into scalding water, strip off the skin, cross them, and tie them together below the breast bone; or cut them off; the head may remain on; if so, dip it in scalding water, and pick it clean; twist the wings back, put the liver between the right wing and the body, and turn the head under the other; rub the outside of each bird with a mixture of pepper and salt; spit them, and put some water in the dripping-pan; for each bird put a bit of butter the size of a small egg, put them before a hot fire, and let them roast quickly; baste frequently, half an hour will do them; when nearly done, dredge them with wheat flour, and baste with the butter in the pan; turn them, that they may be nicely and evenly browned; when done, take them up, set the pan over the fire, make a thin batter of a teaspoonful of wheat flour, and cold water, when the gravy is boiling hot, stir it in; continue to stir it for a few minutes, until it is brown, then pour it through a gravy sieve into a tureen, and serve with the pigeons.

Currant jelly, or apples stewed without sugar, dressed celery, or any other salad, and mashed turnips or squash, may be served with roast birds.

Pigeons or small birds roasted, may be dished thus: lay some small slices of nicely toasted bread on a dish, pour the gravy over, lay a pigeon or bird on each, and serve

Pigeons may be roasted in a hot stove oven; prepare them as directed; lay them on a wire stand or trivet in a dripping-pan; baste and finish as before directed.

Roast quickly and baste very frequently, that they may be nicely done and juicy.

PIGEON CUTLETS.—Divide the pigeons in halves down the breast and back; turn the foot inward so that it may appear like the bone of a chop; rub each over with salt and pepper mixed; dip them in wheat flour or rolled crackers, and fry with slices of fat corned pork or sweet lard or beef dripping, let the fat become hot in the pan before putting the pieces in; put the inside down first; put a tin cover over and fry quickly. When this is done nearly through, turn the other and let it brown; then take them up, put half a wine-glass of hot water in the pan, add a piece of butter the size of an egg; let it become boiling hot; stir in a teaspoonful of browned flour; let it remain over the fire for a few minutes, then put it in the dish and serve; or make the gravy by putting a bit of butter in the pan, after taking up the fry; let it become hot; add a teaspoonful of hot water and turn it into the dish. Port or Madeira wine may used in the gravy instead of water, and currant jelly served with it, or a tablespoonful served into it. Or a lemon cut in slices and fried may be served with the cutlets.

Pigeon cutlets may be broiled and served with or without jelly.

Woodcock, snipe, partridges, quails, etc., may be dressed the same as pigeons. The pheasant or prairie hen, which is the same, or nearly resembles it, may be served the same as chickens.

To Broil Small Birds.—Small birds should be carefully picked that the skin may not be torn; for frying or broiling, split them down the back, spread them flat, and broil very gently over a bright fire of coals; put the inside first to the fire, let them be done nearly through before turning; brown the other side nicely; then take them on to a hot dish, butter them, put a very little salt and pepper over and serve quickly.

When it is not convenient to broil birds, they may be done very nicely in a pan thus:—split them as directed for broiling; put a bit of butter in a frying-pan, let it become hot, and having rubbed the bird over with a little pepper and salt and rolled crackers, put them in the pan and fry them nicely; add a tablespoonful of hot water to the gravy, put it in the dish, and serve.

To Keep Game from Tainting.—Game may often be made fit for eating when apparently spoiled by nicely cleaning it and washing with vinegar and water.

If you have birds which you fear will not keep, pick and empty them; rinse them, and rub them over with salt outside and in; have in readiness a kettle of boiling water, and plunge them in one by one, holding them by the legs and drawing them up and down, so that the water may pass through them, let them remain in for five or six minutes, then hang them in a cool place; when perfectly drained, rub them outside and in with black pepper.

The most delicate birds may be preserved in this way. Thoroughly wash them before roasting or otherwise cooking them.

Pieces of charcoal put about meat or birds, will

preserve them from taint and restore what is spoiling. Poultry or birds drawn and wiped dry, and a bit of charcoal put into the body and over the outside of each, will keep them nicely, or they may be kept in a box lined with zinc, and bits of ice between them. Pepper keeps them secure from flies.

To Roast Birds.—Pick and empty them, (Europeans do not take out the entrails from birds of several kinds; but few Americans have arrived at that state of refinement, therefore no receipt will be given for dressing them, without so doing.) Put a bit of butter and pepper and salt worked into the body, or fill with mashed potatoes, seasoned with a bit of butter, pepper and salt, and moistened with milk; cut off the pinions at the first joint; press the legs close to the ribs, and turn the head backward, sticking the bill between the leg and the body; rub each over with pepper and salt, and hang them on bird spits, and set them before a hot fire; baste with a cup of water and butter; dredge flour or rolled cracker over, and baste continually for the last five minutes; lay slices of toast under to catch the dripping, and serve under the birds.

Small birds may be prepared as for roasting, and broiled whole so as to resemble a roast. Have a good bed of bright coals; set the gridiron rather high over it; put the birds on, with the back down for a few minutes; then turn the sides and breast that they may be evenly done; keep them covered with a tin cover; stir up the coals occasionally; when about half done, put the gridiron nearer the fire to brown the birds; when done, take them on a hot dish, butter them, and serve hot.

Rabbits, Hares, and Squirrels.—Rabbits

hares, and squirrels are chosen, dressed, and cooked, in like manner.

These should not be cooked as soon as killed one direction will be given, which will serve for either.

Cut a hare or rabbit open down the belly, take out the entrails, save the liver, wipe the inside dry, and rub it over with pepper, then hang it in a cool dry place.

The ears of an old hare are dry and tough, and the claws blunt; in a young one, the ears are tender and pliable, and the claws sharp and smooth.

When wanted for dressing, cut off the fore legs at the first joint, raise the skin of the back and draw it over the hind legs; leave the tail whole, then draw the skin over the back and slip out the fore legs; cut the skin from the neck and head, skin the ears, and leave them on; clean the vent, cut the sinews under the legs, bring them forward; run a skewer through one hind leg, through the body and the other hind leg; do the same with the fore legs; lay the head rather back, put a skewer in at the mouth, through the back of the head, and between the shoulders; rinse the inside, wipe it dry, rub it with a little pepper and salt, and fill it with a bread stuffing, or with boiled potatoes, mashed and seasoned the same as bread stuffing; sew up the body, or tie a cord around to keep in the stuffing, let it secure the legs also in their places; it is now ready for roasting; finish the same as for fowls.

In skinning rabbits, cut off the ears, before boiling, hold the head in a pot of boiling water, which will prevent the disagreeable appearance they otherwise have.

Boil the same as fowl, or turkey according to

their weight; serve the same sauce and vegetables with it.

They may be broiled, stewed, or fried the same as chickens, or pigeons; or made a soup.

Squirrels, after having been split and skinned, may be broiled, fried, or stewed; they are best broiled.

EGGS, OMLETS, &c.

To Choose Eggs.—Fresh eggs when held to the light, the white will look clear, and the yolk distinct; if not good, they will have a clouded appearance.

When eggs are stale, the white will be thin and watery, and the yolk will not be a uniform color, when broken; if there is no mustiness, or disagreeable smell, eggs in this state, are not unfit for making cakes, puddings, etc.

Eggs for boiling should be as fresh as possible; a new laid egg will generally recommend itself, by the delicate transparency of its shell.

Eggs may be kept fresh for several weeks, by packing them, the small end downwards, in bran or chaff; keep them in a cool place. A refrigerator, or ice-box, will keep eggs as when first laid for a long time.

To Keep Eggs.—Take fresh laid eggs, dip each one in melted lard, or beef fat, or rub a bit of butter thoroughly over the shell, between the hands; then pack them, the small end downwards, in bran, or chaff; in this way they will keep good for months.

Eggs may be kept good for a year, in the following manner :—

To a pail of water, put of unslacked lime and coarse salt each a pint; keep it in a cellar, or cool place, and put the eggs in, as fresh laid as possible.

It is well to keep a stone pot of this lime water ready to receive the eggs as soon as laid; make a fresh supply every few months. This lime water is of exactly the proper strength; strong lime water will cook the eggs. Very strong lime water will eat the shell.

For making omlets, or frying eggs, it is best to have an omlet pan, which is thick-bottomed, and about six inches in diameter, or across; this is best also for pan-cakes, or fritters, or for frying oysters; the small size of the pan, enables you to turn the omlet, or pan-cake, without danger of breaking; and the thick bottom regulates the heat, so that fritters, etc., may be sufficiently done without burning.

For turning omlets, fried oysters, fried parsley, &c., have a skimmer spoon, which is a flat thin blade, with holes or perforations, that the fry may be taken up without the fat.

To BOIL EGGS, *in their shells.*—Wash the shells clean in cold water before boiling; have a stewpan of boiling water, into which put the eggs; keep it boiling—four minutes for very soft—five, that the yolk only may be soft—six minutes will boil the yolk hard, for eating. Eight minutes are required to boil eggs for salad, or garnish. When done, take them from the boiling water, into a basin of cold water, which will prevent the yolk turning dark or black.

Boiled eggs will become harder, from the heat of the shell, if they lay a few minutes before breaking; if they are not to be served immediately, take them up a minute sooner than otherwise, and put them into a dish with a cover; in this way they will keep hot for ten or fifteen minutes, and become but little harder. If the water is kept fast boiling after the eggs are in, one minute less will do them, than if otherwise.

A more delicate way of eggs in the shells is this: Have a stew-pan of pure water, boiling hot, put the eggs in, cover the stew-pan without putting it over the fire; five minutes will do then for those who like soft eggs, and a minute or two longer for those who like them harder. The white of eggs boiled in this way is more like poached eggs; less firm than in the other manner.

If eggs are boiled in an egg boiler at table, let the water be boiling hot when they are put in, and replenish it when more are wanted; five minutes will be required when the white is wanted soft, six when the yolk only is to be soft.

The most healthful and delicate way of cooking eggs is to poach them thus—have a clean stew-pan with boiling hot water, add to it a little salt; break the eggs one at a time into a cup, and from it slip them into boiling water; when the white is set and firm, which it will be after about five minutes, take each up with a skimmer, and lay them into a dish over a pot of boiling water; cover the dish; when all are done, put a bit of butter, and if liked, sprinkle pepper over them, and serve; in this way they may be kept hot and soft for a long time, so that you may do any number of them.

After boiling eggs as directed for garnishing; when they are quite cold, take off the shell, and cut them lengthwise in two; then cut each half in two or three. This looks well over spinach or lettuce or boiled fish; or cut them in slices across; or the white may be cut in long slips, and the yolk in slices or quarters.

EGGS POACHED IN BALLS.—Put three pints of boiling water into a stew-pan; set it on a hot stove or coals; stir the water with a stick until it runs rapidly around, then having broken an egg into a cup —taking care not to break the yolk—drop it into the whirling water, continue to stir it until the egg is cooked; then take it into a dish with a skimmer and set it over a pot of boiling water; boil one at a time, until you have enough. These will remain soft for a long time.

OMELET AU NATURAL.—Break eight or ten eggs into a basin; add a small teaspoonful of salt and a little pepper, with a tablespoonful of cold water; beat the whole well with a spoon or whisk. In the meantime put some fresh sweet butter into an omlet pan, and when it is nearly hot, put in an omlet; whilst it is frying, with a skimmer spoon raise the edges from the pan that it may be properly done. When the eggs are set and one side is a fine brown, double it half over and serve hot. These omlets should be put quite thin in the pan; the butter required for each will be about the size of a small egg.

STIRRED EGGS.—Break eight or more eggs into a basin, add to them a tablespoonful sweet butter, cut into bits and a teaspoonful of salt, make a little bit of butter hot in a frying pan, pour in the eggs and let them cook. Stir them with a silver spoon until they are just set without becoming hard or brown; serve over toast.

FRENCH OMELET.—Break eight eggs into a basin,

season with a small teaspoonful of salt, and a little pepper, and if liked mace or nutmeg; add two tablespoonfuls of milk or cream; two ounces of butter broke in bits, and a little parsley cut small, if liked, also a finely chopped shalot or white onion well washed.

Beat these ingredients well together with a spoon, put an ounce of butter in a frying pan, let it become boiling hot, and pour the omlet in about half an inch thick; as it is cooking continue to stir it with a spoon, drawing it from the sides to the centre, that it may be evenly done; shake the pan now and then to free the omlet from it; let it fry gently; when it is a fine clear brown, turn it into a dish, and serve.

An Omelet.—Take a rich meat gravy, beat eggs light and put them to it; beat them well together, make a tablespoonful of salted lard hot in a frying-pan; put in the omlet half an inch thick and fry it a delicate brown. When one side is done turn it out on a dish.

Ham Omelet.—Chop some fat and lean ham quite fine; beat up six or eight eggs, and stir the ham, (a teacupful) into them; have a tablespoonful of lard made hot in an omlet pan; put in the omlet and fry it gently. Slip a knife around the edge occasionally, that it may be done nicely; then turn it on a dish. Or, you may make it nearly an inch thick, and when one side is done, turn it and let it brown.

Spanish Omelet.—Make with chopped ham as above directed, add to it two small white oinions finely minced, and finish as directed.

Dutch Omelet.—Break eight eggs into a basin, season with pepper and salt, add two ounces of butter cut small, beat these well together, make an ounce of butter hot in a frying-pan, put the eggs in, continue to stir it, drawing it away from the sides, that it may be evenly done, shake it now and then to free it from the pan; when the under side is a little browned, turn the omlet into a dish, and serve; this must be done over a moderate fire.

SMOKED BEEF WITH EGGS.—Cut some smoked beef in thin shavings or chips, put them into a frying-pan, and nearly fill it with hot water; set it on the fire, and let it boil up once, then pour it off; add to the beef a good bit of lard, twice the size of an egg, for half a pound of the beef; shake a little pepper over, and let it fry for a few minutes over a quick fire; then break two, three, or more eggs into it; stir them together until the eggs are done, then turn it on to a dish.

Or after frying the beef with a little wheat flour dredged over, fry eggs, and serve with it the same as ham.

OMELET—May be made of smoked beef chipped thin, first taking off the outside skin; finish as directed for ham omlet.

A NICE BREAKFAST OF SMOKED BEEF.—Pare off the outside skin of the beef, and shave it thin, then put it in a pan, and if very salt, pour boiling water over it, let it remain for a few minutes, then throw it off; add to the beef a large tablespoonful of lard, to half a pound of it; shake a little pepper over, set it over the fire, when it begins to fry nicely, dredge over a heaping teaspoonful of wheat flour; put to it a teacup of boiling water, stir it together over the fire for a few minutes; when the gravy is thick, it is done.

Have two or three slices of bread toasted a delicate brown, cut them in small squares or lozenges, and put them into a deep dish, then pour the beef and gravy over; a small bit of butter may be put to it before putting it over the toast.

Frizzed Beef.—Pare off the outside skin of the beef, and cut some thin small slices or chips, put them on a gridiron over a bright, clear fire of coals, when they are hot and crisp, take them on to a hot dish, with butter and pepper, and serve.

To Serve Smoked Beef.—Cut off the outside skin, shave the beef thin, and lay it lightly on a plate, and serve for tea.

After a piece of smoked beef has been cut, keep it folded in a coarse paper, and hang it up.

If smoked beef or mutton, or venison hams (which are served in the same manner,) is carefully cut evenly across, instead of cutting it carelessly at one side, it will cut to better advantage, and last longer.

VEGETABLES.

To Preserve Vegetables for Winter Use.—Green stringed beans must be picked when young; put a layer three inches deep, in a small wooden keg or half barrel; sprinkle in salt an inch deep; then put another layer of beans, then salt, and beans and salt in alternate layers, until you have enough; let the last be salt, cover them with a piece of board which will fit the inside of the barrel or keg; and place a heavy weight upon it; they will make a brine.

When wanted for use, soak them one night or more in plenty of water, changing it once or twice, until the salt is out of them, then cut them, and boil the same as when fresh.

Carrots, beans, beet-roots, parsnips, and potatoes, keep best in dry sand or earth in a cellar; turnips keep best on a cellar bottom, or they may be kept the same as carrots, etc. Whatever earth remains about them when taken from the ground, should not be taken off.

When sprouts come on potatoes or other stored vegetables, they should be carefully cut off. The young sprouts from turnips are sometimes served as a salad, or boiled tender in salt and water, and served with butter and pepper over.

Celery may be kept all winter by setting it in boxes filled with earth; keep it in the cellar; it will grow and whiten in the dark; leeks may also be kept in this way.

Cabbage set out in earth, in a good cellar, will keep good and fresh all winter. Small close heads of cabbage may be kept many weeks, by taking them before the frost comes, and laying them on a stone floor; this will whiten them, and make them tender.

Store onions are to be strung, and hung in a dry, cold place.

Pumpkin may be kept for use, thus:—Cut it up, take off the skin, and take out the seeds; put a teacup of water, to a common size pumpkin, and stew it to a mash, over a slow fire; let it dry as much as it will, without burning; then take it up, spread it in pans, or make it in thin cakes, and dry it in a hot sun, or cool oven, after baking; when wanted for use, stew it in milk, or pour hot milk over it, and let it dissolve—then add eggs, &c., for pies. Pumpkins may be kept for a long time, on frames, in a good dry cellar; or they may be cut up, and dried the same as apples. They are then to be stewed with very little water, and used the same as fresh pumpkin.

Parsley should be cut when tender, and a delicate green; then pack it down in sweet butter; one pound of butter will be enough for quarter of a peck of parsley; this butter may be used in drawn butter, or sauce, or for frying, or fricassee. In this way, parsley may be kept perfectly green, and fresh, all winter.

Most vegetables require to be well washed, in plenty of water. Green vegetables are good, in proportion as they are young, and fresh gathered.

Spinach, cucumbers, new potatoes, beets, and turnips, should be put in cold water some time before cooking, or dressing.

OLD POTATOES, *to boil.*—Wash them clean, in two or three waters, take off a bit of the skin from each end, the size of a two shilling piece, or cut off a ring lengthwise, from end to end; then put them into a stew-pan, or pot, and pour boiling water over, to cover them; add a teaspoonful of salt, and cover the pot close; let them boil fast for half an hour, for small ones, or three-quarters of an hour for large; when done, take them up, or pour the water off, and let them set for two or three minutes to dry off; then take the skins off, and serve them plain, in a covered dish.

When old potatoes are not very fine, take off all the skin, and lay them in cold water, for an hour before boiling; skim the pot whilst boiling potatoes.

Mashed Potatoes.—Potatoes are not good for mashing, until they are full grown; peel them, and lay them in water, for an hour or more, before boiling, for mashing.

Old potatoes, when unfit for plain boiling, may be served mashed; cut out all imperfections, take off all the skin, and lay them in cold water, for one hour, or more; then put them into a dinner-pot, or stew-pan, with a teaspoonful of salt; cover the stew-pan, and let them boil for half an hour, unless they are large, when three-quarters of an hour will be required; when they are done, take them up with a skimmer into a wooden bowl or tray, and mash them fine with a potato beetle; melt a piece of butter, the size of a large egg, into half a pint of hot milk; mix it with the mashed patotoes until it is thoroughly incorporated, and a smooth mass; then put it in a deep dish, smooth the top over, and mark it neatly with a knife; put pepper over, and serve. The quantity of milk used, must be in proportion to the quantity of potatoes.

Mashed potatoes may be heaped on a flat dish; make it in a crown, or pine apple; stick a sprig of green celery, or parsley, in the top; or, first brown it before the fire, or in an oven.

Mashed potatoes may be made a highly ornamental dish; after shaping it, as taste may direct, trim the edge of the plate with a wreath of celery leaves, or green parsley; or first brown the outside in an oven, or before the fire.

To Boil New Potatoes.—Scrape the skins from new potatoes, and lay them in cold water, for an hour or more; then put them into a stew-pan, or dinner-pot, and pour boiling water over, to cover them; add a teaspoonful of salt, cover the pot, or pan, let them boil fast for half an hour; try one, if not quite done, cover for a few minutes, then drain the water off; let them stand for a few minutes over the fire; take them into a deep dish, put a bit of butter and pepper over, and serve covered.

POTATOES IN HASTE.—A very nice little dish may be made of cold boiled potatoes, in a very few minutes. Having peeled, cut them in slices, half an inch thick, put them in a stew-pan, pour boiling water over them; cover the stew-pan, and set it over the fire for ten minutes; then drain off all the water, add a small bit of butter, shake pepper over, and serve hot.

Or, having cut the potatoes in slices, put them in a stew-pan, cover them with milk; cover the stew-pan and set it over the fire for five minutes. Work a large teaspoonful of butter with a small one of flour, and put it to the potatoes; shake a little pepper over, and add a little parsley cut fine, if liked. Cover the stew-pan for ten minutes, then turn the potatoes into a deep dish, and serve for breakfast.

Potatoes may be pared and cut in slices and boiled in water with a little salt for twenty minutes, then served with butter and pepper over; or work a teaspoonful of wheat flour with a small bit of butter, and put it to the potatoes a few minutes before they are done; then shake a little pepper over and serve.

FRIED POTATOES.—Boil some potatoes in their skins; when cold, peel them and cut them in slices, quarter of an inch thick; put a large tablespoonful of lard or beef dripping into a frying pan, and set it over the fire; add pepper and salt according to the quantity of potatoes, (a teaspoonful of salt and a saltspoonful of pepper to a dozen small sized potatoes,) when it is boiling hot, put in enough sliced potatoes to cover the bottom of the pan, as soon as one side is a delicate brown, turn the other; when both are done, take them into a hot dish; then fry more: when all are done, put to them a little of the fat in which they were fried, and serve.

Care is necessary in frying potatoes that they are nicely and delicately browned, without being burned or cooked to a crisp; for breakfast or supper, fried potatoes are much liked.

Potatoes may be fried with less time or trouble thus: peel them and chop them small, make some lard hot in the pan; add salt and pepper as before directed, then put the potatoes in; turn them that they may be nicely browned. Serve in a covered dish.

HASHED POTATOES.—Peel and chop some cold boiled potatoes, and put them into a stew-pan with a very little milk or water to moisten them; put to them a small bit of butter and pepper and salt, to taste; cover the stew-pan close, and set it over a gentle fire for fifteen or twenty minutes; stir them once or twice whilst cooking. Serve hot for breakfast.

BAKED POTATOES.—Take as many large and equal sized potatoes as you wish; wash them perfectly clean in two or three changes of water, then wipe them dry, and put them in a quick oven for one hour; serve with cold butter, pepper and salt.

ROASTED POTATOES.—Wash perfectly clean as many potatoes of equal size as you wish; make clean a place on a hot hearth where wood is burnt, lay the potatoes down and cover them with hot ashes; if not very near the fire, add fresh embers occasionally; half an hour or three quarters will roast them, according to their size; when done wipe them clean, and serve with cold butter, salt and pepper. Serve with cold meat for breakfast, dinner or supper.

BROILED POTATOES.—Cut cold boiled potatoes in slices lengthwise, quarter of an inch thick; dip each slice in wheat flour, and lay them on a gridiron over a bright fire of coals; when both sides are browned nicely, take them on a hot dish, put a bit of butter, pepper and salt to taste over, and serve hot.

SWEET OR CAROLINA POTATOES.—The best sweet potatoes are from the southern states; those raised in New Jersey are not nearly as sweet as those from the south.

The best manner of serving sweet potatoes is roasted or baked.

To BAKE SWEET POTATOES.—Wash them perfectly clean, wipe them dry, and bake in a quick oven, according to their size—half an hour for quite small size, three-quarters for larger, and a full hour for the largest. Let the oven have a good heat, and do not open it, unless it is necessary to turn them, until they are done.

ROASTED SWEET POTATOES.—Having washed them clean, and wiped them dry, roast them on a hot hearth as directed for common potatoes; or put them in a dutch oven, or tin reflector. Roasted or baked potatoes should not be cut, but broken open and eaten from the skin, as from a shell.

To BOIL SWEET POTATOES.—Wash them perfectly clean, put them into a pot or stew-pan, and pour boiling water over to cover them; cover the pot close, and boil fast for half an hour; or more if the potatoes are large; try them with a fork; when done, drain off the water, take off the skins, and serve.

Cold sweet potatoes may be cut in slices across or lengthwise, and fried or broiled as common potatoes; or they may be cut in half and served cold.

Sweet potatoes are made pie of, the same as pumpkin pie.

Young Turnips.—Cut off the green leaves ot new turnips, leaving an inch or more of the stalks; pare them, and trim them neatly, then put them into a pot of boiling water, with a teaspoonful of salt; cover the pot, and let them boil fast for half an hour, or until perfectly tender; put butter and pepper over, and serve hot. Or serve with drawn butter over.

Ruta Baga—Or large winter turnip, may be cut in quarters or slices, and boiled with meat, and served with a little butter and pepper over; or boil in water with a little salt; take off the thick outside rind, and cut them in quarters or slices, and boil them for an half an hour or more, until they are soft; then drain off the water, and mash them fine, add a bit of butter and pepper to taste, work them smooth, then put them into a covered dish, smooth the upper surface over, and mark it with a knife blade in flutes, meeting in the centre, or make it in a pyramid or pine-apple, and serve.

Summer Squash.—Young green squashes must be fresh to be fit for eating; if they are so, the outside will be crisp when cut with the nail.

Cut them in quarters, and if not very tender

pare off the outside skin; take the seeds and strings from the inside, and cut the squashes small, then put them into a stew-pan, with a teaspoonful of salt to a common sized squash; pour boiling water on nearly to cover them, cover the stew-pan, and let them boil fast, until they are tender, half an hour is generally enough; take them from the water into a cullender with a skimmer, press the water from them, then take them on to a dish, mash them smooth, add a bit of butter and pepper to taste, put them into a dish, and serve.

Winter Squash.—Cut the large yellow or winter squash small, take off the outside skin, and the inside strings and seeds: then put it into a stewpan, with hot water to cover it, cover the stew-pan for half an hour or longer, until they are tender, take them into a cullender with a skimmer, press out the water, then take them into a dish and mash them perfectly smooth, add a good bit of butter, and pepper and salt to taste; make it in a neat form the same as mashed turnips or potatoes; but do not brown it; put pepper over in spots, and garnish with sprigs of parsley, or celery leaves, if you wish it ornamental.

Sprouts and Greens.—Cabbage sprouts, young beet-tops, and the green leaves of young turnips, are boiled with salt meats, or in clear water, with a little salt.

Cabbage Sprouts.—The leaves must be cut from the stalk end, and washed in plenty of water, let the water boil when they are put in, and boil fast for half an hour; when done, take them from the water into a cullender, press all the water from them, chop them, and serve them with a salad dressing, or with roasted meat, to be eaten with the gravy, and vinegar and mustard. These greens are generally boiled with salt beef or pork, and eaten with vinegar.

Or, they may be served in this manner: having boiled, and pressed all the water from them, lay them close on a steak dish; fry some steaks or cutlets, or some slices of ham or sausages, lay them on the greens, and pour the gravy over. Vinegar may be added at table by those who like it.

The tops of young beets are next in delicacy to spinach. After nicely boiling, and pressing the water from them, put them into a covered dish; put bits of butter and pepper over, and serve. Or, boil beet-tops with salt fat meat, press the water from them, and serve with the meat.

YOUNG BEETS.—Wash fresh pulled young beets; break the tops from them, pick from them all the withered leaves, and put them with the beets into a pot of hot water, cover it, and let them boil fast for half an hour, or longer if the beets are large; then take the tops into a cullender, and press all the water from them; take the beets into a pan of cold water, and rub off the skin with the hand; put the pressed tops in a dish, slice the beets over; make a small cup of vinegar hot, with a bit of butter the size of a large egg, put a small teaspoonful of salt, and a little pepper to it, then pour it over the beets and tops, and serve. When the stalks of beet-tops are long, cut them from the beets and the leaves, tie them in bundles, and boil, and serve like asparagus, with a little white sauce, or drawn butter over, serve the beets in deep vegetable dishes, with the same sauce.

OLD BEETS.—Winter beets should be put in cold water over night to take off the earthy taste which they are apt to have; before boiling wash them clean, put them into a pot of boiling water and boil fast; if not very large, one hour will be sufficient for them; should they be very large, one hour and a half or two hours will be required; when done take them into a pan of cold water, rub the skins off with the hands, and cut them in thin slices, put them into a deep dish, strew a little salt and pepper over and pour on cold vinegar nearly to cover them; prepare them an hour before serving, with roasted or fried meat; if to be served with cold or boiled meat, make a cup of vinegar hot, put a large tablespoonful of butter to it; add pepper and salt to taste, and serve hot. Winter beets may be cut in halves or quarters, and pickled by covering them with cold vinegar.

Beets must be washed, but never cut before boiling, else they will lose their fine color.

SPINACH.—Take off every discolored leaf from the bunches; put them into a large pan or pail of water, and wash each cluster of leaves separately, shaking it well in the water, otherwise it will be gritty or sandy; washing it in this way, through two waters, will generally be enough; have a large kettle of water boiling fast, put in the spinach, press it down; add a teaspoonful of salt and a bit of saleratus, the size of a pea, to a peck of spinach; cover the pot and let it boil fast for fifteen minutes, it will sink when done; then take it into a cullender with a skimmer, press the water from it, cut it small with a knife, press it again, put a good bit of butter and a little pepper to it; put it into a deep dish, smooth the surface over, let it rise high in the centre, cut a cold boiled egg in slices and lay them over, serve hot with a cover; or it may be served on a flat dish; put it neatly on, lay hard boiled and sliced egg over. Spinach is boiled with salt beef, pork or ham. After the meat is done, take it up and press it between two plates that it may cut nicely, meanwhile, put the spinach into the pot, let it boil fast for fifteen minutes, then take it into a cullender, press all the water from it, cut it small, and serve with the meat. To be served with fried meat and gravy: boil it in water with a teaspoonful of salt, press the water from it and serve.

GREEN PEAS.—Shell green peas, until you have a quart; half a peck in the shells will generally produce a quart of shelled peas. Put boiling water to cover them; add a teaspoonful of salt, cover the stewpan and boil fast for half an hour; then take one between your fingers, if it will mash easily, they are done; drain off the water, take them into a deep dish, put to them a small teacup or less of sweet butter and a little pepper; a small teaspoonful of white sugar is a great improvement; serve hot. Small young potatoes, nicely scraped, may be boiled and served with them, or in a separate dish with a little butter over.

Lamb and peas is a favorite dish in the spring of the year; they are nice with poultry, veal, and mutton. A bit of saleratus or carbonate of soda, the size of a pea, put with green vegetables, improves the color, and renders them more healthful; fast boiling keeps the color good.

MARROW-FAT PEAS—Are the late sort, and as their name indicates, are much richer in taste. The shell of these is more of a yellowish green. and has a roughness, which the earlier peas have not; they should be young, and fresh picked. The early pea has a shell of brighter green and smooth, and is very inferior in taste, but recommend themselves by their forwardness, that being their distinguishing merit. The marrow-fat peas are dressed the same as the early peas.

Asparagus.—Choose green stalks of asparagras, the largest are best; cut off the white tough part, wash the green in cold water, and tie it in small bundles, that they may be taken up without danger of breaking; put them in hot water with a teaspoonful of salt, and let them boil fast for half an hour; toast some thin slices of bread a delicate brown; cut off the extreme outside crust, butter each slice freely; then lay them on small oval dishes; untie the asparagus, and lay it on the toast; butter it a little, sprinkle pepper over and serve. Or it may be served without the toast; the toast may be moistened by putting a little of the water in which the asparagus, but boiled, over it.

Vinegar is eaten with asparagus was it is generally added at table by such as like it.

Asparagus may be laid on plain toast; and a little drawn butter poured over both.

Asparagus Stewed.—Cut the green part of a bunch of asparagus in inch or half inch lengths; put it into a stew-pan and let it boil fast for fifteen minutes, then pour very nearly all the water off, work a tablespoonful of butter with a teaspoonful of flour, then stir them into the asparagus. Add pepper and salt to taste; cover the stew-pan for five minutes; and serve poured over toast.

Asparagus Salad.—Divide a bunch of green asparagus into small bundles; tie them, and put them in hot water, with a teaspoonful of salt; let them boil fast for fifteen or twenty minutes, until they are tender; when done, take them into a salad bowl; make a small teacup of vinegar hot, put a bit of butter, the size of an egg, (or a teaspoonful of sweet oil) to it, add a teaspoonful of made mustard; stir them well together, and pour it over the salad.

GREEN BEANS.—Cut the bud and stem end off, and take the strings from the sides of stringed beans; cut them in inch lengths; wash them in cold water, then put them into a stew-pan of hot water, add a teaspoonful of salt, cover the stew-pan, and let them boil fast for half or three-quarters of an hour; take one up, if it will mash easily when pressed between the thumb and finger, they are done. Drain off the water, add sweet butter and pepper to taste; but some nicely toasted bread in squares or diamonds, lay them on a dish, and serve the beans over.

Green beans when good, will be a bright color, and crisp when broken. They should be fresh picked.

BEANS AND CORN, CALLED SUCCATASH.—Take the husks and silk from a dozen ears of sweet corn, and with a sharp knife cut the kernels from the cob, scrape gently what remains on the cob with the knife blade; string a quart or more of green beans, and cut them in inch lengths or shorter; wash them and put them to the corn; put them, with the corn, into a stew-pan, add half a pint of boiling milk or water; cover it close, and let them boil rather gently for three-quarters of an hour; then add a teacup of butter, a teaspoonful of salt, and a saltspoonful of pepper; stir them well together; cover it for ten minutes; take the beans and corn into a dish, with more or less of the liquid, as may be liked.

This dish may be made without butter, by substituting half a pound of nicely corned fat pork, washed in cold water, and cut in slices as thin as a knife blade. No other salt is required.

Lima beans and sweet corn make the finest succatash.

LIMA BEANS.—Lay a quart of shelled Lima beans in cold water for one hour; then put them into a stew-pan, and pour boiling water over to cover them; cover the stew-pan, and let it boil fast for half an hour; then take one between your finger and thumb, if it will mash easily, it is done; drain off nearly all the water, add a small teacup of butter, a teaspoonful of salt, and a little pepper; cover them for a few minutes over the fire, then serve hot.

CARROTS.—When young and small, carrots need only be washed without scraping; leave on about an inch length of the green; put them in a stew-pan with hot water to cover them, and a teaspoonful of salt: let them boil fast for twenty minutes, then take them into a dish, put butter and pepper over, and serve, with boiled meat or poultry.

OLD OR WINTER CARROTS—Must be scraped and washed clean; then boil them tender, slice them, and serve with butter, pepper, and salt over.

Carrots may be sliced before boiling, and served in the same manner. Carrots are mostly used for soups.

CARROTS MASHED.—Scrape off the skin, wash them and boil them tender in a pot of boiling water, then take them up with a skimmer, mash them smooth, add butter, pepper, and a little salt; make them in a form with a knife blade, and serve, with boiled or roast meat.

CAULIFLOWER SALAD.—Boil cauliflower in water, with a little salt, until tender, drain it in a cullender, cut it small, put it in a salad bowl, and serve with a salad dressing, cold or hot.

CAULIFLOWER.—Cut off the stalks, boil the cauliflower in milk and water until it is tender, make a drawn butter and serve over it, or put bits of butter over, strew pepper over, and serve hot.

PARSNIPS.—Young parsnips require only to be scraped before boiling, old ones must be pared thin and sliced, when tender, put butter and pepper over, and serve. Parsnips may be boiled or stewed with salt meat.

FRIED PARSNIPS.—Boil whole parsnips until they are tender, then skin them, and cut them in slices lengthwise, of a quarter of an inch thickness; have a little lard or beef dripping, made hot in a frying-pan, salt it (in proportion, a tablespoonful to a pound,) when it is boiling hot, lay the slices in; when one side is a fine brown, turn the other; when both are done, take them on to a dish, sprinkle a little pepper over, put over a very little of the fat in which they were fried, and serve hot for breakfast or dinner, with fried or roast meat.

PARSNIP FRITTERS.—Boil four or five parsnips; when tender, take off the skin and mash them fine, add to them a teaspoonful of wheat flour and a beaten egg; put a tablespoonful of lard or beef dripping in a frying-pan over the fire, add to it a saltspoonful of salt; when boiling hot, put in the parsnips, make it in small cakes with a spoon; when one side is a delicate brown, turn the other; when both are done, take them on a dish, put a very little of the fat in which they were fried over, and serve hot. These resemble very nearly the taste of the salsify or oyster plant, and will generally be preferred.

CELERY.—Put a bunch of celery in cold water, cut it loose from the stalk end; cut off the green part and any imperfections, and serve in a celery glass, with vinegar, oil, and made mustard in the castor. Or cut the white part in thin slices across, and put it into a salad bowl or deep dish, put a wreath of the most delicate leaves around the edge, put a sprig in the middle, and pour a salad dressing over the whole.

SALAD DRESSING.—Take the yolk of a hard boiled egg, break it fine with a silver fork, add to it the yolk of an uncooked egg, and a teaspoonful of salt with half as much fine pepper, and half a tablespoonful of made mustard, work them smoothly together, adding gradually a tablespoonful of sweet oil, and the same of white wine vinegar. A larger proportion of oil and vinegar may be used if liked.

CABBAGE SALAD.—Take a fine hard head of white cabbage, cut it in two, and shave it across as fine as possible, with a sharp knife, put it in a salad bowl, and pour the dressing over.

This is very good when celery cannot be had, and far less expensive.

This may be served with stewed oysters, boiled or roasted poultry or meat, and with lobster.

COLDSLAW.—Cut a hard white head of cabbage in two, shave one half as finely as possible, and put it into a stew-pan with a bit of butter the size of an egg, one small teaspoonful of salt, and nearly as much pepper; add to it a wine-glass of vinegar; cover the stew-pan, and set it over a gentle heat for five minutes, shake the stew-pan about; when heated through, turn it into a dish, and serve as a salad.

BOILED CABBAGE.—Trim off all the outside leaves of a head of cabbage, cut it in quarters, and put it into a pot of boiling water, with a teaspoonful of salt; cover the pot close, and let the cabbage boil fast for half an hour, or it may require ten minutes longer; when the stalks are tender, take it up on to a cullender, press it slightly, to free it from water, put a little butter and pepper over it, and serve.

Or after having boiled it, chop it fine, put a bit of butter and some pepper to it, and serve hot in a covered dish.

RED CABBAGE.—This is eaten as a salad, prepared as directed for cabbage salad or coldslaw, or shaved fine and pickled.

RADISHES.—Radishes are of three sorts; the long red, the small button or turnip radish, and the winter or white radish.

Radishes should be fresh pulled, and tender, to be in perfection for the palate, or to be healthful; to many persons they are positively injurious.

To prepare them for the table, cut off all the leaves, leaving about an inch of the stalk, trim them neatly, and lay them in cold water for an hour, serve the long ones in a tumbler or celery glass half filled with water; serve the small ones on a plate; they are generally eaten with salt only; they may be served cut in thin slices, with vinegar, pepper and salt over.

LETTUCE.—The early lettuce, and first fine salad are five or six leaves in a cluster; their early appearance is their greatest recommendation; cabbage or white heart lettuce is later and much more delicate; break the leaves apart one by one from the stalk and throw them into a pan of cold water; rinse them well, lay them into a salad bowl or a deep dish, lay the largest leaves first, put the next size upon them, then lay on the finest white leaves; cut hard boiled eggs in slices or quarters and lay them at equal distances around the edge and over the salad; serve with vinegar, oil, and made mustard in the castor.

Or, having picked and washed the lettuce, cut the leaves small; put the cut salad in a glass dish or bowl, pour a salad dressing over and serve; or, garnish with small red radishes, cut in halves or slices, and hard boiled eggs cut in quarters or slices; pour a salad dressing over when ready to serve.

Serve with boiled lobster, boiled fowls, or roasted lamb or veal.

ARTICHOKES.—These are eaten the same as radishes, but more generally sliced thin, with salt, pepper, and vinegar.

Artichokes are served boiled the same as turnips: that is, wash and pare them, throw them into a pot of boiling water, let them boil for half an hour, then take them up with a skimmer into a vegetable dish, put butter, pepper, and salt over, or serve with drawn butter over. White or winter radishes may be boiled the same as artichokes.

CUCUMBERS.—Cucumbers are very unwholesome if not perfectly fresh gathered, which may be ascertained : press the finger nail into the rind, and if fresh it will be crisp, if it is tough or withered, the cucumber is stale.

Cucumbers are eaten with salt only, or sliced, with vinegar, pepper, and salt. Cut off an inch of the stem end, pare off all the green outside or rind, and lay them in cold water or on ice for an hour or more; when served cut them in quarters from end to end, or cut them in slices not thicker than a dollar piece, put them in a deep dish, strew a little salt and pepper over, and nearly cover them with good vinegar, when ready to serve.

Young green onions are sometimes peeled and cut in thin slices, and served with cucumbers.

SHALOTS, OR GREEN ONIONS.—Take off the outer skin or leaf; cut off all but about an inch or two of the green part, and lay them in cold water for an hour, then take them from the water on to a plate, and serve with salt.

Or, cut them in thin slices, sprinkle salt and pepper over, and vinegar nearly to cover them.

WINTER, OR STORE ONIONS.—White onions are used for boiling or pickling; red onions are eaten, cut in thin slices; let them lie in cold water for half an hour, then throw it off; put salt, pepper, and vinegar over; or cut in thin slices and fry as previously directed, with liver or beef.

TO BOIL ONIONS —Take off the skin and outer shell until they are white, put them into a stewpan with a teaspoonful of salt (to a dozen, medium size) and hot water to cover them; cover the stewpan and let them boil for half an hour, or until they are tender, then take them into a dish with a skimmer, put a bit of butter, the size of an egg, to them; sprinkle pepper over, and serve.

Boiled onions are served with roast fowl, goose, or turkey, or boiled or roast mutton.

To Boil Green Corn.—Get the short, full ears of sweet or sugar corn, trim off all the husks, leaving only the last inside leaves; have a kettle of boiling water with a small teaspoonful of salt to each quart; put in the corn and let it boil fast for half an hour, if young and tender, or longer if less tender; when done, drain off all the water, take off the remaining husks; lay a napkin on a large dish, lay the corn on, turn the corners of the napkin over it, and serve, to eat with salt and cold butter.

Or break each ear of corn in pieces, about two inches long, or break each ear in two, tie them in a cloth and put them into a pot of boiling water with a small tablespoonful of salt; let it boil fast for half an hour if young and tender, or longer, if necessary; some corn will require a full hour. When done take it from the water, and serve, folded in a napkin.

Corn may be served in the following manner:—

Take off all the husks, then with a sharp knife cut it from the cob and put it in a stew-pan, with a teacup of water, to a quart of corn cut from the cob, cover it close, and let it simmer gently for one hour; then add a large tablespoonful of butter; pepper and salt to taste, and serve hot.

Sweet or sugar corn is best for boiling. The ears are short and full, and the grains, when broken by the finger nail, are full of a sweet, milky fluid.

Common large ears of white corn may be improved by putting a tablespoonful of white sugar to the boiling water. Or it may be cut from the cob, and finished as directed above, with the addition of the sugar.

ROASTED GREEN CORN.—Strip off all the husk from green corn, and roast it on a gridiron, over a bright fire of coals, turning it as one side is done. Or, if a wood fire is used, make a place clean in the front of the fire; lay the corn down, turn it when one side is done; serve with salt and butter.

SALSIFY, OR, VEGETABLE OYSTER.—Boil and serve as directed for parsnips; either plain boiled, or fried, or made fritters.

EGG PLANT.—Cut an egg plant in thin slices, pare off the purple rind, then strew each slice with salt, and lay them together on a plate, placed slanting that the liquor which exudes may run off, after an hour rinse the slices, wipe them dry, dip each slice in batter or flour, and fry a nice brown, turning them that each side may be a nice brown, fry in seasoned fat or lard, or sweet butter.

MUSHROOMS.—Mushrooms for eating grow in open pasture lands. Those which grow near or under trees, are poisonous.

Good mushrooms first appear very small, of a round form, on a small stalk; they grow very rapidly. The upper part and the stalk are white; as they increase in size the under part gradually opens, and shows a fringed fir of a fine salmon color, which continues more or less until the mushroom has gained some size, and then changes to a dark brown.

These marks should be attended to; and likewise whether the skin can be easily parted from the edge and middle, and whether they have a pleasant smell.

Those which are poisonous, have a yellowish skin, and the under part has not the clear salmon color of genuine mushrooms. They have also a rank smell, and the fringe or fur is white or yellow.

BROILED MUSHROOMS.—Choose the largest sort, lay them on a small gridiron over bright coals; the stalk upwards. Broil quickly, and serve, with butter, pepper, and salt over.

HOMINY.—There are three sizes of hominy; the middle size is best.

Wash a small teacup of hominy in plenty of water, rubbing it between the hands; all that is not good will rise to the top; drain off the first water, then add more; stir it in this; let it settle and pour off the water; then put to it a quart of water, cover it and let it stand all night. In the morning add to it a teaspoonful of salt, and set the vessel which contains it in a kettle of boiling water over the fire. One hour will boil it. The reason for putting the vessel in water is, that otherwise it is very liable to burn. It may be set in an oven, or over a very gentle heat, without danger of burning. When all the water is absorbed, stir it well with a spoon, turn it out in a deep dish, cover it and serve for breakfast, with broiled steak, stewed clams, fried oysters, or chickens.

This is extremely palateable and wholesome, and much liked, though not generally known.

Some hominy is much sweeter than other. It may be eaten with butter for breakfast, or with a sauce of butter, sugar and nutmeg for dessert, the same as rice. Coarse hominy requires five or six hours boiling. Cooked with dried beans and pork, it is called succatash.

TOMATOES.—These are cooked and dressed in a variety of ways.

Tomatoes may be sliced thin, and served with salt, pepper, and vinegar over, for breakfast; or sliced, and strewn with sugar and grated nutmeg, for tea; for dinner they may be stewed or broiled, or baked.

Tomatoes may be preserved in sugar, or as catsup, when out of season. Such as like them, declare them to be equally excellent in each and every form or dressing.

STEWED TOMATOES.—Pour boiling water over six or eight large tomatoes, or a greater number of small ones; let them remain for a few minutes, then peel off the skins, squeeze out the seeds, and some of the juice, by pressing them gently in the hand; put them in a well tinned stew-pan, with a teaspoonful of salt, a saltspoonful of pepper, a bit of butter, half as large as an egg, and a tablespoonful of grated bread or rolled crackers; cover the stew-pan close, and set it over the fire for nearly an hour, shake the stew-pan occasionally, that they may not burn; serve hot.

This is decidedly the best manner of stewing tomatoes; they may be done without the bread crumbs, and with less stewing if preferred.

BAKED TOMATOES.—Wash five or six smooth tomatoes, cut a piece from the stem end, the size of a twenty-five cent piece, put a saltspoonful of salt, half as much pepper, and a bit of butter the size of a nutmeg, in each; set them in a dish or pan, and bake in a moderate oven for nearly one hour.

BROILED TOMATOES.—Having broiled a steak of beef, ham, veal or lamb, on one side, turn it; lay sliced tomatoes over it, sprinkle a little pepper and salt over, and when the meat is done, and dished, put butter over, and serve hot.

SCOLLOPED TOMATOES.—Peel six fine tomatoes, (pour scalding water over, if the skins do not come off readily,) and press the seeds and juice from them, butter a scolloped tin plate, put to the tomatoes two tablespoonsful of bread crumbs, a teaspoonful of salt, and a saltspoonful of pepper, and a piece of butter the size of a small egg, cut it small; put the prepared tomatoes into the buttered dish, and bake half an hour in a quick oven; when done, turn it out. A teaspoonful of sugar added to the preparation is considered an improvement.

WATER-CRESSES.—These are used as a salad; pick out all discolored leaves, wash each cluster separately, and serve in a salad bowl, with cold boiled eggs sliced and put over; or cut the cresses fine, and serve with a salad dressing.

LEEKS.—These are used principally for soups, they may be boiled, and served with toast the same as asparagus.

CABBAGE AND POTATOES.—Chop cold boiled cabbage and potatoes quite fine; put them together, season with butter, pepper and salt, add a very little vinegar or hot water, to moisten without making it wet, put it into a stew-pan over the fire, stir it well, that it may be thoroughly heated, but not burn; then take it into a dish, and serve for breakfast, or with cold boiled salt meat for dinner.

HORSE-RADISH.—Lay fresh horse-radish in a pan of cold water for an hour or more, then pare or scrape off the outer skin, and grate it on a coarse grater; add a little salt to it, moisten with vinegar, and serve with boiled fish or roast meat.

SAUCES

For Meat, Fish, Poultry, or Vegetables.

To Make Drawn Butter.—Put half a pint of milk in a perfectly clean stew-pan, and set it over a moderate fire; put into a pint bowl a heaping tablespoonful of wheat flour, quarter of a pound of sweet butter, and a saltspoonful of salt; work these well together with the back of a spoon, then pour into it, stirring it all the time, half a pint of boiling water; when it is smooth, stir it into the boiling milk, let it simmer for five minutes or more, and it is done.

Drawn butter made after this receipt, will be found to be most excellent; it may be made less rich, by using less butter.

Parsley Sauce.—Make a drawn butter as directed, dip a bunch of parsley into boiling water, then cut it fine, and stir it into the drawn butter a few minutes before taking it up.

Egg Sauce.—Make a drawn butter; chop two hard boiled eggs quite fine, the white and yolk separately, and stir it into the sauce before serving. This is used for boiled fish or vegetables.

Sour Sauce.—Make half a pint of good vinegar hot, stir into it a quarter of a pound of fresh butter, and a teaspoonful of made mustard, and a little pepper, and serve with boiled lobster or fish.

Cold Butter and Vinegar Sauce.—Beat a quarter of a pound of butter to a cream, with a gill of vinegar, and a teaspoonful of pepper; dip a bunch of parsley into scalding water, chop or cut it small, and beat it with the butter; a teaspoonful of made mustard may also be added. Serve with boiled meat or lobster.

BUTTER SAUCE.—Beat a quarter of a pound of butter to a cream, add a teaspoonful of pepper and salt, each; beat it well together, and serve with roast, or baked, or boiled potatoes, and cold meat— or, put it over boiled vegetables.

SHALOT SAUCE.—Take half a pint of water, in which meat has been boiled, add a wineglass of vinegar, and two or three shalots cut fine, and half a teaspoonful of salt; put these into a sauce-pan, over the fire; work a teaspoonful of flour into a piece of butter the size of an egg, and stir them into the hot water, and let them simmer for fifteen minutes. Serve with boiled meat.

TO BROWN FLOUR.—Take some flour into a pan or dish, and set it in the oven or over some coals; stir it about, that it may not burn, but be nicely browned. Keep it in a dredging box for browning gravies.

NASTURTION, OR IMITATION CAPER SAUCE.— Stir some pickled nasturtions into sour, or drawn butter sauce.

ANCHOVY SAUCE.—Soak some anchovies in a basin of cold water, for two or three hours; then put them in a stew-pan, with cold water, and set them on coals to simmer, until the anchovies are dissolved; then strain the water, add to it a wine-glass of red wine, and half a pint of melted butter;

let it simmer for quarter of an hour, then serve with boiled fish, or meat.

OYSTER SAUCE.—Put half a pint of milk into a stew-pan, set it over a fire; mix a tablespoonful of wheat flour with a quarter of a pound of butter; when the milk boils, put to it a pint of small oysters; then pour into the butter and flour, half a pint of boiling water, stirring it all the time; when smooth, add it to the milk and oysters; add a small teaspoonful of salt and pepper, and serve with boiled meat, turkey, or fowls.

MINT SAUCE.—Take nice fresh mint, chop it small, mix with it a teaspoonful of sugar, and vinegar to moisten it. Serve with roast lamb.

ONION SAUCE.—Peel some nice white onions, and boil them tender; press the water from them, chop them fine, and put them to half a pint of hot milk; add a bit of butter, and a teaspoonful of salt, and pepper to taste. Serve with boiled veal, or poultry, or mutton.

LOBSTER SAUCE.—Put the coral, and spawn of a boiled lobster into a mortar, with a tablespoonful of butter, pound it to a smooth mass, then rub it through a sieve; melt nearly a quarter of a pound of sweet butter, with a wineglass of wine, or vinegar; add a teaspooonful of made mustard, stir in the coral, and spawn, and a little salt and pepper; stir it until it is smooth, and serve. Some of the meat of the lobster may be chopped fine, and stirred into it. Madeira wine should be used.

LEMON SAUCE.—Make a drawn, or melted butter sauce, cut a lemon into very thin slices, take out the seeds, and stir the slices into the sauce; give it one boil, then serve over boiled fish, fowl, or meat.

CURRIE POWDER.—This powder is used for flavoring various stews of meat, fish, and poultry; a tablespoonful of the powder for each pound of meat, or less may be used, if liked. Currie powder may be bought at the best groceries, or you may have it made up at the druggists, as follows:

Take thirteen ounces of coriander seed, two ounces of black pepper, one of cayenne pepper, three ounces of cummin seed, and six ounces of pale colored tumeric; the whole pounded very fine; set them before the fire, and let them dry perfectly, turning them frequently; mix them well, and when cold, put it into bottles; cork them tight; this will be good for one year, if kept in a dry place.

CREAM SAUCE.—Put quarter of a pound of butter in a stew-pan, with a small tablespoonful of wheat flour, a teaspoonful of chopped parsley, and the same of young onions of scallians, chopped fine; add a saltspoonful of salt, and the same of pepper, and grated nutmeg; mix these well together, then add a glass of cream, or rich milk, set it over the fire, and stir it with a silver spoon, until it is ready to boil; if it is too thick, add more milk; this sauce should be kept stirring for fifteen minutes. Serve with boiled rabbits, meat, or poultry.

MELTED, OR CLARIFIED BUTTER.—Put quarter of a pound of butter in a stew-pan, by a gentle fire; let it remain until the scum rises, and the milk settles to the bottom; take off the scum carefully with a spoon; then pour the butter carefully from the milk.

APPLE SAUCE.—Peel, quarter, and core, rich tart apples; put to them a very little water, cover them, and set them over the fire; when tender, mash them smooth, and serve with roasted pork, goose, or any other gross meat.

FRIED APPLES.—Wash fine fair apples without paring, and cut them in slices an eighth of an inch thick, and fry in hot lard, or pork fat; serve with fried pork.

FRIED PEACHES.—Take peaches, not fully ripe, wash them, and wipe them; then cut them in slices quarter of an inch thick, and fry in the pan, after pork; serve with the meat. This is a South Carolina dish.

CRANBERRY SAUCE, OR JAM.—Pick a quart of cranberries free from all imperfections, wash them, and put them into a stew-pan, with a teacup of water, and the same of brown sugar; cover the stew-pan, and let them stew gently for one hour; then mash them smooth with a silver spoon; dip a quart bowl in cold water, pour in the stewed cranberries, and set it to become cold; then turn it out on a dish, or glass saucer, and serve with roast pork, ham, goose, or fowls.

DIRECTIONS.

For making and keeping Butter in the best manner. Also, Milk, Cream, Cheese, etc.

To Freshen Salt Butter.—Butter which has been made too salt, may be freshened and made sweet in the following manner: Take two or three pounds of it into a wooden bowl or tray, pour very cold water over it, and work it with a ladle, gently pressing it until the water is colored; then drain it off, add more water, continue to work it, changing the water until it is clear; mix a small teaspoonful of fine white sugar, and a large one of fine salt together for each pound of butter; and after draining off the water for the last time, strew the mixture over; work it thoroughly in with a ladle by folding and gently pressing the butter; then make it in rolls and wrap each in a separate bit of muslin; or pack it down in stone jars, lay a bit of muslin upon it, and put a cover over to keep it from the air; keep it in a cool dry place. Ice water, or cold spring water, is requisite for making good butter.

Delicious Butter.—Lay open three clean coarse towels, one over the other; put a pint of thick cream in the upper one, tie the cream in them as close as possible; then bury it in the earth in a dry place, eighteen inches deep, for twenty-four hours; then put the cream in a cool earthen basin, and stir it with a spoon for five minutes in summer, or fifteen in winter;—when you will have a lump of cool, fresh, and most delicious butter, for the breakfast table. Why not try it?

Butter in Haste, *from Winter Cream, or from*

the Milk of one Cow.—Take milk fresh from the cow, strain it into clean pans, set it over a gentle fire until it is scalding hot; do not let it boil; then set it aside; when it is cold skim off the cream; the milk will still be fit for any ordinary use; when you have enough cream, put it into a clean earthen basin; beat it with a wooden spoon, until the butter is made, which will not be long; then take it from the milk and work it with a little cold water, until it is free from milk, then drain off the water, put a small tablespoonful of fine salt to each pound of butter, and work it in. A small teaspoonful of fine white sugar, worked in with the salt, will be found an improvement—sugar is a great preservative. Make the butter in a roll; cover it with a bit of muslin, and keep it in a cool place.

This receipt was obtained from one who practiced it for several winters.

To Preserve Butter for Winter Use.—Take two parts of the best fine salt, one part finely ground loaf sugar, and one of saltpetre; beat them well together. To each pound of butter, worked perfectly free from milk, put one ounce of this composition; work it well into it, and pack it down in stone pots, or wooden firkins. Butter packed in this way, will be found to equal the best rose butter, and will remain sweet for years, if not exposed to the air.

To make Butter Sweet, *for Winter Use.*—Buy the ordinary packed butter, which is not strong or rank; take out several pounds, and work it with cold water until free from milk; put to each pound a small teaspoonful of fine salt, then pack it close into stone pots or wooden kegs; make a brine of one part saltpetre, one part white sugar, and two

I*

of common salt. To each ounce of this preparation put a gill of water for each two pounds of butter; pour it over the butter; cover the pot or keg, and keep it in a cool place.

Quite indifferent butter may be made sweet and good by pouring this brine over, and allowing it to remain for a few weeks, or longer, before using.

Or you may pack it as directed in the preceding receipt, and arrive at the same result.

Butter packed after these directions has been eaten in the spring of the year in preference to the best grass butter.

To Make Butter.—In order to make butter well, it is necessary that the vessels in which the milk is kept be sweet and clean, and the milk-room or cellar cool and airy in summer.

Large tin pans are mostly used for milk; the broadest are best, allowing a greater surface for the cream to rise.

Vessels in which milk is kept, after being emptied, must first be washed in cold water to take off all the milk, and any remains of cream, then fill them with scalding hot water, which must be suffered to remain until it is nearly cold. One pan may be turned over another, which is filled with hot water, for a few minutes, then change their relative positions, pouring the water from one to the other; this will require less time and water than the other way. Lastly, wash them well in the water, and turn them upside down in the sun. Tin milk pails are best, being most easily kept sweet; white or hard wood pails are generally used, and must be washed well in cold water and then scalded the same as tin pans. Occasionally, scour both pails and pans with soft soap and sand; and afterwards scald them, rinse them in hot water, and dry them in the sun, or by a fire. Or, instead of scalding the milk tins, and other vessels, as above directed, have a large vessel of boiling water, and having first washed them in cold water, dip each pan into the scalding water, turning it around that every part may get its due. Let it remain in for a few minutes, then wipe them dry, and set them by for use; their own heat will assist the drying.

Milk strainers are tin basins, with a fine sieve at the bottom; or with a ring by which to fasten a linen cloth, over a bottomless basin. The ring and cloth must be taken off every time it is used, and first washed in cold water; allow it to remain in the water whilst washing the tins, then wash it out; pour scalding water in it, and lastly, rinse it in cold water and hang it to dry.

A small frame or ladder is wanted to lay across the pan and support the strainer whilst the milk is poured through.

For taking the cream from the milk, a small short-handle tin skimmer or shell is used; a stone jar or pot is best for keeping cream. There should never be more than three days' gatherings for a churning; too long keeping will make bitter butter; wash the jar in cold water, then scald and dry as directed for the tins.

Wooden ware churns are mostly used. The old fashioned barrel churn, is best for small churnings; a larger sort, in which the dasher is suspended and moved back and forth instead of up and down, is less tiresome; the churn is to be kept sweet and clean in the same manner as the other vessels, exposing the inside to the heat of the sun, until thoroughly dry, after each time washing.

A wooden tray and ladle, is also necessary for receiving and working the butter, after it is made.

Care is necessary that the churning is neither too

fast nor too slowly performed. The dashes should be continued at intervals of about a second between them, and steadily, until the butter has come, when a slower and more gentle motion is desirable.

Scald the tray and ladle, then fill it with cold water until the butter is made.

After the butter is fairly gathered, take it from the buttermilk, with the ladle, pressing it against the side of the churn, to free it from the milk; having thrown the water from the tray, put the butter in, pour cold water over, to cover it, and set it in a cool place for half an hour, to harden it; then with the ladle work all the milk from it, changing the water until it is clear; it is best to have ice water if possible, in summer. To each pound of butter put a small tablespoonful of fine salt, and a small teaspoonful of fine white sugar; work it nicely into the butter and make it in rolls, or pack it in wooden or stone vessels, put a bit of muslin, and a cover over to keep the butter from the air.

Butter should be made and kept in a cool cellar or ice house: this direction is particularly for summer, when it must be done in the coolest part of the day, and the coolest possible place. Cold water poured in occasionally, in small quantities, at the dasher, will make butter come better, in summer.

In warm weather, milk is generally ready for skimming, after twenty-four hours' standing, when the cream is wanted for butter.

Cream for table or freezing, twelve hours' standing is sufficient; take off the cream, let the milk remain until the next morning, then skim it and keep the cream for butter.

When the weather is cold, let the milk become scalding hot without boiling, before straining it; after twelve hours it is fit for skimming, and the milk which remains will be sweet and fit for common purposes. Another way to hasten cream is to dip the pans in boiling water before straining in the milk; by turning another pan scalded in the same manner over the pan with the milk, you may greatly facilitate the operation. Another way is to set the pans over vessels of boiling water; this will also cause the cream to rise quickly.

If you churn in winter, pour boiling water into the churn, cover it and let it remain until ready to put in the cream, at which time throw it out. Winter churning should be done in a moderately warm room.

Milk cellars should be under ground or over an ice house. If under ground, a milk room should be paved with brick or stone; and a stone or wooden table in the centre; or a rack or shelf suspended from the ceiling instead. There should be stone or wooden shelves running around three sides; in summer the windows and doors should be close latticed only, that there may be a free current of air. In cold or winter weather the windows should be closely glazed, and the door tight.

The shelves and floor of a milk room should be washed and wiped dry twice a week in summer, and once each week in winter. The place should be cool and sweet, and free from any mustiness, which will affect the milk.

To preserve butter for winter use, see a previous receipt. (page 201.)

Buttermilk and thick sour milk are used to make pot-cheese, or cottage-cheese, as it is sometimes called.

Buttermilk is also a cooling summer drink, and very palateable, sweetened with a little sugar, or syrup, or molasses. A little grated nutmeg may also be added. It is fit for eating only the first day. Bread crumbed into sweetened buttermilk is much liked by children, as well as certain grown persons one might mention.

Thick sour milk, taken from the pan carefully with a skimmer, without breaking, may be served with sugar and nutmeg over. It is both cooling and very palateable, and by most persons preferred to cold custard.

Sour milk and buttermilk are kept for the pigs.

To Make Pot Cheese.—Put butter-milk and thick sour milk together, about one-third buttermilk; put it in a clean vessel over the fire, make it scalding hot, then take the curd from the whey with a skimmer, put it into a muslin or linen bag, tie it up and hang it to drain; after an hour or two, take it down, moisten it slightly with sweet cream, put a little salt to it, work the salt into it, and make it in balls the size of a teacup; press it close with the hands, lay a cloth on a dish to receive the cheese, cover it, then set it in a cool place. These are fine for the breakfast or tea-table.

Lay one on a small plate, and serve with bread and butter, and ripe fruit, or preserves.

Pot-cheese should be made fresh, once or twice a week.

Cows Fed on Turnips.—If cows are fed on turnips, the butter made from their milk has an unpleasant flavor; to counteract which, put a quart of boiling water to every two gallons of milk, and let it stand as usual for cream.

A very small quantity of nitre, dissolved in cold water, and put to the milk, is said to destroy any ill taste.

Artificial Cheese.—Boil one gallon of new milk with two quarts of cream; add six or eight eggs well beaten, and six or seven large spoonsful of wine-vinegar; let it simmer until it comes to a tender curd, then tie it in a cheese-cloth, and hang it to drain for several hours, after which, open the cloth, work some salt to the cheese, then lay a cloth in a cullender or cheese-hoop, put the curd in, fold the cloth over, and lay a weight upon it for one hour or longer, then turn it on to a dish and serve.

MILK CHEESE.—Put five quarts of warm milk into a basin, with two tablespoonsful of rennet water; when the curd is formed, break it gently with the hand, drawing it to the side of the basin or other vessel; let it stand for two hours, spread a cheese cloth over a sieve or round basket, put the curd in, let it drain until all the whey is off, then salt it to taste; then lay a cloth in a cheese-hoop, put the curd in, lay a cloth over; lay a wooden cover, the size of the inside of the hoop over, place a two pound weight upon it, and let it remain for twelve hours; then take it out, put it in a frame, or tie a cloth tight around it, and turn it from one side to the other every day, until dry; then rub the outside with a little butter, and sprinkle pepper over to keep the flies from it; put it to ripen between two pewter plates; if the weather is warm, it will be ready in three weeks.

CHEESE-CREAM.—Make a pint of milk lukewarm, dilute a piece of rennet the size of a pea, in milk, and stir it in; put it over some hot coals until it curds, then drain it, and turn it into a dessert dish, and serve with wine sauce, or with sugar and cream.

To PREPARE RENNET.—Take the stomach of

the calf, empty it, and strew it plentifully with salt, let it lay for a day or two, then stretch it out on two sticks, and dry it in the sun; a piece of dried rennet the size of your hand, is sufficient for a quart of water; a tablespoonful of the water will curd a quart of milk.

CHEESE ROASTED.—Grate three ounces of dry cheese, and mix it with the yolks of two eggs, put four ounces of grated bread, and three of butter; beat the whole together in a mortar, with a dessert-spoonful of made mustard, a little salt, and some pepper; toast some slices of bread, cut off the outside crust, cut it in shapes, and spread the paste thick upon them, and put them in a dutch oven; let them become hot, and slightly browned; serve hot as possible.

To MAKE WELSH RABBIT.—Cut or grate some good cheese, put a bit of butter, and some made mustard to it, put it in a frying pan over the fire, and stir it smooth; a little milk may be added to it; when it is hot, and a smooth paste, spread it on slices of nicely toasted bread, and serve hot.

To MAKE TOAST.—Cut slices from a loaf of wheat bread, let them be smooth, even, and half an inch thick, have a bright fire, and toast them quickly; when both sides are a fine brown, lay the slices on a hot plate, and put a tin cover over until served.

MILK TOAST.—Having toasted the bread nicely, spread it with sweet butter, make some milk hot, add a small bit of butter, and a little salt to it, then pour it over the toast, and serve. Or lay toasted bread in a deep plate or dish; to a pint of milk put a teaspoonful of salt, and a teacup of butter, make it boiling hot, then pour it over the toast; some persons work a small teaspoonful of flour with the butter, and stir it into the milk when it is boiling hot; stir it for a few minutes, then pour it over the toast.

TOAST WITHOUT BUTTER.—Toast some slices of wheat bread, put a pint of milk over the fire, when hot, add a small teaspoonful of salt, and pour it over the toast.

DIRECTIONS

For making Puddings, etc.

FOR BOILING PUDDINGS.—Have a tin form or muslin bag—the former should have a close fitting cover, and be rubbed over the inside with a bit of butter before putting the pudding in it, that it may not stick—the latter should be first dipped into boiling water, then well floured on the inside.

Tin forms may be bought, or small covered pails, of two or three quarts capacity, for large or small puddings; these are more easily kept sweet than are muslin bags. Tie a batter pudding close.

Bread puddings, or those made of corn meal, should be loose, as they swell very much in boiling.

The water must be boiling when the pudding is put in, and continue to boil until it is done. If a pudding is boiled in a bag, it must be turned frequently whilst boiling, otherwise it will stick to the pot.

There must be enough water to cover the pudding if it is boiled in a bag; if boiled in a tin form do not let the water quite reach the top of it.

To boil a pudding in a tin basin, dip a cloth in hot water, dredge it with flour, and tie it closely over the basin.

When the pudding is done, take it from the water, give whatever it is boiling in, one sudden plunge into cold water, then turn it out immediately; this will prevent its sticking. If there is any delay in serving the pudding, cover it with a napkin, or the cloth in which it was boiled; it is best to serve as soon as turned out.

Baked Puddings.—Bread, cornmeal, or rice require a moderate heat; batter or custard require a quick oven; the time required for baking each particular one is given with the receipt for making it.

Eggs for puddings are beaten enough when a spoonful can be taken up clear from strings.

A baked pudding must be served in whatever it is made. It is well to improve their appearance as much as possible. They may be served the same as meat pies, substituting small apples or other small fruit for the parsley or green leaves.

Soufflees, or light puddings, require a quick oven. These should be made so as to be done at the moment for serving; otherwise they will fall and flatten.

Common Custard.—Beat either four or five fresh eggs light; then stir them into a quart of milk; sweeten to taste; flavor with a teaspoonful of peach water, or extract of lemon, or vanilla, and half a teaspoonful of salt; rub butter over the bottom and sides of a baking dish or tin basin; pour in the custard, grate a little nutmeg over, and bake in a quick oven. Three-quarters of an hour is generally enough. Try whether it is done by putting a teaspoon handle into the middle of it; if it comes out clean, it is enough.

Or, butter small cups; set them into a shallow pan of hot water, reaching nearly to the top of the cups; nearly fill them with the custard mixture; keep the water boiling until they are done. The pan may be set in an oven, or over a fire; if over the fire, it is best to brown them with a hot shovel.

MINUTE PUDDING.—Put a quart of milk in a stew-pan over a clear fire; make a batter of a large teacup of wheat flour and enough cold milk; add a teaspoonful of salt, and when the milk is boiling hot, stir the batter gradually to it; continue to stir it until it thickens, and the flour is cooked. Dip a mould or basin into cold water; pour the pudding in and let it cool sufficiently to keep its form, then turn it out and serve with sugar and butter, or wine-sauce.

APPLE FRITTERS, *without Eggs*.—Put of buttermilk or sour milk and water, each half a pint into a basin; dissolve half a teaspoonful of saleratus in a little water; put a teaspoonful of salt to the milk and water, and stir in wheat flour enough to make a smooth batter, then add the saleratus; pare and chop fine five or six large tart apples, and stir them into the batter; have a thick-bottomed frying-pan, put into it a large tablespoonful of sweet lard, set it over the fire, and when it is boiling hot, put in batter by the large spoonful until the pan is full, flatten each a little; let them fry gently; when one side is a delicate brown turn the other; when both are done take them on a dish, add to each a small bit of butter and a teaspoonful of sugar, with a little grated nutmeg, and serve hot.

BOILED APPLE PUDDING, *without Eggs.*—Make a batter the same as for fritters, using double the quantity of milk and water and flour; peel, quarter, and core five or six rich tart apples, and stir them into the batter; tie it into a pudding bag, and boil two hours. Serve with butter and sugar worked together, with a little grated nutmeg.

Huckleberries, cranberries, or ripe peaches may be used instead of apples.

APPLE FRITTERS, *with Eggs.*—Beat two eggs light, and stir them to a pint of milk, and half a pint of water, and flour enough to make a smooth batter, (a pint bowl heaping full is enough flour) pare and core six large tart apples, and chop them small, stir them into the batter, and finish as directed without eggs.

BOILED APPLE PUDDING, *with Eggs.*—Make a batter with two well beated eggs, and a pint and a half of milk, with a pint bowl heaping full of wheat flour; beat it until smooth and light; pare, quarter, and core, five or six large tender tart or sour apples, and stir them into the batter, with a teaspoonful of salt; tie it in a pudding-bag, and boil for two hours. Turn it out on a dish, and serve with sugar, butter, and nutmeg sauce.

APPLE DUMPLINGS.—Pare, quarter, and core, eight fine tender tart apples; make a pie crust, roll it to half an inch thickness, cut it in round pieces, the size of a tea plate; lay as many pieces of apples in the centre as it will contain, gather the edges up, and pinch them together over the apple; have a pot of boiling water, and when the dumplings are all made, drop them in; cover the pot, and let them boil gently, for nearly an hour; then take each one carefully with a skimmer, on to a dish; serve quickly, with butter, sugar, and nutmeg, worked together, or with butter and syrup; to be eaten cut open, and the sauce, or syrup, and butter over.

A more healthful paste may be made for apple puddings, or dumplings, thus:—To a pint of sour milk, or buttermilk, and half a pint of water, put a small teaspoonful of saleratus, dissolved in a little hot water; put wheat flour, into an earthen basin, make a hollow in the centre, add a teaspoonful of salt, and the buttermilk, etc.; work in the flour until it is a soft dough; flour your hands, and divide it in pieces, the size of a common apple; then flatten it between your hands, to about half an inch thickness, or rather less; put a quartered apple in the centre, then draw the edges of the paste together over it, pinch it close; strew some flour over a large dish, and lay each dumpling on, (the gathered side down,) until they are finished; have a pot of boiling water, drop the dumplings in, cover the pot, and let them boil gently for nearly an hour; serve with sugar, or syrup, and butter.

This paste is both light, and delicate; a pie paste is not so; very few persons can eat it without positive injury.

DRIED PEACH DUMPLINGS.—Stew dried peaches without sugar, and finish as directed for apple dumplings.

DRIED APPLE DUMPLINGS.—Pick the apples, and cut out any imperfections, rinse them in cold water, and put them in soak for one night; then stew them with the water in which they were soaked, with more, if necessary; add a lemon, cut in thin slices, if liked; when the apples are tender, put them on dishes to cool; then finish as directed for apple dumplings, the last mentioned paste to be preferred. Any dried fruit may be stewed, and done in this way.

Ripe Peach Dumplings.—Pare, not very ripe peaches, and cut them in halves, or quarters, and finish as directed for apples.

Rhubarb Dumplings.—Peel off the skin from the stalks, cut them in inch lengths, and finish as directed for apple dumplings.

Paste Pudding, *with Fruit.*—Make a pie paste, roll it out to less than half an inch thickness, cover the whole surface, until within two inches of the edge, with apples, peeled and cored, and chopped small, or stewed fruit, such as cranberries, prunes, plums, or any other; then begin at one side, and fold, or roll it neatly; wrap a pudding cloth around it, secure the ends by tying, and, unless very small, boil gently for two hours; take the cloth from it, turn it on a dish, and serve with a sauce of butter, sugar, and grated nutmeg, or wine sauce; cut it in slices across, nearly an inch in thickness.

Instead of pie paste, a more healthful one may be used, as directed for apple dumplings; roll it rather thinner than directed for pie paste.

Snow Balls.—Pick all imperfections from half a pint of rice, put it in water, and rub it between the hands; then pour that water off, put more on, stir it about in it, let the rice settle, then drain the water off; put the rice in a two quart stew-pan, with a teaspoonful of salt, and a quart of water; cover the stew-pan, and set it where it will boil gently for one hour, or until the water is all absorbed; dip some teacups into cold water, fill them with the boiled rice, press it to their shape; then turn them out on a dish, and serve with butter, and sugar, or wine sauce.

PRUNE PUDDING.—Beat two eggs, stir them to a quart of milk, with a teaspoonful of salt, and enough wheat flour to make a rather thick batter; rinse, or wash a handful of prunes, as may be required; sprinkle a little flour over, then stir them into the batter; tie it in a pudding-bag, and boil for two hours; serve with butter, and sugar, or wine sauce.

APPLE CHARLOTTE.—Cut slices of wheat bread or rolls, and having rubbed the bottom and sides of a basin, with a bit of butter, line it with the sliced bread, or rolls; peel tart apples, cut them small, and nearly fill the pan, strewing bits of butter and sugar between the apples; grate a small nutmeg over; soak as many slices of bread, or roll, as will cover it; over which put a plate, and a weight, to keep the bread close upon the apples; bake two hours in a quick oven, then turn it out.

Quarter of a pound of butter, and half a pound of sugar, to half a peck of tart apples.

PEACH CHARLOTTE.—Pare and cut the peaches, which may be ripe, but not soft, and finish as directed for apples. A charlotte may be made of any sort of fruit; dried fruit may be first stewed and sweetened.

A NICE DESSERT—May be made by stewing

fruit of any sort; cherries, currants, cranberries, or apples; make it quite sweet, butter some slices of wheat bread, lay them on a dish, and pour the stewed fruit over and serve hot.

If, for example, cherries are used; pick the stems and imperfections from a quart of them, put to them water rather more than to cover them, add a large teacup of sugar, (for sour cherries,) cover them, and let them stew rather slowly for half an hour, then pour them over the buttered bread, and serve hot.

WHOLE APPLE DUMPLINGS.—Take eight or ten rather small sized, tender tart apples, pare them neatly, and take out the cores with a penknife, roll out some good pie paste, or the one directed for apple-dumplings, to less than half an inch thickness; cut two rounds for each apple, lay it on one of them, then lay the other over, wet the edges on the inside, and join them neatly, then tie each in a bit of muslin, and boil for one hour; serve with butter and sugar, or syrup and nutmeg.

QUAKING PUDDING.—Grate stale bread until you have a teacupful, add to it six well beaten eggs, and a heaping teaspoonful of rice flour; stir them into a quart of milk, add a small teaspoonful of salt, tie it in a well floured pudding cloth, and boil for two hours; when done, turn it out, and serve with wine sauce heaped upon it; it is best to boil it in a basin. This pudding may be baked in a well buttered basin, then turned out, and served with wine sauce upon it; one hour will bake it in a quick oven.

CHEAP BATTER PUDDING.—Beat three fresh eggs with six dessert spoonsful of wheat flour; beat until very light, then stir into it gradually a quart of milk; add one tablespoonful of sweet butter, and two of sugar; of salt and essence of lemon, or peach water, each a teaspoonful; grate half a nutmeg to it, beat it well together, put it into a buttered basin or mould for one hour, in a hot oven; when done, turn it out, or serve in the basin. This pudding may be boiled; omit the sugar, butter, and flavoring, boil two hours, and serve with wine sauce.

RICH BATTER PUDDING.—Beat six eggs with six large spoonsful of wheat flour, until very light, then stir it into a quart of milk, beat them well together, butter a dish, and bake for one hour in a hot or quick oven. Serve with brandy or wine sauce; instead of brandy or wine, lemon juice may be used.

This pudding may be tied in a cloth, and boiled for two hours; serve with a sauce. Or it may be baked in small cups.

CITRON PUDDING.—Beat the yolks of three eggs with two tablespoonsful of wheat flour; when light, add a pint of boiled milk, and a quarter of citron cut small; put it in buttered cups, and bake half an hour in a quick oven; when done, turn them out, and serve with liquid sauce.

COCOANUT PUDDING.—Take the meat of a cocoanut from the shell, and take off the black outside; grate the white meat of a small cocoanut, and stir it into four well beaten eggs, add a quart of milk, and a teaspoonful of salt; line a buttered tin basin with pie paste rolled thin, put the pudding in, and bake for one hour in a hot oven; take it from the basin and serve with wine sauce. This pudding may be boiled, and served with sauce; or add a tablespoon-

J

ful of sweet butter, two large spoonsful of sugar, half a nutmeg, and a teaspoonful of essence of lemon, or peach water; bake in bowls or cups lined with pie paste. Two hours will be required for boiling.

FLOATING ISLAND.—Set a quart of rich milk to boil, when it does so, stir into it two small tablespoonfuls of white sugar, and the beaten yolks of six eggs; flavor with lemon or rose, or peach water; whip the whites to a high froth; when the custard is thick, put it into a deep china dish, and heap the frothed eggs upon it; it may be finished by putting spoonsful of jelly or jam over the frothed eggs, and serve.

TRIFLE.—Cover the bottom of a glass dish with Naples' biscuit, and half a dozen maccaroons broke in half, pour enough brandy or wine over to moisten them; next put spoonsful of jelly or jam over, pour a custard over, made of the yolks of six eggs and a quart of milk, sweetened to taste; whip the whites of two eggs, with quarter of a pound of pulverized white sugar, add a small wine-glass of wine or lemon juice, and when it will stand in a heap, put it on the custard, and serve.

LEMON CREAM, FLOATING ISLAND.—Beat the yolks of twelve eggs to the juice of four lemons, make it sweet with white sugar, and set it over a chafing dish of coals or a furnace; stir it till it become thick, then pour it into a dish, whip the whites of the eggs to a high froth, and serve it on the cream.

CHRISTMAS PLUM PUDDING.—Chop half a pound of beef suet very fine, stone and chop one pound of raisins ; take a pound of currants, picked, washed, and dried ; soak half a sixpenny wheat loaf in a pint of milk ; when it is all imbibed, add to it the chopped suet, raisins, and currants, a tablespoonful of sugar and two well beaten eggs ; put to it one wineglass of brandy or lemon juice, half a nutmeg grated or half a teaspoonful of ground mace, a tablespoonful of ground cinnamon and a small teaspoonful of alspice ; mix it well together, and boil it in a bag or tin form for three hours. When done turn it out and serve.

For sauce, beat quarter of a pound of butter to a cream, then stir into it half a pound of pulverized white sugar, continue to beat it until it is light; a wineglass of wine or brandy may be added.

Plum pudding may be made and kept for a month or more ; having made one as directed, or double its size, and boil twice as long, keep it in the cloth in which it was boiled ; when wanted cut off a piece or slice, put some butter and sugar, and if liked, a little wine over, put it on a plate and set it in a hot stove oven for half an hour, and serve ; or cut a slice, put a bit of butter in a frying pan, let it become hot, lay the pudding in, put over it a tablespoonful of sugar, dissolved in a little wine or water, cover the pan, and when the pudding is hot through, turn it on a dish and serve ; a tablespoonful of wine or hot water may be put in the pan after the pudding ; let it become hot, then put it over the pudding.

Plum Pudding.—Take half a pound of wheat flour, half a pound of raisins stoned and chopped, and the same of currants, picked, washed, and dried ; use milk enough to stir easily with a spoon, add half a pound of suet chopped fine, and four well beaten eggs and a large teaspoonful of mace.

cinnamon and alspice; mix all well together and boil it for two hours and a half in a cloth or tin. Serve with butter and sugar, or wine sauce. Plum pudding, if cold, may be warmed in a pan with some of the sauce.

LEMON PUDDING.—Beat half a pound of fresh butter to a cream with half a pound of white sugar, powdered fine, then add to it eight eggs well beaten, and a large fresh lemon grated with the skin, stir it well together, line a dish with puff paste, fill with the pudding and bake in a quick oven for nearly an hour.

ALMOND PUDDING.—Boil a pint of milk, let it cool; beat three eggs light, with three tablespoonfuls of flour; take the skins from two ounces of shelled almonds and pound them in a mortar to a smooth paste, with a teaspoonful of extract of lemon or peach water; melt one ounce of butter in the milk, add a quarter of a pound of white sugar, then beat all together and bake in a basin or cups.

ALMOND PUDDING.—Take the skins from quarter of a pound of shelled sweet almonds and four or five of bitter, pound them in a mortar with a teaspoonful of extract of lemon or orange-flour water, and a wineglass of wine; grate Naples biscuit or sponge cake until you have a pint bowl of it; add to it quarter of a pound of loaf sugar, half a pound of butter beaten to a cream, and a quart of cream boiled; grate in half a nutmeg and beat all together with six eggs beaten to a froth; line a dish with thin puff paste, put the mixture in and bake for one hour in a quick oven. Serve hot or cold.

ALMOND PUDDING BOILED.—Take the skins from

half a pound of shelled almonds, beat them to a smooth paste with a tablespoonful of rose water or lemon juice; mix a pint bowl of grated bread and a nutmeg grated with quarter of a pound of butter and the yolks of six eggs; beat them well together, add a tablespoonful of flour and a pint of cream or boiled milk, mix them well together, then put in the almonds, beat it until thoroughly mixed, then tie it in a buttered cloth and boil for one hour.

DISH OF SNOW, WHIPT CREAM.—To the whites of three eggs beaten to a froth, add a pint of cream and four tablespoonfuls of sweet wine, with three of fine white sugar and a teaspoonful of extract of lemon or vanilla; whip it to a froth and serve in a glass dish; serve jelly or jam with it.

Or lay lady-fingers or sliced sponge cake in a glass dish, put spoonfuls of jelly or jam over, and heap the snow upon it.

MOCK CREAM.—Beat three eggs light; then add to them, three heaping teaspoonfuls of wheat flour, beat them well together, then stir them into a pint and a half of boiling milk, add to it a saltspoonful of salt and a teaspoonful of essence of lemon or peach water, stir it for five minutes over a gentle fire; when perfectly smooth it is done.

Line a pudding pan, (having rubbed it over with butter,) with puff paste, cut strips of the paste and lay it around the edge, fill it with cream, strew powder sugar over, and set it in a hot oven for half an hour; when nicely browned it is done. This is altogether superior to custard.

CHARLOTTE RUSSE.—There are many varieties of this same charlotte; they are always similarly made, that is, of sponge cake or lady-fingers and whipt cream custard or blanc-mange, or the following: line the sides and bottom of an oval tin basin with lady-fingers closely fitted together or slightly lapped. Beat the whites of three eggs to a high froth with quarter of a pound of powder sugar and half a pint of cream until it is quite thick and light; flavor to taste with lemon or vanilla extract and fill the cake-lined mould, lay sliced sponge cake or lady-fingers over to cover it, and set it on ice for an hour or more. Turn it out on a dish and serve.

Or having lined a basin or mould, or small tin cups with lady-fingers, or sliced Savoy biscuit, or yellow lady-cake, fill them with mock cream, blanc-mange, or custard made of the yolks of eggs, and set them on ice to harden, or let them become cold. Turn them out, and serve.

Make a Charlotte de Russe as follows:—Break an ounce of isinglass small, and put to it a teacup of hot milk or water; set it on a stove until all is dissolved; then strain it through a bit of muslin to half a pound of fine white sugar. When very nearly cold, add it to a quart of cream, already beaten to a froth; continue to beat it for a few minutes, holding the pan on ice; having lined your moulds with lady-fingers, pour your cream in, cover it with lady-fingers or sponge cake sliced. Turn it out and serve.

Isinglass.—There are three sorts of isinglass: American, and English, and Russia, which is three times the price of the others; only one-third as much is required of it as of Cooper's isinglass, for a quart of milk, which is one ounce.

To Clarify Isinglass.—Break an ounce of isinglass small; pour on to it a cup of boiling water, and set it over a gentle heat to dissolve; when entirely dissolved, take off the scum, or strain it through a coarse cloth.

BLANC-MANGE.—Boil a pint of cream and a quart of milk together; clarify an ounce and a half of isinglass, and stir it into the cream; make it sweet with white sugar, and flavor with lemon and rose, or with vanilla, or orange flower water, and a teaspoonful of salt. Let it boil up once, stirring it well. Have ready some earthen moulds dipped in cold water; fill them with the blanc-mange. When perfectly cold turn them out, or when ready to serve.

Red jelly or jam is served with blanc-mange.

Three ounces of almonds skinned or blanched, and pounded to a smooth paste, stirred into the milk with the isinglass, may be considered an improvement. Strain it through a bit of coarse muslin into the moulds.

RIBBON BLANC-MANGE.—Put into a mould some blanc-mange one inch deep; let it become perfectly cold; color some blanc-mange with cochineal or carmine, a fine rose color, and put it an inch deep on the white; when it is also cold and firm, put the same depth of white, and white and red alternately, until the mould is full. When cold, it may be turned out on a dish.

Make rose color with cochineal pounded fine and steeped in a little hot water, or wash off enough from a saucer of carmine; use more or less according as you may wish the color to be.

INDIAN MEAL DUMPLINGS.—Put a pint of yellow corn meal into a large bowl; pour boiling water into it, stirring it all the time; make it a moist paste to mould in your hands; add a teaspoonful of salt, stir it in; make it in balls the size of a teacup, flour the outside, and drop them into a pot of boiling water, and let them boil for one hour. These may be boiled with salt meat. Serve with a sweet sauce or syrup.

BOILED INDIAN MEAL PUDDING.—On half a pint of Indian, or corn meal, pour a quart of boiling milk, stirring it all the time; add a teaspoonful of salt; beat two, three or four eggs, very light; and when the batter is nearly cold, stir them into it; put the pudding into a cloth or tin mould and boil two hours. Serve with a sauce, or with butter and syrup.

YEAST DUMPLINGS.—Make a dough of a pound and a half of wheat flour, with a tablespoonful of baker's yeast, a teaspoonful of salt, and warm milk, set it in a warm place to rise for two hours; when light, flour your hands, knead it down, and make it in balls the size of a small teacup; have a pot of boiling water; take off any scum which may have risen in boiling, drop the dumplings in, and boil fast for half an hour; take them up with a skimmer, and serve with boiled meat, or with a sauce or with butter and syrup.

CHEAP INDIAN PUDDING.—Stir gradually half a pint of Indian (yellow) cornmeal to a quart of boiling milk or water; when it has cooled, add a teaspoonful of salt, and a teacup of chopped suet, or half as much butter; put to it half a nutmeg grated, a teaspoonful of ground ginger, one egg, and a teacup of sugar or syrup. Bake two hours.

BOILED SUET PUDDING.—Into a quart of boiling milk, stir gradually as much sweet corn meal, as will make a thick batter; add a teacup of beef suet chopped fine, and a teaspoonful of salt; tie it loosely in a bag, and boil two hours. Quarter of a pound of raisins may be added to the batter. Serve with syrup.

BOILED BATTER PUDDING.—Beat three eggs very light with a teacup of wheat flour, and a teaspoonful of salt; then stir it into a quart of milk; put it in a tin form, or well floured pudding cloth, and boil fast for two hours. Serve with a wine or other sauce.

BOILED BREAD PUDDING.—Steep broken bits of stale bread in warm milk; when it is soft, beat it as you would beat eggs, until it is a smooth batter; add a teaspoonful of salt, tie it in a pudding-bag, and boil for an hour, or two, according to its size; one quart of milk, and bread enough to make a nice batter, may be boiled two hours; serve with a sauce. Eggs may be added to this pudding, one, two, three, or four.

BAKED BREAD PUDDING.—Break stale bread in small bits, to fill a pint bowl, put it into a quart of warm milk; when it is soft, beat it fine; add two well beaten eggs, half a nutmeg, grated, a bit of butter, the size of a large egg, and two tablespoonsful of sugar, with a teaspoonful of salt; a teaspoonful of lemon extract is an improvement. Bake one hour in a hot oven.

SMALL CUSTARDS.—Boil a quart of milk, beat from four to six eggs light, and when the milk is nearly cold, stir them into it; add a teaspoonful of salt, and two tablespoonsful of sugar; grate half a nutmeg over, and the yellow part of a lemon, or a small teaspoonful of lemon extract.

Butter some custard cups, and nearly fill them; set them in a shallow pan, and fill it nearly to the top of the cups, with boiling water; set it in a hot oven, or on some coals, for half an hour; then take the cups out, wipe them, and serve on a custard stand; or lay a napkin over a large dish, or tray, and set the cups on it. Serve with ripe fruit, with sugar; or with preserves.

BOILED BREAD PUDDING.—Cut three slices, of half an inch thickness, from a sixpenny loaf of wheat bread, take off the outside crust, and cut the slices in small squares; pour enough warm milk over, to moisten them; then beat two eggs light, and stir them into a pint of milk; rub the inside of a tin basin with butter, and having picked and washed half a pound of raisins, put them into the basin, lay the soaked bread on them, pour the milk and eggs over; dip a muslin cloth in hot water, dredge wheat flour over one side, and tie it over the basin; boil for one hour; when done, take the cloth from it, lay a plate over the basin, then turn the pudding upon it. Serve with wine, or other sauce.

BAKED BREAD AND BUTTER PUDDING.—From a baker's sixpenny loaf, cut three slices, of more than half an inch thickness, spread butter, quarter of an inch thick over each slice; butter a two quart basin, cut each slice in four, and strew them with well washed and picked currants, or raisins, and put them in the basin; beat two, or four eggs light, stir them into a quart of milk; add half a grated nutmeg, and a teaspoonful of lemon extract, if liked; make it sweet with three large spoonsful of sugar; pour in the bread and raisins; bake one hour in a hot oven.

This pudding requires nearly quarter of a pound of butter, half a pound of raisins, or currants, and two or more eggs, to a quart of milk.

Egg Pudding.—Beat nine eggs, with nine tablespoonsful of wheat flour, until it is very light; then add, gradually, three pints of boiled milk, and a teaspoonful of salt; bake one hour in a hot oven. Serve with sugar, butter, and nutmeg, or wine sauce.

Rice Flour Pudding.—Beat four eggs light, with a teacup of rice flour; add a quart of milk, and sugar, and spice, to taste, with a teaspoonful of salt; bake in a buttered basin, in a quick oven, for one hour; a heaping tablespoonful of sugar, and half a nutmeg, grated, will make this pudding very nice; or it may be baked without either, and served with a sauce.

Rice Pudding, *without Eggs*.—Wash a small teacup of rice, in two or three changes of water; make a quart of milk sweet, with a teacup of sugar; add a teaspoonful of salt, and half a nutmeg, grated; put the rice to the milk, and bake in a moderate oven, for nearly two hours.

Rice Pudding, *with Eggs*.—Beat two or more eggs light, and stir them into a quart of milk, with a teaspoonful of salt, and a wineglass of rice, well washed; put to it, two tablespoonsful of sugar, half a nutmeg, grated, and a tablespoonful of butter.—Bake one hour, in a quick oven.

Small Puddings.—Beat six eggs, with six tablespoonsful of wheat flour, and stir it into three pints of milk; add a teaspoonful of salt; butter six custard cups, and one pint bowl, and nearly fill them with the batter; bake half an hour in a quick oven; when done, turn the large one on the middle of a dish; turn the small ones around it, and serve with wine sauce over them.

MARROW PUDDING.—Grate stale bread to fill a pint bowl, pour over it a pint of boiling milk; when cold, slice into it a pound of beef marrow, very thin; add four well beaten eggs, and a wineglass of brandy; mix well together; raisins, and currants, may be added: boil two hours, and serve with brandy sauce.

COCOANUT PUDDING.—Grate half a pound of the white meat of a cocoanut; work a pound of fine white sugar into six ounces of butter, beat six eggs light, then add them to the sugar and butter, sprinkle the cocoanut gradually in, stir it well, add a wine-glass of brandy, and a teaspoonful of lemon extract, with half of a grated nutmeg; line a deep dish with a rich pie paste, put the pudding in, set it into a quick oven, roll some puff paste thin, cut it in leaves; when the pudding has been in the oven half an hour, take it out, make a wreath of the leaves around the edge, and return it to the oven for fifteen minutes, then serve.

SWEET POTATO PUDDING.—Make the same as cocoanut; grate the potato after paring off the skin.

RICH LEMON PUDDING.—Grate lemons outside, and pulp and finish the same as cocoanut pudding.

SPONGE CAKE PUDDING. — Take sponge cake which has become quite dry, grate it fine, add enough hot milk to make it a batter; put to it a bit of butter and some currants washed and dried; line deep dishes with pie paste, put the mixture in, and bake in a quick oven for one hour. Beat the white of an egg with quarter of a pound of pulverized white sugar, and a wineglass of wine, until it is light and white, and will stand in a form, heap it on the top of each pudding or pie as soon as taken from the oven, and serve.

OMLET FOR DESSERT.—Beat six eggs light, add a teaspoonful of salt, and four or five maccaroons pounded fine, beat them well together, fry as usual; strew plentifully with sugar, and serve.

CREAM CUSTARD.—Beat six eggs light, stir them into a quart of cream, sweeten with loaf sugar to taste, add half a nutmeg grated, and a teaspoonful of lemon or vanilla extract, or if preferred, peach water. Bake one hour in a quick oven, in a buttered basin, with or without a bottom crust.

DRIED CURRANT PUDDING.—One pound of currants, cleaned and dried, one pound of suet chopped fine, half a pound of wheat flour or bread crumbs, half a nutmeg grated, one teaspoonful of ginger, and one teaspoonful of salt; make it moist with milk, work it well together, tie it in a pudding bag, and boil for two hours; serve with wine or brandy sauce.

APPLES IN BATTER.—Pare and core several small sized apples, set them in a deep dish, make a rich batter, and pour it over them; bake in a quick oven for one hour; serve with wine sauce.

CHERRY PUDDING.—Make a batter the same as

for apple pudding, with or without eggs, (see directions,) take the stems from a quart of sour cherries, stir them into the batter, tie it in a pudding bag, and boil two hours; serve with butter and sugar sauce.

Ripe Currant Pudding.—Make the same as cherry pudding.

Huckleberry, Blackberry Pudding.—Pick the huckleberries or blackberries free from crushed berries or leaves, rinse them in cold water, and finish as directed for cherry pudding.

White Pudding.—Beat two eggs light, and stir them to a pint of cream, add a small teaspoonful of salt; butter a tin basin or pudding pan, cut three slices quarter of an inch thick, from a baker's loaf; rinse in cold water, pick and stone quarter of a pound of raisins, lay them in the pan, cut the bread small, and put it on them; pour the cream over, bake three-quarters of an hour in a quick oven; turn it out, and serve with wine sauce.

Rhubarb Fritters.—Strip off the outer skin from rhubarb stalks, cut them fine, and finish as directed for apple fritters.

Custard Fritters.—Whip the yolks of three eggs with a tablespoonful of flour, half a nutmeg grated, and a small teaspoonful of salt, add half a pint of cream or rich boiled milk; flavor with a glass of brandy, or a teaspoonful of lemon extract or peach water, sweeten to taste, and bake in a buttered dish; when cold, cut it in slices, cut each in small squares or diamonds; make a batter of two eggs beaten very light, to a pint of milk, and flour, to make a thin batter; dredge the pieces of custard with flour; put a tablespoonful of sweet lard or beef fat into a dripping pan, over the fire, put to it a saltspoonful of salt, and when it is boiling hot, take up one of the pieces with a spoonful of the batter, put it into the pan, then take another in the same way, and fill the pan, not too closely; let them fry gently; when one side is done turn the other; serve with white sugar grated over.

JELLY FRITTERS.—Make a batter of two eggs, a pint of milk, and a pint bowl of wheat flour or more, beat it light; put a tablespoonful of lard or beef fat in a frying or omlet pan, add a saltspoonful of salt, make it boiling hot, put in the batter by the large spoonful, not too close; when one side is a delicate brown, turn the other; when done, take them on to a dish with a doyle over it, put a dessertspoonful of firm jelly or jam on each, and serve.

JELLY IN FRITTERS.—Cut some firm jelly in slices; cut each slice in small squares or diamods, dip each into wheat flour or pulverized sugar, then into a batter made as directed for jelly fritters, fry as therein directed; strew fine sugar over, and serve hot for dessert.

CURRANT JELLY PUDDING.—Make a rich pie paste, roll it out to quarter of an inch thickness, spread currant jelly as thickly over the whole surface within an inch of the edge; then roll or fold it neatly; fold a pudding cloth about it, secure the ends and side and boil for two hours, unless very small; serve with a sauce of butter and sugar; cut it in slices across.

Any sort of jelly, preserve or stewed fruit may be made in this way

CURRANT JELLY DUMPLINGS.—Make a rich pie paste, or one more delicate and healthful as directed for apple dumplings; if pie paste is used, roll it to half an inch thickness; roll the other paste thinner; cut it in rounds the size of a tea saucer, put a large tablespoonful of jelly in the centre of each, gather the outer edges and pinch them together, dip your hand in flour and smooth over the outside; lay each one, the gathered side down, on a floured dish; when all are done, drop them in fast boiling water, which must be skimmed before putting them in; cover the pot and let them boil three-quarters of an hour; take them up carefully with a skimmer and serve quickly with a cover over, and butter and sugar sauce.

Cranberry jam, or any other, may be made in this manner, and it is delicious.

EGG PANCAKES.—Beat six eggs light with a pint bowl of wheat flour, add a teaspoonful of salt, and stir gradually into it enough milk to make a smooth, thin batter; put an omlet pan over the fire and let it become hot, rub a bit of sponge, dipped in butter, over the inside of the pan, and put in enough of the batter to run over it, as thin as a dollar piece; shake the pan when you think one side is done enough, and if you can, toss it up so as to turn it, if you cannot, use a pancake turner; when both sides are a delicate brown, take it on a dish, put a little butter over, grate white sugar and a little nutmeg or cinnamon over; fry another, lay on the first one, sprinkle it likewise, and so continue until you have enough; send to the table hot for dessert or supper; cut it in quarters and serve.

JELLY PANCAKES.—Make and fry the pancakes, as above directed; when one is done and taken on to a plate, spread jelly or jam thinly over it, then roll it up like a scroll, lay a napkin on a hot dish, lay the pancake on, make until you have enough and serve.

BREAD FRITTERS.—To a quart bowl of stale bread broken small, put a quart of boiling milk, cover it for ten or fifteen minutes, when it is quite soft beat it with a spoon until it is smooth, add two well beaten eggs, half a nutmeg grated, one tablespoonful of brandy, a large spoonful of sweet butter and a small teaspoonful of salt; beat it light, make an omlet pan hot, put in a bit of butter the size of a large hickory nut, set the pan over a gentle fire, put in the batter by the spoonful, or enough to run over the bottom of the pan, let it fry very gently; when one side is a fine brown turn the other, put butter and sugar with a little grated nutmeg over, or spread wine sauce over, put one above the other, cut them through in quarters, and serve hot.

FOR A PUDDING.—Make as directed for bread fritters, tie it in a bag and boil two hours; serve with wine sauce.

RATAFIA PUDDING.—Boil a quart of cream, break half a pound of dry sponge cake, or Naples' biscuit, in pieces, and put it into the cream; add a teacup of butter, a wineglass of wine, half a nutmeg grated, and a quarter of a pound of fine white sugar; take the skins from two ounces of shelled almonds, pound them to a smooth paste, with a little lemon juice or brandy to keep them from oiling; when the cream, etcetera, is almost cold, add to it the yolks of four eggs, and the almond paste, beat them well together, grate sugar over the top, and bake half an hour in a quick oven.

TRANSPARENT PUDDING.—Beat eight eggs light; put to them half a pound of butter beaten to a cream, stir in half a pound of finely powdered sugar, and half a nutmeg, add a small teaspoonful of lemon extract, set it over the fire, and stir it until it is thick, then set it to cool; rub a pudding pan over with butter, put a strip of puff paste around the edge; put in the pudding, and bake half an hour in a quick oven; serve it hot.

SMALL CURD PUDDINGS.—Take four quarts of milk, make it warm, and put to it a tablespoonful of rennet water; when the curd is formed, strain the whey from it, and put it into a mortar or earthen basin, beat half a pound of fresh butter with it, until it is well mixed, then beat the yolks of six, and the whites of three eggs light, and strain them to the curd, grate two small Naples' biscuit or a penny roll, and stir them altogether; butter small pans or cups, put in the mixture an inch deep, and bake twenty minutes in a quick oven; when done, turn them out on a dish, and having blanched some almonds, cut them in slips, cut citron in slips, and stick them over the puddings, put liquid wine sauce over, and serve.

EGG DUMPLINGS.—Make a batter of a pint of milk, two well beaten eggs, a saltspoonful of salt, and flour enough to make a batter as thick as for pound-cake; have a clean sauce-pan of boiling water, let the water boil fast, drop in the batter by the tablespoonful; four or five minutes will boil them, take them with a skimmer on to a dish, put a bit of butter and pepper over, and serve with boiled or cold meat; for a little dessert, put butter and grated nutmeg, with syrup or sugar over.

GOTHAM PUDDING.—Beat four eggs light, add to them half a pint of milk, a teaspoonful of salt, and a bit of saleratus the size of a small nutmeg, stir in enough flour to make a rather thick batter, add half a pound of currants clean washed and dried; or a quarter of citron cut in slips, beat it until very light, then tie it in a pudding cloth, and boil one hour and a half; turn it on to a dish, put wine sauce over, and serve. This pudding may be boiled in a tin basin, or well buttered mould.

CORN MEAL FRITTERS, *Without Eggs.*—Take a pint bowl of yellow corn meal, put to it a tablespoonful of sweet butter, and a teaspoonful of salt, stir gradually into it enough boiling milk to make a thick batter; put a tablespoonful of sweet lard with a saltspoonful of salt, into a frying pan, let it become boiling hot, put in the batter by the tablespoonful, flatten it out to an even thickness, and let it fry gently until one side is a rich brown, then turn the other; when both are done, take them on a dish, and serve with a bit of butter and syrup, or sugar over.

CORN MEAL FRITTERS, *With Eggs.*—Beat three eggs light, and stir them to a pint of milk, add a teaspoonful of salt, and enough yellow corn meal to make a thin batter; make some lard boiling hot in a frying pan, put in the batter by the spoonful, and fry each side a delicate brown; serve with butter and sugar, or syrup.

BOILED WHEAT AND INDIAN PUDDING.—Put a quart of warm water or milk into a vessel, put to it a large teaspoonful of salt, and half a teaspoonful of saleratus, dissolved in a little water; stir into it one pound of yellow corn meal, and a teacup of wheat flour, add a tablespoonful of baker's yeast, set it in a warm place for three or four hours, then add two well beaten eggs, stir them well into it; tie it in a pudding bag, and boil two hours with a sauce, or with butter and syrup.

To Make Soupon, or Corn Meal Pudding.—Put two quarts of water into a clean dinner pot, or stew-pan, cover it, and let it become boiling hot over the fire; then add a tablespoonful of salt, take off the light scum from the top, have sweet fresh yellow or white corn meal; take a handful of the meal with the left hand, and a pudding stick in the right, then with the stick, stir the water around, and by degrees let fall the meal; when one handful is exhausted, refill it; continue to stir and add meal until it is as thick as you can stir easily, or until the stick will stand in it, stir it awhile longer; let the fire be gentle; when it is done enough, it will bubble or puff up; turn it into a deep basin; this is eaten cold or hot, with milk or with butter, and syrup or sugar; or with meat and gravy, the same as potatoes or rice.

This is the genuine way of making soupon, sometimes called hasty pudding, which however, is a misnomer, few of the old Dutch, around Schenectady or thereabout, would not be disturbed at hearing it called by other than its ancient name, suppon.

An Englishman travelling through that vicinity a long time ago, chanced to stop at the house of an old resident, and desiring refreshment, forthwith was set before him a generous dish of soupon, with milk to correspond, and bowl and spoon for operation, which, being quite hungry, he soon commenced; the novelty recommending itself to his palate, he inquired its name, whereat the good housewife answered him sup-pon; the good natured traveller continued to do so for some time, when he again asked the name, sup-on being the answer, he renewed the attack, and continued until nature revolted at a further burden; now rising with some degree of passion, or to say the least, exhausted patience, he threw back his chair, seized his hat, and turning to the hostess with—"I have done all I can, now if you will not give me the name, pray keep it," he dashed out of the house, the old lady screaming after him in no very gentle tones, "I tell you. sup-on!"

FRIED SOUPON.—Make a soupon as directed, put it in a basin three inches deep; when it is entirely cold, cut it in slices half an inch thick, and fry in a pan with hot lard or butter; it is served for breakfast, with meat and syrup.

DRIED CURRANT FRITTERS.—Make a batter of two eggs well beaten, with quarter of a pound of wheat flour, quarter of a pound of beef suet chopped fine, a wineglass of brandy, enough milk to make a rather thin batter, and a large teaspoonful of salt; add a quarter of a pound of raisins, stoned and chopped, and the same weight of currants, washed and dried; fry in hot lard or beef drippings, as directed for fritters; when done, put a little butter and grated nutmeg over, and a large spoonful of sugar, and serve hot; they may be served with a wine sauce.

GREEN CORN PUDDING.—Grate the corn from three green ears, beat four, five or six eggs light, and stir them into a quart of milk; stir in the grated corn, with a large teaspoonful of salt, and half a nutmeg grated, and if liked, a small teaspoonful of lemon extract or peach water, make it sweet, and bake for one hour in a hot oven. The sugar and spice may be omitted in making, and wine sauce served with the pudding.

OMELET SOUFFLEE.—Beat six eggs, the whites and yolks separately; put to the yolks four dessert spoonsful of white sugar powdered, and the yellow rind of a lemon chopped very fine; mix them thoroughly; whip the whites to a high froth, and add them to the yolks; put quarter of a pound of butter into the pan, over a brisk fire, and as soon as it is completely melted, pour in the mixture, stir it, that the butter may be completely incorporated with the eggs; when it is so, put it in a buttered dish, and set it over hot embers' or ashes; strew powder sugar over the top, and color it with a hot shovel or salamander; this may be done in the oven.

This may be served as soon as possible, as it soon falls, and so the appearance is spoiled.

OMELET SOUFFLEE, *in a Mould.*—Break six fresh eggs, separate the whites from the yolks, put with the latter, three spoonsful of white sugar powdered fine, a dessert spoonful of rice flour, and a teaspoonful of orange flower water; stir these well together; whip the whites of the eggs to a high froth, and *stir* them to the yolks; pour the mixture into a buttered mould, not much more than to half fill it, bake in a moderate oven for half an hour; when done, turn it on to a dish, and serve quickly.

This omelet must be clear; and shake like a jelly.

GRATED COCOANUT, *a Dish of Snow.*—Take a large cocoanut, break it in pieces, pare off the dark outside, and throw them into cold water; grate the white meat on a coarse grater, and with a broad fork, heap it on a flat glass dish; serve with jellies, jam, or tart preserves.

Cranberry or currant jelly in a form, served with this, has a pretty appearance, and is a fine relish.

To Make a Hedge Hog.—Take the brown skins from two pounds of shelled almonds, beat them to a paste in a mortar, moistening them occasionally with a little lemon juice or orange flower water; beat the yolks and whites of seven eggs very light and stir them into a pint of cream with quarter of a pound of powder sugar, stir this gradually into the almond paste, put half a pound of fresh butter into a saucepan and set it over the fire; when it is melted put in the mixture and stir it around, mixing it thoroughly until it is sufficiently firm, and moulded into a hedge hog; stick it full of blanched almonds cut lengthwise in slips and set it in a dish, stir the yolks of four eggs into a pint of boiling cream, sweeten to taste and pour it around the hedge hog in the dish, let it become cold, then serve it as an ornamental dish for dessert or supper.

Frothed Eggs.—Beat the yolks of eight and the whites of four eggs with a tablespoonful of water, a teaspoonful of salt and the juice of one lemon, with sugar to taste; fry this as an omlet, put it on a dish; whip the four remaining whites to a high froth with a pound of white sugar, flavor with lemon or vanilla, heap it on the omlet and set it before the fire or in an oven for a few minutes to brown. Serve for dessert or supper.

Omelet with Sweetmeats.—Beat nine eggs,

the yolks and whites separately, put five tablespoonfuls of fine white sugar to the yolks; add a teaspoonful of lemon extract or peach water, whip the whites to a high froth and stir them with the yolks; put a teacup of butter into the pan, let it become hot, put in the omlet, draw it from the edges of the pan to the middle, and stir it so that it may be evenly done, shake it occasionally so as to free it from the pan; when done, spread jelly or jam over, roll it in the form of a muff, strew powder sugar over, make it with a hot skewer, and serve for dessert.

OMELET GLACEE.—Whip some fresh eggs to a froth with a little salt, finely shred lemon peel and five or six pounded macaroons; beat them well together, then fry as usual, sprinkle white sugar, brown with a salamander and serve.

PUDDING SAUCES.

WINE SAUCE.—Beat quarter of a pound of sweet butter to a cream, add gradually to it quarter of a pound of fine white sugar and a wineglass of wine, with half a nutmeg grated; continue to beat it until it is light and white, then mould it in a neat form and serve.

BRANDY SAUCE.—Make as directed for wine-sauce, substituting brandy for wine.

LIQUID BRANDY OR WINE-SAUCE.—To quarter

of a pound of butter put a quarter of a pound of sugar and a gill of brandy; grate half a nutmeg into it, make it hot and serve. Or it may be beaten well together and served cold.

LEMON SAUCE.—Make as directed for wine-sauce, using lemon in place of wine.

LEMON AND SYRUP SAUCE.—To half a pint of syrup put the juice of two fresh lemons, simmer them together for fifteen minutes, then add half a nutmeg, grated, and a small teacup of butter; stir it smooth. Serve with cornmeal or boiled rice puddings, or with batter or apple puddings.

SWEET SAUCE.—Work a teacup of sugar into a teacup of butter with a teaspoonful of flour and half a nutmeg, grated; when it is a smooth paste, stir gradually into it half a pint of boiling water, set it over the fire for ten minutes, stir it all the time, then turn it into a tureen and serve—with boiled batter or apple puddings. A glass of wine may be added to this, or a lemon sliced thin and cut into dice; put it in before putting it on the fire.

CRANBERRY SAUCE.—Wash a pint of cranberries, and pick out all imperfections, put them in a stew-pan, put a small teacup of water to them, put a large teacup of sugar over, cover them, and let them stew gently for nearly an hour, then add a teacup of butter to them, stir it in, and serve poured over boiled rice, or in a sauce dish.

APPLE SAUCE.—Pare, quarter, and core quarter of a peck of rich tart apples, put them in a stew-pan, with a teacup of water; add some finely chopped lemon peel, and a large cup of sugar, grate half a nutmeg over, and cover the stew-pan; let them stew gently for half an hour, then mash them fine; add a teacup of butter, and serve with boiled rice, or boiled batter pudding.

Rich Lemon Sauce, *for Puddings.*—Boil a fresh skin lemon in plenty of water, until a straw will penetrate it, then cut it in slices, and each slice in quarters; put to them and the juice, a teacup of sugar, and the same of butter, with a large teaspoonful of wheat flour worked into it; put all together into a stew-pan, and stir in gradually half a pint of boiling water; keep it over the fire for ten minutes, stirring it all the time, then serve with half a nutmeg grated over.

Maple Sugar Sauce.—Scrape maple sugar, or grate it until you have a teacupful, put to it a teacupful of hot water, stir it until it is dissolved, let it simmer for a few minutes, then stir in a tablespoonful of butter, and serve with boiled rice.

Cinnamon Sauce.—Make a sauce as directed for sweet sauce; when nearly done, stir in a dessertspoonful of ground cinnamon.

Or work together a teacup of butter and a teacup of sugar, with a large spoonful of ground casia or cinnamon; beat it until light and white, and serve with boiled rice or batter pudding.

Sauce for Plum Pudding.—Take the yolks of three eggs, add a gill of cream, and three tablespoonfuls of white sugar, set it over the fire, stir it until it is thick, then add a glass of brandy to it, stirring it all the time

DIRECTIONS

For Baking and Making Pies, Tarts, &c., and a Few hints for the Economical.

Be careful that the oven, whether of brick, or a range or stove, be perfectly clean, and free from any sugar or fat from anything which may have run over whilst baking.

The delicacy of pastry depends as much upon the baking as the making, therefore strict attention should be paid to the following directions:

Puff paste requires a quick even heat; a hot oven would curl the paste and scorch it.

Tart paste or short paste requires a degree less of heat.

For raised or light crust, the oven may be heated as for puff paste.

A brick oven must be thoroughly heated, that is, have a body of heat, else it will render pastry or cakes heavy; this must be attended to before beginning to bake; there may be sufficient heat to raise, and yet not enough to finish baking.

A range or stove oven is more easily managed; it is necessary to have it thoroughly heated, and a well sustained fire to keep it so, for those things which require the greatest degree of heat; those requiring less will be baked after these are done; there should always be a good heat at the bottom; some stove ovens are so well constructed, as to have a regular heat throughout.

When baking with coal, if the fire is not brisk enough, do not put on more coal, but add a stick or two of hard wood, or if nearly done, put in a stick of pine wood.

Tin summer ovens are very good for small things,

such as cakes, biscuits, and custards, but such as require a body of heat, will not do well in them. The charcoal for heating them should be in rather small pieces, and replenished a little at a time, as it burns away; by this means you may have a steady and more regular heat.

Sheet iron summer ovens are preferable to tin, and are heated in the same manner; these are very convenient for small families. A few cents worth of charcoal will get a nice breakfast for five or six, if rightly managed; thus, after kindling a fire in the furnace, with a few bits of twisted paper or splintered pine wood, and small pieces of charcoal, nearly fill it with coal; set a kettle of water over, then make out biscuit, short-cake, or corn meal bread, as you like; the oven by this time is heated; put them in to bake; two quarts of water will now be nearly boiling, put four even tablespoonsful of coffee in a coffee pot or bowl, add to it a little cold water, and a third of the white of an egg, mix it well together; if it is in a coffee-pot, pour the boiling water from the teakettle on it; cover it, and set it over the fire for ten or fifteen minutes; then set it by for a few minutes to settle, or if it is mixed in a bowl, stir it into the boiling water, and finish in the same manner. After this is done, a small steak may be broiled or fried over the furnace in fifteen minutes; or eggs may be boiled. The whole will require rather more than one hour. This is economy, where a fire is not required for other purposes during the day; and as it is all done within the fireplace, the room in which it is done is not heated by it.

A nice dinner may be cooked for a small family in this manner; make a small bread pudding or custard, have a breast of veal or lamb, or a shoulder, or any small piece; prepare it, and set them side by side in the oven; put vegetables in a pot over the furnace, or peeled potatoes in with the meat, keep up a brisk fire for an hour, and the dinner is done. Half a peck of charcoal will be enough for it.

FINEST PUFF PASTE, *for Puffs.*—Heap one pound of flour in the centre of the paste-board, or slab, make a hollow in the centre, break one egg into it; then add a teaspoonful of salt, and a piece of butter the size of an egg; mix these lightly together, with a little cold water; add the water, a little at a time, until the flour is made a nice paste; work it together, and roll it out to half an inch thickness; then divide a pound of butter in six parts, spread one part over the paste; then fold it, and roll it out again, until you can perceive the butter through; then spread over another part, fold it up and roll out again, and so continue until all is used, and it has been through six turns. It is now ready for making in pies, puffs, or any other purpose; and may be used immediately, or set in a refrigerator or ice box, or other cool place for a day or two, and be improved thereby.

A marble slab, and rolling-pin, are best for pastry, and much more durable; after using them, wash off all the old paste, scrape them clean, wash them first with cold water, then pour scalding water over them, and wipe them dry.

Have a hair sieve ready to sift any flour you may wish to use; this is but little trouble, or delay, and always best to sift flour.

To gild pastry, wet it over when nearly done, with the yolk of an egg, beaten with a little milk.

COMMON PUFF PASTE. *for Pies.*—Put one pound of sifted wheat flour on the slab, or into an earthen basin; make a hollow in the centre, work into it quarter of a pound of lard, and a teaspoonful of salt; when it is mixed through the flour, add as much cold water as will bind it together; then strew a little flour over the paste-board, or table; flour the rolling-pin, and roll out the paste to half an inch thickness; divide half a pound of butter in three parts; spread one evenly over the paste; fold it up, dredge a little flour over it, and the paste-slab, or table; roll it out again, spread another portion of the butter over, and fold, and roll again; so continue until all the butter is used; roll it out to quarter of an inch thickness for pies.

This paste is for the upper crust of pies, or to line tartlet pans, for shells for fruit, or preserves. Puff paste should not be used for the under crust of pies; when not having space enough to rise, it becomes greasy and heavy, and consequently unwholesome. Half a pound of shortening, worked into a pound of flour, with a teaspoonful of salt, and enough water to bind it, will make an under crust rich enough.

A LIGHT PUFF PASTE.—Have one pound of sifted flour, and the same weight of sweet butter; work one-fourth of the butter into the flour, until it is like sand; measure two teaspoonfuls of cream of tartar, and one of soda, rub it through the seive; put it to the flour; add enough cold water to bind it, and work it smooth; dredge flour over the paste-slab, or board, rub a little flour over the rolling-pin, and roll the paste to about half an inch thickness; spread over the whole surface, one-third of the remaining butter, then, fold it up; dredge flour over the paste-slab, and rolling-pin, and roll it out again; then put on another portion of the butter, and fold, and roll again; spread on the remaining butter, and fold, and roll for the last time.

Paste Puffs.—Roll the paste to rather more than half an inch thickness, and cut it in cakes with a tin cutter, the size of the top of a tumbler; then with a wineglass, or tin cutter of that size, mark the size of it in the centre of the larger cake; lay them on tins, wet the tops over with a brush, dipped in an egg beaten with a little sugar, bake in a quick oven for half an hour; when done, take out the centre, and fill with jelly or jam. Serve for dessert or supper.

Paste Tarts.—Roll puff paste to half an inch thickness, cut it in cakes the size of a tumbler; cut the inside from one, leaving a ring the width of a finger; put it on one of the cakes, wet the top over with the yolk of an egg, beaten with a little milk; make several in the same manner, lay them on baking tins, and set them in a quick oven, for nearly half an hour; then put a tablespoonful of jelly, or jam, or rich stewed fruit in the centre of each; strew a little fine sugar over, and return them to the oven for ten minutes.

Family Pie Crust, *Short.*—Put a pound of sifted flour into a bowl, work into it half a pound of sweet lard, or beef dripping, with a dessert-spoonful of salt; when it is thoroughly mixed through, put to it enough cold water to bind it together; flour the paste-slab, or table, and rolling pin, take a part of the paste, and roll it to less than a quarter of an inch thickness.

This will be quite rich enough for health or taste.

A bit of volatile salts, the size of a small nutmeg, dissolved in a little hot water, and put to the paste, with the water to bind it, will make it more light and delicate.

For the upper, or outside crust of a pie, roll the paste out thin, spread a bit of butter, half the size of an egg, over it; fold it up, roll it out again, and cover the pie.

Sweet Paste Jelly Tarts.—Mix half a pound of flour, half a pound of fine white sugar, and half a pound of butter well together, with a bit of volatile salts the size of a pea, (dissolve it in about a tablespoonful of hot water;) when it is all dissolved and cooled, add it to the paste; beat it smooth with a rolling-pin, then roll it out to nearly half an inch thickness; cut it in cakes, the size of the top of a tumbler; wet the top of each over with a little milk, and bake on tins, in a hot oven, for half an hour; when done, heap a tablespoonful of jelly, or marmalade, in the centre of each; grate sugar over and return them to the oven, for ten or fifteen minutes.

Sugar Paste Cream Tarts.—To one pound of flour, put quarter of a pound of sugar, and one beaten egg; work it together with a little cold water, in which is dissolved a bit of volatile salts, half the size of a small nutmeg; roll it as thin as a dollar piece; rub some small tin tartlet pans, and line them with the paste; bake them ten minutes, then fill them with mock cream; grate sugar over, and return them to the oven for a few minutes to brown the tops.

Puff paste may be used instead of the above.

Canellons.—Make a stiff paste with a quarter of a pound of flour, half as much white sugar, and a teacupful of melted butter, and a teaspoonful of essence of lemon; beat the paste well with a rolling pin, and roll it as thin as a dollar piece.

Make little canes of card paper of about three inches in length, and one in diameter; butter the outside well, and wrap each in some of the paste, close it neatly on one side, and bake in a quick oven for ten or fifteen minutes.

When they are done, and cooled a little, take out the paper, and fill them with jelly or marmalade, or fill them with the mixture of which kisses are made.

CANELLON'S GLACES.—Roll out some puff paste quite thin, to about eighteen inches square, and cut it into about twenty-four strips, have by you as many pieces of beach wood turned; let them be about six inches long, three-quarters of an inch in diameter at one end, and not more than half an inch at the other; (or instead of wood, these may be made of card paper or tin,) rub them over with butter, moisten one side of the strips of paste, and wind one around each of the moulds; begin at the smallest end, so as to form a screw four inches in length; lay them on baking tins, rather distant from each other, and half bake them in a quick oven, then take them out; wet them over with beaten egg, roll them lightly in powdered loaf sugar, and return them to the oven for a few minutes, to give them a color; as soon as you take them from the oven, remove the moulds, and lay them to cool. When wanted to serve, fill them with jelly or kiss mixture.

CAKES A LA-POLANAISE.—Take puff paste, roll it a quarter of an inch thick, and cut it in pieces four or five inches square, gather up the four corners of each, have ready some round moulds, dip them in warm water, and put them inside the cakes; then put them in a quick oven; when they

K*

are three parts done, take them out, and wash them over with the beaten white of an egg; sprinkle powdered sugar over, and finish baking. When done, take out the moulds, and fill the cakes with preserve, or jelly, or mock cream.

TRIFLES.—Work one egg, and a tablespoonful of sugar, to as much flour as will make a stiff paste, roll it as thin as a dollar piece, and cut it in small round or squares cakes, drop two or three at a time into boiling lard; when they rise to the surface and turn over, they are done; take them out with a skimmer, and lay them on an inverted sieve to drain. When served for dessert or supper, put a spoonful of jelly on each.

NOTHINGS.—Break two or three fresh eggs into a basin, and work into them enough flour to make a very stiff paste, roll it out to the thickness of a dollar piece; cut them in small cakes, and finish the same as trifles.

These make a very pretty dish; they may be served with jelly or jam, between each two.

REMARKS ON PIE MAKING.—Pies for ordinary desserts are best to be made on plates of six or eight inches diameter, and when served with a variety of puddings, creams, etcetera, should be cut in six or more pieces.

Pumpkin pies should be made on dishes flat at the bottom, nearly an inch deep, with nearly perpendicular sides; generally they should not be larger than a breakfast or dinner plate; for Thanksgiving dinner, pumpkin pie being the crowning dish of the feast, should be made on a dish so large, that each of the guests may be helped to a piece from one and the same pie, which may be ornamented for the occasion, as shall hereafter oe directed.

Mince pies, for Christmas, should be distinguished by their size and ornaments, from those for ordinary occasions.

A New-Year's day table is not finished without its mince pies, which should be made small, not larger than tartlets, or made on the smallest tea or dessert plates, that they may be cut in two or four pieces.

Apple pies should always be served with roast pig or goose.

APPLE PIE.—Rub a pie dish over with a bit of butter; line it with short pie crust rolled thin; pare some rich tart apples, and cut them in small pieces; fill the pie dish an inch thick, lay them evenly over; if the apples are sour, use a teacup of sugar, to a quart bowl of cut apples; strew it over them, then grate half a nutmeg over, strew a saltspoonful of salt evenly over, and half a teaspoonful of ground cinnamon; then cover with a paste or puff paste crust; trim off the edges with a sharp knife, cut a slit in the centre, or make it before putting it over the pie; pass a gigling iron around the pie, half an inch inside of the edge, and bake for nearly an hour in a quick oven; if they are quite small, half an hour will bake them. You may gild the tops by brushing them over with the yolk of an egg, beaten with a little milk, before putting them in the oven, or when half done.

APPLE TART.—Peel and slice some nice tart apples, and stew them, with a small teacup of water, and the same of sugar, to a quart of sliced apples; add half a nutmeg grated, a saltspoonful of salt, and a little grated lemon peel, or lemon extract, or half a teaspoonful of ground cinnamon; set them to become cold; line some small pie plates with rich pie paste, or light puff paste, put in the stewed apples half an inch deep, roll out some of the paste, wet it over slightly with the yolk of an egg, beaten with a little milk, and a teaspoonful of sugar; cut it in strips the width of a finger, and lay it in bars or diamonds across the tart; lay another strip around the edge, trim off the outside neatly with a sharp knife, and bake in a quick oven until the paste loosens from the dish.

DRIED APPLE PIE.—Cut out all imperfections from tart dried apples, (a sharp pair of scissors is best for this purpose) then rinse them in cold water, put them in a vessel and put water over three inches more than to cover them; let them stand one night, then put them over a gentle fire with the water in which they were soaked, cover them and let them stew gently; boil a lemon in water until a straw will pierce the skin; cut it in thin slices, or smaller, and put it to the apples with the juice from it; add half a pound of clean brown sugar for each quart of apples, let them stew until they are soft, then turn them into dishes to become cold.

Rub the pie dishes over with a small bit of sponge, dipped in butter, line them with pie-paste, put in the stewed apple half an inch thick, thinning it towards the edge; roll an upper crust rather thin, cut three or four small slits each side of the middle and put it over the pie; trim them neatly with a sharp knife, and bake in a quick oven for three-quarters of an hour.

DRIED APPLE TART.—Prepare the apples, and make the same as for pie, with the exception of the cover, instead of which, put strips of paste in bars or diamonds.

DRIED PEACH PIE.—Prepare the fruit and finish the same as dried apple pie.

DRIED PEACH TART.—Make the same as directed for dried apple tart.

DRIED PLUM PIE.—Wash dried plums in plenty of water, put them to soak at night in water to cover them; in the morning put them to stew with the same water, put a pound of clean brown sugar to each quart of fruit, let there be plenty of liquid, if not enough, add hot water, cover them and let them stew until the syrup is rich, turn them into flat dishes to become cold. Cover a pie dish with paste, put in the stewed fruit and juice, half an inch deep, dredge a little wheat flour over, and cover with a rich pie or puff paste crust; bake three-quarters of an hour in a hot oven; gild the top over with the yolk of an egg beaten with a little milk, when half done, or grate white sugar over when served.

DRIED PLUM TART.—Prepare the fruit and finish the same as pie with the exception of the upper crust, instead of which put strips of paste over in bars or diamonds, finish with a strip laid around the edge, trim off the outside and bake half an hour in a quick oven, or bake until the crust loosens from the dish.

Or, line some small tartlet pans with tart paste, fill them with the stewed fruit, grate sugar over, and bake in a quick oven until the paste loosens from the pans.

RIPE PLUM PIES.—Stew ripe plums with

water to cover them, put a teacup of brown sugar, or more if they are sour, cover them and let them stew gently until they are soft, then take them in flat dishes to become cold, and finish as directed for dried plums. Tarts may be made as directed for dried plums.

GREEN PLUMS—require to be stewed as directed for ripe plums, with twice as much sugar.

GREEN GAGE PIES OR TARTS.—Stew green gages as directed for ripe plums, grate a little nutmeg to them and finish as directed for dried plums; green gages make delicious pies or tarts.

DRIED CHERRIES.—Rinse a quart of cherries, dried without the stones, in cold water; put them in a stewpan or brass kettle with water, three inches more than to cover them; cover the vessel in which they are and let them stew gently over a moderate fire for half an hour, then put a pound of brown sugar to them and let them stew for half an hour longer; having lined the pie dishes with paste, put in the cherries and juice half an inch deep, strew a small teaspoonful of flour over; roll out an upper crust, enough to cover the pie; make several small incisions on either side of the middle, cut a strip of paste the width of a finger, and lay it around the edge of the pie, put the cover over, trim off the edge, even with the dish, with a sharp knife, and bake in a quick oven until the paste loosens from the plate; about three-quarters of an hour will bake them. This is a fine pie; the top may be gilded as directed, previously.

SOUR CHERRY PIE.—Take the stems from fair ripe cherries, rinse them in a little cold water, line a pie plate with family pie-crust, put in a layer of cherries to cover the surface, put in cold water to half cover them, dredge them white with flour (if the cherries are small put two layers of them) put a large teacup of clean brown sugar to a quart bowl of stemmed cherries, grate a little nutmeg over and cover the pie with a light puff paste or family pie-crust; bake in a moderately quick oven until the pie loosens from the dish; gild the top when half done, or grate sugar over when it is served.

PEACH PIE.—Peaches for pie may be ripe but not soft; pare them, cut them up and finish as directed for apple pies. Unripe peaches may be pared and stewed as directed for apple tart, and baked in a pie or tart.

WHOLE PEACH PIE.—Take small sized peaches, not fully ripe, pare them without cutting them up; line a dish with pie paste, lay the peaches in close together, put in a little water, for a pie the size of a large dinner plate; strew over a small teacup of sugar, dredge a small teaspoonful of flour over, grate half a small nutmeg over, and a saltspoonful of salt, and cover the pie; cut a slit in the centre, and bake for one hour in a quick oven.

CRANBERRY PIE OR TARTS.—Pick a quart of cranberries free from imperfections, put a pint of water to them, and put them in a stew-pan, over a moderate fire; put a pound of clean brown sugar to them, and stew them gently, until they are all soft, then mash them with a silver spoon, and turn them into a dish to become cold, then make them in pies or tarts, and bake. Many persons put flour in cranberry pies; it is a great mistake, as it completely spoils the color of the fruit.

LEMON PIE.—Boil six fresh lemons in fair water until a straw will penetrate the skin, then take them out, chop them fine, and take out the pips; to a pound of light brown sugar put a teacup of water; let it boil, skimming it clear until it is a nice syrup, then put in the lemon and set it to cool; cover a shallow plate with pie-paste, put in the lemon, spread out to nearly the edge, cover with a paste, cut a slit in the centre and bake.

MERINGUE PIE.—This may be made by adding to a nicely made and baked tart, a nice whip, made as follows: to the white of a fresh egg, add two tablespoonfuls of finely pulverized white sugar, flavor with lemon, vanilla, or any other flavor, which may be liked, whip the same as for kisses, then with a knife lay it on the top of the tart, and shape it nicely off at the edges, then set it into an oven and close it for a few minutes until it is delicately browned.

RHUBARB PIE.—Cut the large stalks off where the leaves commence; strip off the outside skin, then cut the stalks in pieces half an inch long; line a pie dish with paste rolled rather thicker than a dollar piece, put in a layer of the rhubarb nearly an inch deep; to a quart bowl of cut rhubarb, put a large teacup of sugar, strew it over with a saltspoonful of salt, and half a nutmeg grated; cover with a rich pie crust, cut a slit in the centre, trim off the edge with a sharp knife, and bake in a quick oven, until the pie loosens from the dish. Rhubarb pies made in this way, are altogether superior to those made of the fruit stewed.

RHUBARB TART.—Peel the stalks, and cut them

in inch lengths; to a quart bowl of pieces, put half a teacup of water, and a teacup of clean brown sugar; cover it, and let it stew gently until it may be mashed, then make it fine with a spoon, add a saltspoonful of salt, and half a nutmeg grated; line small pie dishes or tartlet pans, put in the stewed fruit nearly half an inch deep; roll some paste to half an inch thickness, brush it over with the yolk of an egg, beaten with a little milk, cut it in strips the width of a finger, and lay it across the pie; lay a strip around the edge, then trim it off even with the dish, and bake in a quick oven for a half an hour, or until the paste loosens from the dish; these tarts may be baked without the strips across.

HUCKLE OR WHORTLEBERRY PIE.—Put a quart of picked huckleberries into a basin of water, take off whatever floats, take up the berries by the handful, pick out all the stems and unripe berries, and put them into a dish; line a buttered pie dish with a pie paste, put in the berries half an inch deep, and to a quart of berries put a teacup of brown sugar, and half a teacup of water; dredge a teaspoonful of flour over, strew a saltspoonful of salt, and half a nutmeg grated over; cover the pie, cut a slit in the centre, or make several small incisions on either side of it, press the two crusts together around the edge, trim it off neatly with a sharp knife, and bake in a quick oven for three-quarters of an hour.

RIPE CURRANT PIE.—Make as directed for huckleberry pie; use twice as much sugar, and a puff paste crust.

GREEN CURRANT PIE OR TARTS.—Pick the

currants free from stems, stew them as directed for rhubarb tarts, and make in pie or tarts.

Gooseberry Tarts and Pies.—Take off the stems and blossom end ; wash them and stew them the same as rhubarb for tarts ; make them in pies, or make them in tarts ; strew a little sugar over, and bake.

Green Grapes for Pies and Tarts.—Pick green grapes from the stems, and stew them with a pound of sugar, and half a pint of water, to a quart bowl of grapes ; add a saltspoonful of salt, and half a nutmeg grated, and finish.

Huckleberries stewed with green grapes, make a nice pie ; allow a teacup of sugar for a quart of huckleberries.

Blackberry Pie.—Pick the berries clean, rinse them in cold water, and finish as directed for huckleberries.

Cream Pies.—Scald a quart of sweet cream, beat four or five eggs light, then stir them into the scalding cream ; add a saltspoonful of salt, a teaspoonful of the extract of lemon or peach water, and half a nutmeg grated, if liked ; sweeten to taste, (about two tablespoonfuls of sugar is enough,) have flat pie dishes, with nearly perpendicular sides, rub them over with a bit of sponge dipped in melted butter, line them with pie paste rolled quite thin, set them in a quick oven for ten minutes, then put in the cream nearly to fill them, and bake for half an hour.

These pies, and also pumpkin and custard pies, may be very prettily ornamented, when half baked, with flowers, stars, or letters, cut from thin rolled paste; if letters or love-knots are used, form them of narrow strips of paste; the cream or custard must be firm, before these are put on, otherwise they will sink.

CUSTARD PIES.—Boil a quart of milk, beat four or five eggs light, and stir them gradually into it, and finish as directed for cream pies.

CUSTARD PIE, *a Labor Saving Pie, which makes its own Paste.*—Beat four eggs with four dessert-spoonsful of wheat flour, until they are light, then gradually stir into it a quart of milk; add a saltspoonful of salt, and half a nutmeg grated, with sugar to taste; (about two dessert-spoonsful is enough,) rub a square tin pie-pan over with a bit of butter, and put the mixture in nearly to fill it; bake half an hour in a quick oven.

This is a truly " Native American Democratic Citizen" pie, and being such, could it prove other than excellent?

MOCK CREAM PIES.—Make the cream as directed, (see mock cream,) and finish the same as cream pies; bake them until nicely browned at the top.

RICE PIES.—Pick and wash a wine-glass of rice, and boil it in a quart of milk until soft, then take it from the fire, having beaten three eggs light, stir them gradually into it; add a small teacup of sugar, and a small nutmeg grated, with half a teaspoonful of salt, and a small teaspoonful of extract of lemon or peach water, if liked. Line flat pie dishes with pie paste, nearly fill them with the pie mixture, and bake half an hour in a quick oven.

Rice Flour Pie.—Make this pie as directed for mock cream, using rice flour instead of wheat.

Pumpkin Pie.—Cut up a nice cheese pumpkin, take out the seeds and stringy inside, pare off the rind, and cut the pumpkin small, then put it in a kettle with a teacup of water; cover the vessel, and set it over a gentle fire, until the pumpkin is soft enough to mash when lightly pressed; then set a colander or sieve into a basin, take the stewed pumpkin into it, and press it through into the basin with a ladle or wooden spoon; when it is all rubbed through, add to it milk enough to make a thin batter, to every quart of this batter put four well beaten eggs; make it sweet, a small teacup of sugar, and a saltspoonful of salt, for each quart, is about what will generally be liked; grate in a nutmeg, and a teaspoonful of extract of lemon, and some ground ginger, if liked.

Line flat bottomed pie dishes with pie paste, and nearly fill them with the pumpkin mixture, lay a strip of paste around the edge, trim off the outside neatly, and bake three-quarters of an hour in a quick oven; the top of the pie should be delicately brown. Ornament as directed for cream pies.

A less number of eggs than is mentioned in this receipt, may be used; pumpkin pies are sometimes made without any eggs; these are less delicate, as may be supposed.

Thanksgiving Pie.—Prepare pumpkin pie mixture as directed in the last receipt; take a very large flat pie dish with nearly perpendicular sides, and nearly an inch in depth; the dish should be of earthen or tin and nearly eighteen inches across;

rub it over with a bit of sponge dipped in melted butter, cover it with family pie-crust rolled a quarter of an inch thick; cut a strip of paste, the width of a finger, and put it around the inside edge of the pie, then nearly fill it with the pie mixture, and put it in a moderately hot oven; roll some puff paste to less than quarter of an inch thickness, brush it over with the yolk of an egg beaten with a little milk, and a teaspoonful of sugar, then cut it in small stars; cut some of it in strips the width of a finger or a little narrower; when the pie is half baked so that it is firm or set, lay it on the stars, at a little distance from the edge, and the same distance from each other; put a larger one in the centre; of the strips of paste make letters to spell THANKSGIVING; and put six on either side of the star in the centre, midway between that, and those on the edge, so as to form a curve around the centre; cut a strip of the paste half an inch wide and put it around the edge of the pie, then return it to the oven, and let it remain for twenty minutes or more until it is nicely colored and the paste is cooked.

To serve thanksgiving pie after the table is cleared for dessert, place the large pie in the centre, place around it, puddings, jellies, etc., making this the crown of the feast.

MINCE PIE MEAT.—Take a nice tender piece of beef which is free from gristle, skin, or strings; the tongue is used for making pies as is also a sirloin; the heart, head and skirts are also used for mince pies.

The tongue or sirloin is best, put the meat in hot water to cover it; boil it gently until turning a fork in it will break it, set it to become cold, then take out all the bone and gristle parts; if the tongue is used, peel off the skin; chop it very fine.

To Make Mince Pie Mixture.—Weigh two pounds of the chopped meat, put to it two pounds of suet free from strings or skin, and chopped fine; add two pounds of currants, picked, washed, and dried, and four pounds of peeled and chopped rich tart apples, with the juice of two lemons, and the chopped peel of one; a pint of sweet wine, and one large nutmeg grated, or a teaspoonful of ground mace, three pounds and a half of sugar, quarter of an ounce of ground cloves, or alspice, and the same of cinnamon, and a large tablespoonful of salt; mix the whole well together, put it in a stone pot or jar, cover it close and set it in a cool place for use; mix it well together before using.

Mince Pies.—Line a pie dish with a nice puff paste, rolled to twice the thickness of a dollar piece (first having rubbed the dish over with a bit of sponge dipped in butter) put in the pie mixture half an inch deep, and spread it to within a finger width of the edge; roll out a puff paste crust, turn a plate the size of the one on which the pie is made on to it, and with a knife cut the paste around, the size of the plate, then take the plate off, make three small incisions with the end of the knife on either side of the middle, take it carefully up, and cover the pie with it, press it lightly with the finger against the bottom crust, put it in quick oven for three-quarters of an hour; the top may be brushed over with the yolk of an egg beaten with a little milk. Mince pies made in this way should be served warm.

Domestic Mince Pie Meat.—Boil a nice piece of beef until tender; take out every bit of skin, bone, or gristle, and chop the meat fine; to each pound of chopped meat, put of ground mace, cinnamon, and alspice, each a teaspoonful, with half a teaspoonful of ground cloves, and a large teaspoonful of salt; put to the meat enough syrup or molasses to make it moist, mix it well together, and pack it in a stone jar, dip a paper in brandy, and lay it over; cover the jar, and set it in a cold dry place. This will keep all winter.

To Finish the Pie Mixture.—Pare, core, and chop not very fine some tart juicy apples, put to them one-third as much of the prepared meat; stone one pound of raisins, and cut a quarter of citron in small bits, add a gill of brandy, and enough sweet cider to make the whole quite wet; a peck of apples, pared and chopped with a quart bowl of the prepared meat, and the raisins, citron, and cider, as above mentioned, with a large teacupful of brown sugar, is enough to make six or seven pies the size of a dinner plate; a teacupful of fine chopped suet may be added, if liked.

To Make Mince Pies.—Rub pie dishes over with a bit of spenge dipped in butter, and cover them with a family pie-crust, rolled quite thin; put in the pie mixture half an inch deep, cover the pie with some of the paste, trim it off at the edge, cut a slit in the centre, press the upper against the under crust with your finger, bake three-quarters of an hour in a moderate oven.

These pies may be kept three or four weeks in winter; when wanted, set one in an oven for ten minutes, or serve them cold.

Apple Mince Pies.—One pound of well washed and dried Zante currants, one pound of peeled and chopped apples, one pound of suet chopped fine, one pound of moist sugar, quarter of a pound of raisins stoned and cut in two, the juice of four oranges and two lemons, with the chopped peel of one; add of ground mace and alspice, each a teaspoonful, and a wineglass of brandy; mix them well together, and keep it closely covered in a dry cool place. Bake with two crusts, the same as mince pies.

MERINGUE PIE.—Make any nice rich tart and bake it, then having beaten the whites of two eggs with a quarter of a pound of finely pulverized white sugar, until it may be moulded with a knife, lay it over the tart an inch or less thick, even the sides, and put it into an oven for a few minutes until it is slightly colored, serve hot or cold.

These tarts should be made of preserves or jams or else fruits stewed very rich.

DIRECTIONS

For Making Varieties of Bread, Biscuit, Rolls, Cakes, &c. &c.

INTRODUCTORY REMARKS.—An oven to bake well, should have a regular heat throughout, but particularly at the bottom, without which, bread or cakes will not rise or bake well; bread and cakes are as often spoiled in baking as in making.

Bread or large cakes had better, if convenient, be sent to a competent family baker, if you have not a good baking oven.

Small cakes, such as tea-biscuit, rolls, jumbals, drop cakes, etc., bake nicely in a tin or sheet iron summer oven: these should often be looked to, as those nearest the furnace will first be done; when they are so, either turn the pan about, or remove those that are done, putting the unfinished ones in their places, and fresh ones in place of them.

For baking bread, plum cake, or other large cakes, have round tin pans with sides nearly perpendicular. For cakes, line the pans with white paper, rubbed over with butter. Pans with nearly straight sides bake more evenly, and are more easily iced than slanting sides.

A brick oven for baking bread, should be as hot as you can bear to hold your hand in, whilst counting twenty or twenty seconds; this is an established rule in most farm houses.

Degrees of heating ovens for baking, are—cool or slow heat; moderate or gentle is a degree stronger than slow, and is like a hot breeze or breath; a quick heat is hot, but not intensely; a degree stronger is a hot oven; still stronger is scorching hot, and fit for nothing but destruction.

One accustomed to baking, will readily understand what degree of heat is meant by the terms used; one not accustomed, must need learn.

In using volatile salts or saleratus for bread or cakes, it should be powdered, and dissolved with a little hot water before putting it into the bread or cakes.

A bit of volatile salts the size of a small nutmeg, powdered fine and dissolved with a little hot water and added to a pound or sponge cake will insure a light cake; it is much used by cake bakers; carbonate of soda may be used instead of this. The salts is generally put with the beaten eggs, and beaten with them for ten minutes or more.

Volatile salts should be kept in a glass bottle or jar, with a ground stopper.

Saleratus or bi-carbonate of soda (which may be used in place of saleratus) may be kept in a wooden box with a cover.; it must be kept perfectly dry, the least moisture will spread through and dissolve a large quantity.

An earthen basin is best for beating eggs or cake mixture in.

Cake should be beaten with a wooden spoon or spatula, like an old fashioned pudding stick; butter may be beaten with the like.

Eggs should be beaten with rods, or a broad fork; a silver fork or one made of iron wire is best, as it is broadest; eggs should be clear and fresh for cake.

None but good sweet butter should be used for cake making; should it be rather salt, it will do no harm; butter in the least degree rank or strong will spoil a cake.

It is well as a general rule in cake making to beat the butter and sugar (which must first be made fine) to a light cream; indeed, in the making of pound cake, the lightness of the cake depends as much upon this, as upon the eggs being well beaten; then beat the eggs and put them to the butter and gradually add the flour and other ingredients, beating it all the time.

In common cakes where only a few eggs are used, beat them until you can take a spoonful up clear from strings.

For pound, sponge, or other fine cakes, observe each particular direction.

Before beginning to mix a cake, see that all the ingredients are before you, otherwise by omitting one or more, you may spoil your cake. Cake mixture cannot be beaten too much; it is not enough to beat it whilst mixing, but the operation should be continued after all the parts are added, until the whole is light and creamy.

In receipts in which milk is used as one ingredient, either sweet or sour may be used, but not a mixture of both.

Sour milk makes a spongy light cake; sweet milk makes a cake which is more fine, and cuts like pound-cake.

Almonds for cakes or macaroons may be bought already shelled, for two shillings per pound, which is much cheaper and less troublesome than those in the shell.

Almonds for macaroons and other cakes, should be pounded in a marble mortar, or one made of hard wood (lignum vitæ.)

To blanch almonds, pour boiling water on them, and let them remain in it until the skins may be easily removed, then take it off, throw the almonds into cold water to whiten them, drain them from the water but do not wipe them; the moisture will prevent their oiling.

For making lady-fingers, confectioners have a tin tube as long as your finger, like the spout of a tunnel; to the upper part of this, a little bag is attached, and the cake mixture put in it, and pressed out on to the paper, the size and length desired; the point of the tube may be larger or smaller as may be required; Savoy biscuit mixture, may be baked as lady-fingers, for making charlotte d'russe.

In making cakes, if you wish them to be pleasing to the eye as well as to the palate, use double refined white sugar, although clean light brown sugar makes an equally good cake.

Finely pulverized or ground sugar, which is as

fine as wheat flour, is the sort for icing cakes, and for making fine cakes; where this cannot be had, the sugar must be rolled and sifted, or pounded in a mortar.

To ascertain whether a cake is baked enough, if a small one, take a broom splint, and run it through the thickest part, if it is not done, some of the dough or unbaked cake will be found sticking to it; if done, it will come out clean. If a cake is large, take a teaspoon handle or small knife-blade, instead of the broom splint.

All receipts herein contained, will be found to be just what they are represented, and give full satisfaction, if strictly followed.

To keep cakes as when fresh made: fold a thick napkin about them, and put them into a stone jar, with a close cover; or keep them in a tin box or canister, tightly covered, in a cool dark closet.

To Make Baker's Bread.—To one quart of warm water, put a gill of baker's yeast, stir in the flour to make a thin batter, put it in a large pitcher or tin pail, and let it set in a large pan, in a warm place, all night.

Early next morning, put seven pounds of superfine wheat flour into a wooden bowl or tray, heap it around the sides, leaving a hollow in the centre, dissolve a bit of volatile salts, the size of a small nutmeg, in a little hot water, and when it is cool, put it to the batter, pour it into the hollow of the flour; powder a piece of alum the size of a very small hickory nut, make it as fine as flour, then stir it into the batter, until it is a white foam, add to it a tablespoonful of salt, and gradually, three pints or more of warm water with this; work all the flour into a dough; knead or work it with your two hands, until it is a smooth, shining paste, then strew a little flour over, spread a thick cloth over, and set it in a warm place for two hours, until it has risen to twice its first size, then dip your hands in flour, work it down fine and smooth, cover it, and set it near the fire for an hour; knead it smooth again, make it in loaves, and bake according to their size, in a quick oven; if the mass is divided in two loaves, they will require one hour's baking in a quick oven; if divided in four, half an hour will be sufficient.

To Make Wheat Bread:—Put seven pounds of wheat flour in a large bowl or tray, heap it around the sides, leaving a hollow in the centre; put into it a quart of warm water, add to it a large tablespoonful of salt, half a teaspoonful of saleratus, (dissolved in a little water,) and half a gill of baker's yeast; have three pints more of warm water, and with as much of it as may be necessary, make the whole in a rather soft dough, work it well with both hands, (see directions for kneading bread,) when it is smooth and shining, strew a little flour over, lay a thickly folded cloth over it, and set it in a warm place for four or five hours, then knead it again for fifteen minutes, cover it, and let it set to rise again; when it is like a sponge, work it down again, divide it in loaves, either two or four, and bake in a quick oven, according to their size; one hour, if divided in two loaves; half an hour each, if divided in four.

This bread need only rise once, and if made of the best superfine flour, will be beautifully white and light, and healthful and sweet.

Any who will follow this receipt, either with once rising or twice, will have uniformly white and sweet bread.

In cold weather, bread should be mixed in a

warm room, and not allowed to become cold whilst mixing: have a thickly folded cloth, warm it, and lay it over, and set the bowl in a warm place; if there is any difficulty about its rising, set the bowl or tray over a kettle of hot water. It is as well to mix this bread at night, in cold weather, and cover it close, in a warm room, until morning.

POTATO BREAD.—To make potato bread, pare half a peck of nice potatoes, wash them through two changes of water, put them into a kettle with a teaspoonful of salt, pour over them enough boiling water to cover them, then cover the kettle or pot, and let them boil fast for half an hour, or longer if they are large; then take them from the kettle of boiling water with a skimmer, into a cullender, rub them through it into a dish; put seven pounds of wheat flour into a bowl or tray, make a hollow in the centre, into which put the prepared potatoes; add nearly a gill of baker's yeast, a heaping tablespoonful of salt, and half a teaspoonful of saleratus, dissolved in warm water, (it must be entirely dissolved,) have nearly three quarts of warm water or milk in a pitcher, and with as much of it as may be necessary, make the potatoes and flour into a soft dough or paste; work it with your hands without flouring them, until it will not stick to them, and it is a smooth, glossy mass, then put a cover over the pan, cover it with a thickly folded cloth, and set it in a warm place for five or six hours in warm weather, or all night in winter; it will then be as light as a sponge; dip your hands lightly in flour, and knead or work the bread down until it is fine and smooth, then set it to rise again for two hours; when it is light, work it down again, divide it in three or six loaves, lay them in a large pan to touch each other, (first having rubbed the pan over with a sponge dipped in butter,) let them set for ten minutes, then bake in a quick oven one hour, if divided in three, or half an hour if divided in six.

It is not usual to give home-made bread more than one rising, nor is it necessary, but the bread will be whiter and finer.

Potatoes for bread may be washed through three or more changes of water; put them in a pot with boiling water to cover them, cover the pot, and let them boil fast for forty minutes, if small, or an hour if large, then take them from the water with a skimmer, peel them, and grate them on a coarse grater, or mash them fine, one by one, with a potato beetle, then finish as above directed.

To Make Twist Bread.—Let the bread be made as directed for baker's or for wheat bread, then take three pieces as large as a pint bowl each; strew a little flour over the paste-board or table, roll each piece under your hands, to twelve inches length, making it smaller in circumference at the ends than in the middle; having rolled the three in this way, take a baking tin, lay one part on it, join one end of each of the other two to it, and braid them together the length of the rolls, and join the ends by pressing them together; dip a brush in milk, and pass it over the top of the loaf; after ten minutes or so, set it in a quick oven, and bake for nearly an hour.

Wheat and Indian Bread.—Put three pints of water over the fire, when it is boiling hot, add a large tablespoonful of salt, stir into it sweet white corn meal, until it is a thick batter; continue to stir it for ten minutes, that it may not burn, then turn it into a dish, stir into it a quart of cold water; when it is cool enough to bear your hand in it, pour it into a bowl, in which is seven pounds of wheat flour, heaped around the sides, so as to leave a hollow in the centre; add to it a gill of baker's yeast, and half a teaspoonful of saleratus, dissolved in a little hot water, then work the whole into a smooth dough, work it or knead for nearly an hour, then strew a little flour over it, lay a thickly folded cloth over, and set it in a warm place for five or six hours in summer, or mix at night in winter; when light, work it down, set it to rise again for one hour, then heat the oven, work the bread down, and divide it in loaves, and bake, according to their size, in a quick oven; when taken from the oven, turn them over in the pans, and set them to become cold; if the crust is hard, wrap them in a towel as soon as taken from the oven.

RYE BREAD.—Make the same as wheat and Indian bread, substituting rye flour for wheat. Or thus: to a quart of warm water stir as much wheat flour as will make a smooth batter, stir into it half a gill of baker's yeast, and set it in a warm place to rise; this is called setting a sponge; let it be mixed in some vessel which will contain twice the quantity; in the morning put three pounds and a half of rye flour into a bowl or tray, make a hollow in the centre, pour in the sponge, add a dessertspoonful of salt, and half a small teaspoonful of saleratus, dissolved in a little water, make the whole into a smooth dough, with as much warm water as may be necessary; knead it well, cover it, and let it set in a warm place for three hours, then knead it again, and make it in two or three loaves; bake in a quick oven one hour, if made in two loaves, or less if the loaves are smaller.

RYE BREAD CAKE.—Take from the risen dough,

the size of a small loaf, work into it a small teacup of shortening, make it in a flat cake, rather more than an inch thick, and bake twenty five minutes in a quick oven.

DYSPEPSIA BREAD.—Work three quarts of unbolted wheat meal into a dough, with one quart of warm water, half a gill of baker's yeast, one teacup of molasses, one teaspoonful of salt, and half a teaspoonful of saleratus, dissolved in a little hot water; knead it well, then cover it, and set it in a warm place, until it has risen to twice its original size, then work it down; divide it in two loaves, and bake in buttered basins, in a quick oven.

BROWN BREAD.—Make as directed for dyspepsia bread; add a pint bowl of rye flour, and a little more water, mix it well, and bake.

GRAHAM BREAD.—Make as directed for wheat and indian bread, using unbolted wheat flour instead of superfine.

TO KNEAD BREAD.—After the dough is made, flour the hands, and folding the fingers over the thumb, making what is called a fist, belabor the dough first with one hand then the other on every side, work it in this way until it ceases to stick to your hands; much kneading makes bread both whiter and finer.

Kneading bread will be found a most beneficial exercise for dyspeptics, though not a very gentle one; the arms and chest are brought into full play, quite as much as in the use of dumb bells; it is heartily recommended since good bread and good health are both obtained thereby.

Bread can scarce be kneaded too much, it will

readily be allowed, that the more bread is *needed* the sweeter it will be to the taste when eaten.

BREAD CAKE OR BISCUITS.—Take from risen bread dough, the size of a small loaf, work into it one egg and a large tablespoonful of lard when it is thoroughly amalgamated, flour the hands and make it in balls, the size and shape of a hen's egg; rub a tin pan over with a bit of sponge dipped in butter, lay them in so as to touch each other, until the pan is full, wet the tops over with milk, then set them into a quick oven for twenty minutes, serve hot for breakfast or tea. When eaten, break them open—to cut them would make them heavy.

These cakes are very nice when cold for breakfast or tea.

INDIAN CORN BREAD.—Into a quart of yellow corn-meal stir as much boiling milk or water as will make a very stiff batter; add a teacup of molasses and a large teaspoonful of salt; put to it half a teaspoonful of saleratûs dissolved in a little water, and when rather more than bloodwarm add to it half a gill of baker's yeast, mix it well, set it in a warm place to rise, for two hours, then put it an inch deep in buttered basins, and bake one hour in a moderate oven; serve hot, with cold butter.

INDIAN MEAL BREAD FOR TEA.—Stir a quart of boiling milk into a pint of yellow corn-meal, add to it a teacup of molasses and three or four well beaten eggs, a teaspoonful of salt, then pour it into a buttered basin; bake in a moderate oven for two hours. Or, add to this mixture a tablespoonful of sweet butter — butter saucers, half fill them, and bake half an hour in a quick oven.

PONE OR CORN-MEAL BREAKFAST CAKE.—Into a

quart of milk stir enough yellow corn-meal to make a very thick batter, add to it four well beaten eggs and a teaspoonful of salt; butter small basins or tin pans, fill them one inch deep, and bake for nearly an hour in a moderate oven; do not open the oven in less than forty minutes.

ALBANY BREAKFAST CAKES.—Beat six eggs light and stir them into a quart of milk, add a heaping teaspoonful of salt and a bit of saleratus the size of two peas, dissolved in a little hot water; stir in enough sweet corn-meal to make a thick batter, rub some small tin saucers the size of a tea-saucer with butter and half fill them; bake half an hour in a quick oven, or put the mixture an inch deep in square tin pans; when done cut it in squares and serve hot.

INDIAN MEAL BREAKFAST CAKES.—Pour boiling water into a pint of yellow corn-meal, stirring it all the time, until it is wet; dissolve half a small teaspoonful of saleratus in a little hot water, and add it to the meal with a teaspoonful of salt, two well beaten eggs and a piece of butter the size of a large egg, stir it well together; butter square tin pans, two-thirds fill them and bake in a quick oven for half an hour; cut it in squares and serve hot.

INDIAN MEAL GRIDDLE CAKES.—Put three pints of warm water into a basin or jar, add to it half a gill of baker's yeast, half a small teaspoonful of saleratus dissolved, and a teaspoonful of salt, stir in yellow corn-meal to make a batter, add a pint bowl of wheat flour, and beat the whole smooth, cover it, and set it in a warm place to rise; the batter should not more than half fill the vessel, that it may not rise over the sides: in the morning add two well beaten eggs; make a griddle hot, put on it a teaspoonful of lard, spread it over it, and put the batter on in small cakes; when one side is a delicate brown, turn the other, when both sides are done, take them up on a hot dish; these cakes retain the heat for some time; serve butter and syrup with these, for breakfast.

WHEAT AND INDIAN CRUMPETS.—Put half a gill of yeast into a quart of warm milk, with a teaspoonful of salt, stir in wheat flour to make a good batter; set it in a warm place to rise, in the morning, add a teacupful of melted butter, and a handful of yellow corn meal; bake them on a hot griddle, which must be rubbed over with lard each time before putting on the cakes; a spoonful of batter for each cake.

INDIAN GRIDDLE CAKES.—Beat two eggs light, stir them into a quart of sweet milk, with a teaspoonful of salt, and enough corn-meal to make a good batter, bake as soon as mixed, on a hot griddle, rubbed over with a bit of suet or fat pork, a tablespoonful of batter for each cake.

JOHNNY CAKE.—Put a quart of fresh corn-meal into a basin, add a heaping teaspoonful of salt, stir into it boiling water, until it is all moistened, then with your hands, make it in cakes half an inch thick, and bake them on a hot griddle, rubbed over with a bit of fat pork, or beef suet; let them do slowly; when one side is done, turn the other; they may be baked in an oven for twenty minutes; or put the cake on a flat board or iron plate, and slant it in front of the fire; when one side is done, turn the other; serve hot, split them open, and butter freely; they are eaten with fried pork.

Indian Meal Muffins.—Pour boiling water into a quart of yellow corn meal, stirring it all the time, until it is a thick batter, let it cool; when only warm, add a small teacup of butter, a teaspoonful of salt, and a tablespoonful of yeast, with two well beaten eggs; set it in a warm place for two hours, then stir it smooth, and bake in small cakes, on a hot griddle; when one side is a rich brown, turn the other, lay them singly on a hot dish, and serve. These may be made without the yeast, and baked as soon as mixed.

Oat Meal.—May be prepared for cooking, in the same manner as corn meal; either as soupon, gruel, or Johnny cake.

Rye Short Cakes.—Make as directed in the several receipts for wheat flour.

To Make Baker's Yeast.—Make three tablespoonsful of wheat flour into a smooth batter, with a little cold water, then add to it nearly two quarts more of water, and quarter of a pound of brown sugar, put it to boil, stir it occasionally, then set it to cool; when it is only blood warm, add a gill of good yeast, set the vessel in a warm place, or near the fire for one day, to ferment, then pour off the thin liquor from the top, shake the remainder up, and put it in a bottle for use, or keep it in a covered stone jar; half a gill of this yeast for seven pounds of flour.

Yeast Cakes, called Turnpike Cakes.—Put a quart of hops into two quarts of water, cover them, and let them boil, then strain it hot over a quart of fresh corn meal, stir it well together, when cooled, so as to bear your hand in, add a teacupful of good yeast, or one turnpike cake dissolved in warm water, stir it well, make it in cakes the size of the top of a tumbler, and rather less than half an inch thick, lay them on a board, and set them in a dry, warm, but airy place, to rise and harden, do not put them in the sun; when one side is dry, turn the other, and so turn them from side to side, until they are thoroughly dry and hard; should the weather prove damp, these cakes may be dried near the fire. Keep them in coarse paper bags, in a dry, cool place; half of one of these cakes dissolved in a cup of warm water, is enough for seven pounds of flour. These will remain good for months.

LEAVEN.—Take the scrapings of the tray, and a little of the risen dough, to make a cake as large round as a tumbler; dry it, or put it in cold water to cover it. When wanted, pour off the cold water, and put a pint of warm water to it. Use it instead of yeast. If the leaven is dried, dissolve it in warm water. Keep the leaven from each time baking, which should not be less often than twice each week.

DYSPEPSIA CRACKERS.—Mix a hard dough of unbolted wheat flour, a small quantity of salt, and a very little saleratus; beat it well with a rolling-pin; make it in small round cakes, stick each with a fork, and bake in a moderate oven until crisp and hard.

To MAKE BAKER'S ROLLS.—Put three pounds of wheat flour into a large bowl, make a hollow in the centre, put in a large tablespoonful of yeast, a teaspoonful of salt, and a bit of saleratus the size of half a small nutmeg, dissolved in a tablespoonful of hot water, make it into a soft dough with warm milk, work it or knead until it is smooth and shining, then cover it and set it in a warm place for two hours, then work it smooth again, let it rise again, then work it down and divide it in pieces twice the size of a hen's egg; roll it between your hands to the length of a finger, lay them so as to touch each other, on baking tins, dip your hand in milk and pass it lightly over the tops of the rolls, and set them in a quick oven for fifteen or twenty minutes, until they are baked and the tops a delicate brown, break one open to know if they are done. Serve hot for breakfast, to be broken open—cutting light hot cakes soddens them.

BUCKWHEAT GRIDDLE CAKES.—Put three pints of warm water into a stone pot or jar, add half a gill of baker's yeast, or an inch square of turnpike cake dissolved in a little warm water; add a heaping teaspoonful of salt, and half a small teaspoonful of saleratus, have a pudding stick or spatula and gradually stir in enough buckwheat flour to make a nice batter, beat it perfectly smooth, then cover it and set it in a moderately warm place until morning, a large handful of cornmeal may be put with the flour, and is by many persons considered an improvement.

TO BAKE BUCKWHEAT CAKES.—Set a griddle over a gentle steady fire, when it is hot, rub it over with a bit of suet, or fat fresh pork on a fork; the griddle must be hot but not scorching; put the batter on in small cakes, when one side is nicely browned and about half cooked through, turn them.

These cakes to be in perfection, must be not much thicker than a dollar piece, and both sides a delicate brown. Should the batter prove too thick it may be made thinner with sweet milk, this will also make them bake a finer color. The best of sweet butter and syrup to be served with buckwheat cakes hot from the griddle; should the cakes be preferred thicker than mentioned in this receipt, it is an easy matter to make them so; take care that they are baked through.

Buckwheat may be mixed the same as wheat muffins, and baked on a griddle.

MINUTE PUDDING.—Put a quart of water over the fire, when it boils fast, add a large teaspoonful of salt, stir it round with a pudding stick in one hand, and from the other let fall gradually, (stirring it all the time) enough buckwheat flour to make it thick; continue to stir it for a few minutes, when it will be a thick and smooth pudding; dip a large bowl in cold water, and turn the pudding into it; when it is a little cooled lay a plate over the bowl, then reverse it, and turn the pudding out upon it; serve with butter and sugar or a sauce, for dessert.

BUTTERMILK MUFFINS.—To a quart of thick sour milk or buttermilk put a pint of water, stir into it enough wheat flour to make a smooth but not very thin batter; dissolve a large teaspoonful of powdered saleratus in a little hot water, and stir it in with a heaped teaspoonful of salt; the batter must be perfectly smooth and free from lumps. Bake on a hot griddle, which must first be rubbed over with a bit of fat or lard.

MUFFINS.—Mix with a pint of warm milk, two well beaten eggs, half a teaspoonful of melted butter and half a gill of baker's yeast with a teaspoonful of salt and a bit of saleratus the size of a large pea (dissolved in hot water) stir in enough sifted wheat flour to make a thick batter; set it in a warm place to rise, for three hours in warm weather, or longer in winter; it may be mixed at night for breakfast next morning—put a griddle over the fire, when it is hot, rub it over with some fat, grease the inside of the rings, set them on and half fill them with the batter, or they may be done without rings; when one side is done turn the other; bake a light color, as they are done break each one open, put a bit of butter in each, and set them in front of the fire until served; muffins should never be cut open. Cold muffins may be toasted and served hot.

CRUMPETS.—Put half a gill of yeast into a quart of warm milk, with a teaspoonful of salt, set in a warm place to rise, when light, add a cup of melted butter, stir it in, and bake as muffins.

CREAM TEA CAKES.—Put two pounds of sifted wheat flour into a basin, make a hollow in the centre, and put in half a pint of sour cream, and a cup of melted butter, dissolve half a teaspoonful of saleratus in a little hot water, and put it in with a large teaspoonful of salt, make it a nice soft dough; if necessary add a little more cream or water, flour your hands, and make it out in cakes the size of an egg, rub a tin pan over with a bit of butter, lay the cakes in so as to touch each other, until the pan is full; bake in a quick oven, from fifteen to twenty minutes.

When taken from the pan, they should be broken open at one side, and a bit of butter, the size of a large hickory nut, put in, serve hot; they may be served without the butter in them, with cold butter accompanying.

BUTTERMILK TEA CAKES.—Put two pounds of

sifted wheat flour into a basin, make a hollow in the centre, put in a small teacup of butter, lard, or beef drippings, add a teaspoonful of salt, and a teaspoonful of saleratus, dissolved in a little hot water; mix a pint of thick sour milk or buttermilk, with half a pint of water, and with as much of it as may be necessary, make the flour, etc. into a soft dough; dip your hands in flour, and divide the dough into cakes the size of an egg, roll each one between your hands, to a smooth round cake, rub a bit of butter over a tin pie pan, lay the cake in, flatten it a little, and so continue until the pan is full, putting in the cakes so as to touch each other; set the pan in a quick oven, shut it close, and bake fifteen minutes, then break one open, if it is not done through, return them to the oven for three or five minutes longer.

Tea Rusk.— To a pint of warm milk, put half a gill of baker's yeast, a teaspoonful of salt, and half a small teaspoonful of saleratus, dissolved in a little hot water, put to it enough wheat flour to make a soft dough, mix it well and smooth, cover it, and set it in a warm place for two hours, to rise; when light, add half a teacup of sugar, and a cup of melted butter, work them well into the dough, flour your hands well, and make it in small cakes, (the size of a large egg, or a trifle larger,) lay them close together in a buttered pan, dip your hand in a little sweetened milk, and pass it lightly over the tops of the rusks, set them in a quick oven for half an hour; serve hot.

Egg Rusk.—Melt four ounces of butter in a pint of warm milk, beat seven eggs untill you can take them up by the spoonful, and with these, three ounces of sugar, a gill of yeast, and as much sifted wheat flour as may be necessary, make a soft dough, shake a little flour over it, and set it in a warm place to rise, when light, (which it will be in about two hours,) work it down, cover it, and set it to rise again for one hour, then work it down, rub a baking tin over with a bit of suet, make the rusk in cakes, the size and shape of an egg, lay them on the tin, so as to touch each other, dip a brush in a little sweetened milk, and pass it lightly over the cakes, let them set for ten minutes, then put them in a quick oven, and bake twenty minutes; try if they are done by breaking one open, if not, return them to the oven, and close it for five minutes; they may be wet over a second time, a few minutes before they are done; serve hot with butter, for tea.

VELVET CAKES.—To a pint of warm milk, and two well beaten eggs, put half a gill of yeast and half a teacup of soft butter, and a teaspoonful of salt, stir into it enough wheat flour to make a soft dough, strew some flour over it, lay a warm towel over, and set it in a warm place to rise, (three hours in summer, or until light in winter,) dip your hands in flour and work the dough down; make it in small flat cakes, lay them in a buttered pan, quite near each other, dip your hand in milk, and pass it over the top of each cake, bake in a quick oven for twelve or fifteen minutes. These cakes may be mixed at night, and baked in rolls for breakfast.

LIGHT ROLLS.—Take a piece of risen dough, the size of a small loaf, from mixed bread, work into it a teacup of shortening, and one egg, work it well together, then make it in rolls between your hands, about one inch thick, and the length of the finger, lay them close in a buttered basin, and bake fifteen minutes in a quick oven; do not open the oven until that time has expired, then wet the tops of the rolls over with a little milk, and close the oven for five minutes longer.

FRENCH ROLLS, *for Tea.*—Work quarter of a pound of butter into two pounds of sifted wheat flour, until it is like grated bread, put to it two beaten eggs, two tablespoonsful of baker's yeast, half a teaspoonful of salt, and as much warm milk as will make a soft dough, strew flour over, cover it with a warm cloth, and set it in a warm place to rise, for two hours; then dip your hands in flour, and make it in small rolls, an inch thick, and the length of a finger, bake twenty minutes in a quick oven; five minutes before they are done, wet them lightly over with sweet milk, do it as quickly as possible, and close the oven to finish.

RICE FLOUR SHORT CAKES.—Rub three ounces of butter into half a pound of rice flour, moisten it with cold water, work it smooth, then roll it out thin; cut it in small cakes, and bake ten or twelve minutes in a quick oven.

SHORT CAKES OR PASTE CAKES.—Make a short pie crust, roll it out to half an inch thickness, or thinner if preferred, and cut it in small round cakes with a tumbler or tin cutter of that size; bake fifteen minutes in a quick oven.

These cakes may be made the same as "common puff paste" for pies; serve with preserves, jelly, or stewed fruit, for tea. The cakes may be hot or cold.

COMMON BUNS.—Rub four ounces of butter into two pounds of flour, with four ounces of fine sugar and a teaspoonful of carraway seeds, and the same of salt; add half a gill of yeast, and as much warm milk as will make a soft dough; set it in a warm place to rise, (it will be light after about three hours;) strew a paste-slab and rolling-pin with flour, and roll out the dough to half an inch thickness, and cut them in large round cakes; lay them on baking tins; wet the tops over with milk, strew sugar over each, and put them on tins in a quick oven for fifteen minutes.

CROSS BUNS.—To the above mixture add half a nutmeg grated, half a teaspoonful of ground alspice, and a cup of dried currants, washed and dried; mix it well together; finish as directed for buns; when nearly done, press the form of a cross in the centre of each.

SODA OR MILK BISCUIT.—To a pound of sifted flour put the yolk of an egg; dissolve a teaspoonful of carbonate of soda in a little milk; put it and a teaspoonful of salt to the flour, with as much milk as will make a stiff paste; work it well together; beat it for some minutes with a rolling-pin, then roll it very thin; cut it in round or square biscuits, and bake in a moderate oven until they are crisp.

BUTTER CRACKERS.—Rub four ounces of butter into a pound of flour, with a teaspoonful of salt; when it is like sand, put to it enough cold water to damp it and keep it together; beat it with a rolling-pin until it is smooth; then roll it thin; cut it in small cakes, or make it in small crackers between your hands; lay them on baking tins, and set them in a quick oven for fifteen minutes, or set them in a moderate oven for twenty minutes; let each cracker be about the size of a dollar piece, and nearly half an inch thick.

Milk Biscuits.—Warm two ounces of sweet butter in a gill of sweet milk, and with it wet a pound of flour into a very stiff paste; beat it with a rolling-pin, and work it very smooth; roll it a quarter of an inch thick; cut it in small round cakes; stick each with a fork, and bake ten minutes in a quick oven.

To make Doughnuts.—Take of risen wheat-bread dough the size of a quart bowl; work into it a teacup of butter, two teacups of clean brown sugar, rolled fine, half a nutmeg, grated, a teaspoonful of ground cinnamon, and two eggs; work it to a smooth paste; strew some flour over a paste-table and rolling-pin; put on some of the paste, and roll it to a quarter of an inch thickness; rub more flour over the rolling-pin, if the paste sticks; cut it in small squares, stars, or diamonds; fry in hot fat.

To fry Doughnuts and Crullers.—Have a small iron or porcelain kettle; put into it a pound of lard, set it over a gentle fire; when it is boiling hot, drop a bit of the dough in to try it; if the fat is not hot enough, the cakes will absorb it, and thereby be rendered unfit for eating; if too hot, it will make them a dark brown outside before the inside is cooked: boiling hot is about the heat the fat should be; if it is at a right heat, the doughnuts will in about ten minutes be of a delicate brown outside, and nicely cooked inside: five or six minutes will cook a crulier; try the fat, by dropping a bit of the dough in; if it is right, the fat will boil up when it is put in: keep the kettle in motion all the time the cakes are in, that they may boil evenly: when the cakes are a fine color, take them out with a skimmer on to an inverted sieve.

FRIED CAKES.

DOUGHNUTS.—Take a pound of flour, a quarter of a pound of butter, three quarters of a pound of clean brown sugar, rolled fine, one nutmeg, grated, and a teaspoonful of ground cinnamon; mix these well together; then add a tablespoonful of bakers' yeast, with as much warm milk, with saleratus the size of a pea dissolved in it, as will make a smooth dough; knead it for a few minutes, cover it, and set it in a warm place to rise, for three hours or more, until it is light; then roll it out to a quarter of an inch thickness; cut it in small squares or diamonds, and fry as directed.

DOUGHNUTS, *without Yeast*.—Half a pound of butter, a pint of sour milk or buttermilk, three quarters of a pound of sugar, a small teaspoonful of saleratus dissolved in a little hot water, two well-beaten eggs, and as much flour as will make a smooth dough; flavor with half a teaspoonful of lemon extract, and half a nutmeg, grated; rub a little flour over a paste-board or table, roll the dough to a quarter of an inch thickness; cut them in squares, or diamonds, or round cakes, and fry in boiling lard as directed. These cakes may be made in rings, and fried.

FRIED CAKES.—One quart of milk, half a pound of butter, six eggs, well beaten, one pound of sugar, one pound of currants, washed and dried, or one pound of raisins, stoned, and as much sifted wheat flour as will make a thick batter; beat the eggs until they can be taken up without strings; beat the butter with the sugar to a cream; grate in half a nutmeg; add a teaspoonful of lemon extract, or a wine-glass of brandy, in which rose leaves have been steeped, and a teaspoonful of salt; then stir in flour to make a thick batter; add the raisins or currants; beat it for a few minutes, then fry in boiling lard as directed for doughnuts and crullers. A dessert-spoonful of the batter makes a cake.

PLAIN CRULLERS.—Take half a pint of sour milk or buttermilk, one teacup of butter, two teacups of sugar, three well-beaten eggs, and a small teaspoonful of powdered saleratus, dissolved in a little hot water; add a teaspoonful of salt, half a nutmeg, grated, and a teaspoonful of ground cinnamon; work in as much sifted wheat flour as will make a smooth dough; work it well together; roll the cakes to twice the thickness of a dollar piece; cut it in pieces two inches square; cut it in fingers, twist each a little, and join the ends together, and fry as before directed. These cakes may be cut in rings, stars, baskets, or any other fancy shapes.

RICHER CRULLERS.—One pound of butter, beaten with one pound of finely rolled sugar, and six well-beaten eggs; work them into two pounds of flour, with half a nutmeg, grated; when it is a smooth dough, flour a paste board or table and rolling-pin, and roll it to an eighth of an inch thickness; cut it in rings or crullers, and fry as directed; when done, grate sugar over.

RICHEST CRULLERS.—Beat one pound of butter to a cream, with one pound of finely rolled sugar; add four well-beaten eggs, and half a nutmeg, grated; work the whole into a pound and a quarter of sifted flour; flour the cake board or table, and roll it to the eighth of an inch thickness; cut it as fancy may dictate, and fry as directed.

DELICATE CRULLERS.—Take four eggs, four tablespoonsful of lard, four tablespoonsful of sugar, a teaspoonful of salt, and half a nutmeg grated, a teaspoonful of lemon extract may be added; work into these as much sifted flour as will make a nice dough, roll it to about an eighth of an inch thickness, and fry as directed for doughnuts and crullers.

To make little baskets, cut the paste in strips an inch and a half wide, and three inches long, and with a gigling iron, cut slits across it from one side to the other, within a quarter of an inch of either edge, and quarter of an inch apart; then join the two ends together in a circle, forming the basket; press it down slightly, that the strips may bulge, and so form the basket, like those made for fly traps of paper; as soon as they are taken from the fat, (five minutes will do them,) grate white sugar over.

PREPARED FLOUR.—To one quart of wheat flour, put two heaped teaspoonfuls of cream of tartar, and one of soda, work it through a seive, and make use of it instead of unprepared flour in any of the receipts.

To MAKE WIGS.—Take three pounds and a half of flour, rub into it three quarters of a pound of butter, until it is like grated bread, put to it a pound of sugar, half a nutmeg grated, and a teaspoonful of ground ginger; beat three eggs very light, take a gill of baker's yeast, and a wine-glass of brandy, make a hollow in the flour, and put in the eggs and yeast, with as much warm milk as will make a nice dough; work it smooth, cover it, and set it in a warm place for two hours, then divide it into eighteen or twenty cakes, put them in a buttered pan, at a little distance from each other, brush the top of each over with the yolk of an egg beaten with a little milk, and bake half an hour in a quick oven; serve hot, to be broken open and buttered.

CURRANT BUNS.—Into three pounds and a half of sifted wheat flour, work two pounds of soft lard, add a large tablespoonful of salt, and a teaspoonful of ground alspice; add to it half a gill of baker's yeast, and enough warm water to make a soft dough, cover it, and set it in a warm place for three hours, then stir into it half a pound of currants, picked, washed, and dried; make it in cakes (with a spoon,) an inch thick, and the size of the top of a tumbler; bake twenty minutes in a quick oven.

WAFFLES.—Three teacups of sugar rolled fine, one cup of butter, three well beaten eggs, half a teaspoonful of saleratus, dissolved in a teacup of milk, stir in sifted wheat flour, until it is a thick batter, add to it half a nutmeg grated, and a teaspoonful of lemon extract, put in a teaspoonful of salt, and stir it for some time.

Make the waffle irons hot, dip a sponge in melted butter, and rub it over every part, put a large spoonful or two of the mixture in for each cake, close the iron, and set it over hot coals or a stove; let them remain for six or eight minutes, then turn the iron over; after six or eight minutes open it, if the cake is a nice color, and loosens, take it out; and so continue until you have enough.

WAFFLES,—May be made of soft jumble mixture, or of pound cake; any cake may be baked in waffle irons. Waffles may be made for dessert of a batter, as directed for wheat fritters, pan-cakes, and served with wine sauce over.

YEAST WAFFLES.—Beat three eggs light, put to

them one pint of warm milk, a large tablespoonful of yeast, one tablespoonful of butter, and half a nutmeg, and flour as stiff as you can stir with a spoon, or enough to make a light batter, add a teaspoonful of salt, and set it in a warm place to rise, for two or three hours, then bake them in muffin rings or a waffle iron; put butter and sugar over, and serve hot.

WAFERS.—Two tablespoonsful of white sugar, two ditto of butter, one teacup of flour, half a teaspoonful of lemon extract, or a tablespoonful of brandy, and half a nutmeg grated, work them well together, cut it in bits the size of your thumb, make a wafer iron hot, rub it inside with a bit of butter, put in a bit of the dough, press the irons together upon it, and bake it a delicate brown, then take it out, slip another bit in, and so continue until all are done; or roll the paste as thin as a dollar piece, cut it in small cakes, and bake it four or five minutes in a quick oven.

WAFERS.—Take three quarters of a pound of sugar, three quarters of a pound of flour, the yolks of three eggs, half a nutmeg grated, and a teaspoonful of carroway seeds, if liked; add a quarter of a pound of butter, and work the whole into a smooth paste or dough, cut it in bits half the size of an egg, and bake it in a wafer iron, or roll it out as thin as a dollar piece, cut it in round cakes the size of the top of a tumbler, and bake in a quick oven for a few minutes.

WAFERS AND JELLY.—Make a batter as directed for soft jumbles or Dover cake, rub a square tin pan over with a bit of sponge dipped in soft butter, put in the mixture, not much thicker than a dollar piece, put the pan in a moderate oven for fifteen minutes, or until it is nicely baked, then turn it carefully out, spread it with jelly; when it is cold, bake another, lay it carefully upon the first one, when cold, spread it with jelly, and having baked a third, lay it carefully upon it; serve cut in squares, or cut it round, and serve cut in wedge shaped pieces. Or having baked one of these cakes, spread half of it with jelly, lay the other half upon it; when cold, cut it in pieces three inches long, and one broad; serve for tea or for evening parties.

COMMON JUMBLES.—One teacup of butter, two teacups of sugar, one teacup of sour milk or buttermilk, one small teaspoonful of saleratus, dissolved in a little water, one beaten egg, and half a nutmeg grated, use enough sifted flour to make it so as to mould in well floured hands, roll it quarter of an inch thick, cut it in round cakes, make an opening in the centre with the finger, grate sugar over, lay them in pans or baking tins, and set them in a quick oven for ten or twelve minutes.

JUMBLES.—Three pounds of flour, one pound and a half of butter, one pound of sugar, and six well beaten eggs, add half a grated nutmeg, and a teaspoonful of lemon extract, or a teaspoonful of ground cinnamon; work it well together, then roll it out to eighth of an inch thickness, grate loaf sugar over, cut it in round cakes, make an aperture in the centre of each, lay them on tin plates, and bake ten minutes in a quick oven.

SMALL CAKES.—Three eggs, three tablespoonsful of butter, the same of sugar, three teacups of flour, one teaspoonful of lemon extract, and half a nutmeg grated, work these well together, roll it thin, cut it in small cakes or jumbles, and bake in a quick oven.

TAYLOR CAKES.—Beat one pound of butter to a cream, put it to one pound and a half of flour, one pound of fine sugar, and four eggs well beaten; add half a nutmeg grated, and a teaspoonful of carroway seeds, work it well together, roll it thin, cut it in round cakes, and bake in a moderate oven ten or twelve minutes.

ALMOND JUMBLES.—Beat half a pound of butter to a cream, with half a pound of fine sugar, mix it with a pound of flour, and quarter of a pound of almonds blanched, and shred small, or beaten to a paste with a little lemon juice; work it well together, then roll it eighth of an inch thick, cut it in small round cakes, and bake in a quick oven ten or twelve minutes.

CINNAMON WAFERS.—Pound and sift six ounces of sugar, and put it with an equal weight of fresh butter, beaten to a cream, with an equal weight of sifted flour; add half an ounce of ground cinnamon, and a small egg, stir these well together in an earthen basin, add sufficient milk to make a thin batter; make a griddle quite hot, rub it over with a bit of sponge dipped in soft butter, then lay on it a spoonful of the batter; when one side is done turn the other, when both sides are a fine brown, roll it (still on the griddle) around a small stick, and so continue until all the paste is used.

SPONGE CAKES.—One pound of sifted flour, five eggs well beaten, half a pound of fine sugar, half a nutmeg grated, and a few drops of lemon extract or a teaspoonful of orange flower water, roll it to quarter of an inch thickness, cut it in cakes the size of the top of a tumbler, and bake twelve or fifteen minutes in a quick oven.

WHITE CAKES.—Take half a pound of sifted flour, rub into it one ounce of butter, and quarter of a pound of fine sugar, add one egg, half a teaspoonful of carroway seeds, and as much milk as will make it a paste; roll it out to quarter of an inch thickness, or thinner, cut it in small round cakes, and bake on tin plates in a quick oven, ten or twelve minutes.

ONE TWO-THREE-FOUR CAKE.—One cup of butter, two cups of sugar, three cups of flour, and four eggs. Work the sugar and butter together, put it to the eggs, well beaten, then mix in the flour; add grated nutmeg; flour the cake board or table, and roll the cake to rather more than a quarter of an inch thick; stick each with a fork, and bake fifteen minutes in a quick oven.

SPICE CAKES.—Two pounds of sifted flour, three quarters of a pound of sugar, three quarters of a pound of butter, one tablespoonful of ground spices, one teaspoonful of salt, and two tablespoonsful of yeast; mix it to a nice dough with warm milk, cover it, and set it in a warm place for three hours; then roll it thin; cut it in small cakes, and bake ten or twelve minutes in a quick oven. These may be fried as doughnuts.

RICH SPICE CAKES.—Take one pound and a half of flour, three quarters of a pound of sugar, three quarters of a pound of butter, and half a teacup of mixed spices; work the butter, flour, and sugar together with the spices, until thoroughly incorporated; roll it thin, cut it in small cakes, and bake in a moderate oven.

PORTUGAL CAKES.—One pound of butter worked into one pound of flour and one pound of sugar; add a quarter of a pound of well-washed and dried currants, three well-beaten eggs, and a gill of brandy; mix them well together, and bake in a quick oven.

SPANISH CAKES.—Two pounds of flour, three quarters of a pound of sugar, three quarters of a pound of butter, four eggs, well beaten, one teaspoonful of ground cinnamon, and half a nutmeg, grated; work it well together, roll it in thin sheets, and cut in fancy cakes with tin cutters, such as stars, leaves, hearts, &c.; bake fifteen minutes in a moderate oven.

WINE CAKES.—Mix eight ounces of flour with half a pound of finely-powdered sugar, beat four ounces of butter with two tablespoonfuls of wine; then make the flour and sugar into a paste with it, and four eggs, beaten light; add carroway seeds, and roll the paste as thin as paper; cut the cakes with the top of a tumbler, brush the tops over with the beaten white of an egg, grate sugar over, and bake ten or twelve minutes in a quick oven; take them from the tins when cold.

SOFT GINGERBREAD, *(Molasses.)*—Take half a pint of sour milk or buttermilk, half a pint of molasses, one teacup of butter, or salted lard, or beef fat, one large teaspoonful of saleratus, dissolved in a little hot water, two well-beaten eggs, half a nutmeg, grated, a teaspoonful of ground cinnamon and a large spoonful of ground ginger; mix in sifted wheat flour, until it is a thick batter which you can stir easily with a spoon; beat it well together for some time, then pour it an inch deep in square tin pans, buttered; bake half an hour in a quic oven: to ascertain whether it is done, try as directed in introductory remarks.

GINGER SNAPS.—Half a pint of molasses, a quarter of a pound of brown sugar, carroway seeds and ground ginger, each a tablespoonful, and a quarter of a pound of butter; work the butter into a pound of flour; work it altogether, and form it in cakes not larger than a dollar piece, on baking tins; bake in a moderate oven twenty minutes, when they will be dry and crisp.

SOFT GINGERBREAD, *without Eggs.*—Make as directed for soft gingerbread, omitting the eggs, and using two teaspoonfuls of saleratus instead of one; dissolve it in a teacupful of warm water.

PEARLASH CAKE.—Take half a pint of molasses, half a pint of water, half a teacup of butter, one teaspoonful of ground ginger, one teaspoonful of ground cinnamon, and an even full tablespoon of powdered pearlash; dissolve it in the water; put these ingredients together, then stir in as much sifted flour as will make a stiff batter, beat it well for some time together; with a sponge dipped in soft butter, rub the inside of square tin pans, put in the cake mixture nearly an inch deep, and bake half an hour in a quick oven; when the cake loosens from the sides of the pan, it is done; it may be broken and eaten hot. This is a healthful cake for children, and extremely palatable to all.

Molasses Cup Cakes.—Two cups of molasses, one cup of butter, one cup of milk, one teaspoonful of powdered saleratus dissolved in a little hot water, one teaspoonful of lemon extract, half a nutmeg, grated, and two well-beaten eggs; stir in, by degrees, enough flour to make it as stiff as you can stir easily with a spoon, beat it well until it is very light, rub a two-quart tin basin over with a bit of butter, line it with white paper, and put the cake in it; bake forty minutes in a quick oven; try if it is done, by running a broom splint in at the thickest part; if it comes out clean, it is done. This is a delicious cake.

Honey Cake.—Three pounds and a half of flour, one pound and a half of honey, half a pound of sugar, half a pound of butter, half a nutmeg, grated, a tablespoonful of ground ginger, and one teaspoonful of saleratus, dissolved in a little hot water; work it to a smooth dough, roll it a quarter of an inch thick, cut it in small cakes, and bake twenty-five minutes in a moderate oven.

Ginger Nuts.—Into three pounds and a half of wheat flour work half a pound of butter; add half a pound of sugar and a pint and a half of molasses, half a nutmeg, grated, and a teaspoonful of ground ginger; put to it a large teaspoonful of saleratus, dissolved in a little hot water; make it a nice dough, roll it thin, and cut it in small cakes; put them on baking tins, and bake fifteen minutes in a quick oven.

Wigs.—Take half a pound of butter, half a pound of sugar, one pound and three quarters of flour, one quart of milk, and six eggs; make the milk warm, and melt the butter in it, beat them very light, then stir them into the milk, with half a gill of yeast; put the sugar and flour together, and gradually stir the milk, &c. into it; cover it, and set it in a warm place for three hours; when light, rub some square tin pans over with a bit of butter, put in the mixture nearly an inch deep, and bake twenty minutes in a quick oven; when done, turn them out, break or cut it open, put butter between, and serve hot for tea. This tea cake may be cut in small squares and served hot, to be buttered at table. This mixture may be put half as thick in the pans, and baked fifteen minutes; when cold, cut it in squares; it is very delicate and light for lunch. Saleratus, half the size of a small nutmeg, may be dissolved, and added to the mixture.

CREAM CUP CAKE.—Four cups of flour, two cups of butter, one cup of sour cream, five well-beaten eggs, and one small teaspoonful of saleratus dissolved in a little hot water; beat these together for a long time; add half a nutmeg, grated, and a teaspoonful of lemon extract or orange-flower water; bake in a quick oven, in buttered tins lined with paper; if baked in square tins, put the mixture in an inch deep, and bake twenty-five minutes; in round pans, put it an inch and half, and bake forty minutes.

COMMON CUP CAKE.—One tea cup of butter, two of sugar, four of flour, four well-beaten eggs, one cup of sour milk, one teaspoonful of saleratus, dissolved in a little water, one teaspoonful of lemon extract, or a wineglass of brandy, and half a nutmeg, grated; beat up the mixture well, butter two two-quart basins, line them with white paper, and divide the mixture between them; bake in a quick oven three quarters of an hour.

Soft Jumbles.—Two teacups of sugar, rolled fine, one cup of sweet milk, with half a teaspoonful of saleratus dissolved in it, one cup of butter, beat to cream, and four well-beaten eggs; use sifted flour enough to make it rather thicker than pound cake; beat it well after all the ingredients are in, rub some square tin pans over with a bit of sponge dipped in soft butter, put in the mixture rather more than an inch deep, and bake in a moderate oven three quarters of an hour; when served, cut it in small squares. This mixture makes fine waffles; an ounce of shelled almonds blanched and stirred fine or pounded to a paste may be added to this cake mixture.

Teacup Cake without Eggs.—One cup of butter, two cups of sugar, one cup of sour cream or buttermilk, one teaspoonful of cream of tartar and one teaspoonful of soda, rolled very fine, a gill of brandy, half a nutmeg grated and a teaspoonful of essence of lemon or the yellow rind of a lemon grated; stir in enough sifted wheat flour to make it as thick as pound-cake; beat well; put in an inch deep in buttered basins; bake half an hour in a quick oven.

Soda Cake —Dissolve half a pound of sugar and a teaspoonful of carbonate of soda in a pint of milk; put to it half a pound of butter beaten to a cream and half a nutmeg grated; add gradually enough flour to make a stiff batter, beat it well, put it in shallow pans and bake in a quick oven. If half an inch deep, bake twenty minutes, in a moderate oven. Cut it in small squares to serve.

Cocoanut Cup Cake.—Two cups of sugar, two cups of butter, one cup of milk, one teaspoonful of essence of lemon, half a nutmeg grated, four well beaten eggs and the white meat of a cocoanut grated; use as much sifted wheat flour as will make a rather stiff batter; beat it well, butter square tin pans, line them with white paper, and put in the mixture an inch deep; bake in a moderate oven half an hour, or it may require ten minutes longer.

When cold, cut in small squares or diamonds; this is a rich cake and is much improved by a thin icing. This cake should be made with fine white sugar.

COMPOSITION CAKE.—One pound of sugar, half a pound of butter beaten to a cream, four eggs well beaten, one cup of milk, half a teaspoonful of saleratus, or volatile salts dissolved in a little hot water, half a nutmeg grated, and a teaspoonful of essence of lemon; use as much sifted flour as will make a stiff batter.

Beat these well together until it is light and creamy, then add one pound of raisins, stoned, and cut in two, or one pound of currants, picked, washed, and dried; line square tin pans with buttered paper, put in the mixture an inch deep and bake half an hour in a moderate oven; try it, ten minutes longer may possibly be required. When served cut the cake in squares or oblong pieces; this mixture makes two cakes eight inches wide and twelve long.

To ice this cake, take it from the pans; when cold take off the paper, turn the pan upside down and set the cake upon it; finish as directed. See "To ice a cake."

This cake mixture without the fruit makes fine waffles.

ALMOND CAKE.—Make a batter as directed for

composition cake, blanch quarter of a pound of shelled almonds, cut them in slips and stir them into the cake instead of fruit; finish as directed for that cake.

YELLOW LADY-CAKE.—*A new way to make it.*— Take a pound of fine white sugar with half a pound of butter beaten to a cream, the yolks of eight eggs beaten smooth and thick, one cup of sweet milk, a small teaspoonful of powdered volatile salts or saleratus, dissolved in a little hot water, half a nutmeg grated, a teaspoonful of lemon extract or orange-flower water, and as much sifted wheat flour as will make it as thick as pound-cake batter; beat it until it is light and creamy, then having taken the skins from, and beaten to a paste quarter of a pound of shelled almonds, stir them into the cake, beat them in it, line buttered tin pans with white paper, put in the mixture an inch deep, and bake half an hour in a quick oven, or forty minutes in a moderate oven. This is a delicious cake, never before given in any book, being the result of an experiment of the author of this book.

Lady-cake is usually made with the yolks of eggs, as Savoy cake (two yolks for one whole egg) with the addition of pounded almonds. Ice it as directed for composition cake, when a little dry, mark it with a knife blade in slices the width of a finger, and three inches long.

WHITE LADY-CAKE.—Beat the whites of eight eggs to a high froth, add gradually a pound of white sugar finely ground, beat quarter of a pound of butter to a cream, add a teacup of sweet milk with a small teaspoonful of powdered volatile salts or saleratus dissolved in it; put the eggs to butter and milk, add as much sifted wheat flour as will make it as thick as pound-cake mixture, and a teaspoonful of orange-flower water or lemon extract then add quarter of a pound of shelled almonds, blanched and beaten to a paste with a little white of egg; beat the whole together until light and white; line a square tin pan with buttered paper, put in the mixture an inch deep, and bake half an hour in a quick oven. When done take it from the pan, when cold take the paper off, turn it upside down on the bottom of the pan and ice the side which was down; when the icing is nearly hard mark it in slices the width of a finger, and two inches and a half long.

CITRON HEART CAKES.—Beat half a pound of butter to a cream, take six eggs, beat the whites to a froth, and the yolks with half a pound of sugar, and rather more than half a pound of sifted flour, beat these well together, add a wine-glass of brandy, and quarter of a pound of citron cut in thin slips, bake it in small heart shaped tins, or a square tin pan, rubbed over with a bit of sponge dipped in melted butter, put the mixture in half an inch deep, bake fifteen or twenty minutes in a quick oven; these are very fine cakes.

Shred almonds may be used instead of citron.

WEBSTER CAKES.—Mix a pound and a half of sifted flour with a pound of powder sugar, rub into it a pound of sweet butter, then add ten well beaten eggs, two tablespoonsful of rose or orange flower water, and two tablespoonsful of wine or brandy, with half a pound of well cleansed and dried currants; beat the mixture until it is light and creamy, bake it in square tin pans, lined with buttered paper; put the mixture in half an inch deep, and bake in a quick oven fifteen minutes; when served cut it in squares or diamonds; this cake may be iced, mark it as it is to be cut, before the icing is dry.

PALO-ALTO CAKES.—Beat half a pound of butter to a cream, with half a pound of fine white sugar, put to it five well beaten eggs, a tablespoonful of rose water, the same of brandy, half a nutmeg grated, and half a pound of sifted flour, beat it together until very light; line square tin pans with paper, rubbed over with a bit of sponge dipped in melted butter, put in the mixture half an inch deep, and bake in a quick oven fifteen minutes, or twenty in a moderate oven; when done, take it from the pans, turn them upside down, and set the cake upon them; when the cake is cold, take off the paper, cut it in small fancy shapes; put a little red jelly in the centre of each piece, and with a small syringe, put a border of icing around it.

DOVER CAKE.—Beat half a pound of butter to a cream, with a pound of fine white sugar, add half a pint of milk, four well beaten eggs, one wine-glass of rose water, a wine-glass of brandy, one nutmeg grated, a teaspoonful of ground cinnamon, and half a teaspoonful of saleratus, dissolved in a tablespoonful of hot water, beat in as much wheat flour as will make it as thick as pound-cake mixture, beat well after all the ingredients are in, line round or square tin pans with buttered paper, put the mixture in an inch deep in square, or an inch and a half in round pans, bake in a quick oven; half an hour for square pans, forty-five minutes for round basins.

The addition of currants, raisins, and citron, to this cake, makes one which will keep for months, and improve.

WASHINGTON CAKE.—One pound and three quarters of flour, one pound and a half of sugar, three quarters of a pound of butter, four eggs, half a pint of sour milk, one teaspoonful of saleratus, dissolved in a little hot water.

Beat the sugar and butter together, add the milk and beaten eggs, then put in the dissolved saleratus, and gradually stir in the flour, with a wineglass of brandy or wine, and a small nutmeg grated; beat them well together.

Make it in two round cakes, or bake it in square tin pans, in a quick oven, allow fifteen minutes if half an inch deep, thirty minutes if an inch deep, and forty-five if an inch and a half deep.

TO BAKE CAKES.—Allow fifteen minutes for baking a cake which is half an inch thick or deep, and according as it may be thicker, allow fifteen minutes for each half inch, in a quick oven; in a moderate or gentle oven, five minutes more for each half inch may be allowed; in a slow oven, half an hour would be required for each half inch.

SMALL POUND CAKES.—One pound and a half of sifted flour, seven eggs well beaten, and two teaspoonfuls of cream of tartar and one of soda, sifted in with the flour, one pound of fine white sugar, one pound of butter, and one teaspoonful of essence of lemon or orange flower water, with half a nutmeg grated.

Beat the eggs light, beat the butter and sugar together, then put it with the eggs, and gradually add the flour, beat all together for a few minutes, put it half an inch deep in very small round tins, rubbed with a bit of butter, and bake ten minutes in a quick oven, or bake it in square tins fifteen minutes; cut it small to serve.

POUND CAKES.—One pound and a half of flour, one pound of butter, one pound of fine white sugar, ten eggs, one gill of brandy, half a nutmeg grated, and a teaspoonful of vanilla or lemon extract, or orange flower water.

Beat the butter and sugar to a cream, beat the eggs to a high froth, then put all together, beat it until it is light and creamy, put it in basins lined with buttered paper, let the mixture be an inch and a half deep, and bake in a moderate oven for one hour, then try it; when done, turn it gently out, reverse the pan, and set the cake on the bottom until cold, let the paper remain until the cake is to be cut.

QUEEN CAKE.—Beat one pound of butter to a cream, with a tablespoonful of rose water; then add one pound of fine white sugar, ten eggs, beaten very light, and a pound and a quarter of sifted flour; beat the cake well together; then add half a pound of shelled almonds, blanched, and beaten to a paste; butter tin round basins, line them with white paper; put in the mixture an inch and a half deep; bake one hour in a quick oven.

THANKSGIVING TEA CAKE.—One teacup of butter, one of white sugar, two well-beaten eggs, two teacups heaping full of sifted wheat flour; one teaspoonful of cream of tartar, and half a teaspoonful of soda.

Beat the butter to a cream, with the sugar; then add the two eggs, well beaten; pound the salts and alum to powder, and dissolve them separately; then put them to the sugar and eggs, and gradually stir in the flour; beat it until it is very light—it cannot be beaten too much; cut some citron in thin slices, cut each slice quite small; stir them into the cake; line a tin two quart basin with buttered paper; put the mixture in, and bake in a quick oven.

COCOANUT POUND-CAKE.—One pound of white fine sugar, half a pound of butter, one teacup of sweet milk, one teaspoonful of powdered saleratus, or a bit of volatile salts the size of a small nutmeg, dissolved in a little hot water; one teaspoonful of essence of lemon, and four well beaten eggs.

Beat these ingredients well together, until very light, with as much sifted flour as will make it as thick as pound-cake; then lightly stir in the white meat of a cocoanut, grated; line square tin pans with buttered paper; put the mixture in an inch deep, and bake in a quick oven for half an hour: when done, take it from the pan, reverse the pan, and set the cake on the bottom to cool. This cake should be iced or frosted: mark it in small squares or diamonds, before it is hard.

ALMOND POUND-CAKE.—Make a cake as for cocoanut pound-cake; take the skins from quarter of a pound of shelled almonds; pound them small, but not to a paste, with a little lemon juice, or white of egg; beat them with the cake, instead of cocoanut, and finish in the same manner.

HICKORY-NUT, OR JACKSON CAKE.—Crack some fine hickory-nuts; pick the meats from the shells, until you have half a pint; make a cake as for cocoanut pound-cake; make the nut meats small, and stir them in. Raisins, stoned, and cut in two; or currants, well washed and dried, may be added, and will be an improvement. Put the mixture more than an inch deep in a round tin basin, lined with buttered paper; and bake in a quick oven.

SPONGE CAKE.—One pound of sugar, finely ground; half a pound of sifted flour; eight eggs; one teaspoonful of salt; one tablespoonful of rose brandy; or a teaspoonful of lemon extract.

Beat the yolks of the eggs, flour and sugar together, until it is smooth and light; beat the whites of the eggs to a high froth; then beat all together, until well mixed; one teaspoonful of cream of tartar, and half a teaspoonful of soda sifted dry into the flour.

Butter a square tin pan, line it with paper, and put in the mixture more than an inch deep; bake in a moderate oven.

SMALL SPONGE CAKES.—Beat five eggs light, with half a pound of sugar, and quarter of a pound of flour; flavor with grated nutmeg, and lemon, or orange flower water; add a small teaspoonful of salt; beat it until it rises in bubbles; butter small tins, put in the mixture half an inch deep, and bake twelve or fifteen minutes in a quick oven.

HARRISON CAKE.—Beat two eggs light; add to them half a pound of sugar, a tablespoonful of butter, half a teacup of sweet milk, half a teaspoonful of powdered saleratus, a small teaspoonful of salt, half a nutmeg, grated; and enough flour to make a smooth batter; beat it until it rises in bubbles; put it in buttered pans, and bake in a quick oven; cut it in squares to serve.

DIET BREAD.—One pound of sifted flour, one pound of fine sugar, one teaspoonful of salt, and nine eggs. Make and finish the same as sponge cake.

SAVOY BISCUIT.—Beat the whites of six eggs to a froth, and the yolks, with rather more than half a pound of finely powdered white sugar; then add half a pound of sifted flour, and a teaspoonful of lemon extract, or orange flower water; beat all well together; butter square tin pans; line them with white paper, nearly fill them, and bake in a quick oven.

LAFAYETTE CAKE.—Make a Savoy biscuit, bake it in a round tin basin, about five inches in diameter, with straight sides. When cold, cut it in slices quarter of an inch thick; spread each with jelly, or jam; put it together again; put three or four slices for each cake; ice the top and sides; and while it is soft, mark it to cut in wedge-shaped pieces when served.

This cake may be served without icing; it may be made of Pound Cake, or Dover Cake.

NAPLES BISCUIT.—Beat eight eggs light; add to them one pound of fine white sugar, and one pound of sifted wheat flour; flavor with a teaspoonful of salt, and essence of lemon, or orange flower water; beat it until it rises in bubbles; bake in a quick oven.

BISCUIT AND JELLY SANDWICH.—Bake a Naples biscuit in a basin with straight sides; then cut it in slices, and finish as directed for Lafayette cake.

CAKE TRIFLE.—Bake a Savoy cake, or Naples biscuit; cut out the inside about one inch from the edge and bottom, leaving the shell. In place of the inside, put a custard made of the yolks of four eggs, beaten with a pint of boiling milk, sweetened, and flavored with half a teaspoonful of peach-water; lay on it some jelly, or jam; beat the whites of two eggs, with white ground sugar, until it will stand in a heap; put it on the jelly, and serve.

Spoon Biscuits.—Put the whites of four eggs into a basin; put the yolks in another, with quarter of a pound of fine white sugar, and the yellow part of a lemon, grated; mix these last together, for ten minutes; then whip the whites to a high froth, and put about half of them to the yolks; mix it well; then add the remainder; stir it very gently, and lay it with a spoon on sheets of paper; let each be the thickness and length of a finger, and some little distance apart; strew them with fine white sugar; lay the papers on baking-tins, and as soon as the sugar dissolves, and the biscuits shine, put them in a moderate oven; let it remain open for seven or eight minutes; then close it for fifteen minutes: when cold, take them from the paper with a knife-blade. Almonds, blanched, and cut in slips across, may be stirred into the mixture before putting it on the paper.

Tablets de Patience, or Lady-Fingers.— Take eight eggs; whip the whites to a firm snow. In the meantime, have the yolks beaten up with six ounces of powdered sugar. Each of these operations should be performed at least one hour. Then mix all together with six ounces of sifted flour; and when well incorporated, stir in half a pint of rose, or orange flower water; stir them together for some time.

Have ready some tin plates, rubbed with white wax; take a funnel with three or four tubes; fill it with the paste, and press out the cakes upon the plates, to the size and length of a finger; grate white sugar over each; let them lay until the sugar melts, and they shine: then put them in a moderate oven, until they have a fine color; when cool, take them from the tins, and lay them together in couples, by the backs. These cakes may be formed with a spoon, on sheets of writing paper. Half this quantity will be trouble enough at one time.

LOAF CAKE.—One pound of butter beaten to a cream, two pounds of sugar rolled fine, three pounds of sifted wheat flour, six well beaten eggs, three teaspoonsful of powdered saleratus, dissolved in a little hot water, one tablespoonful of ground cinnamon, and half a nutmeg grated, add one pound of currants, well washed and dried, one pound of raisins stoned and cut in two; work the whole well together, divide it in three loaves, put them in buttered basins, and bake one hour in a moderate oven.

LOAF CAKE.—Make either of the mixtures directed for doughnuts, work into it one pound of currants washed and dried, or a pound of raisins stoned and cut in two; bake in a moderate oven. When served, cut it in slices.

DIET BISCUIT.—Beat the yolks of four eggs for ten minutes, with half a pound of powdered sugar, and rather less flour, beat the whites and the yolks to a high froth, flavor with a teaspoonful of salt and essence of lemon or orange flower water, add the whites to the yolks, stir them gently together, and bake in small tins in a quick oven.

FRENCH TEA CAKE.—Beat ten eggs to a high froth, dissolve half a teaspoonful of volatile salts, with a little hot water, let it stand to cool, then put it to the eggs, and beat for ten minutes, add four ounces of powdered loaf sugar, and the same of sifted flour, beat them well together, line square tin pans with buttered paper, put in the cake mixture, nearly an inch deep, and bake in a quick oven. When served; cut it in squares.

DROP CAKES.—Beat eight eggs very light with one pound of powdered sugar, and twelve ounces of flour; flavor with lemon or rose, and half a nutmeg, grated; if the mixture is not beat enough, the cakes will run into each other; make them in small oblong cakes, on sheets of paper, grate sugar 'over each; bake in a moderate oven; when done, take them from the paper with a knife.

ALMOND DROP CAKES.—Take the skins from an ounce of almonds and pound them fine, with a teaspoonful of lemon extract, beat the yolks of three eggs, and put them to the almonds, then add sugar and flour each an ounce and a half; mix them well together, strew sugar and flour in a tin plate, drop the mixture from a spoon in small cakes, let them be an inch apart; bake in a quick oven.

LEMON DROP CAKES.—Grate the rinds from three large fresh skin lemons, put to it three heaping tablespoonfuls of white fine sugar and a tablespoonful of wheat flour; work the whole together with the white of an egg; make it in small balls on sheets of paper, the distance of an inch apart; bake half an hour in a slow oven.

SUGAR DROP CAKES.—Beat one pound of white sugar with the yolks of seven eggs, beat the whites of ten to a high froth, mix one pound of sifted flour to the yolks and sugar, then stir in lightly the beaten whites; beat the whole well together; drop this mixture on buttered paper; bake in a quick oven, take them from the paper whilst hot, with a knife blade.

Cocoanut Sponge Cake.—Beat the yolks of six eggs with half a pound of sugar and a quarter of a pound of flour, add a teaspoonful of salt, a teaspoonful of lemon essence, and half a nutmeg, grated; beat the whites of the eggs to a froth, and stir them to the yolks, &c. and the white meat of a cocoa-nut, grated; line square tin pans with buttered paper, and having stirred the ingredients well together, put the mixture in an inch deep in the pans; bake in a quick oven half an hour; cut it in squares, to serve with or without icing.

Rout Drop Cakes.—Two pounds of flour, one pound of sugar, one pound of butter, one pound of currants, well washed and dried; mix the whole into a stiff paste, with two eggs, one tablespoonful of rose-water, and one gill of brandy; strew a tin plate with flour and powdered sugar, mixed; put the paste on it in small cakes, and bake in a quick oven.

Rich Fruit Cake.—Make a cake of one pound of flour, one pound of sugar, three quarters of a pound of butter, and ten eggs. First beat the yolks and sugar together, then add the flour and butter, beaten to a cream; and lastly, mix in lightly the whites of the eggs, beaten to a high froth.

Have a pound of raisins stoned and cut in two, two pounds of currants well washed and dried, one pound of citron cut in slips, mace and cinnamon, each a tablespoonful, and a gill of brandy; strew a quarter of a pound of flour over the currants and raisins, then stir all into the cake; line round tin basins with buttered paper, fill them two inches deep, then bake in a quick oven one hour.

This cake is better for keeping several weeks or months.

MRS. MADISON'S WHIM.—Two pounds of flour, two pounds of sugar, two pounds of butter, beaten to a cream, twelve eggs, the yolks beaten with the sugar and the whites beaten to a high froth, two wineglasses of brandy in which rose-leaves have been steeped, two nutmegs, grated, one teaspoonful of saleratus, dissolved in a tablespoonful of hot water. Beat the whole well together until it is light and creamy, then add two pounds of raisins, stoned and chopped; strew a teacup of flour over them before putting them in the cake; line round basins with buttered paper, and put the cake mixture in an inch and a half deep; bake in a quick oven.

This cake will keep good for three months.

WEDDING CAKE.—One pound of flour, nine eggs, the whites and yolks beaten separately, one pound of butter beaten to a cream, one pound of brown sugar, one teacup of molasses, nutmegs grated, or ground mace, one ounce, one teaspoonful of ground alspice, one teaspoonful of cinnamon, and a gill of brandy; beat this mixture well.

Having picked, washed, and dried three pounds of currants, and stoned and cut in two three pounds of raisins, strew half a pound of flour over them; mix it well through, and stir them with a pound of citron, cut in slips, into the cake.

Line round tin pans with buttered paper; put the mixture in an inch and a half or two inches deep, and bake in a moderate oven an hour and a half or two hours. See directions for icing a cake.

PLUM CAKE.—Make a cake of two cups of butter, two cups of molasses, one cup of sweet milk, two eggs, well beaten, one teaspoonful of powdered saleratus, dissolved with a little hot water, one teaspoonful of ground mace or nutmeg, one teaspoonful of ground alspice, a tablespoonful of cinnamon, and a gill of brandy; stir in flour to make a batter as stiff as may be stirred easily with a spoon; beat it well until it is light, then add two pounds of raisins, stoned, and cut in two, two pounds of currants, picked, washed, and dried, and half a pound of citron, cut in slips. Bake in a quick oven.

This is a fine, rich cake, easily made, and not expensive.

TO CLEAN CURRANTS FOR CAKE.—Pick out all the sticks and stones, put the currants in a pan, and more than cover them with water; rub them between your hands, take them up by the handful, pick out any imperfections, and put them into another pan; when all are done, cover them with water, shake them about, take them up in the hand, press the water from them, and spread them on a thickly folded cloth, lay them in the sun or near the fire to dry; turn them and spread them, that they may be thoroughly dried. Keep them in glass jars or boxes lined with paper. Some dried currants require only to be picked over, rinsed in one water, and dried.

RICH BRIDE-CAKE.—Take four pounds of sifted flour, four pounds of sweet fresh butter, beaten to a cream, and two pounds of white powdered sugar; take six eggs for each pound of flour, an ounce of ground mace or nutmegs, and a tablespoonful of lemon extract or orange-flower water.

Wash through several waters, and pick clean from grit, four pounds of currants, and spread them on a folded cloth to dry; stone, and cut in two, four pounds of raisins, cut two pounds of citron in slips, and chop or slice one pound of blanched almonds.

Beat the yolks of the eggs with the sugar to a smooth paste, beat the butter and flour together, and add them to the yolks and sugar; then add the spice and half a pint of brandy, and the whites of the eggs beaten to a froth; stir all together for some time; strew half a pound of flour over the fruit, mix it through, then by degrees stir it into the cake.

Butter large tin basins, line them with white paper, and put in the mixture two inches deep, and bake in a moderate oven two hours. The fruit should be prepared the day before making the cake.

ALMOND SPICE BISCUITS.—Take three pounds of sifted flour, three pounds of almonds, beaten fine, an ounce each of cinnamon and mace, pounded fine, and one pound of powdered sugar. To three pounds of clean brown sugar put a teacupful of water; when it is all dissolved, set it over the fire, let it become boiling hot, take off the scum, and make the other ingredients into a paste with it, make it the size of a rolling-pin, lay it on a sheet of paper, flatten it a little with your hands, keeping it higher in the middle than at the end; put it into a quick oven for nearly an hour; when done, take it out, and whilst hot, cut it in slices the eighth of an inch thick, and dry them in a cool oven.

SCOTCH CAKE.—Take two pounds of wheat flour, sift and dry it, then mix with it a pound of powdered sugar and a quarter of a pound of carroway seeds; put half a pound of butter near the fire until it is melted, then work the flour and sugar to a paste with it; roll it out to half an inch thickness, and cut it in cakes four inches long and three wide; lay them on white paper, crimp the edges neatly with the finger, stick the cakes with a fork, strew some carroway comfits over, and bake them a pale color in a moderate oven.

ALMOND DROPS.—Blanch and pound five ounces of sweet and three ounces of bitter almonds, with a little white of egg, put half a pound of flour on your slab, make a hole in the middle, in which put the almonds, with half a pound of powdered sugar, four yolks of eggs, and a small teaspoonful of salt; work this to a paste; make it in rolls the size of your finger, then cut it in bits the size of a small nutmeg; make them in round balls in your hands, lay them the distance of half an inch apart on sheets of paper; lay them on baking tins, and put them in a moderate oven for fifteen or twenty minutes; take them from the papers with a thin blade knife, whilst warm.

ALMOND MACAROONS.—Pour boiling water over half a pound of shelled almonds, take the skins off, and throw them into cold water; when all are done, take a few at a time in a mortar, and pound them to a smooth fine paste with a little extract of lemon or orange-flower water; add to the paste an equal weight of finely-ground white sugar and the whites of two eggs, not beaten; work it together with the back of a spoon until it is a nice paste; then dip your hand in water, and roll the preparation in balls the shape and size of a large nutmeg; lay some white paper on baking tins, lay them on at the distance of an inch apart; when all are done, dip your finger in water, and pass it gently over the macaroons, this will make them smooth and shining; put them into a slow oven, close it three quarters of an hour, and they are done.

If this receipt is strictly followed, there can be no failure, and the macaroons will be found to equal any made by professed confectioners.

COCOANUT MACAROONS.—Make these the same as almond macaroons, substituting grated cocoanut for powdered almonds; finish the same as almond macaroons.

COCOANUT DROPS.—Break a cocoanut in pieces, and lay it in cold water, then cut off the dark rind, and grate the white meat on a coarse grater; put the whites of four eggs with half a pound of powdered white sugar; beat it until it is light and white, then add to it a teaspoonful of lemon extract, and gradually as much grated cocoanut as will make it as thick as can be stirred easily with a spoon; lay it in heaps the size of a large nutmeg on sheets of white paper, place them the distance of half an inch apart; when the paper is full, lay it on a baking tin, set them in a quick oven; when they begin to look yellowish, they are done; let them remain on the paper until nearly cold, then take them off with a thin-bladed knife.

KISSES.—Beat the whites of four small eggs to a high froth, then stir into it half a pound of finely-ground white sugar; flavor with vanilla or lemon extract, continue to beat it until it will lie on a heap; this being done, lay the mixture on letter-paper, in the size and shape of half an egg, and nearly the distance of an inch apart; if it loses its shape or runs, it is not sufficiently beaten. Then place the paper containing them on a piece of hard wood, (a piece of the head of a flour-barrel,) and put them in a quick oven, without closing it; watch them, when they begin to look yellowish, take them out; take the paper from the wood on to a table, and let them cool for three or four minutes, then slip a thin-bladed knife very carefully under one, turn it into your left hand, take another from the paper in the same manner, and join the two by the sides which were next the paper, then lay the kiss thus made on a dish; handle them very gently whilst making.

These are delicious eating; the outside being hard, and the inside a rich, creamy moisture; and present a beautiful appearance.

Following this receipt for making kisses will insure success, unsurpassed by any professed confectioner, and that, too, without the least difficulty. The time required for finishing is short, after having prepared the mixture.

By placing the paper containing the kisses on a baking-tin, instead of the board, the bottom will be hardened as well as the upper surface. Those made in this manner are not as delicious as the others, as they contain less of the moisture, or cream: they, however, look very well.

This mixture may be put on the paper with a syringe. For that purpose, press it out in a little pyramid, or heap. Or it may be made in any form you choose.

JELLY KISSES.—Kisses, to be served for dessert at a large dinner, with other suitable confectionary, may be varied in this way:—Having made the kisses, put them in a moderate oven, until the outside is a little hardened ; then take one off carefully, as before directed ; take out the soft inside with the handle of a spoon, and put it back with the mixture, to make more ; then lay the shell down. Take another, and prepare it likewise ; fill the shells with currant jelly, or jam ; join two together, cementing them with some of the mixture; so continue until you have enough.

Make kisses, cocoanut drops, and such like, the day before they are wanted.

COCOANUT KISSES.—Make a kiss mixture ; add to it half of a cocoanut, grated (the white meat only) ; finish as directed for kisses.

TO MAKE ICING FOR CAKES.—Beat the white of two small eggs to a high froth ; then add to them quarter of a pound of white sugar, ground fine, like flour ; flavor with lemon extract, or vanilla ; beat it until it is light, and very white, but not quite so stiff as kiss mixture ; the longer it is beaten, the more firm it will become. No more sugar must be added to make it so. Beat the frosting until it may be spread smoothly on the cake.

This quantity will ice quite a large cake, over the top and sides.

TO ICE OR FROST CAKE.—Make an icing as above directed, more or less, as may be required.

Turn over the basin in which the cake was baked, and set the cake on the bottom ; then spread the icing on the sides with a piece of card paper, or Bristol board, about four inches long, and two and a half wide ; then heap what you suppose to be sufficient for the top, in the centre of the cake ; and with the card paper spread it evenly over ;

set it in a warm place to dry and harden, after which, ornament it as you may fancy.

If sugar ornaments are put on, it should be done whilst it is moist or soft.

For small cakes, where a thin icing only is required, it must not be beaten as stiff. Let it be so as to flow for the last coating of a cake that it may be smooth.

ORNAMENTAL FROSTING.—For this purpose, have syringes, of different sizes; draw any one you may choose, full of the icing, and work it in any designs you may fancy—wheels, Grecian border, or flowers look well; or borders of beading. The cake must, of course, first be covered with a plain frosting, which may be white; or colored pink with cochineal, powdered, or carmine: blue, with a little indigo; or brown with a little chocolate, finely grated: green may be made with a little spinach-juice, or a mixture of a little gamboge and indigo—more or less gamboge, according as you want it light or dark green.

ALMOND MERINGUES.—Beat the whites of two large eggs to a high froth; then add to it quarter of a pound of finely ground, double refined sugar; beat it until it is light and firm, so as to retain any form in which you may place it; add to it quarter of a pound of almonds, blanched, and cut in very thin slices, across; form it in rings, on letter paper; put the papers on baking-tins, and put them for a short time in a moderate oven (without closing it), to harden; when cold, take them from the papers, with a thin-bladed knife.

These, like kisses, macaroons, etc., should be made a day before they are wanted, on account of the time required to do them.

Meringues may be made in any fancy form which may be desired.

COCOANUT MERINGUES.—Make as above, using finely chipped cocoanut, instead of almonds.

TO PREPARE COCHINEAL, *to color Pink or Red.*—Take an ounce of powdered cochineal; also an ounce of cream of tartar, and two drachms of alum: put these ingredients into a saucepan, with half a pint of water: when it boils, take it from the fire, and let it cool; pour it off into a bottle, as free from sediment as possible. To keep cochineal any length of time, boil an ounce of it (finely powdered) in three quarters of a pint of water, until reduced to half; then add to it rock-alum, and cream of tartar, each half an ounce (pounded fine); boil them together for a short time; then strain it; when cold, bottle it. If you wish to keep it for a long time, boil an ounce of loaf sugar with it.

ALMOND SPICE BISCUITS.—Blanch half a pound of shelled almonds, and pound them in a mortar, to a smooth paste; break into them two eggs; add half a pound of ground sugar; half a nutmeg, grated; a tablespoonful of ground ginger, and a teaspoonful of ground cinnamon; work it with the back of a spoon to a smooth mass; strew some mixed flour and sugar on a paste slab, and roll it to quarter of an inch thickness; mark it in squares or diamonds, and bake in a moderate oven, twenty or twenty-five minutes.

HAZEL NUTS, OR FILBERTS—May be made in macaroons, or meringues.

COCOANUT CAKE OR CANDY.—Take cocoanut

meat from the shell, pare off the black rind and grate it on a coarse grater, or chip it fine, have half a pound of it; to half a pound of loaf sugar, put two tablespoonfuls of water; when it is dissolved put it over the fire, let it become boiling hot, then stir in the cocoanut, continue to stir it until it is thick, take care not to burn it; pour it on a well buttered pan or marble slab, cut it in whatever forms you think proper when nearly cold.

PISTACHIO BISCOTTES.—Mix together in a pan, quarter of a pound of powdered sugar, quarter of a pound of flour, dried and sifted; and the yolks of five eggs; beat them for ten minutes; add two ounces of pistachios, taken from the shells: then spread it on buttered baking-tins, ten inches long, and five wide; make it of an equal thickness; strew over it two ounces of pistachios, cut crosswise; put this in a slow oven for forty or fifty minutes; then take it out, cut it in pieces rather more than two inches long, and half an inch wide; return them to the oven for a few minutes to dry; almonds may be used instead of pistachios.

PISTACHIO BISCUIT.—Take a pound of pistachio nuts, two ounces of sweet almonds, the whites of sixteen eggs, and the yolks of eight, two ounces of flour, and a pound of powder sugar; blanch and pound the pistachios and almonds, moistening occasionally with the white of egg; beat the whites of the eggs to a high froth, and the yolks with half of the sugar, and the yellow rind of a lemon grated; when both are thoroughly beaten, put them together, beat constantly; whilst doing so, sift over the remainder of the sugar and the flour, then add the almonds and pistachios; make some paper cases, put in the biscuits half as thick as a finger, bake in a moderate oven twenty-five minutes, whip the white of an egg with a tablespoonful of fine sugar, to a smooth paste, and brush the biscuits over with it.

To Make a Pyramid *of Cocoanut Drops, Maccaroons, or Meringue.*—To half a pound of loaf sugar, put an ounce of gum arabic, and two tablespoonsful of water, stir it until it is all dissolved, then set it over a slow fire, stirring it all the time, until it is like melted glue.

Have a tin mould, or make one of stiff paper, rub butter over the outside to prevent the candy from sticking, set it firmly on a plate or table; begin at the bottom, by putting a row around it, stick them together with the prepared sugar, (which must be kept hot,) when this row is cold and firm, add another above it, let that also become firm, then add another, and so continue until the pyramid is finished. When the cement is cold and firm, the pyramid may be taken from the form.

These pyramids are used for ornamental desserts or supper tables, and if there is but one, occupy the centre of the table; when there are several, the centre one should be the largest, and different from the other two, one of which should be placed on either side of it, and at some little distance from it; supposing the centre one to be of almond maccaroons, let those on either side be of meringues or cocoanut maccaroons, or drops; let the centre one be ornamented with a sprig of flowers, or a sugar figure at the top.

These ornamental pieces are suitable for fine desserts or supper table, and should remain untouched whilst the pastry, ices, &c. are served, then these should be broken with a knife, and the fragments placed on the table on flat dishes.

A very ornamental pyramid may be made thus: make a form of the desired height and size, of paste board or stiff paper, make a wreath of green leaves or of green tissue paper, fringed as for motto papers; begin at the top, and wind it round the pyramid, about half an inch apart, until the bottom is reached, arrange among it at intervals, flowers made of colored paper, or flower mottoes or natural flowers; put a crowning ornament at the top, either a choice flower or flowers, or some delicate sugar ornament, let this be for the centre of the table, on either side put boquets in high glass stands, or moulds of jelly or cream.

To Make Mottoes.—Cut white and colored tissue paper in pieces about four inches in width, and five long; cut the two longest sides in fringe of one inch depth; put in the centre of each a sugar or burnt almond, or lozenge, and a motto verse or two; fold the paper neatly around it, leaving the fringed ends out, twist each end close to the candy, then spread out the fringe to look full, like a tassel; so continue until you have enough.

Mottoes may be made in flowers or other fancy forms.

DIRECTIONS

For Setting Refreshment Tables.

Tables of refreshment for an evening party, or New Year's day, are generally arranged in the following manner:

A long table running through the centre of the room, or placed against the broad side of it, covered with a white damask cloth for confectionary, jellies, pastry, cakes, &c.; and a table at each side of the mantel recess or pier; the one for sandwiches, oysters, salads, celery, and wines, if used; the other for chocolate, lemonade, and punch, (if used.)

Or all are sometimes placed on one long table, in this manner:

Cakes, confectionery, jellies, etc., in the centre; at one end, coffee and lemonade, &c.; at the other, oysters, sandwiches, celery, wines, &c.

A long table may be placed at one side of the room, through the centre, or across the end.

In either case, the most ornamental dishes, such as pyramids or stands of jelly, are to be placed in the centre, the smaller ones surrounding it; those directly opposite each other should correspond, both in shape and size.

The dessert for a fine dinner is similar to a supper table; puddings occupying the place of cakes.

The pastry should first be placed on the table, at some little distance apart; next the puddings, charlotte de russe, and ice creams, or jellies and blancmange, and nuts and raisins, together with ripe fruits.

Cherries, grapes, pears, or small apples, peaches,

&c., may be made very ornamental, whether for the table or for evening refreshment, in the following manner:

For grapes, get the most delicate grape leaves, lay them in cold water for a short time, take a small brush like a lather brush, choose the finest bunches of grapes, pick off every imperfection, and with the brush polish them carefully, taking off with it whatever dust may be between them; lay each cluster carefully by, until all are done, then take the leaves from the water, wipe them dry; lay them neatly around the edge of a flat dish, with the stems inward, to cover the plate; lay bunches of grapes around on the leaves, put a bunch in the centre, put another row of leaves upon the grapes, quite within the circumference of the first, lay grapes on it; make another row of leaves and grapes, if you wish.

For peaches, take off all the down with a brush and arrange them in the same way as grapes, with peach or vine leaves between; or put a row of leaves, on them a row of peaches, another row of leaves, and on them bunches of grapes.

Yellow or green burgalo pears make a pretty appearance arranged with grapes and leaves, or with only leaves.

Oranges, apples, and green grapes should always have leaves or mottoes arranged with them.

Cluster raisins are served in place of grapes, with soft shell almonds.

Cherries may be served with their stems on, in a glass bowl, or heaped on flat dishes.

For evening parties, baskets of mixed small cakes, such as lady-cake, macaroons, lady-fingers, almond spice biscuit, composition cake, pound-cake cut small, and other small fancy cakes, are sent round twice during the early part of the evening, with lemonade and glasses of water, and a tray of wine, if used.

Jellies, ice cream and charlotte de ruse or blancmange should be sent in at a late hour, when nearly time for dispersing, and with them or after, a tray with glasses of ice water, and small cakes and wines, and cordials if liked.

Raspberry and strawberry syrup, diluted with water and orgeat is much used instead of lemonade, or with it; small tumblers without handles are used for these; they should not be much more than half-filled.

For a small winter party, lemonade, syrup-water and cakes may be sent around twice during the evening, and will be sufficient.

Or, trays with cups of coffee and tea, with powdered white sugar and cream, followed by a tray of small plates, light biscuit, or short cake or cream cakes, buttered hot, and plates of tongue or ham sliced thin, or dishes of pickled oysters; and later in the evening, fancy cakes with jellies and preserves. This is called a tea-party. Sandwiches may be served instead of hot teacakes, and are much to be preferred, unless a table is set.

When a table is set, which is best, if possible let it be long enough to seat all comfortably, and not very broad, not certainly more than three feet and a half wide.

Put a stand of flowers, or a pyramid in the centre, and if the table is long, have one near each end; place plates of bread and butter sandwich at every corner, and once or twice on either side, if necessary; or instead, let there be small teacakes buttered hot, with plates of tongue and ham sliced very thin, between; place regularly round, cakes of fruit and pound-cake, and baskets of cut-cake, and small fancy ditto; intersperse jellies or jams and preserves with blancmange or grated cocoanut and charlotte de russe or trifle, or floating-island wigs, and tea-rusk may be buttered and served hot.

Have tea and coffee at either end of the table, or let it be served from a side-table.

A tea-table may be set with only the substantials, such as hot cakes, sandwiches, oysters pickled, and tea and coffee; and when they are removed. jellies, blancmange, floating island or trifle, or charlotte de russe, and fancy cakes, preserves, brandied fruit, grated cocoanut to take their places, with glasses of cold water, and wines and cordials if used.

The ornaments and large cakes remain on from first to last.

This makes two courses, and is sufficient without any other refreshment during the evening.

For supper, see "directions for setting refreshment tables." page 325.

An oyster supper is expected to be supplied with oysters in every variety of dressing; roasted in the shell is one of the favorites; also stewed and pickled; oyster chowder and pies with scolloped oysters may also be served.

Dressed celery, celery in glasses and pickles, with bread and butter sandwich, and rolls or crackers, and cold butter should be served with oysters.

With roasted oysters it is necessary to have a small tub or vessel to receive the shells, between each two chairs, and coarse napkins at each plate. Coffee and porter is served at oyster suppers. Tureens or deep dishes of large uncooked oysters should be on the table. Chicken or lobster salad may be served at any but oyster suppers with or without oysters; also broiled or stewed birds or game. At ordinary supper parties it is not customary to sit at table; when a hot supper is served it becomes necessary; hot suppers are by no means popular amongst us.

The information contained in the last few pages, is what has been gathered by observation and study of the subject, and to some it may prove acceptable—such as like it not nor require it, may pass it by without offence.

SANDWICHES.—These are made of different articles, but always in the same manner.

Cold biscuit sliced thin and buttered, and a very thin slice of boiled ham or tongue, or beef, between each two slices.

Home-made bread cuts better for sandwiches than baker's bread; a loaf baked for this purpose is best; take the size of a quart bowl, of risen dough, mould it in a roll, about three inches in diameter, and bake it half an hour in a quick oven.

For bread and butter sandwich cut the bread in slices, not thicker than a dollar piece, spread it evenly with sweet butter before cutting it; let the butter be very thin, lay two slices, the buttered sides together, for each sandwich; when you have enough, arrange them on flat dishes, make them in a circle around the middle of the plate as a common centre, one lapping nearly over the other; put a sprig of parsley in the centre.

Sandwiches may be made with cheese, sliced very thin, between each two slices of buttered bread, also of cold boiled eggs sliced, for luncheon; stewed fruit or jelly or preserve spread thin over buttered bread, makes a fine sandwich for lunch.

Any cold meat sliced thin may be made a sandwich; it is generally spread with made mustard;

the most delectable are those made with boiled smoked tongue or ham.

To Make Coffee.—Get a coffee pot of block tin for making coffee, it is the best, and also the easiest mode. Take off the cover of the top, remove all the loose apparatus, and put in it dry coffee finely ground, up to the inside rim near the bottom, then replace the strainers, press them down into the coffee, fill the top with boiling water, put on the cover and set it on to a hot hearth or on the back of the range when all has run through, fill it again and so continue until the coffee is of the strength desired. If made very strong it may be reduced when served, by half filling the cups with boiling hot milk or water.

To make Chocolate.—Scrape or grate the chocolate, take a tablespoonful of it for half a pint, half-and-half milk and water; put it in a perfectly clean stew-pan, make the chocolate a smooth paste with a little cold milk, and stir it into the milk and water when it boils, cover it for ten minutes or longer; add sugar to taste, unless French chocolate is used, which is prepared sweet enough.

Serve soda biscuit, or rolls, or toast, with it.

To make Green Tea.—Have ready a kettle of water boiling fast, pour some into the teapot, let it remain for a few minutes, then throw it out; measure a teaspoonful of tea for each two persons, put it in the pot, pour on it about a gill of boiling water, cover it close for five minutes, then fill it up; have a covered pitcher of boiling water with it; when two cups are poured from it, fill it up; you will thus keep the strength good and equal.

If the company is large, it is best to have some

of the tea drawn in the covered pitcher, and replenish the tea-pot or urn when it is exhausted.

To MAKE BLACK TEA.—Make as directed for green tea; let it steep, setting on hot coals for ten or fifteen minutes.

HASTY CREAM.—Take a gallon of milk warm from the cow, set it over the fire; when it begins to rise, take it off, and set it by; skim off all the cream, and put it on a plate, then set the stew-pan over the fire again; as soon as it is ready to boil, take it off, and skim again; repeat the skimming until no more cream rises. The milk must not boil.

To KEEP CREAM SWEET.—Cream may be kept sweet twenty-four hours, by scalding it without sugar; by adding as much powdered lump sugar as will make it quite sweet, it may be kept for two days in a cool place.

CREAM SNOW.—Take a pint of sweet cream, mix with it eight teaspoonfuls of white powdered sugar, the whites of two eggs, and a tablespoonful of orange-flower water or a teaspoonful of lemon or vanilla extract; whip it, take off the froth as it rises, and continue to beat it until you have enough.

SYRUP OF CREAM.—Put a pound of white sugar to each pint of fresh sweet cream, boil it, stirring it all the time; put it in a cool place until it is perfectly cold, then put it in one or two-ounce phials, cork and seal them. Prepared in this way, it may be kept for several weeks.

CLOTTED CREAM.—Take four quarts of new

milk from the cow, put it in a pan, and let it stand until the next day; then set it over a very slow fire for half an hour, make it nearly hot, then put it away until it is cold: take off the cream free from milk, beat it smooth with a spoon, sweeten it to taste, and serve with preserves or fruit.

Ice Cream.—Boil a quart of cream, make it sweet with white sugar, flavor with lemon or vanilla extract of orange-flower water; when cold, freeze it as directed to make "Ice Cream." The yolks of three eggs may be beaten, and stirred into it when it is boiling hot.

Cream for freezing may be made boiling hot, then made sweet with loaf sugar, and flavored with vanilla or lemon extract, or with the juice of strawberries, raspberries, or pine-apple; the fruit should be bruised and strained, with a quarter of a pound of sugar to each pint of juice, and stirred into the cream when it is cold.

Vanilla or Lemon Ice Cream.—Take two drachms of vanilla or lemon peel, one quart of milk, half a pound of sugar, a pint of cream, and the yolks of three eggs; beat the yolks well, and stir them with the milk, then add the other ingredients; set it over a moderate fire, and stir it constantly with a silver spoon until it is boiling hot, then take out the lemon peel or vanilla, and, when cold, freeze it.

Ice Cream—May be made thus: Put milk over a gentle fire to boil, stir it occasionally; beat four eggs for each quart until very light, then stir them into the boiling milk, stir it for a few minutes, then set it to become cold; make it very sweet, flavor it to taste, then freeze it. If it is flavored with the juice of berries or pine-apple, bruise the fruit, strain the juice from it, and put it to the cream when cold.

CURRANT-WATER ICE.—Press the juice from ripe currants, strain it clear; to one pint of juice put a pound of loaf sugar, put to it a pint of water, and freeze as directed for cream.

CURRANT-WATER.—Having pressed the juice from ripe currants, strain it clear; put to each pint nearly a pound of white sugar, reduce it with ice-water to your taste; grate nutmeg over, and serve. This is a fine cooling summer beverage. Serve sponge cake with it.

LEMON OR ORANGE SUGAR.—Grate the yellow outside from fresh skin lemons or oranges, put to it an equal quantity of powdered loaf sugar, dry it, and keep it for flavoring cakes, pies, &c.

LEMON OR ORANGE-WATER.—Peel the outside from lemons or oranges, pound it fine in a mortar, pour boiling water over to cover it; cover it close; when cold, bottle it for use.

ROSE BRANDY.—Put fresh-gathered rose-leaves in a bottle, cover them with brandy; for flavoring cakes or puddings.

To KEEP LEMON JUICE.—To every pint of juice put a pound of double-refined sugar; stir it until it is all dissolved, then bottle it; put a teaspoonful of sweet oil on the top, and cork it close. When wanted for use, apply a bit of raw cotton to the oil, and it will immediately be absorbed. Keep it in ounce vials. Put a large tablespoonful of this juice to half a gill of ice-water; or, for hot lemonade use boiling water.

To MAKE LEMONADE.—Squeeze the juice from twelve fine lemons, put to it one pound of loaf sugar, pour a little boiling water to the peels, cover them; when cold, strain it off, and put it to the juice and sugar; put the prepared juice in decanters, and make with ice-water in summer, or boiling water in winter; put a wineglass of this to half a pint of water.

Lemons sliced as thin as a dollar-piece, and the edge cut in notches or points, may be put one in each glass.

Crushed raspberries or strawberries, or thin-sliced pine-apple, may be added to lemon.

ORANGE SHERBET.—Squeeze the juice from oranges, pour boiling water on the peel, and cover it closely, boil water and sugar (a pint to a pound,) to a syrup, skim it clear; when all are cold, mix the syrup juice and peel infusion with as much water as may be necessary for a rich taste, strain it, and set the vessel containing it on ice. Or it may be made the same as lemonade, using one lemon with half a dozen oranges.

ORANGE-WATER ICE.—Take ten or twelve fine oranges, take off the peel, divide them in quarters, and after taking out the pips, pound them with the grated rinds of two oranges, put them into a coarse cloth, and press out all the juice, and put to it a pint of water, in which is dissolved half a pound of sugar. Freeze as directed for ice cream.

ORGEAT.—Take the skins from half a pound of shelled almonds, pound them to a very fine paste, adding a little water occasionally to keep them from oiling. Mix half a gallon of water and some orange flower water, or lemon extract, with two pounds of sugar, to the paste, beat it well together, then strain it two or three times through a jelly bag, stirring it with a wooden spoon.

Serve it in small tumblers half filled, or in decanters. Set it on ice before serving.

STRAWBERRY SHERBET.—Take fourteen ounces of picked strawberries, crush them in a mortar, then add to them a quart of water; pour this into a basin, with a lemon sliced, and a teaspoonful of orange flower water; let it remain for two or three hours.

Put eighteen ounces of sugar into another basin, cover it with a cloth, through which pour the strawberry juice, after as much has run through as will; gather up the cloth, and squeeze out as much juice as possible from it; when the sugar is all dissolved, strain it again; set the vessel containing it on ice, until ready to serve.

STRAWBERRY SYRUP.—Take fine ripe strawberries, crush them in a cloth, and press the juice from them; to each pint of it, put a pint of simple syrup, boil gently for one hour, then let it become cold, and bottle it; cork and seal it. When served, reduce it to taste with water, set it on ice, and serve in small tumblers half filled.

RASPBERRY SYRUP.—Make as directed for strawberry, and serve with sponge or other cake, cut small.

PINE-APPLE SYRUP.—Take the rough coat from a ripe pine-apple, cut it small, and pound it fine, put a teacup of water to it, and squeeze the juice from it through a cloth, put this to enough simple syrup to flavor it, boil it over a gentle fire for a short time, when cold, bottle it; mix it with water to your taste, set it on ice; serve in small tumblers.

LEMON SYRUP.—Flavor simple syrup with extract of lemon.

VANILLA SYRUP.—Flavor simple syrup with vanilla extract.

TO MAKE ICE CREAM.—Ice pots for making ice cream are of two sorts, block-tin and pewter. Of these, pewter is best, the substance to be iced congealing more gradually than in the former, an object much to be desired; when the ice is formed too quickly, it is apt to be rough and coarse, like hail, especially if it is not well worked with a spatula or flat wooden spoon.

The other utensils necessary for the operation, are a deep pail six or eight inches larger in diameter than the ice pot, with a vent peg at the bottom, and a wooden spatula ten or twelve inches long; then having put the cream (or whatever it may be,) into the ice pot, put a layer of ice broken fine, and mixed with coarse salt in the pail; set on the ice pot, fill the space around the sides with ice broken fine, and mixed with coarse salt, nearly to the top of the pot; take care that none of the ice gets into it, strew over the top of the ice a large handful of coarse salt, cover it with a woolen cloth, and let it stand for fifteen minutes; then take the cover from the ice pot, and with the spatula, stir the contents up together, so that those parts which touch the sides of the mould, and consequently congeal first, may be mixed with the liquid in the middle, work it well for ten minutes or so, then replace the cover; take the ice pot by the ears, and stir it back and forth for quarter of an hour, then open the mould a second time, and stir the cream as before. Continue these operations alternately until the cream or whatever it is to be frozen, is perfectly smooth, and free from lumps.

During the process, take care to let out the water which will collect at the bottom of the pail, by means of the vent peg; keep the ice pressed close to the pot.

It is to be served in a mould; after having nicely frozen the cream, put some of it in, press it close to the shape, put in more, and press it close until the mould is full, cover it, and set it in a pail of fine ice, mixed with salt, for one hour; then take it out, wipe the mould dry with a cloth dipped in hot water, then turn it into a deep plate, and serve quickly.

Note to twelfth edition.

Austin's Magic Freezer has superseded all others for freezing creams, and may be had at Berrian's, 601 Broadway.

SYLLABUB.—Take the juice of a large lemon, and the yellow rind pared thin, a glass of brandy, two glasses of white wine, and a quarter of a pound of powdered sugar. Put these ingredients into a pan, and let them remain one night, the next day add a pint of thick cream, and the whites of two eggs beaten together, beat them all together to a fine froth; serve it in jelly glasses.

WINE SANGAREE.—Put a gill of wine (port or Madeira,) into a tumbler, add to it water, hot or cold, nearly to fill it, sweeten with loaf sugar to taste, grate nutmeg over, and serve with sponge cake, lady cake, or Savoy biscuit, cut small.

Wine Jelly.—Into a clean porcelain lined kettle put a quart of water, add to it a pound of crushed sugar, the white, and shells of two eggs. When it is boiling hot, put to it a pint of Madeira wine, and a wineglass of pale brandy with the juice of two lemons and a small stick of cinnamon, stir the whole well together, and having dissolved an ounce and a half of isinglass or gelatine, in a little hot water, stir it in, continue to boil gently, for half an hour or more, then having pared off the yellow rind of the lemons, put them into the jelly strainer, pour the jelly over, and let it drain slowly through. Should it not be perfectly clear, make it hot and run it through a second time, and set it in a cool place.

Calf's Feet Jelly.—Wash and clean a set of large feet, boil them in eight quarts of water, until reduced to four, then strain it, and set it to cool; when cold, take off every particle of fat from the top, take up the jelly, leaving any sediment that may be at the bottom; set it over the fire again, and when it is dissolved, before it is hot, add the whites of six eggs beaten to a high froth, the juice of six lemons, and a pint of Madeira wine, sweeten it to taste, with fine white sugar, let it boil, (skimming it well,) until it is perfectly clear, put some of the yellow skins of the lemons in the jelly bag, and strain the jelly through; this gives a fine amber color; if it is not a good color, strain it again; if not sufficiently firm a jelly, boil over a gentle fire until it is so. A wine glass of pale brandy may be added and a stick of cinnamon.

Calf's Head Cheese.—Take the meat from making the jelly, chop it fine, season with pepper and salt, tie it in a cloth, and press it.

Ivory Dust Jelly.—Boil one pound of ivory dust in five pints of water until reduced to a quart, then strain it and add a quart more water; boil it again to a stiff jelly, add the juice of a lemon and the yellow rind pared thin. Sweeten to taste, strain it into a mould.

JAUNE MANGE.—Break up and boil an ounce of isinglass in rather more than half a pint of water until it is melted, strain it; then add the juice of two large oranges, a gill of white wine, and the yolks of four eggs beaten and strained; sweeten to taste, and stir it over a gentle fire till it boils up; dip a mould in cold water and pour the preparation into it.

To CLARIFY SUGAR FOR CANDIES.—To every pound of sugar put a teacup of water, put it in a brass or copper preserving kettle, over a slow fire, for half an hour, put to it a small quantity of isinglass and gum arabic dissolved together; this will cause all impurities to rise to the surface, skim it off as it rises, boil until it is thick candy; flavor to taste.

All kinds of sugar for candies are boiled as above directed. When boiling loaf sugar, add a tablespoonful of rum or vinegar to prevent it becoming too brittle whilst making.

By pulling loaf sugar after it is boiled to candy, you may make it as white as snow; rub your hands with a bit of butter that the candy may not stick to them; loaf sugar after boiling thick, may be pulled until it is white and made in small rolls and twisted a little, and is commonly called little rock or snow. Sugar boiled to candy may be pulled, twisted, rolled and cut in whatever forms you choose.

To MAKE SIMPLE SYRUP.—Put half a pint of

water to each pound of sugar, when it is all dissolved set it over a gentle fire, let it boil for half an hour; when it is clear and boiling hot, spread a wetted napkin over a basin, pour the syrup in and strain it through; flavor to taste.

LEMON CANDY OR ROCK.—To one pound of loaf sugar put a teacup of water, set it over a slow fire, stir it with a spoon until it is all dissolved, put in a little hot rum or vinegar to clear it; take off any scum that rises.

Try when it is done enough by dipping a spoon in it and raising it; if the threads thus formed snap like glass, it is done enough; rub a square tin pan over with a bit of sponge dipped in soft butter, and pour the candy in as thick as a dollar piece; when nearly cold mark it in narrow strips with a knife.

Before pouring it into the pans, chopped cocoanut, sliced almonds or picked hickory nuts may be stirred into it. Brazil nuts taken from the shells, cut in slices and added to it, are very good.

Or this candy may be poured in the pans half an inch thick; to be broken small when cold.

COMMON LEMON CANDY.—Take three pounds of coarse brown sugar; add to it three teacupsful of water, and set it over a slow fire for half an hour, then put to it a little gum arabic, dissolved in hot water; this is to clear it. Continue to take off the scum, as long as it rises. When perfectly clear, try it by dipping a pipe stem first into it and then into cold water, or by taking a spoonful of it into a saucer; if it is done it will snap like glass. Flavor with lemon extract and cut it in sticks; this may be made sour with lemon juice or a little tartaric acid.

CREAM CANDY.—To three pounds of loaf sugar put half a pint of water, set it over a slow fire for half an hour; then add to it a teaspoonful of gum arabic, dissolved, and a tablespoonful of vinegar. When boiled to candy, bright and clear, take it off; flavor with vanilla, lemon, rose, or orange.

Rub the hands over with a bit of sweet butter, and pull the candy between them until it is white; then stretch it out in wide thin strips and cut it in lengths; or make it in rolls and twist, or braid it.

COMMON TWIST.—To three pounds of common sugar put one pint of water and boil it over a slow fire for half an hour, then skim it clear; continue to boil it until it is candy; try some in a saucer. When boiled enough, take it off, rub the hands with a little butter, take that which is cooled, and pull it as you would molasses candy, until it is white, then twist or braid it, and cut it in strips.

PEPPERMINT, ROSE, OR HOARHOUND CANDY.— Make as for lemon candy, flavor with essence of peppermint or rose, or finely powdered hoarhound.

MOLASSES CANDY (TAFFY.)—Put a pint of common molasses in a stewpan, over a slow fire, let it boil, stir it to prevent its running over the top, or if necessary, take it off; when it has boiled more than half an hour try it, by taking some in a saucer; when cold, if it is brittle and hard, it is done; flavor with lemon, sassafras, or vanilla, and pour it quarter or half an inch deep in buttered tin pans. Shelled peanuts, (ground nuts) or almonds may be stirred into it, enough to make it thick, or but a few.

Molasses candy may be made a light color by pulling it in your hands, having first rubbed them over with a bit of butter, to prevent the candy sticking to them, during the process.

DIRECTIONS

FOR PRESERVING FRUITS.

TO GREEN FRUIT FOR PRESERVING IN SUGAR OR VINEGAR.—Apples, pears, limes, plums, apricots, &c., for preserving or pickling may be greened thus:

Put vine-leaves under, between, and over the fruit in a preserving kettle; put small bits of alum, the size of a pea, say a dozen bits to a kettle full; put enough water to cover the fruit, cover the kettle close to exclude all outer air, set it over a gentle fire, let them simmer; when they are tender drain off the water; if they are not a fine green let them become cold, then put vine-leaves and a bit of saleratus or soda with them, and set them over a slow fire until they begin to simmer; a bit of soda or saleratus the size of a small nutmeg will have the desired effect; then spread them out to cool, after which, finish as severally directed.

Spinach may be used for coloring green, instead of vine leaves.

TO COLOR FRUIT YELLOW.—Boil the fruit with fresh skin lemons in water to cover them, until it is tender; then take it up, spread it on dishes to cool, and finish as may be directed.

To Color Preserves Pink.—By putting in with it a little cochineal, powdered fine, then finish in the syrup.

Preserving Kettles—Should be broad, and not very deep, with a handle at each side; there should be a closely-fitting cover. To preserve in very small quantities, a small ketttle is requisite.

A charcoal furnace or coal stove, or the side of a range, is equally good for preserving. A furnace has the advantage of being portable, so that they may be used in the open air, if necessary.

Jelly bags of fine cambric or flannel are used; these may be made like a lady's reticule, with a string by which to close the top and suspend it whilst dripping. (See tin strainers, page 348.)

Crushed or loaf sugar should be used for best preserves; it is not much higher in price than the best light brown sugar; there is, however, sufficient difference to make it economy for preserving for domestic use, since it is equally nice, except to the eye.

Crushed or loaf sugar need only be dissolved, and made hot, before putting in the fruit.

Refined sugar, which is next in price and quality, need only be dissolved, boiled, and skimmed, to make it clear.

Strawberries, raspberries, cherries, currants, or any other red fruit, should have double-refined sugar, since with brown sugar the color of the fruit and that of the sugar combined, makes a dingy reddish brown, which is not pleasing to the eye; neither will it answer for green fruit.

Summer fruits require more care to keep, than

those done later. A cool, dark closet, is the best place to keep preserves.

Small glass jars, or wide-mouthed bottles, are best for liquid preserves. The best white earthenware, or stone-china small jars, are good.

Pint tumblers of common glass, or white earthenware pots, are proper for jellies, marmalade, or jam.

For peaches, quinces, plums, &c. large glass jars, or stoneware pots, with small tops, are good. There is little or no difficulty in keeping preserves, (if they are properly put up,) after the summer-heat is past.

Glass jars may first be covered with tissue-paper, and fastened against the jar with a little sugar boiled in water, and then tin tight-fitting covers put over.

Glass bottles should first be corked tight, then dipped into coarse sealing-wax, melted.

Jellies, jam, &c. may be secured by first pressing a piece of tissue-paper, fitting the top of the glass closely upon it; then wet another piece with sugar boiled to candy; paste it over the top of the tumbler, and over that put a third piece; this will perfectly secure them. Large jars may be secured in the same manner—putting several pieces of tissue-paper, and securing them each separately with the melted sugar or candy; and over this a close-fitting cover may be put, or a bladder tied over: this last precaution is not necessary.

Glass is best for keeping preserves, as it may then be examined without opening the jars.

Should a thick mould appear on the top of preserves, it must not be disturbed, as it is no evidence of spoiling, but will rather serve to keep them.

Foam or frothiness is the sign of fermentation; and as soon as it is perceived, turn the preserves from the jar or pot into a preserving kettle, and set it over a gentle fire; take off the skim or foam as it rises; when no more rises, take out the fruit with a skimmer, and, having washed the jar with cold water, and perfectly dried it at the fire, put in the fruit; give the syrup one more boil, skim it, and put it in a pitcher to settle; when nearly cold, pour it carefully over the fruit, leaving whatever sediment there may be at the bottom. When perfectly cold, cover them as at first.

To CLARIFY SUGAR, *for Preserving*.—Put into a preserving pan as many pounds of sugar as you wish; to each pound of sugar put half a pint of water, and the white of an egg to every four pounds; stir it together until the sugar is dissolved; then set it over a gentle fire; stir it occasionally, and take off the scum as it rises: after a few boilings up, the sugar will rise so high as to run over the side of the pan; to prevent which, take it from the fire for a few minutes, when it will subside, and leave time for skimming. Repeat the skimming until a slight scum or foam only will rise; then take off the pan, lay a slightly wetted napkin over a basin, and then strain the sugar through it.

Put the skimmings into a basin; when the sugar is clarified, rinse the skimmer and basin with a glass of cold water, and put it to the scum, and set it by for common purposes.

To BOTTLE FRUIT. — Cherries, strawberries, sliced pine-apple, plums, apricots, gooseberries, &c. may be preserved in the following manner—to be used the same as fresh fruit.

Gather the fruit before it is very ripe; put it in wide-mouthed bottles made for the purpose; fill them as full as they will hold, and cork them tight; seal the corks; put some hay in a large saucepan, set in the bottles, with hay between them, to prevent their touching; then fill the saucepan with water to the necks of the bottles, and set it over the fire until the water is nearly boiling, then take it off; let it stand until the bottles are cold, then keep them in a cool place until wanted, when the fruit will be found equal to fresh.

To Preserve Pine-Apples *without Cooking.*—The best pine-apples for preserving are those known as the sugar-loaf and bird's-eye; these are richer in flavor, and the coat or skin being less rough, they are less troublesome to pare; they should not be very ripe.

Pare off the rough outside of the pine-apple, and cut it in thin slices, (not much thicker than a dollar-piece;) have ready a pound of finely-ground white sugar for each pound of fruit; put sugar half an inch deep at the bottom of a small glass jar, then put in a layer of sliced pine-apple nearly an inch deep; on that put sugar as thick as at first, press it down with a spoon as closely as possible; then another layer of pine-apple, then one of sugar, and so continue until the jar is full—sugar being the last.

Put closely-fitting corks in the top, and dip them in melted sealing-wax; set them in a cool dark place until cold weather; or the jars may be secured by pasting tissue-paper, wet with melted sugar, over first; then put a closely-fitting tin cover over.

Many persons use more than a pound of sugar for a pound of fruit. One pound will be found sufficient.

Pine-apples preserved in this way, have much the taste of brandy fruit. They are much liked.

Pine-apples bottled as before directed, should

be served with sugar strewed over, the same as fresh fruit.

PINE-APPLE PRESERVE.—Twist off the top and bottom, and pare off the rough outside of pine-apples; then weigh them and cut them in slices, chips, or quarters, or cut them in four or six, and shape each piece like a whole pine-apple; to each pound of fruit put a teacup of water; put it in a preserving kettle, cover it, and set it over the fire, and let them boil gently until they are tender and clear; then take them from the water, by sticking a fork in the centre of each slice, or with a skimmer, into a dish.

Put to the water, white sugar, a pound for each pound of fruit; stir it until it is all dissolved; then put in the pine-apple, cover the kettle, and let them boil gently until transparent throughout; when it is so, take it out, let it cool, and put it in glass jars: let the syrup boil or simmer gently until it is thick and rich, and when nearly cool pour it over the fruit. The next day secure the jars as before directed.

Pine-apple done in this way, is a beautiful and delicious preserve. The usual manner of preserving it, by putting it into the syrup without first boiling it, makes it little better than sweetened leather

PINE-APPLE JELLY.—Take a perfectly ripe and sound pine-apple, cut off the outside, cut it in small pieces; bruise them, and to each pound put a teacup of water; put it in a preserving-kettle over the fire, cover the kettle, and let them boil for twenty minutes; then strain it, and squeeze it through a bit of muslin: for each pound of fruit take a pound of sugar, put a teacup of water to each pound; set it over the fire until it is dissolved; then add the pine-apple juice: for each quart of the syrup, clarify an ounce of the best isinglass, and stir it in; let it boil, until by taking some on a plate to cool, you find it a stiff jelly. Secure it as directed.

To PRESERVE WHOLE PINE-APPLES.—Get small sized pine-apples, not perfectly ripe; twist off the green top; pare the fruit neatly with a sharp small knife, and with care take out the tough centre, running from top to bottom; take from the green top all but five or six of the inner leaves, and put them and the pine-apples into a preserving kettle; put to them half a pint of water for each pound of fruit; cover the kettle close, and set it over a moderate fire; when they look a uniform color, and are tender, take them carefully on a flat dish: throw a napkin over them; to the water in which they were boiled, put a pound of double refined sugar to each pound of fruit; stir it until it is dissolved; set it over the fire, and let it become boiling hot; then put in the pine-apples and green tops; cover the preserving kettle, and let them boil gently, until they are almost transparent, and of the same appearance throughout: then take them carefully into a tureen, or large glass jar: as soon as they are cooled, put the tops in their places; boil the syrup until it is thick, and not more than half the original quantity; then turn it over the fruit, and when it is cold, secure it with paper, and a close fitting cover.

TIN JELLY STRAINERS.—An excellent article for straining jellies may be procured at Berrian's, 601 Broadway, and which will be found both an economy and a convenience and worth twice its price. It is a double vessel, the outer one to be filled with boiling water. Into the inside put a piece of thin cambric or book muslin, set it in a place where it will be undisturbed, set a vessel for receiving the jelly under the spout, and then pour it into the strainer, let it drip slowly until it has all run through. The water in the outer vessel being hot, the jelly continues liquid until it has all run through.

Should any thing occur to prevent the jelly being sufficiently clear, make it hot, and having rinsed the muslin, replace it and run the jelly through a second time.

To Keep Quinces.—Quinces, to keep, must be gathered when quite ripe, and perfectly sound. Rub off the down, quarter and core them, and put them in wide mouthed bottles, and finish as directed for bottling fruit.

Quinces for Preserving—Should be perfectly ripe and sound. The large apple-quince is preferred for making jelly.

Pare and halve the quinces, and take out the cores; to each pound of fruit, after it is thus prepared, put a teacup of water; put them into a preserving kettle, over the fire; cover it, and let them boil gently, until a broom splint will pierce them; then take them from the water with a skimmer, on to a flat dish; fold a napkin over them; to the water in which they were boiled, put one pound of white sugar to each pound of quinces; stir it until the sugar is dissolved and hot; then put in the quinces; let them boil gently, until they are clear, and the syrup is thick; cut one open; if it is not one color all the way through, let them boil longer, until it is so. Take them into whatever you intend keeping them in; let the syrup cool, and settle for a few minutes; then turn it over the fruit; next day, cover them as directed.

If the quinces are done in brown sugar, put to it the white of one egg for each pound; stir it in, and having boiled the fruit as directed, (with a teacup of water for each pound,) pour the water on the sugar; stir it until it is dissolved; then set it over the fire; take off the scum as it rises: should it be likely to boil over, set it off, or at one side: when no more scum rises, only a light foam, put in the quinces, cover them, and let them boil gently, until they are clear, and a uniform color throughout, and the syrup is thick; then take them into the pot or jar with a skimmer; boil the syrup for a few minutes longer, and turn it over the fruit; the next day cover and secure as directed.

The skins of quinces may be boiled with very little water, until they are soft; then mash them; put them in a bag of muslin, and strain the liquor from them. This may be put with the preserve, or boiled with apples and sugar, to make a jelly; the seed are not fit to use, since they make a jelly or syrup ropy. Quinces are very fine, preserved according to this receipt.

QUINCES IN JELLY SYRUP.—Pare, halve and core as many fine quinces as you wish; take an equal weight of white crushed sugar; put a layer of the quinces in a preserving kettle, turning the core side up; fill the places of the cores with sugar, and strew some over them; put another layer of quinces; fill the cores, and strew them in the same way, until all the sugar and quinces are used; put over them a teacup of water for each pound of fruit; cover the preserving kettle, and set them over a brisk fire, to boil quickly, until the quinces are tender, and the syrup clear. In the meantime, cut some rich tart apples small, and put them into a stew-pan, with very little water; boil them until soft; then put them in a bag, drain the liquor from them; and after taking the quinces from the syrup, put the liquor in, boil it for half an hour; then take it from the fire, let it settle for a few minutes; then pour it over them. When perfectly cold, cover and secure as directed.

To half a peck of apples, after paring, coring, and cutting them small, put a teacup of water; cover them, and let them boil until soft; then drain the liquor from them through a jelly-bag, without pressing it; the pulp may be sweetened and spiced, for tart or sauce. This quantity will be enough for fifty fine quinces.

QUINCE MARMALADE.—Gather the fruit when fully ripe; pare, quarter and core it; boil the skins with as many teacupfuls of water as you have pounds of quinces; when they are soft, mash them, and strain the water from them, and put it to the quinces; boil them until they are soft enough to mash them fine; rub them through a sieve; put to the pulp as many pounds of sugar; stir them together, and set them over a gentle fire, until it will fall from a spoon, like jelly; or try some in a saucer. If it jellies when cold, it is enough.

Put it in pots or tumblers, and when cold, secure as directed for jelly.

QUINCE JELLY.—Quinces for jelly should not be quite ripe, they should be a fine yellow, rub off the down from them, core them, and cut them small; put them in a preserving kettle, with a teacup of water for each pound, let them stew gently until soft, without mashing, put them in a thin muslin bag with the liquor, press them very slightly; to each pint of the liquor put a pound of sugar; stir it until it is all dissolved, then set it over the fire, and let it boil gently, until by cooling some on a plate, you find it a good jelly, then turn it into pots or tumblers, and when cold, secure as directed for jellies.

QUINCE AND APPLE JELLY.—Cut small, and core an equal weight of tart apples and quinces; put the quinces into a preserving kettle, with water to cover them, cover and set it over the fire until they are soft, then add the apples, let them boil until they are almost a pulp, (there should be enough water to cover them,) then put all into a jelly bag, and strain without pressing it; to each pint of the liquor put a pound of white sugar, put it over the fire, and let it boil gently, until by trying some on a flat plate, you find it a fine jelly; when cool, put it in pots or tumblers, the next day cover as directed.

After making the best jelly, squeeze the juice from the pulp, put a teacup of clean brown sugar to a pint of it, boil it, taking off the scum as it rises; when it is a nice jelly, put it in pots.

QUINCE CHEESE.—Pare and core ripe quinces, cut them small, put the parings into a preserving kettle, turn a plate over them, large enough to cover them, then put in the cut quinces, with a small teacup of water for each pound, cover the kettle close, and set it over a gentle fire until they are quite soft, then take them out; strain the water from the parings, to brown sugar, half a pound for each pound of cut quinces, set it over the fire, and stir it until it is dissolved; let it boil, taking off the scum, until only a light foam rises; mash the quinces fine, and put them into the syrup, cover it, and let them boil slowly, (take care that it does not burn,) until it is thick, like a stiff jelly; line earthen flat dishes or boxes with tissue paper, put the marmalade or cheese in to fill them; when cold, lay tissue paper over, and cover with earthen lids. Serve cut in slices for luncheon, tea or supper.

Apples or pears may be put with the quinces, or done in the same manner without the quinces; lemon cut small, should be put with apples or pears, to flavor them.

WATER-MELON PRESERVES.—Cut a water-melon in two, take out the soft inside, leaving only the firm white skin, scrape off the green outside, and cut them in any fancy shapes you choose; stars, crescents, diamonds, and such like, have a pretty appearance.

Color them green, yellow, or pink, by boiling them as directed in remarks at the beginning of this chapter, then spread them out on plates to cool, make the syrup with a pound of sugar and a teacup of water, for each pound of the prepared melon; when the sugar is all dissolved, and hot, put in the melon, let it boil until it is clear, flavor with lemon and ginger, or rose, if colored pink; if they are colored yellow by boiling with lemons, slice the lemons into the syrup; when it is transparent, take the pieces with a skimmer from the syrup, and spread them on flat dishes, let it boil until it is thick; pour it into a pitcher to cool and settle, put the preserve into jars, and pour the syrup carefully over; when cold, cover as directed.

CITRON.—Cut the citron in wedge-shaped slices from stem to bud end, let the outside be nearly an inch thick, take out the seed part, and boil them with lemons, to make them yellow; or green them, as directed at the beginning of this subject, until they are tender, but not soft, then lay them out singly on flat dishes to cool, and finish as directed for water-melon preserve.

Musk-Melon Preserved.—This is begun, continued, and ended, the same as directed for citron.

To Preserve Limes and Lemons.—Green them as directed, then put them in water to cover them, and boil until a straw will pierce the skin through, then make a syrup of one pound of white sugar, and a teacup of water, for each pound of fruit; set it over the fire, when the sugar is all dissolved, and hot, cut a slit on one side of each lime, from end to end, in the middle, or pierce them several times through with a large needle, put them into the syrup, cover the kettle, and let them boil until clear or transparent, put them in pots or jars, boil the syrup quite thick, then turn it over them; when cold, secure as directed.

Lemons may be done in the same manner, or after boiling them tender, cut them in slices or quarters.

Limes and lemons are preserved without the pulp; after having greened and boiled them tender, cut them in two, or only down one side, take out the pulp, make a syrup of sugar, pound for pound, and a teacup of water to each pound of sugar; when it is clear, put in the limes or lemons, and boil gently until they are transparent, then put them in pots with the syrup.

Oranges in Jelly.—Take a dozen of the smallest sized oranges, boil them in three changes of water, until a straw will easily penetrate the skin; take half a pound of white sugar for each pound of oranges, and for each pound of sugar, a small teacup of water; when it is all dissolved, set it over a gentle fire, put in the oranges, cover them, and let them boil gently; when the fruit looks clear, take the oranges up, cut them half way down in quarters, or cut them entirely through; put to the syrup half an ounce of isinglass dissolved in a little hot water, give it one boil, then take some of it into a saucer, if it is not as thick as you wish, boil it a time longer, put the oranges into a deep glass dish, and turn the jelly over them. Apple jelly may be used instead of isinglass.

Lemons may be done in this manner.

This is a highly ornamental dish, and may be made the day before it is wanted. This jelly may be made firm, and the oranges sliced; put an ounce of isinglass to a quart of syrup.

Put the jelly an inch deep in the mould, when it is cold, lay in slices of the preserved orange, put more jelly in, when that is cold, put on more slices, and so continue until the mould is full. When wanted, dip the mould for an instant in hot water, then turn it out on a flat glass dish.

To Preserve Crab Apples or Lady Apples.—Take off the stem, and core them with a pen-knife, without cutting them open, weigh a pound of white sugar for each pound of prepared fruit, put a teacup of water to each pound of sugar, put it over a moderate fire, when the sugar is all dissolved, and hot, put the apples in, let them boil gently until they are clear, then skim them out, and spread them on flat dishes. Boil the syrup until it is thick, put the syrup in whatever they are to be kept, and when the syrup is cooled and settled, pour it carefully over the fruit.

Slices of lemon boiled with the fruit, may be considered an improvement; one lemon is enough for several pounds of fruit.

Crab apples may be preserved whole, with only half an inch of the stem on; three quarters of a pound of sugar for each pound of fruit.

To Preserve Apples.—Pare and core, and cut them in halves or quarters, take as many pounds of the best brown sugar, put a teacup of water to each pound; when it is dissolved, set it over the fire, and when boiling hot, put in the fruit, and let it boil gently until it is clear, and the syrup thick, take the fruit with a skimmer on to flat dishes, spread it to cool, then put it in pots or jars, and pour the jelly over.

Lemons boiled tender in water, and sliced thin, may be boiled with the apples.

To Preserve Pippins in Slices.—Take the fairest pippins, pare them, and cut them in slices quarter of an inch thick, without taking out the cores; boil two or three lemons, and slice them with the apples; take the same weight of white sugar, (or clarify brown sugar,) put half a gill of water for each pound of sugar, dissolve it, and set it over the fire; when it is boiling hot, put in the slices, let them boil very gently until they are clear, then take them with a skimmer and spread them on flat dishes to cool; boil the syrup until it is quite thick, put the slices on flat dishes, and pour the syrup over. These may be done a day before they are wanted; two hours will be sufficient to make a fine dish for dessert or supper.

Apple Jelly.—Pare and core tart, juicy apples, and cut them small, put to them a little water, and boil them in a covered vessel until they are soft, and the liquor glutinous, then strain them without squeezing, put one pound of white sugar to each pint of juice, flavor with lemon extract, and boil until by cooling some in a saucer, you find it a fine jelly, strain it through thin muslin into moulds. Put sugar and grated nutmeg to the apples, from the jelly bag, and stew them to a thick marmalade.

ORANGE JELLY.— Put one quart of water into a sauce-pan with quarter of a pound of hartshorn shavings, or two ounces of isinglass broken small, boil it gently until it is a strong jelly ; take the juice from four large oranges, and two fine lemons, and half the yellow rind from one orange and one lemon, pared thin, put them to the jelly, and make it sweet with loaf sugar, then beat the whites of four eggs to a high froth, mix it in, and let it boil for ten minutes, then run it through a jelly bag once or twice, until it is perfectly clear ; put it in fancy moulds. When you wish to serve it, set the mould for a few seconds in a pan of hot water, turn a flat glass or china dish over the mould, reverse it with the mould upon it, and if the jelly does not immediately loosen, give it a smart tap with the hand.

APPLES IN JELLY.—Pare a dozen Spitzenburg apples, and core them with an apple corer or sharp fruit-knife, without cutting them open ; put them in a preserving kettle with one or two lemons, with water to cover them, boil them very gently, until they are a fine color, and tender, then take them carefully up with a skimmer ; take half a pint of the water in which they were boiled, and half a pound of loaf sugar, let it boil, cut the lemons in thin slices, and put them with the apples into the syrup ; let them boil very slowly, until the apples are clear, then take them into a flat glass dish lay a slice of lemon on the top of each apple; boil the syrup until it is thick, and pour it over them, or dissolve half an ounce of isinglass, and stir it into the syrup, let it boil for five minutes, try some in a saucer, if it is thick enough, strain it over the apples, if not, boil it a little longer first.

This requires but a short time to make, and is a highly ornamental dish for dessert or supper table.

MARMALADE.—This or jam may be made of almost any ripe fruit or fruits, boiled to a pulp, with a little water; the best, however, are peaches, quinces, apples, oranges, and cranberries, &c.

It is usually made, when of ripe fruits, (strawberries or raspberries, for instance,) by crushing fruit and sugar (half a pound or three quarters to a pound of fruit,) together, and boiling it over a gentle fire, to a jellied mass; when done, put it in glass or white earthen ware small pots, and when perfectly cold, cover as directed for jelly.

CANDIED ORANGE OR LEMON PEEL.—Boil the rind from thick skin oranges or lemons, in plenty of water, until they are tender, and the bitterness is out; change the water once or twice, if necessary.

Clarify half a pound of sugar with half a cup of water for each pound of peel; when it is clear, put in the peels, cover them, and boil them until clear, and the syrup almost a candy; then take them out, and lay them on inverted sieves to dry, boil the syrup with additional sugar, then put in the peels, stir them about until the sugar candies around them; then take them on to a sieve, and set them into a warm oven, or before a fire; when perfectly dry, pack them in a wooden box, with tissue paper between.

To Candy Fruit.—After peaches, plumbs, citron, or quinces have been preserved, take it from the syrup, drain it on a sieve; to a pound of loaf sugar, put half a teacup of water, when it is dissolved, set it over a moderate fire, when boiling hot, put in the fruit, stir it continually, until the sugar is candied about it, then take it upon a sieve, and dry it in a warm oven, or before a fire; repeat this two or three times if you wish.

To Preserve Peaches.—Peaches for preserving may be ripe but not soft; cut them in halves, take out the stones, and pare them neatly; take as many pounds of white sugar as of fruit, put to each pound of sugar a teacup of water; stir it until it is dissolved, set it over a moderate fire, when it is boiling hot, put in the peaches, let them boil gently until a pure, clear, uniform color; turn those at the bottom to the top, carefully with a skimmer several times; do not hurry them; when they are clear, take each half up with a spoon, and spread the halves on flat dishes to become cold; when all are done, let the syrup boil until it is quite thick, pour it into a large pitcher, and let it set to cool and settle.

When the peaches are cold, put them carefully into jars, and pour the syrup over them, leaving any sediment which has settled at the bottom, or strain the syrup. Some of the kernels from the peach stones may be put in with the peaches whilst boiling.

Let them remain open one night, then cover as directed.

When brown sugar is used, it is necessary to clarify it; put to each pound of it a teacup of water, and for every four pounds the white of an egg; stir it until the sugar is all dissolved, then set it over the fire, continue to stir it until it is hot, take off the scum as it rises; should it boil so fast as to be in danger of running over, set it off the fire for a few minutes; continue to boil and skim it until clear and only a light foam rises; it is then ready for the fruit.

Peaches will keep perfectly well with seven pounds of sugar to ten of fruit; boil the syrup quite thick.

It is best to do but a few at a time, being less fatiguing and more likely to be carefully done, that they may not be crushed in boiling; peaches should not be boiled so much as to lose their shape.

PEACHES, WHOLE.—Punch the stones from freestone peaches thus: cut around the stem end, then insert a two-pronged fork at the other end, and with it press the stone out, then pare them neatly; to as many pounds of white sugar as of peaches put an equal number of teacups of water, set it over the fire, stir it until hot, then put in the fruit; let it boil very gently until they are clear, and the syrup quite thick, then take them up one at a time very carefully with a large spoon, and lay them on flat dishes to become cold; let the syrup boil a little longer, then turn it into a pitcher to cool and settle; put the peaches into whatever you intend keeping them, and drain the syrup carefully off from any sediment over the fruit. When perfectly cold, cover them as directed.

It is best to do but few pounds at a time.

Or, having stoned and pared the peaches, make the syrup, and pour it boiling hot over them; let them remain until the next day, then put them into a preserving-kettle over a gentle fire, let them boil slowly until they are clear and the syrup rich; then take them on to flat dishes and set them to become cold; crack some of the stones, take the meats from them, take off the brown skin, and put them in the syrup, boil it quite thick; let it settle and cool a little, put the peaches into a jar or pot, pour the syrup over, leaving in the pitcher whatever may have settled at the bottom. The next day, cover as directed.

Cling-stone peaches may be preserved whole, without taking out the stones.

Pour boiling water over ripe but not soft cling-stones, to cover them, cover the dish with a thickly-folded towel until they are cold, then peel off the skins; prepare the syrup, and finish as directed for whole peaches.

BRANDY PEACHES.—Choose fine ripe but not soft cling-stone peaches, brush off the down, put them into a tureen and pour boiling hot water over them, cover them with a thickly-folded cloth for half an hour; when they are nearly cold, pull off the skin; if it will not come off readily, pour over more hot water; make a syrup of half a pound of sugar for each pound of peaches, with a teacup of water for each pound of sugar; when it is boiling hot, put the peaches in, let them boil for a short time, then take them out to cool; boil the syrup quite thick, add to it an equal measure of white brandy, and pour it over the fruit; when perfectly cold, secure it as directed for preserves.

PEACHES, BRANDIED.—Take white peaches, free-stones, brush or wipe the down from them, stick each with a large needle in several places, and put them in cold water to cover them; when all are in, put the kettle over a moderate fire, and keep it scalding hot, without boiling, until the fruit will give to the touch; then take them with a skimmer carefully into cold water, and let them remain ten minutes; after which, drain off the water, and cover them with other; let them remain for ten or fifteen minutes, then drain it off again, and cover lastly with cold water; after they have remained awhile, drain off the water, and put them in bottles. If any of the fruit is in the least degree broken or bruised, lay it aside, as it would spoil the rest.

Take three quarters of a pound of sugar for each pound of peaches, put a teacup of water to each pound of sugar, and set it over the fire; boil it until it is thick, then put with it an equal measure of white brandy, mix it together, and pour it over the fruit.

PEACH MARMALADE.—Peel ripe peaches, stone them, and cut them small; weigh three quarters of a pound of sugar for each pound of cut fruit, and a teacup of water for each pound of sugar; set it over the fire; when it boils, skim it clear, then put in the peaches, let them boil quite fast; mash them fine, and let them boil until the whole is a jellied mass, and thick, then put it in small jars or tumblers; when cold, secure it as directed for jellies. Half a pound of sugar for a pound of fruit, will make nice marmalade.

PEACH JELLY.—Take the late yellow mealy peaches, pare them, and cut them small, mash them fine, and put them over the fire, with a teacup of water for each pound of fruit; stew them for a while, then put them into a jelly-bag, and gently press and wring all the juice from them; add to each pint of juice a pound of loaf sugar; when it is dissolved, set it over the fire, and let it boil, until by cooling some in a saucer, you find it a nice jelly. Less than a pound of sugar may be used for each pound of fruit.

Marmalade is generally preferred to the jelly of peaches.

Another way to make peach jelly, is to stew the peaches with a pint of water for each pound of fruit; boil until it is soft, then strain the liquor from the peaches; to each pint of the liquor, put a pound of loaf sugar and half an ounce of isinglass, dissolved; or some apple jelly. Let it boil up once, then strain it into moulds.

APRICOTS.—These may be preserved in any of the several ways directed for peaches.

TO DRY PEACHES.—Take ripe but not soft peaches, pare them, and take out the stones, and cut them in halves or quarters, or smaller; spread them on flat dishes or boards, and set them where the sun will shine all day upon them; take them in at dusk or sunset; they should not be put out when the weather is damp or cloudy.

Peaches dry nicely in an oven after the baking is done.

Turn peaches whilst they are drying, that they may dry quickly and perfectly, else they will become musty. Keep them in bags tied closely, and hung up.

TO DRY APPLES.—Apples may be dried in the same manner; pare off every particle of the skin, and take out all the core; dry them where no dust may come to them.

The best apples for drying, are those too sour to use in any other way.

PEACH PRESERVE.—Pare, and cut in halves, ripe

peaches, and dry them in a hot sun or warm oven for two days; then weigh them, and make a syrup of one pound of sugar for three of fruit; put a teacup of water to each pound of sugar, and the white of an egg to four pounds; stir it until it is dissolved, then set it over the fire, boil and skim until only a light foam rises, then put in the fruit, and let it boil gently until the syrup is thick and the fruit clear; put in some of the kernels from the stones; when it is perfectly cold, secure it as previously directed.

A piece of paper to fit the inside of the pot or jar, dipped in thick sugar syrup, and laid on the top of the preserve, before closing the jar, will keep them nicely.

Where the fruit is very plenty, this is a safe and excellent way to preserve it either for table or tarts. The fruit must be cooked slowly, and for a long time.

This receipt was obtained from one who practiced it for years, and found the fruit perfectly good for one year. Preserves intended for keeping, should not be disturbed before cold weather.

STRAWBERRIES PRESERVED.—Strawberries for bottling or preserving, except for jam, should be ripe, but not in the least soft.

Make a syrup of a pound of sugar for each pound of fruit. The sugar should be double refined, although refined sugar does very well: the only difference is in the color of the preserve, which is not so brilliant as when done with other than crushed or loaf sugar.

To each pound of sugar put a teacup of water: set it over a gentle fire, and stir it until it is all dissolved; when boiling hot put in the fruit, having picked off every hull and imperfect berry; let them boil very gently in a covered kettle, until by cutting one open you find it cooked through. That will be known by its having the same color throughout. Take them from the syrup with a skimmer, and spread them on flat dishes, and let them remain until cold; boil the syrup until quite thick; then let it cool and settle; put the fruit into jars or pots, and strain or pour the syrup carefully over, leaving the sediment, which will be at the bottom of the pitcher.

The next day, cover with several papers, wet with sugar, boiled to candy; set them in a cool, airy place.

Strawberries keep perfectly well, made with seven pounds of sugar to ten of fruit: they should be done as directed above, and the syrup cooked quite thick.

A pint of red currant-juice, and a pound of sugar for it, to three pounds of strawberries, make the syrup very beautiful.

STRAWBERRY JAM, OR MARMALADE.—Pick ripe strawberries free from every hull; put three quarters of a pound of sugar, for every pound of fruit; crush them together to a smooth mass; then put it in a preserving kettle, over a gentle fire; stir it with a wooden or silver spoon, until it is jelly-like and thick; let it do slowly for some time; then try some on a plate; if when cold it is like jelly, it is enough. Put it in small jars or tumblers, and secure as directed.

Currant-juice, with a pound of sugar to a pint, to four or five pounds of strawberries, and the required quantity of sugar, makes the jam very nice.

Half a pound of sugar for each pound of fruit, will make very fine jam, or marmalade, which is the same, cooked until it is very thick, and reduced; take care that it does not burn.

To Preserve Strawberries Whole.—Another excellent way, is to make the syrup boiling hot; and having picked fine large strawberries free from hulls, (or, if preferred, leave them and half an inch of the stem on,) pour it over them; let it remain until the next day; then drain it off, and boil again; return it hot to the fruit; let them remain for another night; then put them into the kettle, and boil gently for half an hour; cut one in two; if it is done through take them from the syrup with a skimmer, and spread them on flat dishes to cool; boil the syrup until thick and rich; then put the fruit into glass jars; let the syrup cool and settle; then pour it carefully off from the sediment, over the fruit.

Strawberries Stewed for Tarts.—Make a syrup of one pound of sugar, and a teacup of water; add a little white of eggs; let it boil, and skim it until only a foam rises; then put in a quart of berries, free from stems and hulls; let them boil till they look clear, and the syrup is quite thick. Finish as directed for tarts, with fine puff paste.

Raspberries.—These may be preserved wet, bottled, or made jam or marmalade of, the same as strawberries.

Raspberries are very fine, dried in the sun, or a warm oven. They are very fine stewed for table or tarts.

To Stew Dried Raspberries.—Have them dried free from dust; rinse them lightly in cold water; then put them to stew, with water to cover them, and a teacup of sugar to a pint of dried fruit; cover them, and let them simmer slowly for an hour or more, until they are swelled out, and the syrup is rich.

CHERRIES PRESERVED.—Take fine large cherries, not very ripe; take off the stems, and take out the stones; save whatever juice runs from them, take an equal weight of white sugar; make the syrup of a teacup of water for each pound; set it over the fire, until it is dissolved, and boiling hot; then put in the juice and cherries; boil them gently until clear throughout; take them from the syrup with a skimmer, and spread them on flat dishes to cool; let the syrup boil until it is rich, and quite thick; set it to cool and settle; take the fruit into jars or pots, and pour the syrup carefully over; let them remain open until the next day; then cover as directed.

Sweet cherries are improved by the addition of a pint of red currant-juice, and half a pound of sugar to it, for four or five pounds of cherries.

TO DRY CHERRIES.—Take the stems and stones from ripe cherries; spread them on flat dishes, and dry them in a hot sun, or warm oven; pour whatever juice may have run from them, a little at a time, over them; stir them about, that they may dry evenly. When they are perfectly dry, line boxes or jars with white paper, and pack them close in layers; strew a little brown sugar, and fold the paper over, and keep them in a dry place, or put them in muslin bags, and hang them in an airy place.

CURRANTS PRESERVED.—Take ripe currants,

free from stems; weigh them, and take the same weight of sugar; put a teacup of sugar to each pound of it; boil the syrup until it is hot and clear; then turn it over the fruit; let it remain one night; then set it over the fire, and boil gently, until they are cooked and clear; take them into the jars or pots with a skimmer; boil the syrup until rich and thick; then pour it over the fruit.

Currants may be preserved with ten pounds of fruit to seven of sugar. Take the stems from seven pounds of the currants, and crush and press the juice from the remaining three pounds; put them into the hot syrup, and boil until thick and rich; put it in pots or jars, and the next day secure as directed.

CURRANT JAM.—Pick the currants free from stems; weigh three quarters of a pound of sugar for each pound of fruit; strain the juice from half of them; then crush the remainder and the sugar together, and put them with the juice into a bright brass or porcelain kettle, and boil until it is a smooth jellied mass; have a moderate fire, that it may not burn the preserve.

CURRANT JELLY.—Pick fine red but not long ripe currants from the stems; bruise them, and strain the juice from a quart at a time, through a thin muslin; wring it gently, to get all the liquid; put a pound of white sugar to each pint of juice; stir it until it is all dissolved; set it over a gentle fire; let it become hot, and boil for fifteen minutes; then try it by taking a spoonful into a saucer: when cold, if it is not quite firm enough, boil it for a few minutes longer.

Or pick the fruit from stems; weigh it, and put it into a stone pot; set it in a kettle of hot water, reaching nearly to the top; let it boil until the fruit is hot through; then crush them, and strain the juice from them. Put a pound of white sugar to each pint of it; put it over the fire, and boil for fifteen minutes; try some in a saucer. When the jelly is thick enough, strain it into small white jars, or glass tumblers; when cold, cover with tissue paper, as directed. Glass should be tempered, by keeping it in warm water for a short time before pouring any hot liquid into it, otherwise it will crack.

BLACKBERRIES.—Preserve these as strawberries or currants, either liquid or jam, or jelly. Blackberry jelly or jam is an excellent medicine in summer complaint or dysentery; to make it, crush a quart of fully ripe blackberries with a pound of the best loaf-sugar, put it over a gentle fire and cook it until thick, then put to it a gill of the best fourth-proof brandy, stir it awhile over the fire, then put it in pots.

BLACKBERRY SYRUP.—Make a simple syrup of a pound of sugar to each pint of water, boil it until it is rich and thick, then add to it as many pints of the expressed juice of ripe blackberries as there are pounds of sugar; put half a nutmeg grated to each quart of the syrup; let it boil fifteen or twenty minutes, then add to it half a gill of fourth-proof brandy for each quart of syrup, set it to become cold, then bottle it for use. A tablespoonful for a child or a wineglass for an adult is a dose.

BARBERRIES.—Preserve them the same as currants; or they may be preserved in molasses. Pick them from the stems, and put them into a jug or jar with molasses to cover them. The acid soon destroys all taste of molasses. The small winter or frost grape may be done in the same manner.

GOOSEBERRIES PRESERVED.—Take the blossom from the end and take off the stems; finish as directed for strawberries or currants.

TO KEEP RED GOOSEBERRIES.—Pick gooseberries when fully ripe, and for each quart, take quarter of a pound of sugar and a gill of water, boil together until quite a syrup, then put in the fruit and continue to boil gently for fifteen minutes; then put them into small stone jars; when cold cover them close; keep them for making tarts or pies.

CURRANT JELLY WITHOUT COOKING.—Press the juice from the currants and strain it; to every pint put a pound of fine white sugar, mix them together until the sugar is dissolved, then put it in jars, seal them and expose them to a hot sun for two or three days.

PLUMS.—There are several varieties of plums. The richest purple plum for preserving is the damson; there are of these large and small, the larger are called sweet damsons, the small ones are very rich flavored. The great difficulty in preserving plums is that the skins crack and the fruit comes to pieces; the rule here laid down for preserving them obviates that difficulty.

Purple gages unless properly preserved will turn to juice and skins; and the large horse plum (as it is generally known) comes completely to pieces in ordinary modes of preserving; the one recommended herein will keep them whole, full and rich.

To Preserve Purple Plums.—Make a syrup of clean brown sugar, clarify it as directed in these receipts; when perfectly clear and boiling hot, pour it over the plums having picked out all unsound ones, and stems; let them remain in the syrup two days, then drain it off, make it boiling hot, skim it and pour it over again, let them remain in the syrup two days then drain it off; make it boiling hot, skim it and pour it over again; let them remain another day or two, then put them in a preserving kettle over the fire, and simmer gently until the syrup is reduced and thick or rich. One pound of sugar for each pound of plums.

Small damsons are very fine, preserved as cherries or any other ripe fruit; clarify the syrup and when boiling hot put in the plums, let them boil very gently until they are cooked and the syrup rich. Put them in pots or jars; the next day secure as directed.

To Preserve Plums without the Skins.—Pour boiling water over large egg or magnum bonum plums, cover them until it is cold, then pull off the skins.

Make a syrup of a pound of sugar and a teacup of water for each pound of fruit, make it boiling hot, and pour it over, let them remain for a day or two, then drain it off and boil again, skim it clear and pour it hot over the plums, let them remain until the next day, then put them over the fire in the syrup, boil them very gently until clear; take them from the syrup with a skimmer into the pots or jars; boil the syrup until rich and thick, take off any scum which may rise, then let it cool and settle, and pour it over the plums. If brown sugar is used, which is quite as good except for green gages, clarify it as directed.

GREEN GAGES.—These may be greened as directed for greening fruit; when taken out smooth the skins, make the syrup boiling hot and pour it over until the next day or two, then put them in the syrup over the fire and boil very slowly until they look clear, and the syrup is rich and thick; then take them from the syrup with a skimmer, spread them on flat dishes to cool, boil the syrup quite fast, skim it clear, then let it settle and cool; put the plums into jars and pour the syrup over, leaving any sediment which may remain at the bottom.

PLUMS IN BRANDY.—Take twelve pounds of magnum bonum plums which are turned in color, but not ripe; stick each one several times with a coarse needle, put them in cold water and set them over the fire; when the water begins to boil and the plums rise, take them carefully with a skimmer into a pan of cold water; to three pounds of white sugar put three teacups of water, when it is boiling hot, put it over the fruit, let it remain until the next day, put the plums and syrup in a preserving kettle over the fire, boil very gently that the skins may not break; when they are clear take them on flat plates; put to the syrup an equal measure of white brandy, stir it until mixed; put the plums into a glass jar and pour the syrup over, when cold put a tissue paper and close fitting tin cover over.

TO BRANDY GREEN GAGES.—Make a syrup of half a pound of sugar for each pound of fruit, with a teacup of water for each pound of sugar, when boiling hot pour it over the plums, let them remain for a day or two, then boil them in the syrup until they are clear, very slowly, that they may not break; then take them out with a skimmer; boil the syrup fast for a few minutes, skim it; let it cool and settle, then mix with it an equal measure of white brandy and pour it over the plums.

Or, green them as directed, make the syrup as above directed, pour it boiling hot over them, let them remain one night, then put them over the fire, let them boil up once, take them out with a skimmer; boil the syrup thick, mix with it an equal measure of white brandy, put the fruit in glass jars and pour over syrup to cover it.

To Keep Damsons.—Put them in small stone jars or wide mouth-glass bottles, and set them up to their necks in a kettle of cold water; set it over the fire to become boiling hot, then take it off, and let the bottles remain until the water is cold; the next day fill the bottles with cold water and cork and seal them. These may be used the same as fresh fruit. Green gages may be done in this way.

To Preserve Damsons a second way.—Put a quart of damsons into a jar with a pound of sugar strewed between them; set the jar in a warm oven, or put it into a kettle of cold water and set it over the fire for an hour, then take it out, set it to become cold, drain the juice off, boil it until it is thick, then pour it over the plums; when cold, cover as directed for preserves.

Jam of Green Gages.—Put ripe green gages into a kettle with very little water, and let them stew until soft, then rub them through a sieve or colander, and to every pint of pulp, put a pound of white sugar, powdered fine, then put it in a preserving kettle over the fire, stir it until the whole is of the consistence of jelly, then take it off; put the marmalade in small jars or tumblers, and cover as directed for jelly. Any sort of plums may be done in this manner.

To Dry Plums.—Split ripe plums, take the stones from them and lay them on plates or sieves to dry in a warm oven or hot sun; take them in at sunset and do not put them out again until the sun will be upon them; turn them that they may be done evenly; when perfectly dry, pack them in jars or boxes, lined with paper, or keep them in bags; hang them in an airy place.

Pears Dried.—Prepare, and dry them the same as apples.

Pears in Brandy.—Take fine rich, juicy, but not very ripe pears, put them into a sauce-pan with cold water to cover them; set them over a gentle fire and simmer them until they will yield to the pressure of your finger, then take them into cold water; pare them with the greatest care, so that not a single defect may remain; make a syrup of three quarters of a pound of white sugar for each pound of fruit, and a cup of water to each pound of sugar; when the syrup is clear and boiling hot put in the pears, boil them gently until they are done through and clear, and the syrup is rich; now take them with a skimmer into glass jars; boil the syrup thick, then mix with it a gill of white brandy to each pint, pour it over the fruit and when cold put paper and a close fitting cover over.

To Preserve Pears.—Take small rich fair fruit, as soon as the pips are black, set them over the fire in a kettle, with water to cover them; let them simmer until they will yield to the pressure of the finger, then with a skimmer take them into cold water, pare them neatly, leaving on a little of the stem, and the blossom end; pierce them at the blossom end to the core, then make a syrup of a pound of sugar for each pound of fruit; when it is boiling hot pour it over the pears, and let it stand until the next day; when drain it off, make it boiling hot and again pour it over; after a day or two put the fruit in the syrup over the fire, and boil gently until it is clear, then take it into the jars or spread it on dishes, boil the syrup thick, then put it and the fruit in jars.

LARGE BELL PEARS.—May be preserved the same as quinces or citron.

PEAR MARMALADE.—To six pounds of small pears, take four pounds of sugar; put the pears into a saucepan with a little cold water, cover it, and set it over the fire until the fruit is soft, then take them into cold water; pare, quarter, and core them; put to them three teacups of water, set them over the fire; roll the sugar fine, mash the fruit fine and smooth, put the sugar to it, stir it well together until it is thick like jelly, then put it in tumblers or jars, and when cold, secure it as jelly.

TO STEW PEARS.—Pare them and cut them in halves, if large, or leave them whole, if small; put them in a stewpan with very little water, cover them and let them stew till tender, then add a pint bowl of brown sugar to quarter of a peck of pears, let them stew until the syrup is rich; a lemon boiled with the pears and sliced thin when the sugar is put in, improves both flavor and color; or a wineglass of red wine may be used instead.

TO BAKE PEARS.—Wash half a peck of tart

pears, cut the stems so as to leave only an inch length; put them in an iron pot over the fire with half a pint of water and a pint of molasses to them; cover the pot or kettle and let them boil rather gently until the pears are soft and the syrup rich, almost like candy; take care not to scorch it.

To STEW QUINCES.—Pare and cut them in quarters, take out the cores, put them into a stewpan with half enough water to cover them, cover the pan, and let them boil till tender, add half a pound of sugar to each pound of cut quinces, cover them and let them stew until the syrup is rich and thick.

Or, pare, core, and cut the quinces, put the skins and cores in the bottom of a stewpan or preserving kettle, put in the cut quinces and enough water to half cover them; cover the vessel and let them stew till tender, then take them up, bruise the skins and cores, and strain the water from them; take for each pound of quinces (before they were boiled) half a pint of the strained water, and half a pound of sugar boiled to a nice syrup; then put in the boiled quinces and boil until they are sweet and rich.

To STEW PEACHES.—Take small under-ripe peaches, pare them neatly, and put them into a kettle with water nearly to cover them, and set them over a gentle fire; to each quart of peaches, put half pound of sugar; let them stew until the syrup is rich. Serve cold for tea or dessert.

To STEW APPLES.—Pare ripe tart apples, and cut them in quarters or smaller; core them, and put them into a stew-pan, with a teacup of water and the same of sugar to a quart or more of cut apples; then set them over the fire, let them simmer gently for nearly an hour; turn them into a flat dish, and set them to cool. Grate half a nutmeg over, if liked.

Small apples may be stewed in this way without cutting them; pare them, and core them with a small knife or apple-corer; a lemon boiled, and sliced thin, may be stewed with them; a small teaspoonful of lemon extract may be put to them whilst stewing

TOMATOES PRESERVED.—Take the small plum-shaped yellow or red tomatoes, pour boiling water over them, and peel off the skins; make the syrup of an equal weight of sugar, and a teacup of water to each pound, set it over the fire; when all is dissolved, and boiling hot, put in the tomatoes, let them boil very gently; boil one or two lemons in water until the peels are tender, then cut them in slices, and put them with the tomatoes in the syrup; let them boil until the fruit is clear throughout, and the syrup rich; then take the tomatoes on to flat dishes, and set them to become cold; boil the syrup until thick and rich, then set it by to cool and settle; put the fruit into a jar or pots, and pour the syrup free from any sediment over them, or the syrup may be strained.

CANDIED TOMATOES.—Choose the fig or plum-shaped tomato; for every four pounds of tomatoes clarify one pound of sugar; pour boiling water over the tomatoes, cover them for a few minutes, then peel them; when the syrup is boiling hot, put them in, let them simmer very slowly until they look clear, then take them out with a skimmer on to a sieve; set them where they may become cold; boil the syrup until it is quite thick, then put the tomatoes in again, simmer them slowly for nearly an hour, then take them out, and lay them on sieves again; boil the syrup an hour longer, then put in the tomatoes for the last time, let them remain for half an hour, simmering, then take them out, flatten them, and dry them in a hot sun or in a warm oven; when perfectly dry, pack them in glass jars. One or two lemons boiled tender, then sliced, and preserved with tomatoes, imparts a fine flavor.

TOMATO JAM.—Take ripe tomatoes, peel them, and take out all the seeds; put them into a preserving kettle, with half a pound of sugar for each pound of prepared tomatoes; boil one or two lemons soft, then pound them fine; take out the pips, and put them to the tomatoes, and boil slowly; mash them to a smooth mass; continue to stir them until smooth and thick, then put it in jars or tumblers.

GRAPES.—These should be picked from the stem when nearly ripe; take sugar, pound for pound, with a teacup of water for each pound of sugar; clarify it, (unless white sugar is used.) make it boiling hot, and pour it over the fruit; let it remain for a day or two; then drain it off; make it boiling hot; skim it, and pour it over again; after a day or two, put fruit and syrup over the fire; let it boil gently until clear, and the syrup thick; then take the grapes from the syrup with a skimmer; boil the syrup sometime longer; then set it to cool and settle, and strain it over the fruit.

A NEW WAY TO PRESERVE GRAPES.—Pick ripe grapes from the stems; take an equal weight of sugar; put to each pound a teacup of water, and make it boiling hot; squeeze the pulp from the skins, save them, and put the inside or pulp to the syrup, having bruised them, to get the juice; let them boil up once or twice; then strain and squeeze it through a coarse cloth; this will take out the seeds; put in the skins, and return it to the fire; they will fill up after one or two boils; when the syrup is sufficiently thick and rich, turn them into an earthen vessel to cool; put them into glass jars; when perfectly cold, secure them as directed.

GRAPE JELLY.—Take ripe grapes, press them from the skins; then put them in a coarse cloth, and press out all the juice; put half a pound of sugar to each pint of juice, and finish the same as currant jelly.

GRAPES DRIED.—Take fine, large, ripe grapes; place them on sieves or hurdles, and set them in a warm oven, turning them carefully and frequently, until they are perfectly dry.

Or dry them in the sun; take them in at sunset; turn them every day, until they are nicely dry.

Line wooden boxes with paper; pack the bunches carefully in layers, strew a little sugar between and over them; when the box is full, cover or fold paper over, and close the box with a wooden cover.

GRAPES PRESERVED IN BUNCHES.—Take full clusters of grapes, not fully ripe; trim the stems neatly; make a syrup of a pound of sugar, and a teacup of water for each pound of grapes; make it boiling hot, and pour it over them; let them remain for a day or two; then drain off the syrup, boil it again, skim it, and pour it over; after a day or two, put grapes and syrup over the fire; boil very gently, until they are clear, and the syrup rich; take them up carefully; lay them on plates to become cold; boil the syrup for nearly an hour; skim it, let it cool and settle; put the grapes in glass jars, and pour the syrup over.

To Dry Grapes in Clusters.—Take preserves from the syrup, dip them in boiling water, to free them from what may be hanging to them; then dry them in the sun, or a warm oven, turning every day, until perfectly dry: then flatten them, and pack them in boxes.

To Preserve Green Grapes.—Take the largest full sized green grapes, take the seeds from them by means of a large needle; make a syrup of as many pounds of sugar, and pour it hot over them; let them remain a day or two, then boil them in the syrup till clear; boil the syrup thick; then put the preserve in pots. When cold, cover as directed.

To Stew Prunes.—Wash or rinse prunes, as may be necessary, in cold water; put them in a stew-pan, with water to cover them: put over them a teacup of clean brown sugar, for each pound of fruit; cover the stew-pan, and boil rather slowly, until the syrup is thick and rich.

To Preserve Green Ginger Roots.—Boil the roots in plenty of water, until they may be pared neatly; then put them in fresh water; change it once or twice, putting on boiling water each time; let them boil until tender; then take them into cold water. Clarify four pounds of sugar for three and a half of ginger; take the ginger from the water, and wipe it dry; dissolve the sugar with a teacup of water to each pound; put it over the ginger, and let it remain for several days; then drain it off, boil and skim it; let it become cold; then pour it over the ginger; let it remain three or four days; then boil it again, and pour it hot over the ginger; repeat the boiling and skimming, until the ginger is penetrated with the sugar, and the syrup becomes thick and clear.

ALMACKS.—Take four dozen ripe plums, split them; two dozen apples, pared and cored, and the same number of pears, ditto.; stew them without water; when well blended, take out the plum stones, and stir in three pounds of clean sugar; boil them gently, stirring them together, for one hour; then spread it on flat dishes, and dry them in the sun, or a cool oven. When nearly dry, mark it in square cakes.

TRANSPARENT MARMALADE.—Take some Sicily oranges, cut them in quarters, take out the pulp, put it into a basin, take out all the seeds, and skin; put the peels into a little salt and water, and leave them to soak all night, then boil them in a good quantity of spring water until they are tender; cut them in shreds, and put them to the pulp; to every pint of it put one pound of loaf sugar, made fine, and boil them gently together for twenty minutes; if it is not perfectly clear, simmer it for some minutes longer, stirring it gently all the time, when cold, put it in jelly glasses, and secure it as directed for jelly.

To PRESERVE FRUIT, *for Tarts or Common Use.*—Cherries, any sort of plums or apples, may be preserved for the above mentioned uses, in the following manner:

Pit the fruit, gathered when ripe, put them in small jars, strew over each, six ounces of sugar for every pound of fruit, tie over each jar two bladders, or thick papers, tie each one separately; put them up to the neck in a vessel of water, and let them boil gently for three hours, then set it off; let them remain in the water until cold. Keep them in a dry, cool place.

MULBERRY PRESERVED.—Take mulberries when fully ripe, but not soft, weigh three quaters of a pound of sugar for each pint of picked berries: finish as directed for strawberries.

MULBERRY SYRUP.—Put some mulberries into a jug, tie a paper over it, and then put it up to the neck in a kettle of water, let it boil; as the liquor rises from the mulberries, drain it off; to each pint of it put one pound of white sugar, or brown sugar clarified; set it over a slow fire, and boil until about the consistence of molasses, then skim it, and take it off; when cold, bottle it.

NECTARINES PRESERVED.—Take nectarines when nearly ripe, pare them, and cut them in halves, and simmer them in boiling water, until they rise to the surface, then drain them; clarify three quarters of a pound of sugar for each pound of fruit, put it in, and let them boil until nearly clear, then set them away in the syrup; the next day drain the syrup from them, boil it until quite thick, then put in the fruit, and let it boil for a short time; drain off the syrup, and repeat the boiling on the following day, then put it in a tureen, and let it stand for two days, then put the preserves in pots, and secure as directed.

TO CANDY NECTARINES.—Split the fruit, and take out the stones, clarify half their weight of sugar, and put in the fruit, and boil gently until clear, take off the light scum, take them with a skimmer on flat dishes, and cover them with, until the next day, then boil the syrup until it is rather thick, put in the fruit, and let them boil until fairly hot through, take them again on to flat dishes, with a skimmer, as free from syrup as possible, let them remain one night, again boil the syrup, and put in the fruit for a short time; spread it out to dry, and set it in a warm place; dust fine white sugar over, and turn them until they are so.

Peaches, large egg plums, and apricots, may be done in this way.

NECTARINES,—May be bottled as directed for fruits.

CAPILLAIRE.—Take fourteen pounds of sugar, break six eggs in, with the shells, stir into it gradually three quarts of water, set it over the fire, and boil it, and take off the scum until only a light froth rises, add to it a gill of orange flower water, or half as much lemon extract, with a little vanilla, then strain it through a jelly bag, and when cold, bottle it; cork it tight to keep.

A wine-glass of this put to a tumbler of ice water, is much liked, and very refreshing.

Sliced lemon or pine-apple, or crushed strawberries, raspberries, or ripe currants, may be added to it; also a glass of wine, brandy, or rum.

CHERRY WATER.—Put a wine-glass of Capillaire into a tumbler, pound a dozen fine large sour cherries in a mortar, so as to break the kernels, then put them in the tumbler, two-thirds fill it with ice water, and serve with sponge or wine cakes;

or instead of ice water, half fill the tumbler with chipped ice, then put in water.

RASPBERRY VINEGAR.—Put a quart of the best vinegar into a bottle, put in picked raspberries, as many as the bottle will contain, put in a cork, and let it remain for a week, then strain the liquor through a fine muslin, press all the juice from the berries, then measure it; to each pint put one pound and a half of white fine sugar, boil it until the syrup is rich, (keep it covered whilst boiling,) when cold bottle it, flavor ice water with it, and serve with small cakes.

ROASTED FIGS.—These are both palatable and nutritious for persons in delicate health. Take fine large fresh figs, put them on bird spits, and roast them before the fire, or broil them over bright coals, on a gridiron; turn them when half done.

MILK PUNCH.—Half fill a pint tumbler with finely chipped ice, add to it a wine-glass of gin, rum, or brandy, and a tablespoonful of fine white sugar, stir it around, then fill it up with milk; grate nutmeg over, and serve.

Or put together of milk and gin, or rum or brandy, a wine-glass each, add a large tablespoonful of white sugar, stir it until the sugar is dissolved, then fill it up with milk; grate nutmeg over, and serve with small cakes.

LEMON BRANDY.—Put the yellow rind of two fine fresh lemons, into a bottle of brandy, after two days strain it; boil two ounces of loaf sugar in a teacup of water, to a nice syrup, let it become cold, then mix it with the brandy.

STRAWBERRY SHERBET.—Take one pound of picked strawberries, crush them to a smooth mass, then add three pints of water, the juice of a lemon, and a tablespoonful of orange flower water; let it stand for three or four hours, put a pound of fine white sugar into another basin, put over it a large cloth or napkin, and strain the strawberries through it, wring it, to extract as much of the juice as possible; stir it until the sugar is dissolved, then strain it again, and set it on ice for an hour, before serving in small tumblers half filled.

CREAM SHERBET.—Put the yolks of six eggs, and a dessert-spoonful of orange flower water, into two quarts of cream, boil it up once in a covered stew-pan, then strain it; add to it three quarters of a pound of fine white sugar, and stir it until it is dissolved.

When cold, set it on ice, or freeze it the same as ice cream.

LEMON SHERBET.—Dissolve a pound and a half of white sugar in a quart of water, take nine large lemons, wipe them clean, and cut each in two; squeeze them so as to extract the juice and the essence from the peel; stir into it the sugared water, then strain it, and freeze the same as ice cream.

To Prepare Ripe Fruits or Melons for Table.

RIPE PEACHES CUT SMALL.—Take fair ripe peaches, pare off the skin, and cut them in slices, not very small, quarters or eighths is best, if the fruit is very ripe; put them into a deep glass dish, and strew fine sugar plentifully over; serve for dessert or tea-table.

To Prepare Strawberries and Raspberries.—Take them carefully up by the handful, pick out every imperfection or hull, have a basin of cold water, and pass them quickly through it, without allowing them to remain for an instant, and put them into a deep china or glass dish ; when all are done, strew them plentifully with powdered white sugar, and serve ; or serve dishes of fine sugar with them, without the sugar upon them ; rinsing the berries in this way, will take none of the richness from them, but freshen them, and take off any sand which may be upon them ; it is particularly necessary with strawberries, after a rain, as you will find by examing the rinsing water.

Strawberries should never be touched after picking them, until within an hour of serving. Putting on sugar for longer than this, draws out the juice, and discolors them. Should it be put in the morning, to be used at tea, or in the evening, they would in all probability become sour. Ripe berries may be kept from one day to the other, by setting the dish containing them on ice, or in a cool, dark place.

Ripe peaches should on no account be cut or sugared more than an hour or two before serving. The same remark applies to raspberries and blackberries.

Peaches, strawberries and raspberries are prepared and sugared in this way, to be served with ice cream ; or with sponge cake or wine cakes in the evening.

Blackberries—Are prepared for table the same as strawberries or raspberries.

Huckle or Whortleberries.—Put them into a basin, with plenty of cold water ; take off the floating berries and stems; take up a handful at a time; pick out any unripe or crushed ones, or stems or leaves; shake the water from them, and put them into a bowl or deep dish; serve sugar with them, or strew it over.

RIPE CURRANTS FOR TEA.—Pick them from the stems, and put them into a basin of water; shake them about; then take them up by the handful; shake off the water, and put them into a deep dish; mix plenty of sugar with them, and serve. These are better for standing for an hour before serving.

RIPE CHERRIES FOR TEA.—Pick them from the stems; rinse them in cold water, and throw out any imperfect ones; then take the stones from them, over the dish in which they are to be served; mix sugar with them.

MUSKMELONS AND CANTELOPES—Are prepared for table by cutting them in two from end to end; and after taking out the seeds and inside, cut them in slices, as the flutes indicate; serve with pepper and salt. There is great choice in this fruit, some being sweet and spicy, whilst others are comparitively insipid. Nutmeg melons are incomparably best.

WATERMELONS.—These should be put in cold water, which should be changed several times, for three or more hours before serving; or put them on ice, or in a refrigerator.

Unripe or over ripe watermelons are very unwholesome. When good, the inside cuts firm, the seeds are black, and they have a delicious sweetness. The inside may be either white, or pink, or red

DIRECTIONS

For Making Mangoes, and Other Varieties of Pickles.

CUCUMBERS.—Cucumbers for pickling should be fresh gathered, not longer than a finger, and an inch thick. The gherkin or cluster cucumber, has a rough, prickly outside, and they are rather thicker for the length than the ordinary pickle.

Make a strong brine of salt and water, which will bear an egg; let the pickles remain in this twenty-four hours; then take them from the brine, lay them in a tub, make vinegar boiling hot, with whole pepper, and alspice, and mustard-seed, if liked; pour it over the pickles, and let them remain until the next day. Then drain it off, boil it again, pour it over, and cover the pickles with a thickly folded cloth; drain off the vinegar the next day; add a few bits of alum the size of a pea to it; make it boiling hot, and again pour it over the pickles; let them remain for a day or two; then cut one in two; if it is not a fine green throughout, scald the vinegar again, and pour it over. After a few days, assort the pickles; put those of each size together in jars; cover them with cold vinegar, put a cloth and cover over the jars. These pickles will keep perfectly well for years. Put the largest and softest in jars to be used first.

Cucumber pickles may be put down in a strong salt and water brine, to be greened and pickled as they may be wanted. Keep them under the brine. When wanted, freshen them in two or three changes of water, for two or three days, until by cutting one open, you find it but little salt; then pour scalding vinegar over them three times, and keep them covered.

Or, after taking them from the brine, put them into a kettle, with vine leaves, and a few very small bits of alum, and a bit of saleratus the size of half a small nutmeg, to one hundred pickles; cover them close, and let them simmer very slowly until they are a fine green; then take them off, and put them in cold vinegar.

Pickles for present use should be put up separately from those intended for keeping.

Another way to make them is: make a strong brine, which will float an egg, put the pickles in for twenty-four hours, then take them from it, put them into a bright brass kettle, with vinegar and water to cover them, with a few bits of alum the size of a pea, scattered between, to harden them; fold a thick coarse towel over them, and simmer very gently until they are green; if they do not become sufficiently so after an hour or more, put in a bit of saleratus the size of a small nutmeg, for a kettle full.

When a fine green, take them with a skimmer into a stone pot or wooden vessel, and cover with cold cider vinegar; put in whole pepper, cloves, alspice, and mustard seed.

GREEN PEPPERS.—These are pickled the same as cucumbers. It is best to slit one seam, and take out the seeds or core, that they may be less strong; if they are preferred strong, slit them, and soak in salt and plenty of water for several days; the last mentioned receipt for cucumbers, is the best for peppers.

The best peppers for pickling are those thick skinned and green; they may be stuffed with white onions, green beans sliced, horseradish, and mustard seed, the same as melon mangoes.

MELON MANGOES.—Get the late, small, smooth, green melon; they should not be larger than a teacup, take a piece from the stem end, large enough to allow you to take the seeds from the inside; scrape out all the soft, without cutting the other, then secure each piece to its own melon; lay them in rows in a stone or wooden vessel, as you do them.

Make a strong brine of salt and water, pour it over the melons, and let them remain twenty-four hours.

Prepare the following stuffing: sliced horseradish, very small cucumbers, green beans, nasturtions, white small onions, mustard seed, whole pepper, cloves and alspice; put the beans in a little water, with the white onions; having peeled them, and set them over the fire, give them one scald, and spread them out to cool; scald the pickles and cool them.

Rinse the melons in clear water, then wipe each dry, proceed to fill them: put a cucumber, one or two small onions, and two or three beans, with sliced horseradish and mustard seed, into each melon, put on the piece belonging to it, and sew it with a coarse needle and thread, lay them in a stone pot or wooden vessel, the cut side up, when all are in, strew over the cloves and pepper, make vinegar (enough to cover them,) boiling hot, and put it over, then cover with a folded towel, let them stand for one night, then drain off the vinegar, make it hot again, and pour it on, cover as before; repeat this scalding four or five times, if necessary, until the mangoes are a fine green; three times is generally enough.

Be sure that the melons are green, and fresh gathered; the proper sort are the last on the vines, and green and firm.

If you wish to keep some until the next summer, choose the most firm, put them in a jar, and cover with cold fresh vinegar; tie thick paper several thicknesses over.

To Pickle Onions.—Peel the onions until they are white, scald them in strong salt and water, then take them up with a skimmer; make vinegar enough to cover them, boiling hot, strew over the onions whole pepper and white mustard seed, pour the vinegar over to cover them, when cold, put them in wide mouthed bottles, and cork them close. A tablespoonful of sweet oil may be put in the bottles before the cork.

The best sort of onions for pickling, are the small white buttons.

To Pickle Nasturtions.—Pick them, and put them in glass bottles, with cold vinegar to cover them; a little salt may be added.

Another Way to Pickle Onions.—Peel the onions, boil some strong salt and water, and put it over them, cover, and let them stand twenty-four hours, then take them up with a skimmer; make some vinegar boiling hot, put to it whole pepper and mustard seed, and pour it over the onions to cover them; when cold, cover close.

To Pickle Plums Like Olives.—Make a pickle of vinegar, mustard seed, and a little salt, make it boiling hot, then put it over green plums, gathered before they begin to turn, let them remain one night, then drain off the vinegar, make it hot again, and pour it over the plums; when cold, cover close. Plums may be taken before the stone is formed, and pickled in the same manner.

To Pickle Green Beans.—Pick sound, tender green beans, put them in a kettle with salt and water, and a very small bit of saleratus, set them over the fire for a few minutes, to scald, when they are a fine green, take them off, take them from the water with a skimmer, make vinegar (enough to cover them,) boiling hot, put to it mustard seed and whole pepper, turn it over the beans, let them remain until the next day, then drain off the vinegar, add a very small bit of alum, make it hot, and again pour it over the beans. Keep them in glass jars with tin covers.

To Pickle Walnuts and Butternuts.—Gather the nuts when so young that you may pierce them with a pin, put them in water to cover them, and change it every day for three weeks, to extract the bitterness; to enough vinegar to cover them, put cloves, alspice, and mustard seed, and salt, make it boiling hot, and put it over the walnuts; let them remain for a day or two, then boil it again; boil it and put it over three times.

Or after soaking them in water as directed, put them in salt and water, with vine leaves, and a bit of saleratus, let them scald up once, then take them out, and pour the boiling vinegar over; drain it off after twenty-four hours, boil it up, and again pour it over the pickle; repeat the scalding once again.

Peaches Pickled.—Brush the down from green peaches, cling-stones, put them in salt and water, with leaves and a bit of saleratus, set them over a moderate fire to simmer slowly, until they are a fine green, then take them out, wipe them dry, and smooth the skins; take enough vinegar to cover them, put to it whole pepper, alspice, and mustard seed, make it boiling hot, and turn it over the peaches; repeat the scalding three successive days.

WALNUT CATSUP.—Bruise to a mass, one hundred and twenty green walnuts, gathered when a pin could pierce one; put to it three quarters of a pound of salt, and a quart of good vinegar; stir them every day for a fortnight, then strain and squeeze the liquor from them through a cloth, and set it aside, put to the husks half a pint of vinegar, and let it stand all night, then strain and squeeze them as before; put the liquor from them to that which was put aside, add to it one ounce and a quarter of whole pepper, forty cloves, half an ounce of nutmeg sliced, and half an ounce of ginger, and boil it for half an hour closely covered, then strain it; when cold, bottle it for use.

Secure the bottles with new corks, and dip them in melted rosin.

TO MAKE CIDER VINEGAR.—After cider has become too sour for use, set it in a warm place, put to it occasionally the rinsings of the sugar basin or molasses jug, and any remains of ale or cold tea; let it remain with the bung open, and you will soon have the best of vinegar.

TOMATO CATSUP.—Take one gallon of skinned tomatoes, four tablespoonsful of salt, four ditto of whole black pepper, half a spoonful of alspice, eight pods of red pepper, and three spoonsful of mustard, boil them together for one hour, then strain it through a sieve or coarse cloth, and when cold, bottle for use; have the best velvet corks.

Q*

ANOTHER TOMATO CATSUP.—Take ripe tomatoes to fill a jar, put them in a moderate oven, and bake them until they are dissolved, then strain them through a coarse cloth or sieve; to every pint of juice put a pint of vinegar, half an ounce of garlic sliced, quarter of an ounce of salt, and the same of white pepper finely ground; boil it for one hour, then rub it through a sieve, boil it again to the consistence of cream; when cold, bottle it, put a teaspoonful of sweet oil in each bottle, cork them tight and keep in a dry place.

OYSTER CATSUP.—Take fine fresh oysters, rinse them in their own liquor, then pound them in a marble mortar, and to a pint of oyster put a pint of sherry wine; boil them up, add an ounce of salt, two drachms of cayenne pepper, let it boil up once again, rub it through a sieve; when cold, put it in bottles and cork and seal them.

TO MAKE MUSTARD.—Put a large tablespoonful of the flour of mustard into a teacup, with a large saltspoonful of salt, mix with it gradually enough cold water to make a smooth, quite thin paste.

TO PICKLE RED CABBAGE.—Cut the cabbage in thin slices across, put a layer of it in a stone pot, strew a little pepper and salt over, then put another layer of sliced cabbage, strew it with salt and pepper, and so continue, until you have enough, then cover with cold vinegar; turn a plate (large enough to cover it) upon the cabbage and cover the pot.

TO PICKLE BEETS.—Wash beets in cold water, take them of as nearly one size as possible; boil them according to the size, from three quarters of an hour to an hour and a half, then take them into a pan of cold water, rub off the skins with your hands, then cut them in halves or quarters, lengthwise, and put them into cold vinegar, with whole pepper and some salt. Beets must not be cut before boiling, only washed clean; old beets which have been kept in earth should be put in soak the night before boiling.

To Pickle Tomatoes.—Take the round smooth green tomatoes, put them in salt and water, cover the vessel and put them over the fire to scald; that is, to let the water become boiling hot, then set the kettle off; take them from the pot into a basin of cold water; to enough cold vinegar to cover them, put whole pepper and mustard seed; when the tomatoes are cold take them from the water, cut each in two across, shake out the seeds and wipe the inside dry with a cloth, then put them into glass jars, and cover with the vinegar, cork them close or with a close fitting tin cover.

Radish Pods.—Pickle these the same as beans

A few hints on the Management of Pickles, Preserved Fruit, &c.

Pickles should always have vinegar enough to cover them; those intended for immediate use, should be kept in wide top stoneware pots or jars; keep a cloth folded upon the pickles, and the pot covered with a plate or wooden vessel managed in the same way; pickles should occasionally be looked over, that the softest and least likely to keep well, may be used first. Store pickles or those intended for use the following summer, should be assorted from the remainder when first made; choose those most firm and equal sized, put them into stone or glass ware, with fresh vinegar to cover them; cover the vessel close with several thicknesses of paper over, or a tin cover, or if wide mouthed bottles are used, cork them tight.

Beans, radish pods, tomatoes, small cucumbers, green plums and nasturtions may be put in a jar together for assorted pickles, with a few onions if liked; it is generally preferable to keep onions separately, since there are many persons to whom they are extremely offensive.

Mangoes should be kept in a jar or pot by themselves. Green peppers should be kept separate from other pickles; if put with cucumbers, they are known to lose taste, whilst the pickles become too strong for eating; five or six peppers amongst two or three hundred cucumbers will make them sufficiently strong.

Should the vinegar on pickles become white or weakened, turn it off, scald and skim it and return it to them either hot or cold. Pickles should be taken from the vinegar with a wooden spoon or fork; stirring them up by putting in the hand will spoil the vinegar.

The vessels in which pickles have been, whether of glass, wood, or stone, will never be fit for preserved fruit; whatever be the cause, they will surely spoil if put in them. After the pickles are used, throw out the vinegar, wash the vessels first in cold water, then pour hot water into them, cover and let it remain until cold, then wash, wipe, and dry them near the fire or in the sun, and set them away for future use; wooden ware will require to be wet occasionally, or to be kept in a damp place, that they may not become leaky.

Should catsups seem frothy or foam, put them in a bright brass or porcelain kettle over the fire, boil slowly, and skim until no more rises, then turn it into an earthen vessel to cool, after which, put it in bottles and stop them tight.

A cool dark closet is the best place for pickles, catsups, and preserves.

Preserves should be disturbed as little as possible; for this reason, it is best to keep them in small vessels, that not more than enough for three or four times use will be disturbed; take them out with a silver spoon.

Mrs. Cowing's Peach Pickles.—Take ripe sound cling-stone peaches, remove the down with a brush like a clothes brush; make a gallon of good vinegar hot, add to it four pounds of brown sugar, boil and skim it clear; stick five or six cloves into each of the peaches, then pour the vinegar hot over them, cover the vessel, and set it in a cold place for eight or ten days, then drain off the vinegar, make it hot, skim it, and again turn it over the peaches; let them become cold, then put them into glass jars, and secure as directed for preserves. Free-stone peaches may be used.

Pickled Plums.—Take any sort of plums—damsons are best—assort them that all may be sound, and put them into a stone jar or pot; to a gallon of good vinegar put four pounds of clean brown sugar, make it boiling hot, skim it clear, and pour it over the plums to nearly or quite cover them; cover the vessel and set it by for a day or two; then drain off the liquid, set it to boil again, skim it clear, and pour it over the fruit, as before directed; let it remain, as before, then put the whole together into a preserving kettle, set it over a slow fire, and let them simmer until the syrup is quite a jelly; then turn them into jelly pots, and when cold, cover with paper, and keep the same as currant jelly, in a cool dry place.

REMARKS

ON THE

ARRANGEMENT AND FURNITURE OF THE BREAKFAST AND DINING-ROOM FOR FAMILIES.

The dining or breakfast-room should be cool, light, and airy, with not much more than the indispensable furniture.

In summer, the floor covered with a straw-matting or an oil-cloth; in winter, with a dark, warm-looking carpet.

A sideboard, or narrow tables, at the side or end of the room, for the convenience of dessert and changes of dishes; or else have dumb waiters, (which are stands supporting large trays.)

Most modern houses are built with sliding-closets: when the dining-room is above the kitchen, this is almost indispensable: or, the waiters' pantry—between the dining-room and kitchen—has an open communication with it, that the dishes may be passed to and from the cook, without the delay and awkwardness of opening and shutting the doors: or, when there are no servants in attendance, it is convenient to have the dessert arranged on a tray covered with a white napkin, and placed on a stand or small table at the left hand of the mistress or head of the table, and one on the other hand, for receiving empty plates, &c.

For Breakfast.

Have a white cloth, with the folds regular and perceptible; let each dish be polished with a soft napkin as it is placed upon the table, otherwise there is apt to be a dimness, from having been put together before they were perfectly dried; and further, to remove the traces of the necessary handling, in putting them to their places and returning them to the table.

The plates may be put in a pile at the left hand of the carver, or at regular intervals around the table. A vast difference may be made in the appearance and neatness of the table, by the manner in which the knives and forks, and spoons, and other paraphernalia, are placed.

The coffee-urn or pot should have on its brightest face, and all the recommendative warmth of its nature—ready for a free outpouring; the cream or boiled milk should not lack heat, and, not "to waste its sweetness" on the unappreciating air, should be contained in a covered pitcher of tin or other metal; the sugar-basin, whether of the same as the other dishes, or of metal, should be bright and covered, with a large-sized tea or sugar-spoon beside it; the cups and saucers may be placed in heaps of three, within the circle of the sugar, slop, and cream vessels. Let the urn or coffee-pot be set at the right-hand side of the one who serves it; and if tea is used, let it be placed on the same side in a line with it; the one to be least called for, to stand at the outer corner of the tray—which may be placed at the middle of the broadside of the table, or at one end.

Before putting the dishes on it, the tray should be covered with a white napkin, fringed at the ends.

Small napkins or doyles, folded in four and ironed very smoothly, may be laid at each plate, which should be reversed, or turned the bottom side up, and the knife and fork at the right-hand side, or the knife at the side and a silver fork in front of the plate. Since so it is, that many Americans dislike the use of a silver fork—finding it exceedingly clumsy and awkward—it is best to place the one belonging to the knife with it, at the side of the plate, leaving it optional which to make use of.

Let the cruet-stand or castor occupy the centre of the table. If there are more than five or six persons, have two small plates of butter, one at either end of the table, and opposite each other; let there be two plates of bread or rolls, or one of either of these, and the other place for hot griddle cakes, or corn bread, or toast.

Opposite the tray or head of the table, let the steak, or fry, (or whatever principal dish,) be placed, with the carving knife and fork before it, and dishes of hominy or boiled rice, or mashed potatoes and boiled eggs or hash, opposite each other, and the plates of bread, between the steak-dish and tray, having one of the plates of butter between each two, and the castor in the centre; also one or two salt-stands filled with fine salt and neatly marked with a teaspoon or otherwise, and a salt-spoon across each, may be placed diagonally opposite each other. These, with a pitcher of ice-water and several tumblers, occupying the corners of the table on either side of the carver, complete the breakfast-table.

If there is a servant or waiter in attendance, let such stand at the left hand of the mistress or head of the table, with a small tray, and pass the cups to and from her, presenting it at the left-hand, by the right hand, without turning; it is very awkward to receive it at the other hand, being obliged to pass back the elbow, and, if in the least embarrassed, in danger of tilting the cup.

Bills of Fare comprising some of the many combinations suitable for simple family breakfasts. For the relief of young housekeepers

Coffee and tea, or chocolate, either or both; broiled beefsteak, or veal or lamb, fried or broiled; with boiled hominy or mashed potatoes, or potatoes fried, baked, or roasted; and sliced wheat bread and corn breakfast-cakes or griddle-cakes.

Broiled or fried chicken; or clams stewed, or fritters, or fried; or broiled or fried ham, with eggs fried, boiled, poached, or omlet; with mashed or fried potatoes, and such warm and cold bread as may be desired.

Salt or fresh fish, fried or broiled, and hot rolls or cold bread, with tea or coffee, constitute a very popular family breakfast in summer; there may be the addition of such a variety of bread, hot or cold, as may be preferred; and mashed, or fried, or roasted potatoes; or boiled hominy; also dressed cucumbers, or stewed tomatoes, and stewed fruit or ripe berries.

Clam omlet will generally be liked by those who are fond of clams.

Green sweet corn, boiled, and served with cold meat or steaks, is suitable for breakfast. Smoked beef, fried or frizzled, or salt cod, relish; or a bit of salmon or smoked shad, broiled, with the other requisites, make a nice relishing breafast.

Hashed meat, or meat and potato hash, is suitable at any time, and with any other dishes.

Hot rolls or muffins, warm biscuits, velvet cakes or bread cakes, and twisted bread or rye bread, or short cakes, are some of the varieties of bread for summer breakfasts, together with dry and milk toast.

Bread for breakfast should be cut in slices nearly half an inch thick, and arranged neatly on a folded napkin or doyle, on flat plates. Rye bread one day old, cut in this way, is much liked.

None but the best sweet butter should be brought to the breakfast or tea-table.

For Winter Breakfasts.

Fried oysters; or soft-shell clams, fried; or fried or broiled chicken; or tripe, broiled or fried; with boiled hominy, or hot corn bread and rolls; and tea or coffee.

Buckwheat griddle-cakes, with fried steaks, ham, or sausages, or cold meat or hash, are a popular breakfast for winter. With many families, buckwheat cakes are the constant breakfast, with some little varieties of meat, and tea or coffee, during the winter. It will be found more healthful to vary occasionally, with corn griddle-cakes, or muffins, or some other hot cakes. The best of sweet butter, and syrup, should be served with these cakes.

Head-cheese, with rolls and coffee, make a nice breakfast; also fried sausages; or meat or cod-fish cakes. A shoulder of lamb may be boned and broiled; or a breast may be nicely and thoroughly broiled; or lamb or chickens stewed.

Cold meat, sliced, and fried potatoes, and parsnips, fried; with boiled hominy, or corn bread or griddle-cakes, may be liked.

Pine Apple cut and sugared for serving at tea or dessert.

Pare off the rough outside and cut it in thick small pieces rather than slices, and strew them plentifully with pulverized white sugar, an hour or two before serving.

Oranges cut in the same manner to serve for dessert or supper.

Luncheons, Suppers, and Desserts require similar preparation and arrangement, with the addition of cold meats, salads, sardines, &c., or oysters fried, stewed, or roasted, or any of the other thousand-and-one tit-bits too numerous to mention.

Arrangement of Table and Bills of Fare for Tea.

SUMMER.

Let a pure white cloth be neatly laid; let the tray be covered with a white napkin; and on it, as for breakfast, the sugar, cream, and slop-basin, containing the spoons and the cups and saucers within them. Let it be placed in the middle of one side or at one end. Put around the tables as many small plates as may be wanted, with a small knife in front of each, or at its side; at the other end or side, opposite the tray, let the dish of ripe or stewed fruit be set, with a large spoon and a pile of small saucers in front or at the side of it. On either side, at some little distance from it, let there be plates, with bread sliced, about the eighth of an inch in thickness; or let one dish be of hot wigs, or rusk, or tea-biscuit. Let a fine mould of butter occupy the centre of the table; let its knife be beside it; and on each side a small plate, the one with cold meat, ham, or tongue, sliced thin. (and a fork to help it;) the other with sliced cheese, or a fresh pot-cheese. A pitcher of ice-water, with small tumblers surrounding it, may occupy one corner, and a basket or plate of cake the other.

Or a glass-dish of custard may occupy the place mentioned for the fruit, and it (the fruit) be distributed in small saucers, with fine white sugar heaped on the centre of each, and placed upon each plate: this gives the table a very pretty appearance. Or, the custard baked in small cups, may occupy the places of the saucers of fruit.

Smoked beef, chopped thin, or Bologna sausages, sliced, may be served at tea; also, cheese; this may be sliced or grated.

For Winter Tea-Table.

The same appurtenances, with the addition of forks, are requisite, with perhaps an urn of coffee, for winter tea-table.

Oysters pickled, in the place of cold meat, or stewed in the place of fruit, or instead of the stew, a bit of broiled fish, or ham or fried oysters, with hot tea-biscuit, and rusks or wigs, and stewed or preserved fruit, and fancy cakes.

Grated cocoanut, with tart preserves, or currant jelly, or cranberry jam, may be served thus: grate the white meat of a cocoanut, and put it in a flat glass dish, then turn a mould of jelly upon the middle of it.

The Dinner-Table.

This requires quite a different arrangement, not having the tray of cups, etc.

First, lay the cloth smoothly and evenly, place the castor in the centre, with a glass salt dish at some little distance on either side of it; lay the plates around the table at regular and proper distances, leaving elbow room for each person, turn the plates down as directed for breakfast, set a tumbler on each plate, with a fringed napkin, in which is folded a piece of bread, cut an inch thick and two and a half inches long, or a cold roll instead ; place the napkin in the tumbler, or upon the plate, and the tumbler on the cloth in front of it ; put a knife at the side of the plate and the silver fork in front.

When two dishes of meat are served, one should be roast, and the other stewed, fried, or boiled, or cold, and placed one at either end of the table; a boiled fish or meat pie, or poultry, may occupy one end of the table instead; boiled potatoes and spinach may be served with and placed in front of roast beef or veal, and mashed potatoes and pickles, or a dressed salad with cold meat, with such other vegetables as may be in season; boiled beets or asparagus may be served instead of spinach; and peas and new potatoes with lamb; a small plate of butter or a fancy mould, and a plate with a doyle spread over it, with properly cut bread and a pitcher of ice water, may be dispensed in the intermediate places, or at the corners. When the meat and vegetables are removed, let the table be brushed free from crumbs with a small table brush on to a small tray.

For the dessert, have a large tray covered with a white napkin, on which place the pastry, puddings, and small plates, with the spoons, knives, and forks for dessert, as many as there may be persons; let fruits, nuts, and creams, and jelly or blancmange, be distributed over the table as may be, also the pastry and puddings, plates, etc.; if there are pies and puddings, or cream, let there be a knife, fork, and spoon and plate and saucer, for each person.

For a dinner of invited friends without much ceremony, pies or tarts and cheese, and some fruit or nuts and raisins, or pudding or blancmange and jelly, or jam or icecream, is amply sufficient.

For family dinner, the dessert is generally of one of these, or melon, or boiled rice with a sauce, or some other simple dessert, of which a great many may be found in this book. A successive variety of fish, flesh, and fowl, is conducive to health, besides pleasing one's palate.

For large dinners, soup is always the first dish, and after it is fish or boiled meat, with potatoes, plain, boiled, and mashed, and such sauces as may be proper with the fish and meat; after these come the roasts, with every variety of seasonable vegetable; small dishes of fried or stewed meat or poultry, and oyster and meat pie or chicken-salad and currie, sweetbreads and ragout, may be interspersed throughout the table, those opposite each other to be dished in like manner, to give the whole a tasteful and regular appearance, with the castors, butter and salt stands, of which last there should be one to every four persons.

After these are done with, the cloth is cleared, and the crumbs and bits of bread are brushed from it on to a small salver by means of a table brush; then is placed the dessert.

Whatever pyramids or other ornaments there may be, should be placed, the most conspicuous and ornamental in the centre, and others (of which there should be duplicates) on either side of it, at greater or less distance apart, according to the number of them; next distribute the pastry regularly, according to the several varieties; next, the puddings and blancmange or charlotte de russe, or fruit and icecream; and lastly, nuts and raisins, or grapes and jellies, instead of charlotte de russe.

Bills of Fare for Ceremonious Family Dinners.

SUMMER.

At one end of the table, a tureen of soup with a pile of plates beside it, or a boiled fish with potatoes and its proper sauce—at the other end, a roast of meat or poultry with potatoes and seasonable vegetables. For dessert, pastry, with pudding, or ripe fruit, or nuts and raisins.

A roast of meat, or a boiled and roasted ham, with mashed potatoes and spinach or asparagus, at one end, and a boiled lobster and lettuce, or a lobster salad with bread, butter, &c., at the other. Dessert—boiled pudding or rice, with a sauce; pastry may be added; or, instead of any of these, a baked pudding or custard, and paste cakes or jelly tarts.

A fine boiled fish, with potatoes and sauce, and a meat pie or pot pie with pickles or salad; with pastry and ripe fruit or melon, or a boiled pudding or boiled rice. Pine apple may be pared and sliced or cut small, and strewed plentifully with sugar an hour before serving.

Holiday Dinners.

Great attention should be paid to the arrangement of the table, which should abound in appropriate ornaments, such as evergreens for Christmas and New Year, national emblematic devices for Fourth of July, &c.

Roast turkey and mince pies for Christmas and New Year, are with us what roast beef and plum pudding are to the English.

To Arrange a Christmas Dinner.

Place a high pyramid of evergreens (made as before directed) in the centre of the table. Let a roasted turkey of uncommon size occupy the middle or centre of one side of the table, on one end let there be a cold boiled ham, and at the other, fricasseed chicken or a roast pig; with the turkey serve mashed potatoes and turnips, boiled onions and dressed celery, or other salad with apple sauce—near the ham place fried or mashed potatoes and pickles or mangoes: and with the pig or fricassee, the same as with the turkey; large pitchers of sweet cider (or where that is not desired, ice water) should be placed diagonally opposite each other, on two corners of the table; boiled turkey with oyster sauce may occupy the place of the fricassee, or instead, a fine oyster pie.

For dessert, there should be one or two very large and ornamental mince pies, one sufficiently large that each of the company may be helped from it, in token of common interest, is desirable.

Icecreams and jellies and jams and ripe fruits and nuts, with sweet cider and syrup water of different sorts, or wines, complete the dessert. Biscuit and jelly sandwich may be served at dessert, or paste puffs and charlotte de russe or blancmange with stands of jelly.

New Year's Dinner—a Cold Collation.

In New York city, where it is the custom for ladies to remain at home to receive the calls of their gentlemen friends, there is no time nor occasion for dinners; should it be desirable, it would be similar to that for Christmas, or instead—a cold roasted turkey, (bone it if you can) cold boiled ham or tongue, a large glass salad-bowl of pickled oysters, or an oyster pie with dressed celery or a chicken salad, with jelly puffs and tarts and small mince pies, blancmange, de russe and jellies and icecream and fancy cakes, with syrup water and orgeat or lemonade for temperance, or wines and punch.

The manner of celebrating New Year's day by calls, is a peculiarity of our own, and having so few which are " native here," many of our wisest and best, have wished that this might in no wise be slighted. Many a feud-divided family have been united, and misunderstanding friends been brought together, under the all-pervading hospitality and genial influence which distinguishes the day.

Fourth of July.

There is generally a cold collation on this day.

Let the centre of the table be ornamented by a pyramid of evergreens or laurel, which may be made thus: make a stand or frame not less than three feet high, make a long wreath of the richest laurel or evergreens, and beginning at the top, wind it around the frame until the bottom is reached: at the summit, let there be a miniature flag of our country, or a small bust or statue of Washington, and at regular distances downward, small silk flags with the coat of arms and mottoes of each several State in the Union; or instead of the flags, take as many streamers of different shades of colored ribbons as there are States, or stars cut from gold or silver paper. The flags may be painted by ladies whose national feelings and talents inspire them to the work.—A cold boiled ham and cold roasted poultry may be placed on one end of the table, or at the middle of one side, and lobster and chicken salads at the sides or end, with bread and butter sandwich and crackers and soda biscuit; such pasty, jelly tarts, jellies, floating island or blancmange and baskets of cut cake and maccaroons, as may be desired, may be distributed around the table; and syrup water and lemonade, with a fine bowl of temperance beverage and bottled soda, which will generally leave a more clear recollection, than wines, cordials, and champagne.

Thanksgiving Dinner.

The substantials for Thanksgiving dinner are similar to those for Christmas, whilst pumpkin pie crowns the dessert, (see Thanksgiving pie,) and the pyramids are of macaroons, &c.

A Fine Temperance Beverage.

To the juice of a dozen fine fresh lemons, pressed so as to extract the essence from the skins, put one pound of double refined sugar; to one quart of picked raspberries or strawberries (or a pint of preserved fruit), put half a pound of fine sugar—pare a ripe pine apple and cut it in thin slices, and each slice in four or six pieces, and put with it half a pound of sugar; stir the lemon juice with the sugar until it is all dissolved, crush the strawberries, and slightly bruise the pine-apple; put the lemon into a large bowl, and add to it three quarts of ice water, then add the strawberry and pine-apple, stir it until the sugar is all dissolved, then set the bowl on ice for an hour before serving. Dip it from the bowl into small tumblers, three parts fill them, and serve with sponge cake cut small, Palo Alto cakes and small sugar cakes.

Bottled fruit, or pine-apple preserved without cooking, may be used in winter.

Champagne Punch

May be made as above directed, with the addition of a bottle of champagne. Or another punch may be made by putting to the Temperance Beverage, of brandy and rum half a pint each, or more according to the quantity required. Sprigs of fresh green mint added to it, and put into a tumbler half filled with finely chipped ice, with glass tubes for sipping it, will make mint julap.

COOKERY FOR INVALIDS.

MISCELLANEOUS RECEIPTS.

To Make Water Gruel.—Put a quart of water or milk into a stew-pan, and set it over the fire; into a pint bowl put a heaping tablespoonful of sweet corn meal, and a small teaspoonful of salt, make it a smooth batter with milk; when the water or milk in the stew pan is boiling hot, stir it into the batter, and let it boil gently for half an hour; when served, it may be sweetened with loaf sugar and a little nutmeg grated over, for a relaxed state of the system, or sweeten with brown sugar, make it with water, and boil a few raisins with it, when the opposite is the case. A bit of butter and a wineglass of wine, or a tablespoonful of brandy, may be added to water gruel, when it is wanted for a strengthening nourishment. Water gruel is generally given after a dose of castor oil, or after an emetic, or almost any thorough medicine.

Oat-Meal Gruel.—Make precisely as directed for corn meal; these gruels, made thus, are extremely nourishing and grateful to the palate, with only salt or sugar, &c. Infants, before weaning, and immediately after, are apt to be fond of gruel or panada

Arrowroot.—This is very nourishing and light, either for invalids or infants; make it with milk or water—put a pint of either into a stew-pan, make it boiling hot, add a saltspoonful of salt, put a heaped teaspoonful of ground Bermuda arrowroot into a cup, make it smooth with cold milk, stir it into the stew-pan, and let it simmer for two or three minutes; then turn it into a bowl, sweeten and grate nutmeg over, if liked; should it be preferred thin, use less arrowroot.

This should be made only as much as is wanted at a time, since it will become as thin as water if heated over. Arrowroot may be made in small quantities, by mixing a teaspoonful smooth in a cup with cold water or milk, then pour upon it, stirring it all the time, boiling milk or water to make it thick or thinner to your taste—add a few grains of salt and sugar to taste.

CARRAGAN MOSS.—Wash and pick a tablespoonful of Irish moss, and put it into a tin cup, pour on it half a pint of boiling water, and set it on a stove or coals for a short time; when it is all dissolved, add sugar and nutmeg to taste. This may be made with milk, to resemble custard, and is wonderfully nourishing and delicate. Delicate infants may be fed on it when they will take no other nourishment.

ARROWROOT BLANCMANGE.—Put a quart of milk to boil, take an ounce of Bermuda arrowroot ground fine, make it a smooth batter with cold milk, add a teaspoonful of salt; when the milk is boiling hot, stir the batter into it, continue to stir it over a gentle fire (that it may not be scorched) for three or four minutes, sweeten to taste with double refined sugar, and flavor with lemon extract or orange flower water, or boil a stick of cinnamon or vanilla bean in the milk before putting in the arrowroot; dip a mould into cold water, strain the blancmange through a muslin into the mould, when perfectly cold turn it out; serve currant jelly or jam with it.

RICE-FLOUR BLANCMANGE.—Make as directed for arrowroot blancmange, a small teacupful of ground rice to a quart of milk.

THICKENED MILK, (*Milk Soup.*)—Put a quart of milk over the fire to boil, put a teacupful of wheat flour into a basin, sprinkle over it enough water to make it damp, then work it between the hands until it forms in small smooth rolls, put a teaspoonful of salt to the milk, and when it is boiling hot, stir in the flour, let it boil gently for ten or twelve minutes, then turn it into a tureen, add sugar and nutmeg if liked, or without either.
This is very light and nourishing for invalids or children, except in cases of constipation, which boiled milk increases.

MILK PORRIDGE.—Make a quart of milk boiling hot: make a tablespoonful of wheat flour, a smooth batter with cold milk; add a teaspoonful of salt, and stir it into the boiling milk; continue to stir it for five minutes then put it into a basin or tureen; sweeten to taste; flavor with nutmeg or cinnamon This is very nourishing and agreeable either for children or adults. Sweetened with loaf sugar, and nutmeg grated plentifully over it, will make it a most excellent remedy for looseness or dysentery. Or, boiled milk without the thickening, sweetened with loaf sugar, and flavored with grated nutmeg, has the same effect.

BUTTERMILK POP.—Make a quart of buttermilk boiling hot, wet a tablespoonful of corn meal or wheat flour, and make it a smooth batter with water, and stir it into the milk, with a teaspoonful of salt; continue to stir it for five minutes when wheat flour is used, or fifteen when it is made with corn meal. Sweeten to taste with sugar or syrup, and add nutmeg or ground cinnamon, if liked. This is eaten with bread broken into it.

GREEN CORN SOUP, *(very excellent.)*—Cut the corn from the cob, (sweet corn to be preferred;) put it into a stew-pan, with a quart or more of sweet milk: add a teaspoonful of salt; let it boil gently for half an hour, then add a bit of sweet butter the size of an egg, and pepper to taste; and serve with rolls or toast. A blade of mace may be added to the flavor if liked.

TOAST WATER.—Cut a slice from a wheat loaf; toast it dry and brown without burning; put it into a pitcher, and pour over it a pint or more of water. A very little lemon-juice may be added to it, with sugar, if desired.

APPLE-WATER.—Cut tart apples quite small; pour boiling water over them, and set it where it will simmer gently for half an hour; then strain off the liquor; sweeten to taste, and serve. Or, take baked apples, and finish in the same manner.

BAKED APPLES.—Put tart or sweet apples into a pan, and set it into a moderate oven for nearly an hour, or a full hour for sweet apples, until they are soft enough to mash.

LEMON WATER.—Cut a small fresh skin lemon in very thin slices; put them into a pitcher, pour a pint of boiling water over; cover it, and let it stand until cold; then sweeten to taste, and serve

To MULL CIDER.--Take a pint of sweet cider; reserve a teacupful of it; then to the remainder put an equal quantity of water, and set it to boil, with a teaspoonful of whole alspice; beat three eggs very light, and by degrees stir the cold cider to them; then stir them into the boiling cider and water; continue to stir it until smooth; sweeten to taste; grate a little nutmeg over, and serve hot in tumblers, with doughnuts or crullers.

MULLED WINE.—Make the same as directed to mull cider, of port, or Madeira.

RICE MILK.—Wash a large teaspoonful of rice, and put it to a quart of sweet milk, with a teaspoonful of salt; cover it, and set it over the fire for nearly an hour; then take it up; add sugar to taste, with nutmeg or ground cinnamon.

SAGO.—Let it soak for an hour or more in cold water, to take off the earthy taste; then rinse it through another water; put a teacupful into a dish; pour over it a quart of boiling water, and let it boil gently for nearly an hour; then sweeten to taste; grate nutmeg over, and serve—or, serve with a sauce.

SAGO MILK.—Soak the sago; then finish as rice milk.

TAPIOCA.—Make as directed for rice.

BARLEY WATER.—Put a large tablespoonful of well-washed pearl-barley into a pitcher; pour over it boiling water; cover it, and let it remain till cold; then drain off the water; sweeten to taste, and, if liked, add the juice of a lemon, and grated nutmeg.

BROTH, IN HASTE.—Chop some roast meat or broiled steak quite fine; to a teacupful put a pint or more of boiling water; cover it, and set it over a gentle fire for ten minutes; season to taste. This broth for invalids or children is both excellent and convenient. A cracker may be rolled fine, and put with the meat before putting on the water.

PANADA.—Break stale bread or soda crackers small, and put them into a bowl; put a bit of butter to it, and pour boiling water over, to make it quite wet; work it fine with a spoon; add sugar and nutmeg to taste, and more water, to make it thinner. Raisins, picked free from stems, and rinsed in cold water, may be put in with the bread, when there is no objection to the effect produced by them—they being laxative.

PRUNES, STEWED.—Rinse or wash the prunes, as may be necessary; then put them into a stew-pan, with a teacupful of clean brown sugar to a pound, and water more than to cover them; cover the pan, and let them stew gently for nearly an hour, until they are soft, and the syrup is rich.

To REMOVE STAINS FROM THE HANDS.—Dampen the hands first in water, then rub them with tartaric acid, or salt of lemons, as you would with soap; rinse them and rub them dry. Tartaric acid, or salt of lemons, will quickly remove stains from white muslin or linens. Put less than half a teaspoonful of the salt or acid into a tablespoonful of water; wet the stain with it, and lay it in the sun for an hour; wet it once or twice with cold water during the time: if this does not quite remove it, repeat the acid water, and lay it in the sun. Tomato juice will remove stains from the hands.

TOMATO PIE.—Take the yellow small tomatoes, ripe but not soft; pare them with a sharp knife; cut them in two across; take out the juice and seeds; then cut the tomatoes small, and season and finish as directed for apple pie. (see page 251.)

TOMATO TART.—Pare and take the seeds from the tomatoes; cut them small, and stew them with sugar and nutmeg, with a very little water or lemon juice; make it quite sweet, and finish as directed for apple tart. (see page 251.)

RHUBARB PRESERVE.—Strip off the outer skin; cut the stalks in inch lengths, and finish as directed for tomatoes

WATER-MELON PICKLES.—Prepare the rind of watermelon as directed for sweetmeat preserve, and put them into cold, spiced vinegar; or, cut them in strips the length and breadth of a finger.

LARGE PLUMS—May be pared with a sharp knife, then preserved the same as directed for peaches.

RIBS OF BEEF.—A fine roasting-piece of beef from the ribs may first be boned, which is a great improvement.

A FORE-QUARTER OF VEAL.—The bone may be taken from a shoulder of veal, without cutting it off; stuff the place of it with potato or bread-stuffing.

ADDITIONAL RECEIPTS

RICE PIE.

Boil a pint of milk, with a pint of cold milk mix smoothly three heaping tablespoonfuls of rice flour and four well beaten eggs, flavor with extract of lemon, (or boil lemon peel in the milk), then stir the eggs, milk, &c., into the boiling milk—sweeten to taste—let it cool; add a wineglass of Madeira wine, if liked, and some nutmeg, line dishes with pie paste, and finish the same as pumpkin.

RICE CUSTARD.

Boil one quart of milk, to one tablespoonful of rice flour, put one beaten egg, and enough of cold milk to make a batter, then stir it into the boiling milk, sweeten to taste—add nutmeg and peach water or lemon extract, a teaspoonful of either, strain it, and serve.

A FRENCH DESSERT.

Beat four eggs to a quart of milk, sweeten and flavor to taste, cut slices of baker's bread and steep them until thoroughly saturated, then fry in hot butter, and serve.

VERMICELLI PUDDING.

Put two ounces of vermicelli into a quart of milk, and boil it over a gentle fire until dissolved, then let it cool, add three well beaten eggs, bake in a quick oven for one hour, and serve with wine or brandy sauce.

SUET PUDDING.

Make a stiff batter with one quart of milk, and as much sifted wheat flour as may be necessary; add three well beaten eggs and two ounces of beef suet, chopped fine, tie it in a bag, and boil for two hours ; serve with a sauce.

TAPIOCA PUDDING.

Put a coffee cup full of tapioca into two quarts of milk, and set it near the fire for an hour, or put it in hot milk— let it cool, then add six well beaten eggs, sweeten to taste, flavor with lemon or peach water or nutmeg, and bake for one hour in a hot oven.

COCOANUT PUDDING.

Boil one quart of milk, when cool, add six well beaten eggs and a piece of butter the size of an egg, and the white meat of a cocoanut, grated fine, flavour, and sweeten to taste ; put it into a buttered pan ; grate two crackers over, and bake in a quick oven—when it is done, it will rise in the middle.

PLUM PUDDING.

Grate a sixpenny loaf of baker's bread, and moisten it with milk, then add to it half a teacup of wheat flour, three-quarters of a pound of butter, half a pound of brown sugar, half a teaspoonful of saleratus, one pound of raisins, stoned, one pound of currants, half a pound of citron, one wine glass of brandy, one nutmeg, grated, and ground cinnamon and alspice, each a teaspoonful — tie it in a cloth, and boil for five hours ; serve with a sauce.

POTATO PUDDING.

Boil one pound of potatoes, and grate them fine, add half a pound of sugar, and six beaten eggs, one wine glass of brandy, grated orange peel, cinnamon and nutmeg, each a teaspoonful—bake in a quick oven, and serve.

ORANGE PUDDING.

One pound of butter with one pound of sugar beaten to a froth, eight eggs well beaten, a fresh lemon, grated, (the pip taken out), the skins of three oranges boiled, and beaten to a pulp, and the juice strained ; add the orange and lemon juice after the eggs—add a wineglass of wine or brandy and nutmeg—bake in a quick oven.

APPLE PUDDING.

Eight large pippens, pared, boiled tender, and mashed, half a pound of butter, half a pound of sugar, six eggs beaten, the juice of a sweet orange, and the rind grated, and a glass of wine—bake in a quick oven.

BAKED INDIAN PUDDING.

Boil three pints of sweet milk, and stir into it one pint of Indian meal, when cold, add five well beaten eggs, a teaspoonful of salt, half a pound of raisins, stoned, and a quarter of a pound of butter, sweeten and spice to taste, and bake nearly two hours in a quick oven.

CHARLIE'S APPLE PUDDING.

Butter a pudding dish well, then put in an inch deep of chopped apples, strew over sugar and spice, with a few bits of butter, then an inch deep of bread crumbs or rolled crackers, then another layer of apples, spice, &c., and lastly crackers or bread crumbs; then again apples, and so fill the dish; press the whole firmly down by turning a plate over it—bake six hours.

MARLBOROUGH PUDDING.

Half a pound of grated apples, half a pound of fine white sugar, half a pound of butter, six eggs well beaten, the peel of one lemon grated, and the strained juice of two; line the dish with pie paste, put the pudding in, and bake in a quick oven.

FLOUR PUDDING BAKED IN CUPS.

Five heaping teaspoonfuls of wheat flour beaten with five eggs, add as much milk as will make a thin batter, sweeten with two table spoonfuls of sugar, add half a nutmeg, grated, and a little lemon extract, bake in little buttered cups, in a quick oven

PLAIN INDIAN PUDDING.

Take a quart of milk, boiling hot, stir into it two teacups of yellow corn meal, add two eggs well beaten, and a teaspoonful of salt, with a teacup of light brown sugar, and a bit of butter the size of an egg ; add nutmeg, cinnamon, and a little ginger, and bake two hours.

CARROT PUDDING.

Grate half a pound of carrots, and half a pound of bread, add half a nutmeg, grated, a teaspoonful of salt, and the same of cinnamon, put to it four table spoonfuls of sugar, four well beaten eggs, half a pound of butter, melted, one glass of wine and a pint of milk, beat the whole together, put it into a buttered dish, sprinkle fine sugar over, and bake.

BREAD CAKE.

Take three pounds of risen dough, one pound of butter, one pound of sugar, one pound of currants, six beaten eggs, one glass of brandy, one nutmeg, grated, and half a teaspoonful of alspice ; work the butter, sugar and eggs well together, then work it into the dough, make it in a loaf, and bake the same as bread.

DROP BISCUITS.

Take a piece of butter, the size of an egg, one quart of milk, four beaten eggs, and to make a batter so thick as to drop without running; add grated nutmeg and lemon extract—let it stand one hour, then drop it on a floured tin, in small cakes, and bake in a quick oven, to a fine brown color.

A SPONGE CAKE.

Take twelve eggs, and their weight of sugar, and half their weight of flour, beat the yolks and sugar together, then add the flour, and lastly, the white, having beaten them to a high froth, stir them lightly together, add half a grated nutmeg, put it into a paper-lined pan, and bake quickly.

SPONGE CAKE PUDDING.

Take two eggs, with their weight in sugar, and half their weight in flour, flavor with lemon or rose water; make a mixture as for rice pie—put the sponge cake mixture into a buttered basin, and when the pie mixture is cold pour it over, and bake.

DELICATE CAKE.

One pound of fine white sugar, one pound of flour, seven ounces of sweet butter, beaten to a cream—the whites of eight eggs beaten to a froth, half a nutmeg, grated, and some lemon extract, if liked, or a little rose water—bake in a paper-lined pan. Almonds blanched and pounded to a paste may be added or substituted for butter.

ALBANY CAKES.

Two pounds and a half of flour, half a pound of sugar, one teacup of sour milk, one egg, one teacupful of saleratus, dissolved in a little water, one tablespoonful of rose water or brandy, and half a nutmeg, grated, or a teaspoonful of ground cinnamon, roll out very thin, and bake in a quick oven for ten minutes.

A GENERAL RULE FOR MAKING SPONGE CAKE.

Take the weight of the eggs used in sugar, and half the weight of flour, beat the yolks and sugar together, then add the flour, and, lastly, the whites, having beaten them to a high froth, stir them thoroughly together, put it into a paper-lined basin, or pan, and bake in a quick oven; the cake may be flavored with lemon, rose, or vanilla extracts, and a little nutmeg, or with a little brandy. Pounded almonds or grated cocoanut, may be added to sponge cake mixture.

A COCOANUT CAKE.

Grate the white meat of one cocoanut—take half a pound of flour, three quarters of a pound of sugar, six ounces of butter, and six beaten eggs for the cake, flavor to taste, when well beaten, stir in the cocoanut, and bake as pound cake.

INDIAN BREAKFAST CAKE.

Take a quart of milk, scalding hot, stir into it as much corn meal as will make a thick batter, add of salt and saleratus, in fine powder, each a teaspoonful, and when a little cooled, two well beaten eggs, bake in buttered pans, in a quick oven.

INDIAN BREAKFAST CAKE.

Wheat flour, one pint bowlful, Indian or corn meal ditto, three well beaten eggs, one tablespoonful of butter, and a pint of milk—bake in small pans, buttered—a quick oven.

INDIAN CAKES.

Make a quart of milk boiling hot, stir it into a pint of sweet white Indian meal, after it has quite cooled, add four beaten eggs, one tablespoonful of wheat flour, one tablespoonful of butter, and a teaspoonful of salt; bake in shallow pans in a quick oven.

INDIAN GRIDDLE CAKES.

One quart of milk, one pint of corn meal, four well beaten eggs, four tablespoonfuls of flour, and one teaspoonful of salt, beat it well together, and bake on a griddle or in a pan.

MUFFINS.

One pint of milk, a bit of butter the size of a large nut, two well beaten eggs, and two tablespoonfuls of yeast— warm the milk and butter together, then add the other ingredients — let it set in a warm place for an hour, or more, and bake in rings on a griddle.

WASHINGTON BREAKFAST CAKE.

One pound and a half of flour, two ounces of butter, one pint of milk, three well beaten eggs, two tablespoonfuls of sugar, and a small teaspoonful of salt, beat it well together put it in pans an inch deep, and bake in a quick oven.

PEACH POT PIE.

Make a paste of one teacup of water and half a cup of shortening, (if lard or beef dripping is used, salt it,) and as much wheat flour as will make a nice paste; take a small iron pot, butter the sides, roll out your paste, reserve enough to cover the top of the pie, put some around the sides, leaving the bottom uncovered, the size of a teaplate; pare half a peck of peaches, and cut them in two, leaving half a dozen with the stones in. If you have more paste, cut it in slips, and put it in with the peaches; put them in the pot, strew half a pound of sugar over, grate nearly a nutmeg over, cut a tablespoonful of butter in bits, and strew them in, add a teacup of water, and a small teaspoonful of salt, put the top crust over, cut a slit in the middle, cover the pot, and set it over a gentle fire for one hour, when it may be put in a hot oven to brown. Apples or cherries may be done in the same manner.

STRAWBERRY SHORT CAKE.

Make a short cake of sour milk or cream, make it in a cake the size of a dinner plate, bake it, then break it through the middle, make a pint of strawberries liquid with sweet cream, and sweeten with white sugar, spread it over the lower part of the cake, put the top over, let it stand for an hour then cut it in wedge shape pieces, and serve.

PORK AND APPLE PIE.

Line a tin with a pie paste, nearly fill it with peeled and quartered tart apples, cover it with thin slices of fat salt pork, add pepper, put a top crust over, and bake in a quick oven for one hour. This is an old-fashioned farmer's pie, and eaten with the addition of syrup, a very much relished dinner.

CRACKLINGS.

Take of cold veal or poultry, and one-half as much ham, chopped fine, mix with them an equal quantity of bread crumbs, add to it beaten eggs to moisten it, make it in small flat cakes, and fry a nice brown in salted lard or beef drippings. Potatoes may be used instead of bread crumbs.

NOODLES AND BEEFSTEAK

Break two eggs into wheat flour enough to make a stiff paste, then roll out to the thickness of a knife blade, let it lay half an hour, then strew a little flour over, roll it up, and with a sharp knife shave across it as fine as possible, put them into boiling water for fifteen minutes, then take them out with a skimmer. Fry a fat beefsteak with plenty of gravy, have ready two tablespoonfuls of grated cheese, put half your noodles on a steak dish, strew half the grated cheese over, lay on the steak, put over it the noodles and the remainder of the cheese, pour the gravy over, and serve. The cheese may be omitted.

TO MAKE NOODLES FOR SOUP.

Make as directed above, and drop them into the soup fifteen minutes before taking it up, instead of putting them in boiling water—they are preferred to macaroni or vermicelli.

TOMATO CATSUP.

Cut one bushel of tomatos in thin slices, and put them in layers in an earthen vessel, strewing salt between each layer, one quart of salt for the whole quantity; let them remain for twelve hours, then stew them slowly until quite soft, rub them through a fine sieve, put them again to stew, add one gallon of vinegar, eight tablespoonfuls of mustard powder, six tablespoonfuls of black pepper, four ditto cayenne, two ditto alspice, cloves ditto; let it simmer for one hour and a half, let it become cold, then bottle and seal it. A porcelain kettle, or an earthen pipkin, is the only safe article for making catsup, the action of the acid on metals being so very poisonous; an earthen pipkin of yellow ware, is decidedly the best vessel for stewing tomatos.

ADDITIONAL IN TWELFTH THOUSAND.

BROWN GRAVY SOUP.

Put into a soup-pot the bones of roast beef and broiled steak bones, together with the root end of tongue, poultry giblets and carcass and a knuckle of veal and the bone of a ham—the meat having been all cut off—let them simmer with water to cover them for four or five hours or longer, then pour it through a colander into a deep basin or stone pot, and set it away until the next day, when take off the cake of fat from the top and pour it off free from sediment; put it into the soup-pot, add a blade of mace and three or four whole cloves, with a small bit of dried red pepper, thicken with two or three table-spoonfulls of nicely browned flour; have some nicely toasted bread cut into dice on the tureen, and pour over the soup.

MUSHROOMS WITH BEEFSTEAK.

Take a dozen or more nice fresh mushrooms, skin them and wash them thoroughly through several waters, then having taken them from the water put them into a stewpan with less than half a teaspoonful of salt and the same of pepper, and a tablespoonful of port wine or water, and half a tablespoonful of butter. Cover the saucepan, set it over the fire, shake it frequently, dredge in a tea-spoonful of flour, let it stew about twenty minutes, then pour it over a broiled beefsteak, and serve hot.

TOMATOS WITH BEEFSTEAK.

Take the skins from a dozen ripe tomatos, put them into a stewpan with a tea-spoonful of salt and the same of pepper, add a small bit of butter, dredge in a tea-spoonful of flour, (either browned or not as may be preferred), let them stew for at least half an hour, then having broiled and nicely seasoned a beefsteak as previously directed, pour over the tomatos and serve hot. A tea-spoonful of sugar put to the tomatos whilst stewing is considered a great improvement by some tastes, or a tea-spoonful of made mustard.

TO FRY SAUSAGES.

Original and superior receipt.

Put the sausages into a frying pan, pour boiling water over to cover them, cover the pan and set them on the back of the fire for ten or fifteen minutes, then take them from the water with a skimmer or into a colander, roll each one singly in wheat flour until it is all white, then having a frying pan with boiling hot lard or pork fat, put in the sausages, roll them over that they may be browned on every side, then serve hot.

TOMATOS FRIED.

Take four tomatos, and without skinning them cut them into rather thick slices (quarter of an inch), flour them, make a little butter or lard hot in a frying pan, put in the sliced tomatos, and when one side is browned turn the other and do likewise, serve in a dish or over a broiled steak or chicken.

POTATO CAKES,

To serve with Roast Ducks.

Having boiled some potatos, chop them fine, season with pepper and salt, to one dozen large sized potatos put a table-spoonful of butter, break into them one fresh egg, then stir them well together, form them in cakes about half an inch thick, and put them in the pan under the duck (or else fry them), and serve with them.

PEACHES PRESERV'D WITHOUT COOKING,

To equal the finest Brandy Peaches.

Brush the down from the peaches and put them into a deep basin, pour boiling water over to cover them, then cover it with a thickly folded towel, let it remain until the water is nearly cold, take them out one by one and rub off the skins with a coarse towel, put a layer of them in the jar or can, cover them with a thick layer of the best pulverized white sugar, then put another layer of peaches, and peaches and sugar alternately until the jar or can is full, the sugar being last, and immediately close and seal them,—set them in a cool, dry, dark place.

Peaches may be cut in halves, or smaller, and done in the same manner. See pine apples without cooking.

Green Gages may be preserved without cooking, the same as peaches.

GREEN CORN FRITTERS.

Cut sugar corn from the cob, scrape whatever of the milk of the corn may remain on the cob;—to a quart bowl of the cut corn put a tea cup of wheat flour and two beaten eggs, with enough milk to make a batter; make a little sweet butter hot in a frying pan, and make the fritters of a table-spoonful of the batter; turn them, that both sides may be nicely browned.

RICE CAKES.

These are made of cold boiled rice with eggs and milk, and a very little wheat flour to make a batter. Bake on a griddle or in a fryingpan, with nice sweet butter, for breakfast or a side dish at dinner, or for dessert with ground cinnamon and fine sugar.

CORN STARCH OR FARINA.

Made as directed for blanc mange, on the packages, with the addition of a little lemon or vanilla flavor, as may be liked, poured into moulds first dipped in cold water, and set on ice for six or more hours. Serve with sweet cream.

POTATOS BAKED IN CUPS.

Mash potatos with butter, and season with salt and pepper. Butter some earthen tea cups and fill them with the prepared potato and bake them in an oven. Or, having shaped them in cups or bowls, wet them over with beaten egg and brown them in an oven or before the fire; or, instead of the egg, dredge with wheat flour, and baste with a little butter.

PEACH FRITTERS.

Made the same as apple fritters.

CREAM OF TARTAR BISCUIT.

To a quart of fine wheat flour put two tea-spoonfuls of cream tartar and one of soda, rub it through a sieve, add a tea cup of sweet butter, work it through the flour, then wet it into a paste with enough sweet milk; work it as little as possible, and let the paste be as soft as can be rolled out on a well floured paste board, let them be an inch thick, cut them in small round or square cakes, and bake in a hot oven for ten or fifteen minutes.

Rolls may be made in the same manner, omitting the butter and adding a teaspoonful of salt; roll them between the hands in cakes the length of a finger, and bake.

CREAM OF TARTAR COOKIES.

To a quart of flour put two tea-spoonfuls of cream of tartar and one of soda, pass it through a sieve, add to it two tea cups of brown sugar, one tea cup of butter, and one or two eggs, with enough milk to make it a paste, add a grated nutmeg, roll half an inch thick and cut in small cakes.

DELICIOUS AND DELICATE MINCE PIES.

Boil a fine piece of beef, free from strings or fat; when it is tender put it into a colander and let it become cold, then chop it very fine, put to it enough of the very best Stuart's syrup to slightly moisten it or rather hold it together, add to it ground cinnamon or cassia, ground cloves, alspice and mace or nutmeg as it may suit the taste to have it more or less highly spiced; pack it down close in an earthen or stone jar, dip a bit of muslin in syrup (one side) and press it upon the prepared meat.—keep it in a cool place. When wanted for use take a pint bowl of the meat, add to it a quart of the very best pippin or greening apples, pared and chopped not too finely, put to it a pint of the best Madeira wine and a wine glass of brandy, a tea cup of nicely cleaned and dried zante currants, and the same of raisins stoned and chopped, and a quarter of citron cut small; mix all well together, add enough sugar to make it really sweet, and it is ready for the paste. Cider of the best sort may be used instead of wine, and the juice of two lemons instead of, or in addition to the brandy.

LARDED SWEETBREAD.

Parboil two or three sweetbreads, let them become cold, then lard them down the middle with bits of fat bacon, and on each side with bits of lemon peel, and beyond that with a little pickled cucumber cut small, then stew them gently under a rich gravy thickened with a little flour, add a little mushroom powder, a small pinch of cayenne pepper, a little salt, and a squeeze or two of lemon juice.

SWEETBREADS ROASTED.

Trim off the tough part, then scald them for a few minutes in a stewpan of water and a little salt (the heart sweetbreads), then take them out into a basin of cold water until cool, have an egg beat up in a dish, and also have ready some fine bread crumbs and clarified butter. Run a skewer through the sweetbreads and fasten on the spit, egg them all over, shake bread crumbs over, then sprinkle clarified butter over, and then bread crumbs again and roast them for a quarter of an hour, take them from the skewer and make a gravy of butter and a little browned flour with hot water or a little lemon juice, and a shake of cayenne. Make it hot and serve in the dish under the sweetbread.

SWEETBREADS FRIED.

Prepare them as for roasting, then fry in butter made hot, turn them to brown them nicely, then make a little gravy with water or lemon juice, and serve.

SWEETBREADS STEWED.

Parboil them, then put them into a stew-pan with a little water or milk: work a little butter and flour together, and add it with a blade or two of mace, some salt and white pepper, and, if liked, a little chopped parsley. Garnish with thin slices of lemon.

VEAL COLLOPS.

Cut the veal from the leg or other lean parts into pieces the size of a large oyster; have a seasoning of pepper, salt, and a little ground mace, or sweet herbs; rub some over each; then dip them into beaten egg, and afterwards into fine bread crumbs or rolled crackers, and fry in sweet butter, the same as oysters. These both look and taste like oysters.

SWEETBREADS LIKE OYSTERS.

Boil the sweetbreads tender in water and a little salt; then pound or mash them fine; add bread crumbs, a little butter, pepper, and salt, and lemon juice. Season them nicely; then add enough beaten egg to bind all together. Make them in cakes the size of an oyster, and fry and serve.

WHITE MINCE OF VEAL.

Chop some cold veal very fine; season with a little mace, white pepper, and a little water, and a bit of butter worked to a paste with wheat flour: a cup of cream may be added at the last.

A wine-glass of Madeira or Port wine, instead of the cream, may be added, and makes another dish.

VEAL CAKES.

Take three quarters of a pound of lean veal, quarter of a pound of beef suet, half the rind of a lemon chopped fine, a little mace, pepper, salt, and a very little white onion. Mix these together; beat them well in a mortar, make them into small cakes, and fry them a nice brown.

JULIENNE SOUP.

This soup is composed of carrots, turnips, leeks, onions, celery, cabbage, parsley, and other vegetables: the roots are cut in thin slips, about an inch long; the vegetables are halved, and then sliced. Fry or stew the roots in a little butter, and stew the other vegetables in a little of the broth, before adding all the broth. For a Julienne root cutter, see Berrian, 601 Broadway.

MACCARONI WITH CHEESE.

Simmer quarter of a pound of maccaroni in a quart of milk, until the pipes are well swelled and tender; then butter a pudding dish, put in a layer of maccaroni; strew it plentifully with grated cheese and bits of butter; then another layer of maccaroni, and grated cheese and butter, and maccaroni, alternately, until the dish is full, the cheese being last; then put over the whole bits of butter, or melt the butter and put it over; then put it into a moderate oven until it is nicely browned. Serve hot.

The cheese for this purpose should be cut and allowed to become dry before it is grated. Pineapple, or old English or Parmesan, should be used. The milk in which the maccaroni is steeped must also be added, if not all absorbed.

MACCARONI SWEET.

Boil two ounces of maccaroni in a pint of milk, with a bit of lemon peel and a stick of cinnamon. When the pipes are swelled to their utmost size without breaking, lay them on a custard dish; pour a custard over them whilst hot. Serve cold.

FARINA PUDDING.

Put a quart of milk into a farina kettle: when it is boiling hot, stir in enough of the dry farina, stirring it all the time, to make it quite thick. Add a small teaspoonful of salt. When it has boiled for twenty minutes or half an hour, take it from the fire, have ready the yolks of three eggs, beaten smooth: stir the hot farina with a spoon, adding by degrees the beaten yolks, and stirring it vigorously all the time, that it may be well blended. Butter a pudding dish large enough to contain it, pour it in, and brown it in a hot or quick oven, fifteen or twenty minutes before serving.

Wine, Brandy, or Lemon Sauce. See page 240.

This is an original receipt, and makes a most delicate pudding, superior to cocoanut, but having that peculiar flavor.

FARINA.

This most excellent article of food may be prepared in a variety of ways. Made as directed in the preceding receipt, before adding the eggs, with the addition of a little sugar and lemon or vanilla flavor, or a stick of cinnamon, (boiled in the milk before adding the farina,) and served cold with sweet cream, it is one of the most acceptable of summer desserts. Dip a jelly mould first in cold water, pour in the boiled farina, and when cold set it on ice. Serve the following day.

Farina may be colored yellow with the yolk of one egg, and served in the same manner. The mould should be an ear of corn when this is done.

CORN STARCH

May be prepared and served the same as farina.

CORN STARCH CUSTARD.

Set a quart of milk to boil, (use a farina kettle,) to three well-beaten eggs add a large tea-spoonful of corn starch, beat it smooth, then stir it into the boiling milk; continue to stir it, and let it boil for twenty minutes; then turn it into a china dish, or when cooled, a glass bowl. Set it in a cold place, or on ice. Having beaten the white of the eggs to a high froth with a table-spoonful or two of pulverized sugar, heap it on before serving.

The corn starch should be sweetened to taste, and flavored with lemon or vanilla.

APPLE PUDDING.

Grate a stale loaf of baker's bread, butter a pudding dish well with sweet butter, strew it plentifully with bread crumbs; then having cored and sliced rich tart or sour apples, (pippins or greenings are best,) put a layer of them on the bread; strew plentifully with light brown sugar and bits of butter, with grated nutmeg or cinnamon; then another layer of bread crumbs and apples, bread, &c., alternately, until the dish is full—the bread and butter and spice being the last. Bake two hours in a moderate oven.

This is a delicious pudding.

CHICKEN SALAD.

Take the white meat of a chicken, either boiled, roasted, or fricasseed; cut it small, or mince it fine; take the same quantity or more of white tender celery, cut small; mix the celery and chicken together an hour or two before it is wanted; then add the salad dressing, (see page 186.) Mix the whole together, put it on a dish, make it in an oval form, spread some of the dressing over the outside. Garnish with the most delicate leaves of celery around the edge, and the white of the egg cut in rings, and green pickles cut in thin lengthwise slices—small cucumber pickles are to be used. Pickled beets may be added, cut in slices, and then in diamonds or stars, alternately with the green pickles and eggs.

LOBSTER SALAD

Must be made and dressed in the same manner as directed for chicken salad, adding the green inside and soft parts of the lobster, and garnish with the small claws of lobster.

POTATO SALAD.

Chop cold boiled potatos in square pieces, rather small, and dress the same as any other salad.

Lettuce, celery, potatos, water-cresses, or cabbage, with cold boiled beets, green pickles, may be used for salads.

SOFT CRABS.

Scald the crabs: take off the claws and spongy part and sand; wipe them dry, and broil or fry them nicely. Season with sweet butter, and pepper and salt.

SUET FRUIT PUDDING.

WITHOUT EGGS.

To one pound of wheat flour, add one tea-spoonful of cream of tartar, and half as much soda—rub it through a sieve; chop one pound of beef suet finely, free it from strings and shreds, and put it to the flour with a pound of chopped raisins or currants, one teacup of syrup, one table-spoonful of ground cinnamon, half a table-spoonful of allspice, and the same of cloves, with a little ground mace or nutmeg; tie it in a floured cloth, and boil three hours—serve with brandy sauce. Citron may be added, or the pudding may be made with it alone.

DELICIOUS CORN BREAD.

Measure a quart of sweet, freshly ground corn meal, add to it a large teacup of wheat flour, two tea-spoonfuls of cream of tartar, and one tea-spoonful of soda in powder; work the whole through a sieve, then add to it a table-spoonful of sweet butter, and the same of syrup; add three well beaten eggs and enough milk to make a batter; beat it well—it should not be much thicker batter than griddle cakes. Butter tin pans or basins, fill them an inch or more deep, and bake in a quick oven for one hour or more. This cannot be surpassed.

STRAWBERRY SHORT-CAKE.

Beat together a large table-spoonful of butter with two of sugar; add one well beaten egg; rub two even tea-spoonsful of cream of tartar in three cups of flower and add them; dissolve one even tea-spoon of soda in a cup of milk, add it last; bake in a flat pan in a quick oven. When done let it get cold, cut in three layers or in half, as you please, cover one layer with strawberries, sprinkle them with sugar; put on a layer of the cake, put another layer of strawberries and sugar, lay on the top layer and dust sugar over.

The strawberries are (I think) nicer if a syrup is made by putting three large spoonsful of sugar in one and a half gills of water; let it dissolve and boil a few moments to form a syrup, remove from the fire, put the berries in, shake them well, and when cool put on the cake in layers.

PAN'D OYSTERS.

Take fifty large oysters, rinse them with a little clean water and let them drain. Then put them in a stew-pan with quarter of a pound of butter, and sufficient salt; red and black pepper to season them well. Put the pan over a clear fire and stir while cooking. When the oysters begin to shrink, remove them from the fire, and serve immediately in a well heated covered dish.

TERRAPINS.

Take four terrapins and let them simmer in a kettle of boiling water for ten minutes; then take them out, and remove the nails and loose skin. Throw out the water just used, rinse the kettle thoroughly and fill it again with clean salted water, boiling hot; then wash the terrapins in warm water, return them to the kettle, and let them boil until thoroughly tender. The time required to boil a terrapin will depend somewhat upon its size and age, but when it is done sufficiently, the body will split at the side, and the claws become very tender. When done, take them out of the kettle and let them get cool; then remove the shells, and carefully clean the terrapins, being very particular to remove the gall, sandbag, entrails and all the spongy parts. Cut the meat very fine, place it in a stew-pan with three tea-spoonsful of flower, mixed with a pound of fresh butter, until thoroughly smooth; then put the pan over a clear fire, and season with salt, red and black pepper. When it comes to boil add half a pint of Madeira wine. Let it simmer a few minutes, being careful to stir it well; remove from the fire, and serve it in a well heated covered dish. For two terrapins use only half the above ingredients.

BEEF.

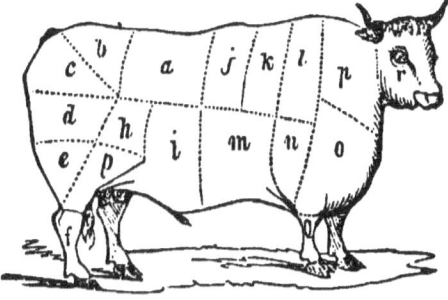

- a   The Sirloin.
- b   The Rump, or Round.
- c   Edge-Bone.
- d   Buttock.
- e   Mouse-Buttock.
- f   Leg.
- g   Thick Flank.
- h   Veiny Piece.
- i   Plate Piece.
- j   Ribs.
- k   Prime Ribs.
- l   Chuck Ribs.
- m   Brisket.
- n   Shoulder.
- o   Clod.
- p   Neck.
- q   Shin.
- r   Head.

MUTTON.

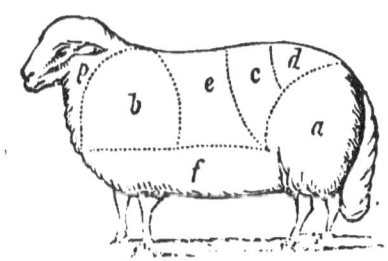

- a   Leg.
- b   Shoulder.
- c   Loin.
- d   Loin.
- e   Neck.
- f   Breast.

VEAL.

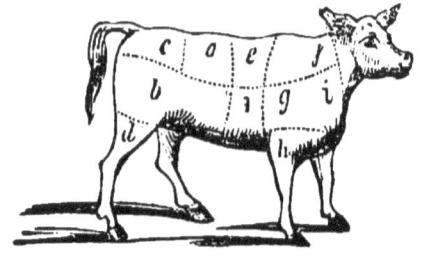

- a Loin, best end.
- c Chump End.
- b Fillet.
- d Knuckle.
- e Neck, best end.
- f Breast, best end.
- h Knuckle.
- g Blade-Bone.
- j Scrag, or Neck.
- l Breast.

PORK.

- a Ham.
- b Hind Loin.
- c Fore Loin.
- d Spare-Rib.
- e Hand, or Spring
- f Belly.

HINTS

ON THE

ETIQUETTE OF THE DINNER TABLE.

Without a perfect knowledge of the art of carving, it is impossible to perform the honors of the table with propriety; and nothing can be more disagreeable to one of a sensitive disposition, than to behold a person, at the head of a well-furnished board, hacking the finest joints, and giving them the appearance of having been gnawed by dogs.

It also merits attention in an economical point of view; a bad carver will mangle joints so as not to be able to fill half a dozen plates from a sirloin of beef, or a large tongue; which, besides creating a great difference in the daily consumption in families, often occasions disgust in delicate persons, causing them to loathe the provisions, however good, which are set before them, if helped in a clumsy manner.

One cannot, therefore, too strongly urge the study of this useful branch of domestic economy; and I doubt not that whoever pays due attention to the following instructions, will, after a little practice, without which all precept is unavailing, speedily acquire the reputation of being a good carver.

A few hints are prefixed on the etiquette of the dinner table, which will be found useful. In that, however, much must be left to a quick and observant eye, and a determination to render yourself as agreeable as possible.

As Host.—The important day on which you feast your friends being arrived, you will be duly prepared to receive the first detachment. It were almost needless to observe that the brief interval before dinner is announced, may be easily filled up by the common-place inquiries after health, and observations on the weather; as the company increases, provided they were previously acquainted, you will find your labors in keeping up the conversation very agreeably diminished.

While your guests are awaiting the announcement of dinner, it will be expedient that you should intimate to the gentlemen of the party, as unobtrusively as possible, which lady you wish each to take in charge, that, when the moment arrives for your adjournment to the dining-room, there may not be half a dozen claimants for the honor of escorting *la plus belle* of the party, while some plain *demoiselle* is under the painful necessity of escorting herself. Such a scene as this should be carefully provided against by the mode above suggested.

When dinner is announced, you will rise and request your friends to proceed to the dining-room, yourself leading the way, in company with your most distinguished female visitor, followed immediately by the hostess, accompanied by the gentleman who has the best claim to such an honor. The remainder of the guests then follow, each gentleman accompanied by the lady previously pointed out to him.

Arrived at the dining-room, you will request the lady whom you conducted to take her seat on your right hand; then, standing behind your chair, you will direct all your visitors to their respective seats.*

Having taken your seat, you will now dispatch soup to each of your guests, from the pile of plates placed on your right hand, without questioning any whether you shall help them or not; but, dealing it out silently, you will first help the person at your right hand, then at your left, and so throughout the table.

You will not ask to be allowed to help your guests, but supply a plate in silence, and hand it to your servants, who will offer it to such of the company as are unprovided. Never offer soup or fish a second time.

If a dish be on the table, some parts of which are preferred to others, according to the taste of the individuals, all should have the opportunity of choice. You will simply ask each one if he has any preference for a particular part; if he replies in the negative, you are not to repeat the question, nor insist that he must have a preference.

Do not attempt to eulogize your dishes, or apologize that you cannot recommend them,—this is extreme bad taste; as also is the vaunting of the excellence of your wines, &c. &c.

Do not insist upon your guests partaking of particular dishes. Do not ask persons more than once, and never force a supply upon their plates. It is ill-bred, though common, to press any one to eat; and, moreover, it is a great annoyance to be crammed like turkeys.

Neither send away your plate, nor relinquish your knife and fork, till your guests have finished.

Soup being removed, the gentleman who supports the lady of the house on her right, should request the honor of taking wine with her; this movement will be the signal for the rest. Should he neglect to do this, you must challenge some lady.

Until the cloth be removed, you must not drink wine except with another. If you are asked to take wine, it is a breach of etiquette to refuse. In performing this ceremony, (which is very agreeable if the wine be good,) you catch the person's eye, and bow politely. It is not necessary to say anything.

If you have children, never introduce them after dinner, unless particularly asked for, and then avoid it if possible.

Never make any observations to your servants at dinner, other than to request them to provide you with what you require, or to take away that which may be removed.

With the dessert, you will have a small plate, two wine-glasses, and *doyles*, placed before each guest. If fresh fruit be on the table, as pears, apples, nectarines, &c., a knife with a silver or silver-plated blade should be placed by the side of each plate; a steel blade, in addition to being discolored by the juices, imparts an unpleasant flavor to the fruit.

As GUEST.—To dine out, it is usually understood that you must be invited; there are, however, some *gentlemen*, who have attained to that high degree of refinement which enables them to dispense with such a stupid ceremony. They drop in as dinner is being served up, when it is impossible that the party on whom they intrude can do other than request them to stay and dine, though we suspect he has a much stronger *inclination* to kick the unwelcome guest into the street.

We would recommend you to eschew such practices; but when invited, return an answer in plain terms, accepting or declining. If you accept, be there at the appointed time. It is inconvenient, on many accounts, to yourself and to your friends, either to be too late or too early.

You will probably have to wait a little time before dinner is announced. During this short period, render yourself as agreeable as possible to the assembled company.

Your host will doubtless point out to you the lady he wishes you to escort to the dining-room. You will be in readiness to attend upon her the moment you are summoned to adjourn. Offer her your right arm, and follow in order. Should you have to pass down stairs, you will give the lady the wall. You will take your seat at the table on the right hand of the lady you conducted.

Being seated, soup will be handed round. When offered, take it; but if you prefer fish, pass it on to your neighbor.

You must not ask for soup or fish a second time; it will not be offered—you would not be so rude or selfish as to keep the company waiting for the second course, that you may have the pleasure of demolishing a double portion of fish.

Fish must be eaten with a silver fork, as the acid in the sauce, acting on the steel of an ordinary fork, gives an unpleasant flavor to the dish. For this reason, also, a knife should not be used in eating fish.

If asked whether you have a preference for any dish, or any particular part of a dish, answer plainly and distinctly as you wish.

Pay as much attention to your companion on your left, as politeness requires, but do not be unnecessarily officious. People do not like to be stared at when eating.

When you are helped to anything, do not wait until the rest of the company are provided. This is very common in the country, but shows a want of good breeding.

Do not allow your plate to be overloaded with a multifarious assortment of vegetables, but rather confine yourself to one kind. When you take another sort of meat, or a dish not properly a vegetable, you must change your plate.

If you have the honor of sitting on the right hand of the hostess, you will, immediately on the removal of soup, request the honor of taking wine with her.

Finally, to do all these things well, and to be *au fait* at a dinner party, be perfectly at your ease. To be at ease is a great step towards enjoying your own dinner, and making yourself agreeable to the company. Fancy yourself at home; performing all the ceremonies without any apparent effort. For the rest, observation and your own judgment will be the best guide, and render you perfect in the etiquette of the dinner-table.

CARVING.

In carving, your knife should not be too heavy, but of a sufficient size, and keen edge. In using it, no great personal strength is required, as constant practice will render it an easy task to carve the most difficult articles; more depending on address than force.

The dish should be sufficiently near to enable the carver to reach it without rising, and the seat should be elevated so as to give command over the joint.

Show no partiality in serving, but let each person have a share of such articles as are considered best; for however you conciliate the one you favor, you must bear in mind that you make enemies of the other guests.

FISH

Requires very little carving. It should be carefully helped with a fish-slice, which, not being sharp, prevents the flakes from being broken; and in salmon and cod these are large, and add much to their beauty. A portion of the roe, milt or liver should be given to each person.

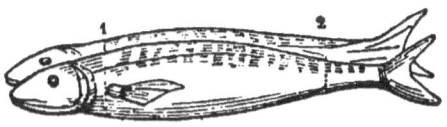

Mackerel.

In helping, first cut off the head at 1, as that part is very inferior and unsavory: then divide down the back, and give a side to each. If less is asked for, the thickest end, which is the most choice, should be served. Inquire if the roe is liked. It may be found between 1 and 2. That of the female is hard, of the male, soft.

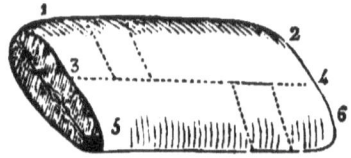

Salmon

Is rarely sent to the table whole, but a piece cut from the middle of a large fish, which is the best flavored part of it. Make an incision along the back 1-2, and another from 5-6; then divide the side about the middle, in the line 3-4; cut the thickest part, between 1-3, 2-4, for the lean, the remainder for the fat. Ask which is preferred, and help as the fancy of your guests may demand. When the fish is very thick, do not venture too near the bone, as there it has an ill flavor, and is discolored.

In paying your respects to a whole Salmon, you will find the choice parts next the head, the thin part next; the tail is considered less savory.

Carp, Perch, Haddock, Etc.

will be easily helped, by attending to the foregoing directions. The head of the Carp is esteemed a delicacy, which should be borne in mind.

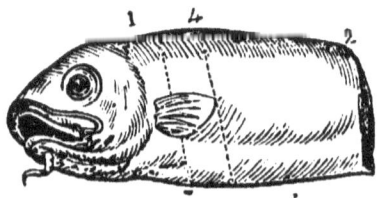

Cod's Head and Shoulders.

Introduce the fish-slice at 1, and cut quite through the back, as far as 2. Then help pieces from between 3 and 4; and with each slice give a portion of the sound, which lines the under side of the back bone. It is thin, and of a darker color than the other part of the fish, and is esteemed a delicacy.

Some persons are partial to the tongue and palate, for which you must insert a spoon into the mouth. The jelly part is about the jaw; the firm part within the head, on which are some other delicate pickings; the finest portions may be found about the shoulders.

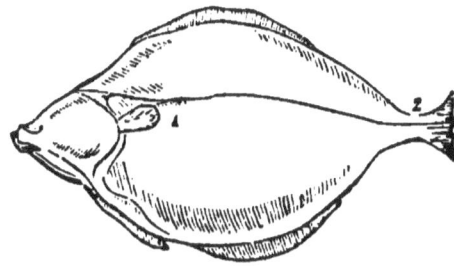

Turbot.

The under side of this fish is the most esteemed, and is placed uppermost on the dish. The fish-slice must be introduced at 1, and an incision made as far as 2; then cut from the middle, which is the primest part. After helping the whole of that side, the upper part must be attacked, and as it is difficult to divide the back bone, raise it with the fork, while you separate a portion with the fish-slice. This part is more solid, and is preferred by some, though it is less delicate than the under side. The fins are esteemed a nicety, and should be attended to accordingly.

Brill, Soles, Plaice,

and *flat* fish in general, may be served in the same manner as a Turbot.

JOINTS.

In helping the more fleshy Joints, such as a Sirloin of Beef, Leg of Mutton, Fillet of Veal, cut thin smooth slices, and let the knife pass through to the bones of Mutton and Beef.

It would prevent much trouble, if the joints of the loin, neck and breast, were cut through by the butcher, previous to the cooking, so that when sent to table, they may be easily severed. Should the whole of the meat belonging to each bone be too thick, one or more slices may be taken off between every two bones.

In some boiled joints, round and aitch-bone of beef for instance, the water renders the outsides vapid, and of course un fit to be eaten; you will therefore be particular to cut off and lay aside a thick slice from the top, before you begin to serve.

Saddle of Mutton.

This is an excellent joint, and produces many nice bits. Cut the whole length of it close to the back bone, and take off some long thin slices in that direction. The upper division consists of lean; the fat may be easily got at by cutting from the left side.

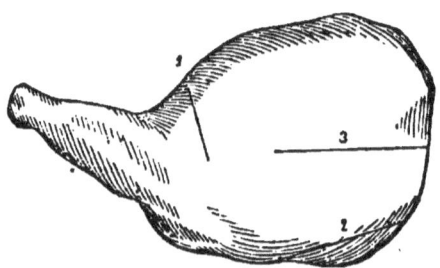

Shoulder of Mutton.

Cut in to the bone at the line 1, and help thin slices of lean from each side of the incision; the prime part of the fat lies at the outer edge, at 2.

Should more meat be required than can be got from that part, cut on either side of the line 3, which represents the blade bone, and some good and delicate slices may be procured. By cutting horizontally from the under side, many "nice bits" will be obtained.

Loin of Mutton.

As the bones of this joint are divided, it is very easily managed. Begin at the narrow end, and take off the chops; when the joints are cut through, some slices of meat may be obtained between the bones.

Haunch of Mutton.

consists of the leg and part of the loin, cut so as to resemble a haunch of venison. It must be helped at table in a similar manner.

CARVING.   443

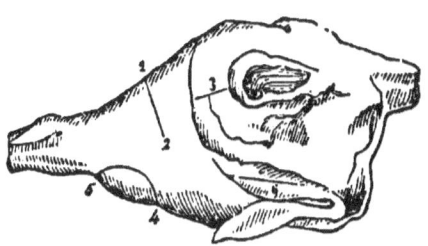

Leg of Mutton.

The finest part is situated in the centre, at 1, between the knuckle and farther end; insert the knife there, and cut thin, deep slices each way, as far in as 2. The outside rarely being very fat, some neat cuts may be obtained off the broad end, at 3. The knuckle of a fine leg is tender, though dry, and many prefer it, although the other is the most juicy. There are some good cuts on the broad end of the back of the leg, from which slices may be procured lengthways.

The cramp bone is by some esteemed a delicacy: to get it out, cut down to the thigh bone, at 4, and pass the knife under it in a semi-circular course, to 5.

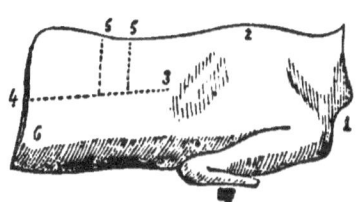

Fore Quarter of Lamb.

First divide the shoulder from the scoven, which consists of the breast and ribs, by passing the knife under the knuckle, in the direction of 1, 2, 3 and cutting so as to leave a fair portion of meat on the ribs; lay it on a separate dish; the other part, which, after being sprinkled over with pepper and salt, should be divided in the line 3–4. This will separate the ribs from the gristly part, and you may help from either, as may be chosen, cutting as directed by the lines 5, 6.

Shoulder of Lamb

must be carved like a shoulder of mutton, of which it is a miniature edition.

Leg of Lamb.

Follow the directions given for leg of mutton, at page 422.

Loin of Lamb

may be helped similar to a loin of mutton. See page 421. This, and the two foregoing, being small joints, should be helped sparingly, as there is very little meat on them, especially when first in season.

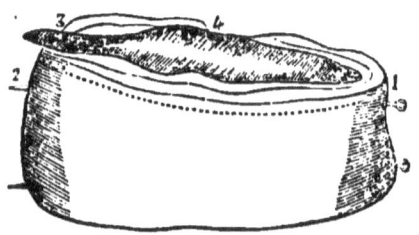

Aitch-Bone of Beef.

Cut off and lay aside a thick slice from the entire surface, as marked 1–2, then help. There are two sorts of fat to this joint, and no tastes differ, it is necessary to learn which is preferred. The solid fat will be found at 3, and must be cut horizontally; the softer, which resembles marrow, at the back of the bone, below 4.

A silver skewer should be substituted for the one which keeps the meat properly together while boiling, and it may be withdrawn when you cut down to it.

Round of Beef.

This joint is so very easy to attend to, that we have not deemed it necessary to give a drawing of it; it only requires a steady hand and a sharp knife. The upper surface being removed, as directed for the aitch-bone of beef, carve thin slices, and give a portion of fat with each.

You must cut the meat as even as possible, as it is of consequence to preserve the beauty of its appearance.

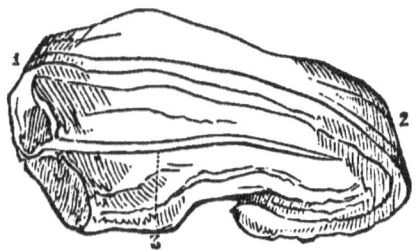

Sirloin of Beef.

There are two modes of helping this joint. The better way is by carving long thin slices from 1 to 2; the other way is by cutting it across, which, however, spoils it. The most tender and prime part is in the direction of the line 3; there will also be found some delicate fat, part of which should be given with each piece.

Ribs of Beef

may be carved similar to the sirloin, always commencing at the thin end of the joint, and cutting long slices, so as to give fat and lean together.

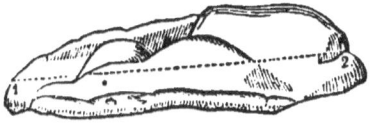

A Breast of Veal

is composed of the ribs and brisket, which must be separated by cutting through the line 1–2; the latter is the thickest and has gristles. Divide each portion into convenient pieces and proceed to help.

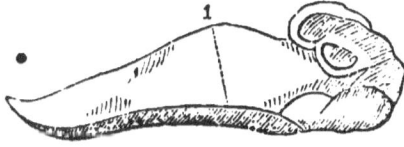

A Tongue.

Cut nearly through the middle, at the line 1, and take thin slices from each side. The fat is situated underneath, at the root of the tongue.

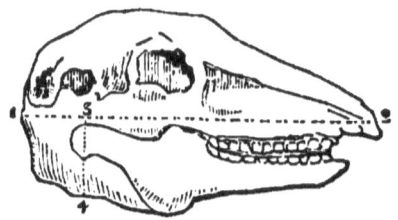

A Calf's Head.

Cut thin slices from 1 to 2, and let the knife penetrate to the bone. At the thick part of the neck end, 3, the throat sweetbread is situated; carve slices from 3 to 4, and help with the other part. Should the eye be asked for, it must be extracted with the point of the knife, and a portion given. The palate, esteemed a delicacy, is situated under the head, and some fine lean may be found by removing the jaw-bone; portions of each of these should be helped round.

A Loin of Veal

should be jointed previous to being sent to table, when each division may be easily cut through with a knife. The fat surrounds the kidney, and portions of each should be given with the other parts.

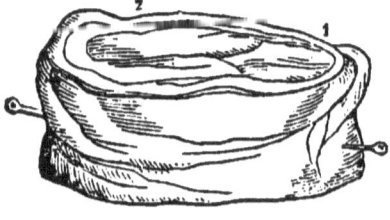

Fillet of Veal

resembles a round of beef, and should be carved similar to it, in thin and very smooth slices, off the top. Cut deep into the flap, between 1 and 2, for the stuffing, and help a portion of it to each person

Slices of lemon are always served with this dish.

CARVING.

Roast Pig.

As this is usually divided as above, before sent to table, little remains to be done by the carver. First separate a shoulder from the body, and then the leg; divide the ribs into convenient portions, and send around with a sufficiency of the stuffing and gravy. Many prefer the neck end between the shoulders, although the ribs are considered the finest part; but as this all depends on taste, the question should be put. The ear is reckoned a delicacy.

Should the head not be divided, it must be done, and the brains taken out, and mixed with the gravy and stuffing.

A Loin of Pork

is cut up in the same manner as a loin of mutton. See page 421.

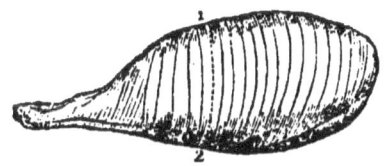

Leg of Pork

Commence carving about midway, between the knuckle and farther end, and cut thin deep slices from either side of the line 1. For the seasoning in a roast leg, lift it up, and it will be found under the skin at the large end.

Hand of Pork.

Cut thin slices from this delicate joint, either across near the knuckle, or from the blade bone, as directed for a shoulder of mutton. This forms a nice dish for a tete a tete dinner; there is not sufficient for a third person.

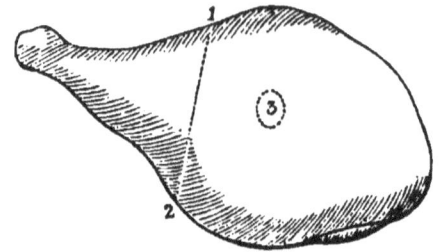

Ham.

The usual mode of carving this joint, is by long delicate slices, through the thick fat, in the direction of 1-2, laying open the bone at each cut, which brings you to the prime part at once. A more saving way is to commence at the knuckle and proceed onwards.

Some persons take out a round piece at 3, and enlarge the hole, by cutting thin circular slices, with a sharp knife. This keeps the meat moist, and preserves the gravy, but seldom looks handsome.

POULTRY, GAME, ETC.

The carving-knife for poultry is smaller and lighter than the meat carver; the point is more peaked, and the handle longer.

In cutting up a turkey, goose, duck, or wild fowl, more prime pieces may be obtained by carving slices from pinion to pinion, without making wings; this is an advantage when your party is large, as it makes the bird go farther.

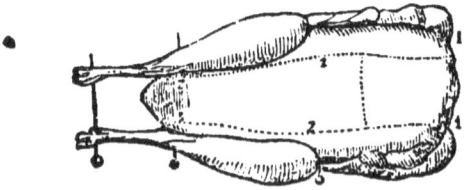

A Fowl.

It will be more convenient, in carving this, to take it on your plate, and lay the joints, as divided, neatly on the dish. Fix your fork in the middle of the breast, and take the wing off in the direction of 1-2; divide the joint at 1, lift up the pinion with your fork, and draw the wing towards the leg, which will separate the fleshy part more naturally than by the knife; cut between the leg and body at 3 to the bone, 2, give the blade a sudden turn, and the joint will break if the fowl is not old. When a similar operation is performed on the other side, take off the merrythought, by cutting in to the bone at 4, and turning it back, which will detach it; next remove the neck bones and divide the breast from the back, by cutting through the whole of the ribs, close to the breast. Turn up the back, press the point of the knife about half way between the neck and rump, and on raising the lower end it will separate easily. Turn the rump from you, take off the sidesmen, and the operation is complete.

The breast and wings are the most delicate parts, but the leg is more juicy in a young bird. Great care should be taken to cut the wings as handsome as possible.

A Partridge

is cut up in the same manner as a fowl, only, on account of the smallness of the bird, the merrythought is seldom divided from the breast. The wings, breast, and merrythought, are the finest parts of it, but the wing is considered the best, and the tip of it is reckoned the most delicious morsel of the whole.

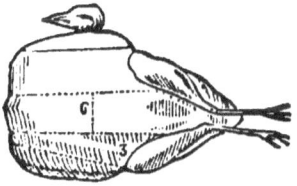

A Pheasant.

Fix your fork in the centre of the breast, and make incisions to the bone at 1-2, then take off the leg in the line 3-4, and the wing at 3-5; sever the other side in the same manner, and separate the slices you had previously divided on the breast. In taking off the wings, be careful not to venture too near the neck, or you will hit on the neck bone, from which the wing should be divided. Pass the knife through the line 6, and under the merrythought towards the neck, which will detach it. The other parts may be served as directed for a fowl.

The breast, wings, and merrythought, are the most delicate parts, although the leg has a high flavor.

A Turkey.

The finest parts of this bird are the breast and wings; the latter will bear some delicate slices being taken off. After the four quarters are severed, the thighs must be divided from the drum-sticks, which, being tough, should be reserved till last. In other respects, a turkey must be dealt with exactly as recommended for a fowl, except that it has no merrythought.

Give a portion of the stuffing, or forced-meat, which is inside the breast, to each person.

Woodcocks, Grouse, etc.,

are carved similar to a fowl, if not too small, when they may be cut in quarters, and helped.

Snipes, being smaller, should be divided in halves.

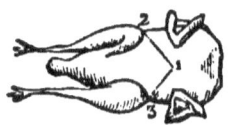

Pigeons.

The usual way of carving these birds is to insert the knife at 1, and cut to 2 and 3, when each portion may be divided into two pieces, and helped. Sometimes they are cut in halves, either across or down the middle: but as the lower part is thought the best, the first mode is the fairest.

Should they be very large and fine, they may be served like fowls.

A Goose.

Take off the wing by putting the fork into the small end of the pinion, and press it close to the body ; divide the joint at 1 with the knife, carrying it along as far as 2. Remove the leg, by cutting in the direction of 2–3, and divide the thigh

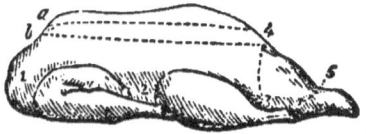

from the drumstick; then sever the limbs on the other side, and cut some long slices from each side of the breast, between the lines a and b.

To get at the stuffing, the apron must be removed, by cutting from 4 to 5 by 3. It is rarely necessary to cut up the whole of the goose, unless the company is large; but the merrythought may be taken off. There are two sidebones by the wing, which may be cut off, as likewise the back and lower sidebones. The best pieces are the breast and thighs

A Duck.

Remove the legs and wings as directed above for a goose, and cut some slices from each side of the breast. The seasoning will be found under the flap, as in the other bird. Should it be necessary, the merrythought, sidebones &c., can be detached in the same manner as recommended for a fowl.

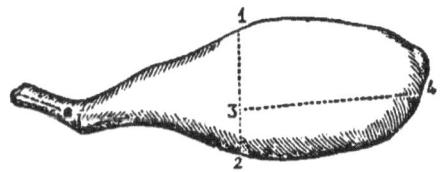

Haunch of Venison.

First let out the gravy, by cutting in to the bone across the joint at 1–2; then turn the broad end towards you, make as deep an incision as you can from 3 to 4, and help thin slices from each side. The greater part of the fat, which is much esteemed, will be found on the left side; and those who carve must take care to proportion both it and the gravy to the number of the company.

Hare.

Insert the point of the knife inside the shoulder at 1, and divide all the way down to the rump at 2: do the same on the

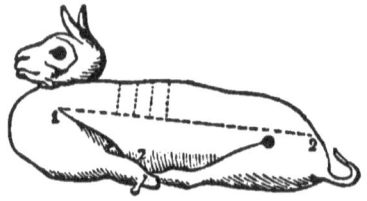

other side, and you will have the hare in three pieces. Pass the knife under the rise of the shoulder at 2–1, to take it off. The leg may be severed in a similar manner; then *behead it*, cut off the ears close to the roots, and divide the upper from the lower jaw. Next place the former flat on a plate, put the point of the knife into the forehead, and divide it through the centre, down to the nose. Cut the back into convenient portions, lay the pieces neatly on the dish, and proceed to serve the company, giving some stuffing, (which will be found in the inside,) and gravy to each person.

The prime parts are the back and legs; the ears are considered a luxury by some, as are the head and brains; they may be distributed to those that like them.

Should the hare not be very tender, it will be difficult to divide the sides from the back, but take off the legs, by cutting through the joints, which you must endeavor to hit. You will then be able to cut a few slices from each side of the back. Next dissever the shoulders, which are called the sportsman's joints, and are preferred by many. The back, &c., may then be carved as directed above.

Rabbit.

The directions for cutting up a hare will be amply sufficient to enable the carver to dispose of this animal. The best part is the shoulders and back, which must be divided into three or four pieces, according to its size. The head should not be given unless asked for.

Babbit's Yeast Powder is one of the improvements of the day. May be used in making biscuits, instead of cream of tartar and soda.

"What Cheer" Cakes.

An old friend with a new name. See "Turnpike" Cakes, page 277 of this book. Much trouble may be saved by purchasing a box of these yeast cakes, as they are the same as directed in the above mentioned recipe.

INDEX.

	PAGE
A-LA-MODE BEEF	82, 83
A-LA-POLONAISE, CAKES	249, 250
ALBANY BREAKFAST CAKES	275
ALBANY CAKES	416
ALMACKS	381
ALMOND BISCOTTES	322
ALMOND CAKE	300, 301
ALMOND DROP CAKES	311
ALMOND DROPS	316
ALMOND JUMBLES	293
ALMOND MACAROONS	316, 317
ALMOND MERINGUES	320, 321
ALMOND POUND-CAKE	306
ALMOND PUDDING, baked	220
ALMOND PUDDING, boiled	220, 221
ALMOND SPICE BISCUITS	315, 321
AMBER COLOR, for Soups	14
ANCHOVY SAUCE	196, 197
APPLE AND PORK PIE	418
APPLE AND QUINCE JELLY	352
APPLE CHARLOTTE	215
APPLE DUMPLINGS	212, 213
APPLE DUMPLINGS (Dried)	213, 214
APPLE DUMPLINGS (Whole)	216
APPLE FRITTERS, with Eggs	212
APPLE FRITTERS, without Eggs	211
APPLE JELLY	356, 357
APPLE MINCE PIE	263, 264
APPLE PIE	251
APPLE PIE (Dried)	252
APPLE PUDDING, baked	414, 420
APPLE PUDDING, boiled, with Eggs	212
APPLE PUDDING, boiled, without Eggs	212
APPLE PUDDING, CHARLIE'S	414
APPLE SAUCE for Goose, etc.	199
APPLE SAUCE for Puddings	241, 242
APPLE TART	251, 252

	PAGE
APPLE TART (Dried)	252, 253
APPLE-WATER	409
APPLES, baked	409
APPLES, CRAB, to preserve	355, 356
APPLES, fried	199
APPLES in Batter	229
APPLES in Jelly	357, 358
APPLES, LADY, to preserve	355, 356
APPLES, PINE (see *Pineapples*)	346
APPLES, to dry	363
APPLES, to preserve	356
APPLES, to preserve for Tarts or Common Use	381, 382
APPLES, to stew	376, 377
APRICOTS, to preserve	363
ARRANGEMENT AND BILL OF FARE FOR TEA-TABLE, IN SUMMER AND WINTER	401, 402
ARRANGEMENT AND FURNITURE OF BREAKFAST AND DINING-ROOM	398-407
ARROW-ROOT BLANC-MANGE	408
ARROW-ROOT, to cook	407, 408
ARTICHOKES, to boil	188
ARTICHOKES, to prepare for Table	188
ARTIFICIAL CHEESE	206, 207
ASPARAGUS, CHOICE OF	182
ASPARAGUS SALAD	182, 183
ASPARAGUS, to boil	182
ASPARAGUS, to stew	182
BACON, to fry or broil	109, 110
BAKERS' BREAD, to make	268, 269
BAKERS' ROLLS, to make	278, 279
BAKERS' YEAST, to make	277
BAKING Bread, Biscuit, Rolls, Cakes, etc., Directions for	264-268
BAKING, heating Ovens for	265

INDEX.

	PAGE
BAKING of Cakes	304
BAKING Pies, Tarts, etc., Directions for	243–245
BALLS, EGG, for Soup	28
BALLS, SNOW	214, 215
BARBERRIES, to preserve	369, 370
BARLEY-WATER	410
BASS, SEA, to cook	39
BASS, STRIPED, to boil	41
BASS, STRIPED, to fry	41
BATTER, Apples in	229
BATTER PUDDING, boiled	225
BATTER PUDDING, Cheap	216, 217
BATTER PUDDING, Rich	217
BEAN SOUP (Dried)	21
BEAN SOUP (Green)	20, 21
BEANS AND CORN	183, 184
BEANS AND PORK, to boil	115
BEANS, Green, to boil	183
BEANS, Green, to pickle	392
BEANS, LIMA, to cook	184
BEEF, Aitch-bone of, to carve	444
BEEF, A-la-mode	82, 83
BEEF AND ONION STEW	78, 79
BEEF AND POTATO HASH	75, 76
BEEF, a Round of, to stew	72, 73
BEEF, BOUILLI	73
BEEF BROTH	25
BEEF CAKES	76
BEEF, Cold, to serve	84
BEEF, Corned	66, 67
BEEF, Corned, to boil with Vegetables	110
BEEF, Frizzed	170
BEEF HEAD-CHEESE	71
BEEF HEART, to bake	73, 74
BEEF HEART, to roast	73, 74
BEEF HEART, to stew	74
BEEF, Joints of	433
BEEF KIDNEYS, to cook	74, 75
BEEF LIVER, to cook	70, 71
BEEF LIVER, to smoke	67
BEEF, Minced	80
BEEF, Pickled	63
BEEF, Potted Head of	71
BEEF, Proper pieces of, for smoking	67
BEEF, Ribs of, to carve	445
BEEF, Ribs of, to roast	411
BEEF, Roast, Vegetables for	81

	PAGE
BEEF, Round of, to carve	444
BEEF, Round of, to cook (French receipt)	83
BEEF, Sirloin of, to carve	445
BEEF, Salted or Corned, to keep for years	66, 67
BEEF, Salted, to boil with Vegetables	169
BEEF, Sandwich	329
BEEF, Shin of, Soup	23, 24
BEEF SKIRTS, to cook	66, 72
BEEF, Smoked	75
BEEF, Smoked, a Breakfast of	169, 170
BEEF, Smoked, to make an Omelette of	169
BEEF, Smoked, to serve	170
BEEF, Smoked, with eggs	169
BEEF SOUP	24, 25
BEEF STEAK AND NOODLES	419
BEEF STEAK, Mushrooms with	420
BEEF STEAK, Onions with	71
BEEF STEAK PIE	77, 78
BEEF STEAK PUDDING	78
BEEF STEAK, Tomatoes with	420, 421
BEEF STEAKS, Choice of	76
BEEF STEAKS, fried, with Gravy	79
BEEF STEAKS, to broil	76, 77
BEEF STEAKS, to fry	77
BEEF STEAKS, to fry (to taste like a broil)	77
BEEF to bake	81, 82
BEEF to choose	65, 66
BEEF, to hash	75
BEEF, to keep sweet	65, 66
BEEF TONGUE, to carve	445
BEEF TONGUES, to pickle	66, 67
BEEF, to pickle	68
BEEF, to roast	80, 81
BEEF, to salt for immediate use	67, 68
BEEF, to smoke	75
BEEF, to stew (Ragout)	72
BEEF TRIPE	68
BEEF TRIPE, to broil	70
BEEF TRIPE, to clean	68, 69
BEEF TRIPE, to fricassee	70
BEEF TRIPE, to fry	69
BEEF TRIPE, how to make Rolla Cheese with	69, 70
BEETS, to pickle	394, 395
BEETS, old, to cook	179, 180

INDEX.

	PAGE
BEETS, young, to cook	170
BEET TOPS, to cook	178, 179
BEVERAGE, a Temperance	406
BILL OF FARE for a Family Breakfast	400
BILL OF FARE for Tea-Table in Summer	401, 402
BILL OF FARE for Tea-Table in Winter	402
BIRD'S NEST, to make, of Macaroni, etc.	156, 157
BIRDS, small, to broil	161
BIRDS, small, to fry	161
BIRDS, small, to roast	162
BIRDS, to cook (see *Poultry* and *Game*)	135–164
Ducks	152–154
Partridges	160
Pigeons	154–160
Quails	160
Small Birds	161–162
Snipe	160
Woodcock	160
BIRDS, to keep from tainting	161, 162
BIRDS, to roast	162
BISCOTTES, Almond	322
BISCOTTES, Pistachio	322
BISCUIT AND JELLY SANDWICH	308
BISCUIT, Directions for baking	264–268
BISCUIT, Directions for making	264–323
BISCUITS, Almond Spice	315, 321
BISCUITS, Cream of Tartar	423
BISCUITS, Diet	310
BISCUITS, Drop	415
BISCUITS, Milk	285, 286
BISCUITS, Naples	308
BISCUITS, or Bread Cake	274
BISCUITS, Pistachio	322, 323
BISCUITS, Savoy	307, 308
BISCUITS, Soda	285
BISCUITS, Spoon	309
BLACKBERRIES, to prepare for Table	336
BLACKBERRIES, to preserve	369
BLACKBERRY PIE	258
BLACKBERRY PUDDING	230
BLACKBERRY SYRUP	369
BLACK FISH, to boil	41
BLACK FISH, to broil	39
BLACK FISH, to fry	39, 40
BLACK FISH, to stew	40
BLACK TEA, to make	331
BLANC-MANGE, Arrow-root	408
BLANC-MANGE, Ribbon	223
BLANC-MANGE, Rice-flour	408
BLANC-MANGE, to make	223
BOLOGNA SAUSAGES, to make	102
BOUILLI, Beef	73
BRAINS, Calf's, to make a Dish of	86
BRANDIED PEACHES	361, 362
BRANDY, Green Gages in	372, 373
BRANDY, Lemon	384
BRANDY PEACHES	361
BRANDY PEACHES, to preserve Peaches without cooking, equal to	422
BRANDY, Pears in	374
BRANDY, Plums in	372
BRANDY, Rose	383
BRANDY SAUCE	240
BRANDY SAUCE, Liquid	240, 241
BREAD AND BUTTER PUDDING, baked	226, 227
BREAD AND BUTTER SANDWICH	329
BREAD, Bakers', to make	268, 269
BREAD, Brown	273
BREAD CAKE	415
BREAD CAKE, or Biscuit	274
BREAD, Corn, Delicious	431
BREAD, Diet	307
BREAD, Directions for baking	264–268
BREAD, Directions for making (see *Cakes* and *Rolls*)	264–274
BREAD, Dyspepsia	273
BREAD FRITTERS	233
BREAD, Graham	273
BREAD, Indian Corn	274
BREAD, Indian Meal	274
BREAD, Potato	270, 271
BREAD PUDDING, baked	225
BREAD PUDDING, boiled	225, 226, 233
BREAD, Rye	272
BREAD, Saleratus in	265, 266
BREAD, to knead	273, 274
BREAD, Twist	271
BREAD, Volatile Salts in	265, 266
BREAD, Wheat and Indian	271, 272
BREAD, Wheat, to make	269, 270
BREAKFAST, Bill of Fare for	400
BREAKFAST CAKES, Albany	275
BREAKFAST CAKES, Cornmeal	274, 275
BREAKFAST CAKES, Indian	417

	PAGE		PAGE
BREAKFAST CAKES, Indian Meal.	275	BUTTERMILK, Uses of	205, 206
BREAKFAST CAKES, Washington	417, 418	BUTTERNUTS, to pickle	392
BREAKFAST, Family, Bill of Fare for	400	CABBAGE AND MILK SOUP	16, 17
		CABBAGE AND POTATOES, to cook together	194
BREAKFAST OF SMOKED BEEF	169, 170	CABBAGE, Red, to dress	187
BREAKFAST-ROOM, Arrangement and Furniture of	398–407	CABBAGE, Red, to pickle	394
BREAKFAST-TABLE, Arrangement of	398–400	CABBAGE SALAD	186
		CABBAGE, Savoy	118
BREAKFAST, Winter, Bill of Fare for	400, 401	CABBAGE SOUP	30
		CABBAGE SPROUTS, to boil	173
BRIDE CAKE (Rich)	314, 315	CABBAGE, to boil	187
BRILL, to carve	441	CABBAGE, to prepare for boiling	119
BROTH, Beef (see *Soup*)	25	CAKE, Almond	300, 301
BROTH, Chicken	27	CAKE, Almond Pound	300
BROTH, Mutton	28, 29	CAKE, Bread	415
BROTH, to make in haste	410	CAKE, Breakfast (Cornmeal)	274, 275
BROTH, Veal	28	CAKE, Breakfast (Indian)	417
BROWN BREAD	273	CAKE, Breakfast (Washingt'n)	417, 418
BROWN GRAVY SOUP	420	CAKE, Bride (Rich)	314, 315
BROWNING FOR GRAVIES	31	CAKE, Cocoanut	416, 417
BROWNING FOR SOUPS	14, 31	CAKE, Cocoanut Cup	299, 300
BUCKWHEAT CAKES, to bake	279, 280	CAKE, Cocoanut, or Candy	321, 322
BUCKWHEAT GRIDDLE CAKES	279	CAKE, Cocoanut Pound	306
BULLHEAD SOUP, to make	19	CAKE, Cocoanut Sponge	312
BUNS, Common	284, 285	CAKE, Common Cup	298
BUNS, Cross	285	CAKE, Composition	300
BUNS, Currant	290	CAKE, Cornmeal Breakfast	274, 275
BUTCHERS' MEAT, Directions for buying and dressing	65–130	CAKE, Cream Cup	298
		CAKE, Cup (see *Cup Cake*)	298
BUTTER, Clarified	193	CAKE, Delicate	416
BUTTER (Cold) and Vinegar Sauce	195, 196	CAKE, Dover	303
		CAKE, French Tea	310, 311
BUTTER CRACKERS	285	CAKE, Fruit (Rich)	312, 313
BUTTER, Delicious, to make	200	CAKE, Harrison	307
BUTTER, Directions for making and keeping	200–206	CAKE, Hickory-nut	306
		CAKE, Honey	297
BUTTER, Drawn, to make	195	CAKE, Indian Breakfast	417
BUTTER, Melted	198	CAKE, Jackson	306
BUTTER, Salt, to freshen	200	CAKE, Johnny	276
BUTTER SAUCE	196	CAKE, Lady (White)	301, 302
BUTTER, Toast without	209	CAKE, Lady (Yellow)	301
BUTTER, to make	202–206	CAKE, Lafayette	208
BUTTER, to make in haste	200, 201	CAKE, Loaf	310
BUTTER, to make sweet for winter use	201, 202	CAKE, One-Two-Three-Four	294
		CAKE, Ornamental Frosting for	320
BUTTER, to preserve for winter	201	CAKE, Pearlash	296
BUTTERED LOBSTER, to prepare	49	CAKE, Plum	314
BUTTERMILK MUFFINS	280	CAKE, Queen	305
BUTTERMILK POP	409	CAKE, Rye Bread	272, 273
BUTTERMILK TEA CAKES	281, 282	CAKE, Scotch	315, 316

T*

INDEX. 457

	PAGE		PAGE
CAKE, Short, Strawberry	418, 431, 432	CAKES, Spice	294
CAKE, Soda	299	CAKES, Spice (Rich)	294, 295
CAKE, Sponge	307, 415	CAKES, Sponge (Small)	293, 294, 307
CAKE, Sponge (Cocoanut)	312	CAKES, Sponge, to make	416
CAKE, Sponge Pudding	416	CAKES, Sugar Drop	311, 312
CAKE, Strawberry Short	418, 431, 432	CAKES, Taylor	293
CAKE, Tea (French)	310, 311	CAKES, Tea (Buttermilk)	281
CAKE, Tea, Thanksgiving	305, 306	CAKES, Tea (Cream)	281
CAKE, Teacup, without Eggs	299	CAKES, Tea (Wigs)	297, 298
CAKE, to clean Currants for	314	CAKES, to bake	304
CAKE, to Frost or Ice	319, 320	CAKES, to keep fresh	263
CAKE TRIFLE	303	CAKES, to make Icing for	319
CAKE, Washington	301	CAKES, Turnpike	277, 278
CAKE, Washington Breakfast	417, 413	CAKES, Veal	426
CAKE, Wedding, to make	313	CAKES, Velvet	283
CAKES A-LA-POLONAISE	249, 250	CAKES, Volatile Salts in	265, 266
CAKES, Albany	416	CAKES, Webster	302, 303
CAKES, Albany Breakfast	275	CAKES, "What Cheer" or Turnpike	277
CAKES, Almond Drop	311		
CAKES, Beef	76	CAKES, White	294
CAKES, Buckwheat Griddle	279	CAKES, Wine	295
CAKES, Buckwheat, to bake	279, 280	CAKES, Yeast	277, 278
CAKES, Buttermilk Tea	281, 282	*₊* *Other Cakes will be found under their respective names.*	
CAKES, Citron Heart	302		
CAKES, Codfish	35	CALF'S BRAINS, a dish of	86
CAKES, Cream Tea	281	CALF'S FEET JELLY	333
CAKES, Cup (Molasses)	297	CALF'S FEET, Roasted	94, 95
CAKES, Directions for baking and making	264-268	CALF'S FEET, Stewed	95
		CALF'S HEAD (a fine dish)	86, 87
CAKES, Drop	311, 312	CALF'S HEAD CHEESE	86, 333
CAKES, Fried	237, 238	CALFS' HEAD SOUP	26, 27
CAKES, Griddle (Buckwheat)	279	CALF'S HEAD, to carve	446
CAKES, Griddle (Indian)	275, 276	CALF'S HEAD, to cook	85-87
CAKES, Indian	417	CALF'S LIVER, to cook	85
CAKES, Indian Griddle	276	CANDIED LEMON PEEL	353
CAKES, Indian meal Breakfast	275	CANDIED ORANGE PEEL	353
CAKES, Indian meal Griddle	275, 276	CANDIES, to clarify Sugar for	339
CAKES, Lemon Drop	311	CANDY, Cocoanut	321, 322
CAKES, Molasses Cup	297	CANDY, Cream	341
CAKES, Palo-Alto	303	CANDY, Hoarhound	341
CAKES, Paste	284	CANDY, Lemon (Common)	340
CAKES, Portugal	295	CANDY, Molasses (Taffy)	341, 342
CAKES, Pound	305	CANDY, Peppermint	341
CAKES, Pound, small	304	CANDY, Rose	341
CAKES, Rice	422	CANDY, Twist, Common	341
CAKES, Rout Drop	312	CANELLONS	248, 249
CAKES, Saleratus used in	265, 266	CANELLONS GLACES	249
CAKES, Short	284	CANTELOPES, to prepare for Table	387
CAKES, Short, Rice Flour	284		
CAKES, Short, Rye	277	CANVAS-BACK DUCKS, to cook	153, 154
CAKES, Small, to make	292, 293	CAPER SAUCE, Imitation	196
CAKES, Spanish	295	CAPILLAIRE	383

458 INDEX.

	PAGE
CAROLINA POTATOES (see *Sweet Potatoes*)	176
CARP, to carve	440
CARRAGAN MOSS	408
CARROT PUDDING	415
CARROTS, Mashed	184, 185
CARROTS, Old or Winter, to cook	184
CARROTS, to boil	184
CARVING, Directions for	439–452
CATFISH OR BULLHEAD SOUP	19
CATSUP, Oyster	394
CATSUP, Tomato	393, 394, 419
CATSUP, Walnut	393
CAULIFLOWER SALAD	195
CAULIFLOWER, to boil	155
CELERY, to prepare for Table	186
CHAMPAGNE PUNCH	406, 407
CHARCOAL, use of, in cooking	244, 245
CHARLIE'S APPLE PUDDING	414
CHARLOTTE, Apple	215
CHARLOTTE, Peach	215
CHARLOTTE RUSSE	221, 222
CHEESE, Artificial	206, 207
CHEESE, Calf's Head	86, 208
CHEESE, Cottage	205, 206
CHEESE, Cream	207
CHEESE, Head (see *Head-Cheese*)	71, 86, 97
CHEESE, Macaroni with	427
CHEESE, Milk	207
CHEESE, Pot	206
CHEESE, Quince	352, 355
CHEESE, Roasted	208
CHEESE, Rolls, to make	69, 70
CHEESE SANDWICHES	329
CHERRIES, a Dessert of	216
CHERRIES, Dried	234
CHERRIES, Ripe, for Tea	357
CHERRIES, to dry	367
CHERRIES, to preserve	367
CHERRIES, to preserve for Tarts or common use	381, 382
CHERRY PIE (Dried)	254
CHERRY PIE (Sour)	254, 255
CHERRY PUDDING	229, 230
CHERRY WATER	383, 384
CHICKEN BROTH	27
CHICKEN CURRIE	139
CHICKEN PATTIES	142, 143
CHICKEN PIE	140, 141
CHICKEN PIE, to serve	63
CHICKEN POT-PIE	141, 142

	PAGE
CHICKEN POT-PIE, to dish a	142
CHICKEN SALAD	429, 430
CHICKEN SALAD, in form of a Nest	143
CHICKEN SOUP, White	22
CHICKEN SOUP, Yellow	21, 22
CHICKEN, to boil (see *Fowl*)	136, 137
CHICKEN, to broil like a Steak	139, 140
CHICKEN, to fry	140
CHICKEN, to prepare for cooking	135, 136
CHICKEN, to roast	137–139
CHICKENS SCOLLOPED	142
CHICKENS, Stuffing for	135, 136
CHOCOLATE, to make	350
CHOP, Lamb, like a Crown	122
CHOPS, Mutton, broiled	130
CHOPS, Mutton, fried	129, 130
CHOPS, Pork, to cook	109
CHOWDER, Clam, to make	55, 56
CHOWDER, Fish, to make	47
CHOWDER, Oyster, to make	61, 62
CHOWDER, to make	47
CHRISTMAS DINNER, how to arrange	404, 405
CHRISTMAS PLUM PUDDING	218, 219
CIDER, to mull	409, 410
CIDER VINEGAR, to make	393
CINNAMON SAUCE	242
CINNAMON WAFERS	293
CITRON HEART CAKES	302
CITRON PUDDING	217
CITRON, to preserve	353, 354
CLAM CHOWDER, to make	55, 56
CLAM FRITTERS, to make	53
CLAM, Hard-shell, Omelette	53
CLAM PIE, to make	53, 54
CLAM POT-PIE, to make	54, 55
CLAM SOUP	29
CLAMS, Hard-shell, Choice of	51, 52
CLAMS, Hard-shell, to boil	52
CLAMS, Hard-shell, to fry	52, 53
CLAMS, Hard-shell, to stew	52
CLAMS, Sand (small) to make Chowder with	61, 62
CLAMS, Scolloped	56
CLAMS, Sea, to cook	55
CLAMS, Soft-shell, Season for	50
CLAMS, Soft-shell, to boil	50, 51
CLAMS, Soft-shell, to fry	51
CLAMS, Soft-shell, to stew	51
CLAMS, time required to stew	52
CLAMS, to pickle	55

INDEX. 459

	PAGE
CLARIFIED SUGAR FOR PRESERVING	345
CLOTTED CREAM	331, 332
COCHINEAL, to prepare, to color pink or red	321
COCOANUT CAKE	416, 417
COCOANUT CAKE OR CANDY	321, 322
COCOANUT CUP CAKE	299, 300
COCOANUT DROPS	317
COCOANUT DROPS, Pyramid of	323, 324
COCOANUT, Grated—a Dish of Snow	258, 239
COCOANUT KISSES	319
COCOANUT MACAROONS	317
COCOANUT MERINGUES	321
COCOANUT POUND CAKE	306
COCOANUT PUDDING	217, 218, 228, 413
COCOANUT SPONGE CAKE	312
COD, baked	37
COD, Cold boiled, to make a Dish of	35, 36
COD, Fresh, Description of	36
COD, Fresh, to boil	35
COD, Fresh, to broil	36
COD, Salt, stewed	35
COD'S HEAD AND SHOULDERS, to carve	440, 441
CODFISH CAKES	35
CODFISH, Dried, to boil	34, 35
CODFISH, Salt, to boil Potatoes with	112
CODFISH STEAKS, fried	36, 37
COFFEE, to make	330
COLD BUTTER AND VINEGAR SAUCE	195, 196
COLD COLLATIONS	405, 406
COLDSLAW, to make	186, 187
COLLATION, Cold, for Fourth of July	405, 406
COLLATION, Cold, for New Year's Day	405
COLLOPS, Veal	426
COLORS FOR SOUPS	14
COMPOSITION CAKE	300
COOKED MEATS, to make Soup from	11, 12
COOKERY FOR INVALIDS	407
COOKIES, Cream of Tartar	424
COOKING, to preserve Peaches without	422
COOKING, to preserve Pine-apples without	346, 347
COOKING, Use of Charcoal in	244, 245
CORN BREAD, Delicious	431
CORNED BEEF, to boil with Vegetables	119
CORNED BEEF, to keep for Years (see *Beef*)	66, 67
CORNED PORK, to boil with Vegetables	117, 118
CORN, Green, Fritters	422
CORN, Green, Soup	409
CORN, Green, to boil	190, 191
CORN, Green, to roast	191
CORN, Green, to serve	190
CORN-MEAL BREAKFAST CAKE	274, 275
CORN-MEAL FRITTERS, with Eggs	235
CORN-MEAL FRITTERS, without Eggs	235
CORN-MEAL PUDDING	236, 237
CORN STARCH CUSTARD	429
CORN STARCH, to prepare	423, 428
COTTAGE-CHEESE	205, 206
CRAB APPLES, to preserve	355, 356
CRABS, Soft, to cook	430
CRABS, to boil	50
CRABS, to choose	50
CRACKERS, Butter	285
CRACKERS, Dyspepsia	278
CRACKLINGS	418, 419
CRANBERRY JAM	199
CRANBERRY PIE	255
CRANBERRY SAUCE	199
CRANBERRY SAUCE, for Puddings	241
CRANBERRY TARTS	255
CREAM CANDY	341
CREAM CHEESE	207
CREAM, Clotted	331, 332
CREAM CUP CAKE	298
CREAM CUSTARD	229
CREAM, Hasty	331
CREAM, Ice (see *Ice Cream*)	332
CREAM, Lemon, Floating Island	218
CREAM MOCK	221
CREAM OF TARTAR BISCUIT	423
CREAM OF TARTAR COOKIES	424
CREAM OF TARTAR ROLLS	423
CREAM PIE	258, 259
CREAM SAUCE, to make	198
CREAM SHERBET	385
CREAM SNOW	331
CREAM, Syrup of	331
CREAM TARTS, Sugar Paste	248
CREAM TEA CAKES	281

CREAM, to cause to rise quickly............................204, 205
CREAM, to keep sweet.......... 331
CREAM, Whipt................... 221
CROSS BUNS..................... 285
CRULLERS, Delicate..........288, 289
CRULLERS, Plain............... 288
CRULLERS, Richer.............. 288
CRULLERS, Richest............. 288
CRULLERS, to fry.............. 286
CRUMPETS, to make............. 281
CRUMPETS, Wheat and Indian.... 276
CUCUMBERS, to choose.......... 189
CUCUMBERS, to pickle........388, 389
CUCUMBERS, to prepare for Table. 189
CUP CAKE, Cocoanut........299, 300
CUP CAKE, Common.............. 298
CUP CAKE, Cream............... 298
CUP CAKES, Molasses........... 297
CUPS, Flour Pudding baked in... 414
CUPS, to bake Potatoes in..... 423
CURD PUDDINGS, small.......... 234
CURRANT BUNS.................. 290
CURRANT FRITTERS (Dried)...... 237
CURRANT JAM................... 368
CURRANT JELLY.............368, 369
CURRANT JELLY DUMPLINGS..... 232
CURRANT JELLY, Lamb Steaks with.....................122, 123
CURRANT JELLY PUDDING........ 231
CURRANT JELLY, without cooking........................... 370
CURRANT PIE (Green)........257, 258
CURRANT PIE (Ripe)............ 257
CURRANT PUDDING (Dried)....... 229
CURRANT PUDDING (Ripe)........ 230
CURRANT TARTS (Green).....257, 258
CURRANT-WATER................. 333
CURRANT-WATER ICE............. 333
CURRANTS, for Cake, to clean.... 314
CURRANTS, Ripe, for Tea........ 387
CURRANTS, to preserve......367, 368
CURRIE, Chicken............... 139
CURRIE, Mutton................ 129
CURRIE POWDER, to make........ 198
CUSTARD COMMON............210, 211
CUSTARD, Corn Starch.......... 429
CUSTARD, Cream................ 229
CUSTARD FRITTERS..........230, 231
CUSTARD PIE, which makes its own paste.................... 259
CUSTARD PIES.................. 259

CUSTARD, Rice................. 412
CUSTARDS, small...........225, 226
CUTLETS, Pigeon............... 160
CUTLETS, Pork, to cook........ 109
DAMSONS, to pickle............ 397
DAMSONS, to preserve.......... 373
DELICATE CAKE................. 416
DESSERT, a French............. 412
DESSERT, a Nice...........215, 216
DESSERT AT DINNER, Arrangement of................... 403
DESSERT, Hominy as............ 192
DESSERT OF PINE-APPLES........ 401
DESSERT, Omelette for......... 229
DESSERT, Oranges as........... 401
DIET BISCUIT.................. 310
DIET BREAD.................... 307
DINING-ROOM, Arrangement and Furniture of.............398-407
DINNER, a Christmas, how to arrange....................404, 405
DINNER, Arrangement of Dessert at............................ 403
DINNER, a Thanksgiving........ 406
DINNER, Duties of Guest at...437, 438
DINNER, Duties of Host at....435-437
DINNER, New Year's............ 405
DINNERS, Family....115, 116, 119, 120
DINNERS, Family (Summer), Bill of Fare for................ 404
DINNERS, Holiday.............. 404
DINNERS, Large, to serve....403, 404
DINNER-TABLE, Arrangement of (see *Table*)..............402-404
DINNER-TABLE, Etiquette of...435-438
DOUGHNUTS, to fry............. 286
DOUGHNUTS, to make.........286, 287
DOUGHNUTS, without Yeast...... 287
DOVER CAKE.................... 303
DRAWN BUTTER, to make......... 195
DRESSING, Salad............... 186
DROP BISCUITS................. 415
DROP CAKES.................... 311
DROP CAKES, Almond............ 311
DROP CAKES, Lemon............. 311
DROP CAKES, Sugar.........311, 312
DROP CAKES, Rout.............. 312
DROPS, Almond................. 316
DROPS, Cocoanut............... 317
DROPS, Cocoanut, Pyramid of 323, 324
DUCK, to carve................ 451

INDEX.

	PAGE
Duck, Veal roasted to look like a	91, 92
Ducks, Canvas-back, to cook	153, 154
Ducks, Roast, Potato Cakes to serve with	421
Ducks, to choose	152, 153
Ducks, to roast in a Pot	154
Ducks, Wild, to cook	152, 153
Dumplings, Apple	212, 213
Dumplings, Apple (Dried)	213, 214
Dumplings, Apple (Whole)	216
Dumplings, Currant Jelly	232
Dumplings, Egg	234
Dumplings, Egg, for Soup	28
Dumplings, Indian Meal	223, 224
Dumplings, Peach (Dried)	213
Dumplings, Peach (Ripe)	214
Dumplings, Rhubarb	214
Dumplings, Yeast	224
Dutch Omelette	168, 169
Dyspepsia Bread	273
Dyspepsia Crackers	278
Eels, Choice of	44
Eels, to bake	44, 45
Eels, to fricassee	45
Eels, to fry	45
Eels, to prepare for cooking	44
Egg Balls for Soup	28
Egg Dumplings	234
Egg Dumplings for Soup	28
Egg Pancakes	232
Egg Plant, to cook	191
Egg Pudding	227
Egg Rusk	282, 283
Egg Sauce	195
Eggs and Ham, fried	114
Eggs, Apple Fritters with	212
Eggs, Apple Fritters without	211, 212
Eggs, Apple Pudding with	212
Eggs, Apple Pudding without	212
Eggs, Corn-meal Fritters with	236
Eggs, Corn-meal Fritters without	235
Eggs, Frothed	239
Eggs, Omelettes, etc. (see *Omelettes*)	164–169
Eggs Poached, with Fried Ham	114
Eggs, Rice Pudding with	227
Eggs, Rice Pudding without	227
Eggs, Soft Gingerbread without	296
Eggs, Stirred	167
Eggs, Suet Fruit Pudding without	430, 431
Eggs, Teacup Cake without	299
Eggs, to boil (in their Shells)	165–167
Eggs, to choose	164
Eggs, to keep	164, 165
Eggs, to make a French Omelette with	167, 168
Eggs, to make an Omelette *au Naturel* with	167
Eggs, to make an Omelette with	168
Eggs, to poach	166
Eggs, to poach in Balls	167
Eggs, with Smoked Beef	169
Etiquette of the Dinner-Table	435–438
Evening Parties, Refreshments for	326, 327
Family Breakfast, Bill of Fare for	400
Family Dinners	115, 116, 119, 120
Family Dinners (Summer), Bill of Fare for	404
Family Pie Crust, Short	247, 248
Fare, Bill of, for Family Br'kfast	400
Fare, Bill of, for Family Dinners	401
Fare, Bill of, for Tea	401, 402
Farina Pudding	
Farina, to cook	423, 428
Feet, Calves', roasted	94, 95
Feet, Calves', stewed	95
Figs, Roasted	384
Filbert Meringues	321
Fingers, Lady	309, 310
Fish, Black, to boil	41
Fish, Black, to fry	39, 40
Fish, Black, to stew	40
Fish Chowder, to make	47
Fish, Directions for carving	439–441
Brill	441
Carp	440
Cod's Head and Shoulders	440, 441
Haddock	440
Mackerel	439
Perch	440
Plaice	441
Salmon	440
Soles	441
Turbot	441

INDEX.

	PAGE
FISH, Directions for cooking (see under respective names; also *Shell Fish*)	33–47
Bass, Striped	41
Black Fish	39
Cod	34–37
Eels	44, 45
Haddock	37
Halibut	41
Herrings	47
Mackerel	45, 46
Perch	41
Pike or Pickerel	47
Salmon	41–44
Sea Bass	39
Shad	37, 38
Trout	46
FISH, Flat, to carve	441
FISH, General Remarks on	32, 33
FISH, Rules for choosing	32
FISH, Salt, to prepare for cooking	34
FISH, Sauces for	195–199
FISH, Shell, to cook	48–64
FISH SOUP	21
FISH, to boil	32, 33
FISH, to broil	33, 34
FISH, to fry	33, 34
FISH, to serve Horse-radish with	194
FLAVORING STEWS, Powder for	198
FLOATING ISLAND	218
FLOATING ISLAND, Lemon Cream	218
FLOUR GRAVY, for Veal Chops	88, 89
FLOUR, Prepared, to make	260
FLOUR PUDDING, baked in Cups	414
FLOUR, to brown	196
FOURTH OF JULY, a Cold Collation for	405, 406
FOWL, Boiled, Stuffing for	136
FOWL, Roast, Stuffing for	135, 136
FOWL, to boil (see *Chicken*)	136, 137
FOWL, to broil like a Steak	139, 140
FOWL, to carve	448, 449
FOWL, to fry	140
FOWL, to roast	135–137
FRENCH DESSERT, a	412
FRENCH OMELETTE, to make	167, 168
FRENCH RECEIPT FOR COOKING ROUND OF BEEF	83
FRENCH ROLLS FOR TEA	284
FRENCH TEA-CAKES	310, 311
FRICASSEED EELS	45

	PAGE
FRICASSEED GOOSE	150
FRICASSEED TRIPE	70
FRICASSEED TURKEY	147, 148
FRIED CAKES	287, 288
FRIED OYSTERS (see *Oysters*)	57
FRITTERS, Apple, with Eggs	212
FRITTERS, Apple, without Eggs	211, 212
FRITTERS, Bread	233
FRITTERS, Clam	53
FRITTERS, Corn-meal, with Eggs	235
FRITTERS, Corn-meal, without Eggs	235
FRITTERS, Currant, Dried	237
FRITTERS, Custard	230, 231
FRITTERS, Green Corn	422
FRITTERS, Jelly	231
FRITTERS, Jelly in	231
FRITTERS, Oyster, to make	56, 57
FRITTERS, Parsnip	185, 186
FRITTERS, Peach	423
FRITTERS, Rhubarb	230
FRIZZED BEEF	170
FROSTING FOR CAKE	319, 320
FROSTING, Ornamental	320
FROTHED EGGS	239
FRUIT CAKE, Rich	312, 313
FRUIT, General Directions for preserving	343–345
FRUIT, Kettles for preserving	343
FRUIT, Paste Pudding with	214
FRUIT, Preserved, Management of	395–397
FRUIT PUDDING, Suet, without Eggs	430, 431
FRUIT SANDWICH	329
FRUIT, to bottle	345, 346
FRUIT, to candy	359
FRUIT, to color Green, for preserving in Sugar or Vinegar	342
FRUIT, to color Yellow, for preserving	342, 343
FRUIT, to keep fresh	345, 346
FRUIT, to preserve for Tarts	381, 382
FRUITS, Directions for preserving (see under their respective names)	342–395
Almacks	381
Apple Jelly	356, 357
Apples in Jelly	357, 358
Apples, to dry	363

INDEX.

FRUITS, Directions for preserving (*continued*).

	PAGE
Apples, to preserve	356
Apples, to stew	376, 377
Apricots	363
Barberries	369, 370
Blackberries	369
Cherries	367
Citron	353, 354
Crab, or Lady Apples	355, 356
Currant Jam	368
Currant Jelly	368–370
Currants	367, 368
Damsons	373
Ginger, Green	380, 381
Gooseberries	370
Grape Jelly	379
Grapes	378–380
Grapes, to dry	380
Green Gages	372–374, 422
Lady Apples	355, 356
Lemon or Orange Peel	358
Lemons	354
Limes	354
Marmalade, to make	358
Marmalade, Transparent	381
Mulberries	352
Musk-melons	354
Nectarines	352, 353
Orange Jelly	357
Oranges in Jelly	354, 355
Peach Jelly	362, 363
Peach Marmalade	362
Peaches	359–364
Peaches, Brandy	361, 362
Peaches, to dry	363
Peaches, to preserve without cooking	422
Pear Marmalade	375
Pears, Brandy	374
Pears, to bake	375, 376
Pears, to dry	374
Pears, to preserve	374, 375
Pine-apple Jelly	347, 348
Pine-apples	346–348
Pippins in slices	356
Plums	370–374
Plums, Brandy	372
Plums, purple	371
Plums, to dry	374
Quince and Apple Jelly	352

FRUITS, Directions for preserving (*continued*).

	PAGE
Quince Cheese	352, 353
Quince Jelly	351
Quince Marmalade	351
Quinces	349–351
Raspberries	366
Rhubarb Preserve	411
Strawberries	364–366
Strawberry Jam, or Marmalade	365, 366
Tomatoes	377
Tomatoes, Candied	377, 378
Tomato Jam	378
Watermelons	353

FRUITS, Ripe, or Melons, to prepare for Table 385–387

	PAGE
Blackberries	386
Cantelopes	387
Cherries	387
Currants for Tea	387
Huckleberries or Whortleberries	386, 387
Muskmelons	387
Peaches, Ripe	385
Raspberries	386
Strawberries	386
Watermelons	387

GAME, etc., to carve 448–450
GAME, to cook (see *Fowl*) 135–164

	PAGE
Ducks, Canvas-back	153, 154
Ducks, Wild	153, 154
Partridges	160
Pheasant	160
Pigeons	154–164
Prairie Hen	160
Quails	160
Snipe	160
Squirrels	162–164
Hares	162–164
Rabbits	162–164
Woodcock	160

GAME, to keep from tainting 161, 162
GINGERBREAD, Molasses 295, 296
GINGERBREAD, Soft 295, 296
GINGERBREAD, Soft, without Eggs 296
GINGER NUTS 297
GINGER ROOTS (Green), to preserve 380, 381
GINGER SNAPS 296

INDEX.

	PAGE
GLACEE, Omelette	240
GLACES, Canellons	249
GOOSE, Fricasseed	150
GOOSE POT-PIE	150
GOOSE, Roast, Vegetables for	151
GOOSE, Stewed, to make a Ragout of	151, 152
GOOSE, to brown-stew a whole	151
GOOSE, to carve	450, 451
GOOSE, to choose a	148
GOOSE, to roast a	148–151
GOOSEBERRIES, Red, to keep	370
GOOSEBERRIES, to preserve	370
GOOSEBERRY PIES	258
GOOSEBERRY TARTS	258
GOTHAM PUDDING	235
GRAHAM BREAD	273
GRAPE JELLY	379
GRAPE PIE (Green)	258
GRAPE TARTS (Green)	258
GRAPES, Green, to preserve	380
GRAPES, to dry	379
GRAPES, to dry in clusters	380
GRAPES, to preserve	378
GRAPES, to preserve (a new way)	378, 379
GRAPES, to preserve in Bunches	379
GRAVIES, Browning for	31
GRAVY FOR VEAL CHOPS	83, 89
GRAVY, Ham	111
GRAVY SOUP (Brown)	420
GRAVY SOUP, Stock for	29, 30
GRAVY, Stock for	29, 30
GREEN BEAN SOUP	20, 21
GREEN BEANS, to boil	183
GREEN BEANS, to pickle	392
GREEN CORN FRITTERS	422
GREEN CORN PUDDING	237, 238
GREEN CORN SOUP	400
GREEN CORN, to boil	190, 191
GREEN CORN, to roast	191
GREEN CORN, to serve	190
GREEN CURRANT PIE	257, 258
GREEN CURRANT TARTS	257, 258
GREEN GAGE PIE	254
GREEN GAGE TARTS	254
GREEN GAGES, Jam of	373, 374
GREEN GAGES, to brandy	372, 373
GREEN GAGES, to preserve	372
GREEN GINGER ROOTS	380, 381
GREEN GRAPE PIE	258

	PAGE
GREEN GRAPE TARTS	258
GREEN GRAPES, to preserve	380
GREEN GRAPES, for Pies and Tarts	258
GREEN ONIONS, to prepare for Table	189
GREEN PEA SOUP	17, 18
GREEN PEAS, to cook	181
GREEN PLUM PIE	254
GREEN TEA, to make	330, 331
GREEN, to color Fruit, for preserving	342
GREEN, to color Soups	14
GREENS, to boil	178
GRIDDLE CAKES, Buckwheat	279
GRIDDLE CAKES, Indian	276, 417
GRIDDLE CAKES, Indian-meal	275, 276
GROUSE, to carve	450
GRUEL, Oatmeal, to make	407
GRUEL, Water, to make	407
HADDOCK, to carve	440
HADDOCK, to cook	37
HALIBUT, Cold boiled, to serve	41
HALIBUT, to boil	41
HALIBUT, to broil	41
HALIBUT, to fry	41
HAM AND EGGS, Fried	114
HAM, Boiled with Vegetables—a Family Dinner	115, 116
HAM, Fried, Poached Eggs with	114
HAM GRAVY	111
HAM OMELETTE	163
HAM SANDWICH	320
HAM, to boil	107, 108
HAM, to broil	110, 111
HAM, to carve a	448
HAM, to fry	110
HAMS, dry salted	99
HAMS, Mutton	127
HAMS, to choose	107
HAMS, to cure	98, 99
HAMS, to smoke (see *Pork*)	99
HANDS, to remove Stains from the	411
HARD-SHELL CLAMS (see *Clams*)	51
HARE SOUP	23
HARE, to carve	451, 452
HARES, to choose, dress, and cook	162–164
HARRISON CAKE	307
HARSLET, Pigs', to make a Dish of	104

	PAGE		PAGE
HARSLET, Sheep's, hashed (see Mutton)	121, 127, 128	INDIAN MEAL GRIDDLE CAKES	275, 276
		INDIAN MEAL MUFFINS	277
HASH, Potato and Beef	75, 76	INDIAN PUDDING, Baked	414
HASTE, to make Soup in	31	INDIAN PUDDING, Cheap	224
HASTY CREAM	331	INDIAN PUDDING, Plain	415
HAZEL-NUT MERINGUES	321	INDIAN PUDDING, to make	120
HEAD, a Beef's, Potted	71	INVALIDS, Cookery for	407
HEAD, a Calf's, to carve	446	ISINGLASS, Kinds of	222
HEAD, a Calf's to cook	85–87	ISINGLASS, to clarify	222, 223
HEAD, a Hog's, to pickle	100	ISLAND, Floating	213
HEAD, a Pig's, to prepare for baking	102, 103	ISLAND, Floating, Lemon Cream	213
		IVORY DUST JELLY	338, 339
HEAD-CHEESE, Beef	71		
HEAD-CHEESE, Calf's	86, 338	JACKSON CAKE	306
HEAD-CHEESE, Pork	97	JAM, Cranberry	199
HEART, Beef's, to bake or roast	73, 74	JAM, Currant	368
HEART, Beef's, to stew	74	JAM OF GREEN GAGES	373, 374
HEART CAKES, Citron	302	JAM, Raspberry	366
HEDGE HOG, to make a	239	JAM, Strawberry	365, 366
HERRINGS, fresh, to boil	47	JAM, Tomato	378
HERRINGS, to cook	47	JARS FOR PRESERVED FRUIT	344
HICKORY-NUT CAKE	306	JAUNE MANGE	339
HOARHOUND CANDY	341	JELLY AND BISCUIT SANDWICH	308
HOG, to cut up a	95, 96	JELLY AND WAFERS	291, 292
HOG'S HEAD, Pickled	100	JELLY, Apple	356, 357
HOG'S LARD	96	JELLY, Apples in	357, 358
HOLIDAY DINNERS	404	JELLY, Calf's Feet	338
HOMINY, as Dessert	192	JELLY, Currant	368, 369
HOMINY, boiled	192	JELLY, Currant, Dumplings	232
HONEY CAKE	297	JELLY, Currant, Pudding	231
HORSE-RADISH, to prepare	194	JELLY, Currant, without cooking	370
HUCKLEBERRIES, to prepare for Table	386, 387	JELLY FRITTERS	231
		JELLY, Grape	379
HUCKLEBERRY PIE	237	JELLY IN FRITTERS	231
HUCKLEBERRY PUDDING	230	JELLY, Ivory Dust	338, 339
		JELLY KISSES	318, 319
ICE CREAM, Lemon	332	JELLY, Orange	357
ICE CREAM, to make	332, 333, 336, 337	JELLY, Oranges in	354, 355
ICE CREAM, Vanilla	332	JELLY PANCAKES	232, 233
ICE, Currant-water	333	JELLY, Peach	362, 363
ICE, Orange-water	334	JELLY, Pine-apple	347, 348
ICING FOR CAKES	319	JELLY, Quince	351, 352
INDIAN AND WHEAT BREAD	271, 272	JELLY, Quince and Apple	352
INDIAN AND WHEAT CRUMPETS	276	JELLY SANDWICH	329
INDIAN BREAKFAST CAKE	417	JELLY STRAINERS	348, 349
INDIAN CAKES	417	JELLY SYRUP, Quinces in	350, 351
INDIAN CORN BREAD	274	JELLY TARTS, Sweet Paste	248
INDIAN GRIDDLE CAKES	276, 417	JELLY, Wine	338
INDIAN MEAL BREAD	274	JOHNNY CAKE	276
INDIAN MEAL BREAKFAST CAKES	275	JUICE, Lemon, to keep	333, 334
INDIAN MEAL DUMPLINGS	223, 224	JULIENNE SOUP	427

	PAGE
JULY FOURTH, a Cold Collation for	405, 406
JUMBLES, Almond	293
JUMBLES, Common	292
JUMBLES, Soft,	299
JUMBLES, to make	292
KETTLES, Preserving	343
KIDNEYS, Beef, to cook	74, 75
KISSES	317, 318
KISSES, Cocoanut	319
KISSES, Jelly	318, 319
KRAUT, Sour, to make,	112, 113
KRAUT, Sour, to serve	113
LADY APPLES, to preserve	355, 356
LADY-CAKE, White	301, 302
LADY-CAKE, Yellow	301
LADY-FINGERS, to make	267, 309, 319
LAFAYETTE CAKE	308
LAMB, a Breast of, to broil,	121, 122
LAMB CHOP, like a Crown	122
LAMB, Fore Quarter of, to carve	443
LAMB, Joints of	121
LAMB, Leg of, to carve	444
LAMB, Loin of, to carve	444
LAMB, Quarter of, boiled	124
LAMB, Quarter of, roasted or baked	123, 124
LAMB, Shoulder of, to carve	444
LAMB SOUP	25, 26
LAMB STEAKS, with Wine or Currant Jelly	122, 123
LAMB STEWED WITH PEAS	122
LAMB, to choose	121
LAMB, to roast a Pig like	105
LARD, to make	96, 111
LARDED SWEETBREAD	424, 425
LEEKS, Uses of	194
LEAVEN, to make	278
LEMONADE, to make	334
LEMON AND SYRUP SAUCE	241
LEMON BRANDY	381
LEMON CANDY, Common	340
LEMON CANDY OR ROCK	340
LEMON CREAM, Floating Island	218
LEMON DROP CAKES	311
LEMON ICE CREAM	332
LEMON JUICE, to keep	333, 334
LEMON PEEL, Candied	358
LEMON PIE	256

	PAGE
LEMON PUDDING	229
LEMON PUDDING, Rich	228
LEMON SAUCE, for Meat	197, 198
LEMON SAUCE, for Puddings	241
LEMON SAUCE, for Puddings, Rich	242
LEMON SHERBET	385
LEMON SUGAR	333
LEMON SYRUP,	336
LEMON WATER	333, 409
LEMONS, to preserve	354
LETTUCE, to prepare for Table	188
LIGHT ROLLS	283, 284
LIMA BEANS, to cook	184
LIMES, to preserve	354
LIQUID BRANDY OR WINE SAUCE (see Sauce)	240, 241
LIVER, Beeves', to cook	70, 71
LIVER, Beeves', to smoke	67
LIVER, Calf's, to cook	85
LOAF CAKE	310
LOBSTER, Boiled, Sour Sauce for	48, 49
LOBSTER, Buttered	49
LOBSTER, Choice of	48
LOBSTER SALAD	49, 50, 420
LOBSTER SAUCE	197
LOBSTER SOUP, to make	16
LOBSTER, to boil	48
LOBSTER, to broil	49
MACARONI SOUP	23
MACARONI, Sweet	427
MACARONI WITH CHEESE	427
MACAROONS, Almond	316, 317
MACAROONS, Cocoanut	317
MACAROONS, Pyramid of	323, 324
MACKEREL, Fresh, to cook	45
MACKEREL, Salt, to dress	46
MACKEREL, to dry	45, 46
MACKEREL, to carve	439
MACKEREL, to Salt	46
MAIGRE, Soup, to make	20
MANGE, Blanc, to make	223
MANGE, Jaune	339
MANGOES and other Pickles, Directions for making	388–397
MANGOES, Melon	390, 391
MAPLE SUGAR SAUCE	242
MARLBOROUGH PUDDING	414
MARMALADE	358
MARMALADE, Peach	362

INDEX. 467

	PAGE
MARMALADE, Pear	375
MARMALADE, Quince	351
MARMALADE, Raspberry	365
MARMALADE, Strawberry	365, 366
MARMALADE, Transparent	351
MARROWFAT PEAS, to cook	181, 182
MARROW PUDDING	223
MEAL, Corn (see *Corn Meal*)	235
MEAL, Indian, Dumplings	223, 224
MEAT, Directions for boiling and serving with Vegetables	112
MEAT from which Soup has been made, to serve cold	12
MEAT, Joints of, to carve	441-448
MEAT, Mince Pie	261-263
MEAT PIE, to serve	63
MEAT SANDWICH	329
MEAT, Sauces for	195-199
MEAT, Sausage	100
MEAT, Soup without	19
MEATS, cooked, to make Soup from	11, 12
MEATS, Directions for buying and dressing	65-130
MEATS, Directions for cooking (see *Beef, Lamb, Mutton, Pork* and *Veal*)	65-130
MELON MANGOES	390, 391
MELON, Water, Preserves	353
MELTED BUTTER, to prepare	198
MERINGUE PIE	256, 264
MERINGUES, Almond	320, 321
MERINGUES, Cocoanut	321
MERINGUES, Filbert	321
MERINGUES, Hazelnut	321
MERINGUES, Pyramid of	323, 324
MILK AND CABBAGE SOUP	16, 17
MILK BISCUITS, to make	286
MILK, Cellar for	205
MILK CHEESE, to make	207
MILK OR SODA BISCUIT	285
MILK, Oysters stewed with	59
MILK PORRIDGE	408, 409
MILK PUNCH	384
MILK, Rice	410
MILK, Sago	410
MILK SOUP	403
MILK, Tapioca	410
MILK, Thickened	408
MILK, Thick Sour, Use of	206
MILK TOAST	263, 299

	PAGE
MILK, to destroy the Unpleasant Flavor of, from cows feeding on turnips	206
MILK, to keep	202, 203
MINCED BEEF	80
MINCE PIE, Apple	263, 264
MINCE PIE, Meat	261
MINCE PIE MEAT, Domestic	262, 263
MINCE PIE MIXTURE, to finish	263
MINCE PIE MIXTURE, to make	262
MINCE PIE, to be served warm	262
MINCE PIE, to make	263
MINCE PIES, Delicious	424
MINCE, White, of Veal	426
MINT SAUCE	197
MINUTE PUDDING	211, 280
MISCELLANEOUS RECEIPTS	407-432
MIXTURE, Mince Pie, to finish	263
MIXTURE, Mince Pie, to make	262
MOCK CREAM	221
MOCK CREAM PIE	259
MOCK TURTLE SOUP	20
MOCK VENISON, to make	126, 127
MOLASSES CANDY (Taffy)	341, 342
MOLASSES CUP CAKES	297
Moss, Carrigan	408
MOTTOES, to make	324
MOULD, Omelette Souffle in a	238
MOULD on Preserves	344
MRS. COWING'S PEACH PICKLES	397
MRS. MADISON'S WHIM	313
MUFFINS	417
MUFFINS, Buttermilk	280
MUFFINS, Indian Meal	277
MUFFINS, to make	280, 281
MULBERRIES, to preserve	382
MULBERRY SYRUP	382
MULLED CIDER	409, 410
MULLED WINE	410
MUSCLES, to cook	64
MUSCLES, to stew	64
MUSHROOMS, Description of	191, 192
MUSHROOMS, to broil	192
MUSHROOMS with Beefsteak	420
MUSKMELON, Preserved	354
MUSKMELONS, to prepare for Table	387
MUSTARD, to make	394
MUTTON, a Breast of, to broil	129
MUTTON, a Shoulder of, to broil	129
MUTTON BROTH	28, 29

	PAGE		PAGE
MUTTON CHOPS, Broiled	130	OMELETTE with Sweetmeats	239, 240
MUTTON CHOPS, Fried	129, 130	ONE-TWO-THREE-FOUR CAKE	294
MUTTON CURRIE	129	ONION AND BEEF STEW	78, 79
MUTTON HAMS	127	ONION SAUCE	197
MUTTON, Haunch of, to carve	442	ONION SOUP	22
MUTTON, Haunch of, to cook	128, 129	ONIONS, Beefsteak with	71
MUTTON, Joints of	433	ONIONS, Green, to prepare for Table	189
MUTTON, Leg of, boiled	130		
MUTTON, Leg of, to carve	443	ONIONS, Store, to dress	189
MUTTON, Leg of, to roast	125	ONIONS, to boil	189, 190
MUTTON, Loin of, to carve	442	ONIONS, to pickle	391
MUTTON, Observations on	125, 126	ONIONS, Winter, to dress	189
MUTTON Pasty, to eat like Venison	126	ORANGE JELLY	357
MUTTON, Saddle of, to carve	442	ORANGE PEEL, Candied	358
MUTTON, Shoulder of, to carve	442	ORANGE PUDDING	413, 414
MUTTON STEAKS, to broil	130	ORANGE SHERBET	334
MUTTON, to make Mock Venison from	126, 127	ORANGE SUGAR	333
		ORANGE-WATER	333
MUTTON, to make taste like Venison	126	ORANGE-WATER ICE	334
		ORANGES as Dessert	401
		ORANGES in Jelly	354, 355
NAPLES BISCUIT	308	ORGEAT	334, 335
NASTURTIUM, or Imitation Caper Sauce	196	ORNAMENTAL FROSTING	320
		ORNAMENTS for Pies	258, 259
NASTURTIUMS, to pickle	391	OVENS, Remarks on	343, 344
NECTARINES, to bottle	383	OX-HEAD SOUP	17
NECTARINES, to candy	382, 383	OYSTER CATSUP	394
NECTARINES, to preserve	382	OYSTER CHOWDER, to make	61, 62
NEW-YEAR'S DAY, a Cold Collation for	405	OYSTER FRITTERS, to make	56, 57
		OYSTER PIE, to make	62, 63
NEW-YEAR'S DINNER	405	OYSTER PIE, to serve	63
NOODLES AND BEEFSTEAK	419	OYSTER SAUCE	197
NOODLES for Soup, to make	419	OYSTER SOUP, to make	15, 16
NOTHINGS, to make	250	OYSTER SUPPER, Directions concerning	328, 329
NUTS, Ginger	297		
		OYSTER, Vegetable, to cook	191
OATMEAL GRUEL, to make	407	OYSTERS AU PARMESAN	63
OATMEAL, to cook	277	OYSTERS, Choice of	56
OLIVES, to pickle plums like	391, 392	OYSTERS, Panned	431, 432
OMELETTE AU NATUREL	167	OYSTERS, Pickled, to serve	61
OMELETTE, Dutch	168, 169	OYSTERS, Scolloped	63, 64
OMELETTE for Dessert	229	OYSTERS, Season for	56
OMELETTE, French	167, 168	OYSTERS, Small, to fry	58
OMELETTE GLACEE	240	OYSTERS, Small, to pickle	61
OMELETTE, Ham	168	OYSTERS, Sweetbreads like	426
OMELETTE of Hard-shell Clams	55	OYSTERS, to boil	58, 59
OMELETTE of Smoked Beef	169	OYSTERS, to broil	58
OMELETTE SOUFLEE	238	OYSTERS, to feed	56
OMELETTE SOUFLEE in a Mould	238	OYSTERS, to fricassee	59
OMELETTE, Spanish	168	OYSTERS, to fry	57
OMELETTE, to make an	168	OYSTERS, to fry in Batter	57

INDEX.

	PAGE		PAGE
OYSTERS, to pickle (No. 1)	59, 60	PEACHES, Fried	190
OYSTERS, to pickle (No. 2)	60, 61	PEACHES, Ripe, to prepare for Table	385, 386
OYSTERS, to roast	58		
OYSTERS, to stew with Milk	59	PEACHES, to dry	363
OYSTERS, to stew with Wine	63	PEACHES, to pickle	392, 393
		PEACHES, to preserve	359, 360
PALO-ALTO CAKES	303	PEACHES, to preserve whole	360, 361
PANADA	410	PEACHES, to preserve without cooking (equal to Brandy Peaches)	422
PANCAKES, Egg	232		
PANCAKES, Jelly	232, 233		
PANNED OYSTERS	431, 432	PEACHES, to stew	376
PARMESAN, Oysters au	63	PEARLASH CAKE	296
PARSLEY SAUCE	195	PEAR MARMALADE	375
PARSNIP FRITTERS	185, 186	PEARS, Large Bell, to preserve	375
PARSNIP STEW	120	PEARS, to bake	375, 376
PARSNIPS, to boil	185	PEARS, to dry	374
PARSNIPS, to fry	185	PEARS to preserve	374, 375
PARTIES, Evening, Refreshments for	326, 327	PEARS, to preserve in Brandy	374
		PEARS, to stew	375
PARTRIDGE, to carve	449	PEA SOUP (Green)	17, 18
PARTRIDGES, to cook	160	PEAS, Green, to cook	181
PARTY, Tea, Directions about	327, 328	PEAS, Lamb stewed with	122
PARTY, Winter, Refreshments for	327	PEAS, Marrowfat, to cook	181, 182
PASTE CAKES	284	PEAS (Split) Soup	21
PASTE JELLY TARTS, Sweet	248	PEEL, Orange and Lemon, to candy	358
PASTE PUDDING, with Fruit	214		
PASTE, Puff, Common (for Pies)	245, 246	PEPPERMINT CANDY	341
PASTE, Puff, Finest (for Puffs)	245	PEPPERS, Green, to pickle	388, 389
PASTE, Puff, Light	246	PERCH, to carve	440
PASTE PUFFS	247	PERCH, to fry	41
PASTE TARTS	247	PHEASANT, to carve	449, 450
PASTY, MUTTON, to eat like Venison	126	PICKLE for beef	66, 67
		PICKLED BEEF	68
PASTY, VENISON	133, 134	PICKLED CLAMS	55
PATIENCE, Tablets de	309, 310	PICKLED OYSTERS	59–61
PATTIES, Chicken	142, 143	PICKLED PORK	96
PEACH CHARLOTTE	215	PICKLED SALMON	43
PEACH DUMPLINGS (Dried)	213	PICKLES, Directions for making (see under their respective names)	388–397
PEACH DUMPLINGS (Ripe)	214		
PEACH FRITTERS	423		
PEACH JELLY	362, 363	Beets	394, 395
PEACH MARMALADE	362	Butternuts	392
PEACH PICKLES, Mrs. Cowing's	397	Cabbage, Red	394
PEACH PIE (Dried)	253	Cucumbers	388, 389
PEACH PIE (Ripe)	255	Green Beans	392
PEACH PIE (Whole)	255	Green Peppers	389, 390
PEACH POT-PIE	418	Melon Mangoes	390, 391
PEACH PRESERVE	363, 364	Nasturtiums	391
PEACH TART (Dried)	253	Onions	391
PEACHES, Brandied	361, 362	Peaches	392, 393, 397
PEACHES, Brandy	361	Plums	391, 392, 397

INDEX.

	PAGE
PICKLES, Directions for making (continued).	
Tomatoes	395
Walnuts	392
PICKLES, Management of	395-397
PICKLES, Peach, Mrs. Cowing's	397
PICKEREL, to cook	47
PICKLES, to color Green	342
PICKLES, Water-melon	411
PIE, a Labor-saving	259
PIE, Apple	251
PIE, Apple (Dried)	252
PIE, Beefsteak	77, 78
PIE, Blackberry	258
PIE, Cherry (Dried)	254
PIE, Cherry (Sour)	254, 255
PIE, Chicken	140, 141
PIE, Chicken, to serve	63
PIE, Clam, to make	53, 54
PIE, Cranberry	255
PIE, Cream	258, 259
PIE CRUST, Family (Short)	247, 248
PIE, Currant (Green)	257, 258
PIE, Currant (Ripe)	257
PIE, Custard, which makes its own Paste	259
PIE, Gooseberry	258
PIE, Grape (Green)	258
PIE, Green Gage	254
PIE, Huckleberry	257
PIE, Huckleberry and Grape	258
PIE, Lemon	256
PIE-MAKING, Remarks on	250, 251
PIE, Meat, to serve	63
PIE, Meringue	256, 264
PIE, Mince, Apple	263, 264
PIE, Mince, Meat for	261
PIE, Mince, Meat for Domestic	262, 263
PIE, Mince, Mixture, to finish	263
PIE, Mince, Mixture, to make	262
PIE, Mince, to be served Warm	262
PIE, Mince, to make	263, 424
PIE, Mock Cream	259
PIE, Oyster, to make	62, 63
PIE, Oyster, to serve	63
PIE, Peach (Dried)	253
PIE, Peach (Ripe)	255
PIE, Peach (Whole)	255
PIE, Pigeon	158, 159
PIE, Pig's Feet	106, 107
PIE, Plum (Dried)	253

	PAGE
PIE, Plum (Green)	254
PIE, Plum (Ripe)	253, 254
PIE, Pork and Apple	413
PIE, Pumpkin	260
PIE, Rhubarb	256
PIE, Rice	259, 412
PIE, Rice Flour	260
PIE, Sweet Potato	177
PIE, Thanksgiving	260, 261
PIE, Tomato	411
PIE, Veal	92, 93
PIE, Whortleberry	257
PIES, Custard	259
PIES, Directions for baking and making (see *Puddings* and *Tarts*)	243-264
PIES, Mince, Delicious	424
PIES, Ornaments for	258, 259
PIES, Puff Paste for	245, 246
PIG, Roast, Sauces to serve with (see *Pork*)	104
PIG, Roast, to carve	447
PIG, to bake a	104
PIG, to roast a	103
PIG, to roast like Lamb	105
PIG'S CHEEK, to cook	108
PIG'S FEET Pie	106, 107
PIG'S FEET, soused	106
PIG'S HARSLET, to make a Dish of	104
PIG'S HEAD, to prepare for baking	102, 103
PIGEON CUTLETS	160
PIGEON PIE	158, 159
PIGEON POT-PIE	159
PIGEONS, Choice of	154, 155
PIGEONS, to broil	155
PIGEONS, to carve	450
PIGEONS, to fry	155, 156
PIGEONS, to make a Bird's Nest of	156, 157
PIGEONS, to roast	159, 160
PIGEONS, to stew brown	157, 158
PIGEONS, to stew (White)	156
PIKE OR PICKEREL, to cook	47
PINE APPLE, Dessert of	401
PINE-APPLE JELLY	347, 348
PINE-APPLE PRESERVE	347
PINE-APPLE SYRUP	335, 336
PINE-APPLES, to preserve whole	348
PINE-APPLES to preserve without cooking	346, 347

	PAGE
PINK, to color Preserves	343
PINK, to prepare Cochineal for coloring	321
PIPPINS, to preserve in Slices	356
PISTACHIO BISCOTTES	322
PISTACHIO BISCUIT	322, 323
PLAICE, to carve	441
PLANT, EGG, to cook	191
PLUM CAKE	314
PLUM PIE (Dried)	253
PLUM PIE (Green)	254
PLUM PIE (Ripe)	253, 254
PLUM PUDDING	219, 220, 413
PLUM PUDDING, Christmas	218, 219
PLUM PUDDING, Sauce for	242
PLUM TART (Dried)	253
PLUMS, General Remarks on	370
PLUMS, Green Gage, to brandy	372, 373
PLUMS, Green Gage, to preserve	372
PLUMS, Large, to preserve	411
PLUMS, Purple, to preserve	371
PLUMS, to dry	374
PLUMS, to pickle	397
PLUMS, to pickle like Olives	391, 392
PLUMS, to preserve for Tarts, or Common Use	381, 382
PLUMS, to preserve in Brandy	372
PLUMS, to preserve without the Skins	371
POACHED EGGS	166
POACHED EGGS, in Balls	167
POACHED EGGS, with Fried Ham	114
PODS, Radish, to pickle	395
PONE, or Corn-meal Breakfast Cake	274, 275
POP, Buttermilk	409
PORK, a Hand of, to carve (see Pig)	447
PORK, a Leg of, to carve	447
PORK, a Loin of, to carve	447
PORK AND APPLE PIE	418
PORK AND BEANS, to bake	115
PORK AND BEANS, to boil	115
PORK, a Pickle for	99, 100
PORK CHEESE, soused	93
PORK, Choice of	95, 96
PORK CHOPS, to cook	109
PORK, Corned, and Beans	115
PORK, Corned, to boil with Vegetables	117, 118

	PAGE
PORK CUTLETS, to cook	109
PORK, Fresh, to stew	105, 106
PORK, General Remarks on	95, 96
PORK HAMS (see Hams)	107
PORK, Head Cheese	97
PORK, Joints of	434
PORK, Leg of, to bake or roast	105
PORK, Leg of, to boil	103
PORK, Loin of, to roast	105
PORK, Pickled	96
PORK, Salt, to fry or broil	109, 110
PORK, Sauces to serve with	104
PORK SAUSAGES, Meat for	100
PORK SAUSAGES (to eat cold), to make	101, 102
PORK SAUSAGES, to make	100, 101
PORK, Smoked, to make a Stew of	108
PORK, Spare-rib of	96
PORK STEAKS, to cook	109
PORK, Tenderloin of	105
PORK, to salt (Farmers' Way)	98
PORRIDGE, Milk	408, 409
PORTABLE SOUP, to make	14, 15
PORTER-HOUSE STEAKS	76
PORTUGAL CAKES	295
POTATO AND BEEF HASH	75, 76
POTATO AND VEAL PIE	93
POTATO BREAD	270, 271
POTATO CAKES, to serve with Roast Ducks	421
POTATO PUDDING	413
POTATO SALAD	430
POTATOES AND CABBAGE, to cook together	194
POTATOES baked in Cups	423
POTATOES, Cold, Boiled, to prepare for Table	174
POTATOES (New), to boil	173, 174
POTATOES (Old), Mashed	173
POTATOES (Old), to boil	172
POTATOES, Sweet, to bake	176
POTATOES, Sweet, to boil	176, 177
POTATOES, Sweet, to roast	176
POTATOES, to bake	173
POTATOES, to boil with Codfish	112
POTATOES, to broil	176
POTATOES, to cook in haste	174
POTATOES, to fry	174, 175
POTATOES, to hash	175
POTATOES, to prepare for Soups	13

	PAGE		PAGE
POTATOES, to roast	175, 176	PUDDING, Batter, Rich	217
POTATOES, Veal minced with	92	PUDDING, Beef Steak	78
POT-CHEESE, to make	296	PUDDING, Blackberry	230
POT-PIE, Chicken	141, 142	PUDDING, Bread and Butter, baked	226, 227
POT-PIE, Chicken, to Dish a	142		
POT-PIE, Clam, to make	54, 55	PUDDING, Bread, baked	225
POT-PIE, Goose	150	PUDDING, Bread, boiled	225, 226, 233
POT-PIE, Peach	413	PUDDING CARROT	415
POT-PIE, Pigeon	159	PUDDING, Charlie's Apple	414
POT-PIE, Veal	93, 94	PUDDING, Cherry	229, 230
POULTRY, Boiling of	136	PUDDING, Citron	217
POULTRY, Choice of	135	PUDDING, Cocoanut, baked	228, 413
POULTRY, Game, etc., to carve	448–450	PUDDING, Cocoanut, boiled	217, 218
POULTRY, General Remarks on (see *Chickens* and *Fowl*)	135	PUDDING, Corn-meal	236, 237
		PUDDING, Currant	230
POULTRY, Roasting of	135, 136	PUDDING, Currant, Dried	229
POULTRY, Sauces for	195–199	PUDDING, Currant Jelly	231
POULTRY, to keep from tainting	161, 162	PUDDING, Egg	227
		PUDDING, Farina	428
POUND-CAKE, Almond	306	PUDDING, Flour, baked in Cups	414
POUND-CAKE, Cocoanut	306	PUDDING, Gotham	235
POUND-CAKES, Small	304	PUDDING, Green Corn	237, 238
POUND-CAKES, to make	305	PUDDING, Huckleberry	230
POWDER, CURRIE, to make	198	PUDDING, Indian, baked	414
PREPARED FLOUR, to make	289	PUDDING, Indian, Cheap	224
PRESERVED FRUIT, Jars for	344	PUDDING, Indian, Plain	415
PRESERVES, Foam on	344, 345	PUDDING, Indian, to make	120
PRESERVES, Mould on	344	PUDDING, Lemon	220
PRESERVES, Peach	363, 364	PUDDING, Lemon, Rich	228
PRESERVES, Pine-apple	346-348	PUDDING, Marlborough	414
PRESERVES, Rhubarb	411	PUDDING, Marrow	228
PRESERVES, Strawberry	364, 365	PUDDING, Minute	211, 230
PRESERVES, Sugar for	343	PUDDING, Orange	412, 414
PRESERVES, to color Green	342	PUDDING, Paste, with Fruit	214
PRESERVES, to color Pink	343	PUDDING, Plum	219, 220, 413
PRESERVES, to color Yellow	342, 343	PUDDING, Plum, Christmas	218, 219
PRESERVING FRUITS, Directions for	343–345	PUDDING, Plum, Sauce for	242
		PUDDING, Potato	413
PRESERVING, to clarify Sugar for	345	PUDDING, Prune	215
PRUNE PUDDING	215	PUDDING, Quaking	216
PRUNES, to stew	380, 410, 411	PUDDING, Ratafia	233
PUDDING, Almond, baked	220	PUDDING, Rice Flour	227
PUDDING, Almond, boiled	220, 221	PUDDING, Rice, with Eggs	227
PUDDING, Apple, baked	414	PUDDING, Rice, without Eggs	227
PUDDING, Apple, boiled	429	PUDDING SAUCES, to make	240–242
PUDDING, Apple, boiled, with Eggs	212	Apple Sauce	241, 242
		Brandy or Wine Sauce	240
PUDDING, Apple, boiled, without Eggs	212	Brandy or Wine Sauce, Liquid	240, 241
PUDDING, Batter, boiled	225	Brandy Sauce	240
PUDDING, Batter, Cheap	216, 217	Cinnamon Sauce	242

INDEX. 473

PUDDING SAUCES, to make (continued).
  Cranberry Sauce 241
  Lemon and Syrup Sauce..... 241
  Lemon Sauce................ 241
  Lemon Sauce, Rich.......... 242
  Maple Sugar Sauce.......... 242
  Plum Pudding, Sauce for.... 242
  Sweet Sauce 241
  Wine Sauce..............240, 241
PUDDING, Sponge Cake......229, 416
PUDDING, Suet............412, 413
PUDDING, Suet, boiled........224, 225
PUDDING, Suet, Fruit, without Eggs....................430, 431
PUDDING, Sweet Potato.......... 228
PUDDING, Tapioca.............. 413
PUDDING, Transparent............ 234
PUDDING, Vermicelli............ 412
PUDDING, Wheat and Indian...235, 236
PUDDING, White................ 230
PUDDINGS, baking of............ 210
PUDDINGS, boiling of......,..209, 210
PUDDINGS, Curd, Small.......... 234
PUDDINGS, Etc., Directions for making (see *Pies, Tarts,* and *Dumplings*) 209–242
PUDDINGS, Lemon Sauce for..... 242
PUDDINGS, Small............227, 223
PUFF PASTE, Common (for Pies).. 245
PUFF PASTE, Finest (for Puffs) ... 245
PUFF PASTE, Light.............. 246
PUFFS, Paste.................... 247
PUMPKIN PIE 260
PUMPKINS, to preserve........171, 172
PUNCH, Champagne..........406, 407
PUNCH, Milk.................... 384
PYRAMID, an Ornamental........ 324
PYRAMID of Cocoa-nut Drops, Macaroons, or Meringue, to make a 323, 324

QUAHOGS (see *Clams*)............ 52
QUAILS, to cook 169
QUAKING PUDDING.............. 216
QUEEN CAKE.................... 305
QUINCE AND APPLE JELLY...... 352
QUINCE CHEESE...........352, 353
QUINCE JELLY.............351, 352
QUINCE MARMALADE............ 351
QUINCES in Jelly Syrup......350, 351

QUINCES, to keep............... 349
QUINCES, to preserve.........349, 350
QUINCES, to stew............... 376

RABBIT, to carve 452
RABBIT, Welsh, to make......... 208
RABBITS, to choose, dress, and cook......................162–164
RADISHES, Kinds of............. 187
RADISHES, to prepare for Table 187,188
RADISH PODS, to pickle.......... 395
RAGOUT, Beef, to make.......... 72
RAGOUT, Veal................89, 90
RAGOUT, to make a, of stewed Goose....................151, 152
RASPBERRIES, Dried, to stew..366, 367
RASPBERRIES, to prepare for Table 386
RASPBERRIES, to preserve 366
RASPBERRY JAM................ 366
RASPBERRY MARMALADE........ 366
RASPBERRY SYRUP.............. 335
RASPBERRY VINEGAR........... 384
RATAFIA PUDDING.............. 233
RECEIPTS, Miscellaneous......407–432
RED CABBAGE, to dress......... 187
RED CABBAGE, to pickle......... 394
RED, to color Soup.............. 14
RED, to prepare Cochineal for coloring..................... 321
REFRESHMENTS for a Winter Party........................ 327
REFRESHMENTS for Evening Parties.....................326, 327
REFRESHMENT TABLES, Directions for setting.........325–329
RENNET, to prepare..........207, 208
RHUBARB DUMPLINGS............ 214
RHUBARB FRITTERS............. 230
RHUBARB PIE................... 256
RHUBARB PRESERVE............. 411
RHUBARB TART.......,.......256, 257
RIBBON BLANC-MANGE........... 223
RICE CAKES.................... 422
RICE CUSTARD 412
RICE-FLOUR BLANC-MANGE 408
RICE-FLOUR PIE................ 260
RICE-FLOUR PUDDING........... 227
RICE-FLOUR SHORT-CAKES....... 234
RICE MILK..................... 410
RICE PIE 259, 412
RICE PUDDING with Eggs........ 227

U*

INDEX.

	PAGE
RICE PUDDING without Eggs	227
ROAST PIG, to carve (see *Pig*)	447
ROCK OR LEMON CANDY	340
ROLLA CHEESE, to make	69, 70
ROLLS, Bakers', to make	278, 279
ROLLS, Cream of Tartar	423
ROLLS, Directions for baking	265
ROLLS, Directions for making	264
ROLLS, French, for Tea	284
ROLLS, Light	283, 284
ROOM, Breakfast, Arrangement and Furniture of	398–407
ROOM, Dining, Arrangement and Furniture of	398–407
ROSE BRANDY	333
ROSE CANDY	341
ROUT DROP-CAKES	312
RUSK, Egg	282, 283
RUSK, Tea	282
RUSSE, Charlotte	221, 222
RUTA-BAGA TURNIPS, to boil	119, 120
RUTA-BAGA TURNIPS, to cook	177
RYE BREAD	272
RYE BREAD CAKE	272, 273
RYE SHORT-CAKES	277
SAGO MILK	410
SAGO, to cook	410
SALAD, Asparagus	182, 183
SALAD, Cabbage	186
SALAD, Cauliflower	185
SALAD, Chicken	143, 429, 430
SALAD DRESSING	186
SALAD, Lobster	49, 50, 430
SALAD, Potato	430
SALAD, Red Cabbage	187
SALAD, Water-cresses used as	194
SALERATUS, Use of, in Bread or Cakes	265, 266
SALMON, Dried or Smoked, to broil	43, 44
SALMON, Salt, a Dish of	44
SALMON, Salt, to cook	44
SALMON, Spiced, to pickle	43
SALMON, to bake	42
SALMON, to boil	41, 42
SALMON, to broil	42
SALMON, to carve	440
SALMON, to dry, or smoke	43
SALMON, to tell when fresh	41
SALMON TROUT, to cook	43

	PAGE
SALSIFY, to cook	191
SALT FISH, to soak (see *Fish*)	34
SANDWICHES, to make	329, 330
Beef Sandwich	329
Biscuit and Jelly	303
Bread and Butter	329
Bread for	329
Cheese	329
Cold Meat	329
Eggs, Cold, boiled	329
Fruit	329
Ham	329
Jelly	329
Tongue	329
SANGAREE, Wine	337
SAUCES for Meat, Fish, Poultry, or Vegetables	195–199
Anchovy Sauce	196, 197
Apple Sauce	199
Apples, Fried	199
Butter, Clarified	198
Butter, Cold, and Vinegar Sauce	195, 196
Butter, Drawn, to make	195
Butter, Melted	198
Butter Sauce	196
Caper Sauce, Imitation	196
Cranberry Sauce, or Jam	199
Cream Sauce	198
Currie Powder	198
Egg Sauce	195
Flour, to brown	196
Lemon Sauce	197, 198
Lobster Sauce	197
Mint Sauce	197
Nasturtium Sauce	196
Onion Sauce	197
Oyster Sauce	197
Parsley Sauce	195
Peaches, Fried	199
Shalot Sauce	196
Sour Sauce	195
Sour Sauce, for boiled Lobsters	48, 49
Venison Sauce	134
SAUCES for Puddings	240–242
Apple Sauce	241, 242
Brandy or Wine Sauce	240
Brandy or Wine Sauce, Liquid	240, 241
Brandy Sauce	240

INDEX.

	PAGE
SAUCES for Puddings (*continued*).	
Cinnamon Sauce	242
Cranberry Sauce	241
Lemon and Syrup Sauce	241
Lemon Sauce	241
Lemon Sauce, Rich	242
Maple Sugar Sauce	242
Plum Pudding, Sauce for	242
Sweet Sauce	241
Wine Sauce	240, 241
SAUCES, to serve with Roast Pig or Pork	104
SAUSAGE MEAT, Beef	66
SAUSAGE MEAT. Pork	100
SAUSAGE MEAT, to cook with Vegetables	117
SAUSAGES, Bologna, to make	102
SAUSAGES, Fried, Vegetables with	117
SAUSAGES, Pork, Meat for	100
SAUSAGES, Pork, to make	100, 101
SAUSAGES, to fry	421
SAUSAGES, Veal	87
SAVOY BISCUIT	307, 308
SAVOY CABBAGE	118
SAVOY SOUP	29
SCOLLOPED CLAMS	56
SCOLLOPED OYSTERS	63, 64
SCOLLOPED TOMATOES	191
SCOLLOPS, to boil	50
SCOTCH CAKE	315, 316
SEA BASS, to cook	38
SEA CLAMS, to cook	55
SHAD, baked	38, 39
SHAD, broiled	38
SHAD, fried	37, 38
SHAD, to dry or smoke	40
SHAD, when in season	37
SHALOT SAUCE	196
SHALOTS, to prepare for Table	189
SHEEP'S HARSLET, hashed	127, 128
SHELL-FISH, Directions for cooking (see under respective names)	48–64
Clams, Hard-shell	51–55
Clams, Sea	55
Clams, Soft-shell	50, 51
Crabs	50
Lobsters	48–50
Muscles	64
Oysters (see *Oysters*)	56–64
Scollops	50

	PAGE
SHERBET, Cream	385
SHERBET, Lemon	385
SHERBET, Orange	384
SHERBET, Strawberry	335, 385
SHIN OF BEEF SOUP	23, 24
SHORT-CAKE, Strawberry	418, 431, 432
SHORT-CAKES	284
SHORT-CAKES, Rice Flour	284
SHORT-CAKES, Rye	277
SIMPLE SYRUP, to make	339, 340
SKIRTS, Beef, to cook	66, 72
SMALL BIRDS, to broil (see *Birds*)	161
SMALL CAKES, to make	292, 293
SMALL PUDDINGS	227, 228
SMOKED BEEF (see *Beef, Smoked*)	75
SNAPS, Ginger	296
SNIPE, to cook	160
SNOW, a Dish of,—Cocoa-nut grated	238, 239
SNOW, a Dish of,—Whipt Cream	221
SNOW-BALLS	214, 215
SNOW CREAM	331
SODA CAKE	299
SODA or Milk Biscuit	285
SOFT CRABS, to cook	430
SOFT GINGER-BREAD	295, 296
SOFT GINGER-BREAD, without Eggs	296
SOFT JUMBLES	299
SOFT-SHELL CLAMS (see *Clams*)	50
SOLES, to carve	441
SOUFFLEE, Omelette	233
SOUFFLEE OMELETTE, in a Mould	233
SOUP BEEF	24, 25
SOUP, Brown Gravy	420
SOUP, Bullhead	19
SOUP, Cabbage	30
SOUP, Cabbage and Milk	16, 17
SOUP, Calf's Head	26, 27
SOUP, Catfish	19
SOUP, Chicken, White	22
SOUP, Chicken, Yellow	21, 22
SOUP, Clam	29
SOUP, Dried Bean	21
SOUP, Egg Balls for	28
SOUP, Egg Dumplings for	28
SOUP, Fish	21
SOUP, Green Bean	20, 21
SOUP, Green Corn	409
SOUP, Green Pea	17, 18
SOUP, Hare	23

	PAGE		PAGE
Soup in Haste	31	Spinach, with fried Sausages	117
Soup, Julienne	427	Split Peas Soup	21
Soup, Lamb	25, 26	Sponge Cake	307, 415
Soup, Lobster	16	Sponge Cake, Cocoanut	312
Soup, Macaroni	28	Sponge-cake Pudding	229, 416
Soup, Maigre	20	Sponge Cakes, General Rules for making	416
Soup, Milk	408		
Soup, Milk and Cabbage	16, 17	Sponge Cakes, small	293, 294, 307
Soup, Mock Turtle	20	Spoon Biscuits	309
Soup, Noodles for	410	Sprouts, Cabbage, to boil	178, 179
Soup, Onion	22	Squash, Summer, to cook	177, 178
Soup, Ox-head	17	Squash, Winter, to cook	178
Soup, Oyster	15, 16	Squirrels, to choose, dress, and cook	162-164
Soup, Pea (Green)	17, 13		
Soup, Portable	14, 15	Stains, to remove from the Hand	411
Soup, Savoy	20	Starch, Corn, Custard	429
Soup, Shin of Beef	23, 24	Starch, Corn, to cook	423
Soup, soon made	31	Steaks, Beef, Choice of (see *Beefsteak*)	76
Soup, Split Peas	21		
Soup, Stock for Gravy	29, 30	Steaks, Codfish, fried	36, 37
Soup, to prepare Vegetables for	12-14	Steaks, Lamb, with Wine or Currant Jelly	122, 123
Soup, Turtle, to make	18, 19		
Soup, Veal	25, 26	Steaks, Mutton, to broil	130
Soup, Vegetable, for Summer	30, 31	Steaks, Pork, to cook	109
Soup, Vegetables for	12, 13	Steaks, Porter-house	76
Soup, Vermicelli	28	Steaks, Sirloin	76
Soup, without Meat	19	Steaks, Venison, fried	131, 132
Soupon, fried	237	Steaks, Venison, to broil	132
Soupon, to make	236, 237	Stew, Beef and Onion	78, 79
Soups (see *Broth*)	11-31	Stew of Smoked Pork, to make	108
Soups, Browning for	31	Stew, Parsnip	120
Soups, Directions for making	11-14	Stews, Powder for flavoring	198
Soups, Thickening for	13	Stock for Gravy	29, 30
Soups, to color brown	14	Stock for Gravy Soup	29, 30
Soups, to color green	14	Store Onions, to dress	189
Soups, to color red	14	Strainers, Jelly	348, 349
Soups, to color yellow	14	Strawberries, to prepare for Table	396
Soups, Vegetables for	12-14		
Soups, white, to make	14	Strawberries, to preserve	364, 365
Sour Kraut, to make	112, 113	Strawberries, to preserve Whole	366
Sour Kraut, to serve	113		
Sour Sauce	193	Strawberries to stew for Tarts	366
Sour Sauce for boiled Lobsters	48, 49	Strawberry Jam	365, 366
Spanish Cakes	295	Strawberry Marmalade	365, 366
Spanish Omelette	168	Strawberry Sherbet	385, 385
Spice Biscuits, Almond	315, 321	Strawberry Short-cake	418, 431
Spice Cakes, Rich	294, 295	Strawberry Syrup	385
Spice Cakes, to make	294	Striped Bass, to boil	41
Spiced Salmon, to pickle	46	Striped Bass, to fry	41
Spinach, boiled	118, 119	Stuffing for boiled Fowl	136
Spinach, to cook	180, 181	Stuffing for roast Fowl	135, 136

INDEX. 477

	PAGE
SUCCOTASH, to make	116, 117, 183, 184
SUET FRUIT PUDDING, without Eggs	430, 431
SUET PUDDING	412, 413
SUET PUDDING, boiled	224, 225
SUGAR DROP CAKES	311, 312
SUGAR for Preserves	343
SUGAR, Lemon	333
SUGAR, Orange	333
SUGAR PASTE CREAM TARTS	248
SUGAR, to clarify for Candies	339
SUGAR, to clarify for preserving	345
SUMMER SQUASH, to cook	177, 178
SUMMER VEGETABLE SOUP	30, 31
SUPPERS, Oyster, Directions about	328, 329
SWEETBREAD, Larded	424, 425
SWEETBREADS LIKE OYSTERS	426
SWEETBREADS, to fry	425
SWEETBREADS, to roast	425
SWEETBREADS, to stew	425
SWEETBREADS, Veal	87, 88
SWEET MACARONI	427
SWEETMEATS, Omelette with	239, 240
SWEET OR CAROLINA POTATOES	176
SWEET PASTE JELLY TARTS	248
SWEET POTATO PIE	177
SWEET POTATO PUDDING	228
SWEET POTATOES, to bake	176
SWEET POTATOES to boil	176, 177
SWEET POTATOES, to roast	176
SWEET SAUCE	241
SYLLABUB	337
SYRUP AND LEMON SAUCE	241
SYRUP, Blackberry	369
SYRUP, Jelly, Quinces in	350, 351
SYRUP, Lemon	336
SYRUP, Mulberry	382
SYRUP OF CREAM	331
SYRUP, Pine-apple	335, 336
SYRUP, Raspberry	335
SYRUP, Simple, to make	339, 340
SYRUP, Strawberry	335
SYRUP, Vanilla	336
TABLE, Arrangement of, for Breakfast	398–400
TABLE, Dinner, Arrangement of	402–404
TABLE, Dinner, Etiquette of	435–438
TABLE, Tea, Arrangement of and Bills of Fare for, in Summer and Winter	401, 402
TABLE, to prepare Ripe Fruits or Melons for	385–387
TABLES, Refreshment, Directions for setting	325–329
TABLETS DE PATIENCE	309, 310
TAFFY, to make	341, 342
TAINTING, how to keep Game from	161, 162
TAPIOCA MILK	410
TAPIOCA PUDDING	413
TART, Apple	251, 252
TART, Apple (Dried)	252, 253
TARTS, Cranberry	255
TARTS, Currant (Green)	257, 258
TARTS, Etc., Directions for baking and making	243–264
TARTS, Gooseberry	258
TARTS, Grape (Green)	258
TARTS, Green Gage	254
TARTS, Paste	247
TARTS, Peach (Dried)	253
TARTS, Plum (Dried)	253
TARTS, Rhubarb	256, 257
TARTS, Strawberries stewed for	366
TARTS, Sugar Paste Cream	248
TARTS, Sweet Paste Jelly	248
TARTS, Tomato	411
TARTS, to preserve Fruit for	381, 382
TAYLOR CAKES	293
TEA, Black, to make	331
TEA-CAKE, French	310, 311
TEA-CAKE, Thanksgiving	305, 306
TEA-CAKES, Buttermilk	281, 282
TEA-CAKES, Cream	281
TEA-CAKES—Wigs	297, 298
TEACUP CAKE without Eggs	299
TEA, French Rolls for	284
TEA, Green, to make	330, 331
TEA, Indian-meal Bread for	274
TEA-PARTY, Directions about	327, 328
TEA, Ripe Cherries for	397
TEA, Ripe Currants for	397
TEA RUSK	289
TEA-TABLE, Directions for setting	327, 328
TEA-TABLE, Summer, Arrangement of, and Bill of Fare for	401, 402

478 INDEX.

	PAGE
TEA-TABLE, Winter, Arrangement of, and Bill of Fare for	402
TEA, to serve Pine-apples at	401
TEMPERANCE BEVERAGE, a	405
TERRAPINS	432
THANKSGIVING DINNER, a	405
THANKSGIVING PIE	260, 261
THANKSGIVING TEA-CAKE	395, 396
TOAST, Milk	298, 299
TOAST, to make	298
TOAST, Water	400
TOAST without Butter	299
TOMATO CATSUP	393, 394, 419
TOMATO JAM	373
TOMATO PIE	411
TOMATO TART	411
TOMATOES, Candied	377, 378
TOMATOES, Scolloped	194
TOMATOES, to bake	193
TOMATOES, to broil	193, 194
TOMATOES, to fry	421
TOMATOES, to pickle	395
TOMATOES, to preserve	377
TOMATOES, to serve raw	193
TOMATOES, to stew	193
TOMATOES with Beefsteak	420, 421
TONGUE, a, to carve	445
TONGUE SANDWICH	329
TONGUES, Beeves', to pickle	67, 68
TONGUES, Beeves', to smoke	67
TONGUES, Pigs', to smoke	95
TRANSPARENT MARMALADE	331
TRANSPARENT PUDDING	231
TRIFLE	213
TRIFLE CAKE	338
TRIFLES, to make	259
TRIPE, Beef	69
TRIPE, Beef, to broil	70
TRIPE, Beef, to clean	68, 69
TRIPE, Beef, to fricassee	70
TRIPE, Beef, to fry	69
TRIPE, Beef, to make Rolla Cheese with	69, 70
TROUT, Salmon, to cook	43
TROUT, to cook	43
TURBOT, to carve	441
TURKEY, Fricasseed (Brown)	147, 148
TURKEY, Fricasseed (White)	147
TURKEY, Roast	144–146
TURKEY, to boil	146, 147
TURKEY to carve	450

	PAGE
TURKEYS, Choice of	143, 144
TURNIPS, Green Leaves of, to boil	178
TURNIPS, Ruta-baga, Directions for boiling	119, 120, 177
TURNIPS, to destroy the Unpleasant Flavor imparted to Milk by Cows feeding on	206
TURNIPS, Winter, to cook	177
TURNIPS, Yellow, to boil	119, 120
TURNIPS, Young, to boil	177
TURNPIKE CAKES, to make	275, 276
TURTLE SOUP (Mock)	20
TURTLE SOUP, to make	18, 19
TWIST BREAD	271
TWIST, Common Candy	341
VANILLA ICE CREAM	332
VANILLA SYRUP	336
VEAL, a Breast of, to carve	445
VEAL, a Fillet of, to carve	446
VEAL, a Loin of, to carve	446
VEAL AND POTATO PIE	93
VEAL BROTH	23
VEAL CAKES	426
VEAL, Choice of	84, 85
VEAL CHOPS, Gravy for	88, 89
VEAL CHOPS, to fry or broil	88, 89
VEAL CHOPS, to stew	89
VEAL COLLOPS	426
VEAL, Fore Quarter of, to dress a	411
VEAL, Joints of	434
VEAL, Minced with Potatoes	92
VEAL PIE	92, 93
VEAL POT-PIE	93, 94
VEAL, Roasted to look like a Duck	91, 92
VEAL SAUSAGES	87
VEAL SOUP	25, 26
VEAL, stewed brown	89
VEAL, stewed with Vegetables (Ragout)	89, 90
VEAL SWEETBREADS	87, 88
VEAL, to boil	55
VEAL, to hash	92
VEAL, to roast	90, 91
VEAL, White Mince of	426
VEGETABLE OYSTER, to cook	191
VEGETABLE SOUP for Summer	30, 31
VEGETABLES boiled with Ham (a Family Dinner)	115, 116

INDEX. 479

VEGETABLES, Directions for boiling and serving Meat with.. 112
VEGETABLES for Roast Beef...... 81
VEGETABLES for Roast Goose.... 151
VEGETABLES for Soups..........12–14
VEGETABLES, Sauces for......195–190
VEGETABLES, to boil with Corned Beef......................... 119
VEGETABLES, to boil with Corned Pork....................117, 118
VEGETABLES, to boil with Salted Beef......................... 119
VEGETABLES, to cook, etc. (see also under their respective names)..................170–194
   Artichokes...............188, 189
   Asparagus...............182, 183
   Beans.. 183
   Beans Lima................... 184
   Beets 179, 180
   Cabbages..........186, 187, 194
   Cabbage Sprouts 178, 179
   Carrots 184, 185
   Cauliflower 185
   Celery 186
   Cucumbers................... 189
   Egg Plant 191
   Green Corn (see *Corn*)....190, 191
   Hominy...................... 192
   Horse-radish 194
   Leeks 194
   Lettuce 188
   Mushrooms..............191, 192
   Onions 189
   Parsnips..................185, 186
   Peas 181, 182
   Potatoes (see *Potatoes*)...... 172
   Radishes 187, 188
   Salsify, or Vegetable Oyster.. 191
   Shalots...................... 189
   Spinach.................180, 181
   Squash..................177, 178
   Sweet Potatoes..........176, 177
   Tomatoes................192–194
   Turnips 177
   Water-cresses................ 194
VEGETABLES, to preserve for Winter Use................170–172
VEGETABLES, Veal stewed with 89, 90
VEGETABLES with fried Sausages 117
VELVET CAKES.................. 283

VENISON, a Pretty Dish of........ 134
VENISON, Choice of.............. 131
VENISON, Haunch of, to carve ... 451
VENISON, Mock, to make.....126, 127
VENISON, Mutton Pasty, to eat like......................... 126
VENISON PASTY.............133, 134
VENISON, roasted...........132, 133
VENISON SAUCE.................. 134
VENISON STEAKS, fried.......131, 132
VENISON STEAKS, to broil........ 132
VENISON, to make Mutton taste like......................... 126
VENISON, to stew................ 132
VERMICELLI PUDDING........... 412
VERMICELLI SOUP................ 28
VINEGAR AND COLD BUTTER SAUCE...................195, 196
VINEGAR, Cider, to make........ 393
VINEGAR, Raspberry 384
VOLATILE SALTS, Use of, in Bread or Cakes................265, 266

WAFERS AND JELLY..........291, 292
WAFERS, Cinnamon.............. 293
WAFERS, to make............... 291
WAFFLES, to make 290
WAFFLES, Yeast............290, 291
WALNUT CATSUP................. 393
WALNUTS, to pickle 392
WASHINGTON BREAKFAST-CAKE.. 417
WASHINGTON CAKE.............. 304
WATER, Apple................... 409
WATER, Barley.................. 410
WATER, Cherry 383, 384
WATER-CRESSES, to dress........ 194
WATER, Currant 333
WATER GRUEL, to make 407
WATER, Lemon.............383, 409
WATER, Orange................. 333
WATER, Toast 409
WATERMELON PICKLES........... 411
WATERMELON PRESERVES....... 353
WATERMELONS, to prepare for Table......................... 387
WEBSTER CAKES............302, 303
WEDDING CAKE, to make........ 313
WELSH RABBIT, to make........ 208
"WHAT CHEER" CAKES, or Turnpike Cakes.............. 277
WHEAT AND INDIAN BREAD..271, 272

	PAGE
WHEAT AND INDIAN CRUMPETS..	276
WHEAT AND INDIAN PUDDING	235, 236
WHEAT BREAD, to make	269, 270
WHIM, Mrs. Madison's	313
WHIPT CREAM	221
WHITE CAKES	294
WHITE LADY-CAKE	301, 302
WHITE MINCE OF VEAL	426
WHITE PUDDING	230
WHITE SOUP, Chicken	22
WHITE SOUPS, Directions about	14
WHORTLEBERRIES, to prepare for Table	286, 387
WHORTLEBERRY PIE	257
WIGS, to make	289, 290, 297, 298
WILD DUCKS, to cook	152, 153
WINE CAKES	295
WINE JELLY	338
WINE OR BRANDY SAUCE, Liquid	240, 241
WINE, Oysters stewed with	63
WINE SANGAREE	337
WINE SAUCE	240
WINE SAUCE, Liquid	240, 241
WINE, to mull	420

	PAGE
WINE, to stew Oysters with	63
WINTER BREAKFAST, Bill of Fare for	400, 401
WINTER PARTY, REFRESHMENTS for	327
WINTER SQUASH, to cook	178
WINTER, to preserve Vegetables for Use in the	170–172
WINTER TURNIPS, to cook	177
WINTER USE, to preserve Butter for	201
WOODCOCKS, to carve	430
WOODCOCKS, to cook	160
YEAST, Bakers', to make	277
YEAST CAKES, to make	277, 278
YEAST DUMPLINGS	224
YEAST POWDER, Babbit's	452
YEAST, to make Doughnuts without	287
YEAST WAFFLES	290, 291
YELLOW LADY-CAKE	301
YELLOW SOUP	14
YELLOW, to color Fruit for preserving	342, 343
YELLOW TURNIPS, to boil	119, 120

THE END.

Popular Books Sent Free of Postage at the Prices annexed.

The Reason Why: General Science. A careful collection of some thousands of reasons for things, which, though generally known, are imperfectly understood. A book of condensed scientific knowledge for the million. By the author of "Inquire Within." It is a handsome 12mo volume, of 356 pages, printed on fine paper, bound in cloth, gilt, and embellished with a large number of wood cuts, illustrating the various subjects treated of. This work assigns reasons for the thousands of things that daily fall under the eye of the intelligent observer, and of which he seeks a simple and clear explanation.

EXAMPLE.
Why does silver tarnish when exposed to the light? Why is the sky blue? This volume answers 1,325 similar questions. Price $1 50

The Biblical Reason Why: A HAND-BOOK FOR BIBLICAL STUDENTS, and a Guide to Family Scripture Readings. By the author of "Inquire Within," &c. Beautifully illustrated, large 12mo, cloth, gilt side and back. This work gives Reasons, founded upon the Bible, and assigned by the most eminent Divines and Christian Philosophers, for the great and all-absorbing events recorded in the History of the Bible, the Life of our Saviour, and the Acts of his Apostles.

EXAMPLE.
Why did the first patriarchs attain such extreme longevity?
Why is the Book of the Prophecies of Isaiah a strong proof of the authenticity of the whole Bible?
This volume answers upwards of 1,400 similar questions. Price $1 50

The Reason Why: Natural History. By the author of "Inquire Within," "The Biblical Reason Why," &c. 12mo, cloth, gilt side and back. Giving Reasons for hundreds of interesting facts in connection with Zoology, and throwing a light upon the peculiar habits and instincts of the various Orders of the Animal Kingdom.

EXAMPLE.
Why do dogs turn around two or three times before they lie down?
Why do birds often roost upon one leg?
This volume answers about 1,500 similar questions. Price $1 50

The Corner Cupboard; or, *Facts for Everybody.* By the author of "Inquire Within." "The Reason Why," &c. Large 12mo, 400 pages, cloth, gilt side and back, illustrated with over One Thousand Engravings. Embracing Facts about—I. Things not generally known. II. Things that ought to be known. III. Things worth knowing. The "Corner Cupboard" is

A Complete Confectioner.	A Complete Lady's Book.
A Complete Cook.	A Complete Gentleman's Book.
A Complete Family Doctor.	A Complete Boy's Book.
A Complete Gardener.	A Complete Girl's Book.
A Complete Father's Book.	A Complete Master's Book.
A Complete Mother's Book.	A Complete Servant's Book.
A Complete Family Book.	A Complete Amusement Book.

A Friend at Everybody's Elbow in Time of Need.
It tells about the food we consume, the clothes we wear, the house we live in, and facts from the Arts and Sciences, as well as from Literature, Manufacture, Commerce, Anatomy, Physiology, the Garden and Field, the whole forming a Complete Encyclopedia of Useful Knowledge. Whether in the parlor or the kitchen, the chamber or the boudoir, at home or abroad, it may be very appropriately called the Family's Ready Adviser. Price $1 50

Epitome of Braithwaite's Retrospect of Practical Medicine and Surgery, Containing a condensed summary of the most important cases; their Treatment and all the Remedies, and other useful matters embraced in the Forty Volumes—the whole being alphabetically classified, and supplied with an addenda, comprising a Table of French Weights and Measures, reduced to English Standard—a List of Incompatibles—a complete List of the Muscles, their Origin, Insertion, and Uses, respectively—Explanations of the principal Abbreviations occurring in Pharmaceutical Formulæ—a Vocabulary of Latin Words most frequently used in Prescriptions, and a Copious Index. By WALTER S. WELLS, M. D. Two volumes, large 8vo., each volume containing over 900 pages of closely printed matter. Substantially bound in sheep. Price, for the Set $10 00

Send Cash Orders to **DICK & FITZGERALD, 18 Ann St., N. Y.**

Popular Books Sent Free of Postage at the Prices annexed.

The Sociable; or, *One Thousand and One Home Amusements.*
Containing Acting Proverbs, Dramatic Charades, Acting Charades, or Drawing-room Pantomimes, Musical Burlesques, Tableaux Vivants, Parlor Games, Games of Action, Forfeits, Science in Sport and Parlor Magic, and a choice collection of curious mental and mechanical Puzzles, &c., illustrated with nearly 300 Engravings and Diagrams, the whole being a fund of never-ending entertainment. By the author of "The Magician's Own Book." Nearly 400 pages, 12mo, cloth, gilt side stamp. "The Sociable; or, One Thousand and One Home Amusements," is a repertory of games and other entertainments, calculated for the use of family parties, the fireside circle or those social gatherings among friends and neighbors which pass away the winter evenings with so much animation and delight. It is impossible for any company to exhaust all the sources of irreproachable mirth and mutual enjoyment produced in this volume.
Price..$1 50

The Magician's Own Book; or, *A Complete Guide to the Art of Conjuring.*
Being a Hand-Book of Parlor Magic, and containing several hundred amusing Magical, Magnetical, Electrical, and Chemical Experiments, Astonishing Transmutations, Wonderful Sleight-of-Hand and Card Tricks, Curious and Perplexing Puzzles, Quaint and Entertaining Tricks and Questions in Numbers, Secret Writing explained, Sleights and Subtleties in Legerdemain, &c., together with all the most noted Tricks of Modern Performers. Illustrated with over 500 Wood Engravings, 12mo, cloth, gilt side and back stamp, 400 pages. Here is the whole process made simple of manipulating the cards, and performing Tricks with Sleight-of-hand. Price..$1 50

Parlor Theatricals; or, *Winter Evenings' Entertainment.*
Containing Acting Proverbs, Dramatic Charades, Acting Charades, or Drawing-room Pantomimes, Musical Burlesques, Tableaux Vivants, &c. By the author of "The Sociable," "The Magician's Own Book," "The Secret Out," &c. 12mo, gilt side and back, illustrated with descriptive engravings and diagrams.
Price..75 cts.

The Book of 1,000 Tales and Amusing Adventures.
Containing over 500 engravings and 450 pages. This is a magnificent book, and is crammed full of the narratives and adventures of travelers, the romantic tales of celebrated warriors, amusing stories in Natural History, besides a thousand things relating to curious trials, entertaining sports, pastimes and games. In this capital work we have our old friend Peter Parley again, and he tells his stories as well as ever. The book is worth ten times the price we ask for it. Price..$1 50

Ladies' Guide to Crochet. By Mrs. ANN S. STEPHENS.
Copiously illustrated with original and very choice designs in Crochet, etc., printed in colors, separate from the letter press, on tinted paper. Also with numerous wood-cuts printed with the letter press, explanatory of terms, etc. Oblong, pp. 117, beautifully bound in extra cloth, gilt. This is by far the best work on the subject of Crochet yet published. There are plenty of other books containing Crochet patterns, but the difficulty is, they do not have the necessary instructions how to work them, and are, therefore, useless. This work, however, supplies this much-felt and glaring deficiency, and has the terms in Crochet so clearly explained, that any Crochet pattern, however difficult, may be worked with ease.
Price..$1 25

10,000 Wonderful Things.
Comprising the Marvelous and Rare, Odd, Curious, Quaint, Eccentric, and Extraordinary, in all Ages and Nations, in Art, Nature, and Science, including many wonders of the world, enriched with hundreds of Authentic Illustrations. Edited by EDMUND FILLINGHAM KING, M. A., author of "Life of Newton." &c., &c. 12mo, cloth, gilt side and back. In the present work, interesting scenes from Nature, curiosities of Art, Costumes, and Customs of a by-gone period, rather predominate; but we have devoted many of its pages to descriptions of remarkable occurrences, beautiful landscapes, stupendous waterfalls, and sublime sea pieces. Price......$1 50

Send Cash Orders to **DICK & FITZGERALD, 18 Ann St., N. Y.**

Popular Books sent Free of Postage at the Prices annexed.

The American Boy's Book of Sports and Games.

A Repository of in and out door Amusements for Boys and Youth. Illustrated with nearly 700 engravings, designed by White, Herrick, Weir and Harvey, and engraved by N. Orr. 600 pp., 12mo. Extra Cloth, gilt side and back, extra gold, $3.50. Extra cloth, full gilt edges, back and side, $1.00. This is, unquestionably, the most attractive and valuable Book of its kind ever issued in this or any other country. It has been three years in preparation, and embraces all the sports and games that tend to develop the physical constitution, improve the mind and heart, and relieve the tedium of leisure hours, both in the parlor and the field. The engravings are in the first style of the art, and embrace eight full page ornamental titles, illustrating the several departments of the work, beautifully printed on tinted paper. The book is issued in the best style, being printed on fine, sized paper, and handsomely bound in extra cloth, with gilt side and back. The following will give an idea of its contents:

Part I—The Play-Ground; or, OUT-DOOR GAMES WITH AND WITHOUT TOYS. Including Games of Activity and Speed; Games with Toys, Marbles, Tops, Hoops, Kites, Archery, Balls; with Cricket, Croquet and Base-Ball.

Part II—Athletic and Graceful RECREATIONS. Including Gymnastics, Skating, Swimming, Rowing, Sailing, Horsemanship. Riding, Driving, Angling, Fencing and Broadsword.

Part III—Amusements with Pets. Comprising Singing and Talking Birds, Pigeons. Domestic and Aquatic Fowls, Rabbits, Squirrels, Mice, Guinea Pigs, Raccoon and Opossum, Dogs, Salt and Fresh Water Aquaria.

Part IV—Play-Room Games for RAINY DAYS. Including Round Games and Forfeits, Board and Slate Games, and Table and Toy Games.

Part V—Evening Amusements. Comprehending Comic Diversions, Parlor Magic, Tricks with Cards, Scientific Recreations and Puzzles.

Part VI—Mechanical and Miscellaneous AMUSEMENTS. Including Carpentry, Painting, Gardening, Postage Stamps and Fragments.

"Trump's" American Hoyle; or, Gentlemen's Handbook of Games.

Containing clear and complete descriptions of all the Games played in the United States, with the American Rules for playing them, including Whist, Euchre, Besique, Cribbage, All-Fours, Loo, Poker, Brag, Piquet, Écarté, Boston, Cassino, Chess, Checkers, Backgammon, Dominoes, Billiards, and a hundred other games. To which is appended an Elaborate Treatise on the Doctrine of Chances.

Reasons why the "American Hoyle" must be the Standard Authority for all Games played in the United States:

Because it is an American Book, prepared with great care, with the aid and counsel of a large number of the best players both amateur and professional, in this country.

The Rules, descriptions, definitions and technicalities are all simplified and adapted to the several games as they are actually played here.

Many of our games are peculiarly American, and cannot be intelligibly described except by an American who understands them, while those of foreign origin have become so changed by American modifications, as to make the European rules and descriptions as likely to mislead as to instruct.

In preparing this work the best or greatest weight of authority for each particular game has been taken upon disputed points.

The important games of Chess, Draughts, and Backgammon are illustrated with over 150 diagrams of games, problems and critical positions, all of which have been carefully played upon the board since the work was stereotyped, and nearly 100 errors (which appear in English Game Books and their American reprints) have been corrected.

All the games played in the United States, whether of home or foreign origin, are given as they are played by Americans at the present day.

12mo., 500 pages, cloth, gilt side and back, profusely illustrated. Price..**$2 00**.

Brisbane's Golden Ready Reckoner,

Calculated in Dollars and Cents, being a useful Assistant to Traders in buying and selling various sorts of commodities, either wholesale or retail, showing at once the amount or value of any number of articles; or quantity of goods, or any merchandise, either by the gallon, quart, pint, ounce, pound, quarter, hundred, yard, foot, inch, bushel, etc., in a easy and plain manner. To which are added, Interest Tables calculated in dollars and cents, for days and for months, at six per cent., and at seven per cent., per annum, alternately; and a great number of other Tables and Rules for calculation, never before in print. Bound in boards, cloth back. By WILLIAM D. BRISBANE, A. M., Accountant, Bookkeeper, &c. Price......**35 cts.**

Send Cash Orders to DICK & FITZGERALD, 18 Ann St., N. Y.

Popular Books sent Free of Postage at the Prices annexed.

Parlor Theatricals; *or, Winter Evenings' Entertainment.* Containing Acting Proverbs, Dramatic Charades, Acting Charades, or Drawing-room Pantomimes, Musical Burlesques, Tableaux Vivants, &c.; with Instructions for Amateurs; how to Construct a Stage and Curtain; how to get up Costumes and Properties, on the "Making Up" of Characters, Exits and Entrances; how to arrange Tableaux, etc. Illustrated with Engravings. Paper covers, price 30 cts. Bound in boards, cloth back, ... 50 cts.

The Parlor Magician; or, *One Hundred Tricks for the Drawing-Room*, containing an Extensive and Miscellaneous Collection of Conjuring and Legerdemain; Sleights with Dice, Dominoes, Cards, Ribbons, Rings, Fruit, Coin, Balls, Handkerchiefs, etc., all of which may be Performed in the Parlor or Drawing-Room, without the aid of any apparatus; also embracing a choice variety of Curious Deceptions, which may be performed with the aid of simple apparatus; the whole illustrated and clearly explained with 121 engravings. Paper covers, price 30 cts. Bound in boards, with cloth back .... 50 cts.

The Book of 500 Curious Puzzles. Containing a large collection of entertaining Paradoxes, Perplexing Deception in numbers, and Amusing Tricks in Geometry. By the author of "The Sociable," "The Secret Out," "The Magician's Own Book." Illustrated with a Great Variety of Engravings. This book will have a large sale. It will furnish Fun and Amusement for a whole winter. Paper covers, price .... 30 cts. Bound in boards, with cloth back .... 50 cts.

Book of Riddles and Five Hundred Home Amusements, containing a Choice and Curious Collection of Riddles, Charades, Enigmas, Rebuses, Anagrams, Transpositions, Conundrums, Amusing Puzzles, Queer Sleights, Recreations in Arithmetic, Fireside Games, and Natural Magic, embracing Entertaining Amusements in Magnetism, Chemistry, Second Sight, and Simple Recreations in Science for Family and Social Pastime, illustrated with sixty engravings. Paper covers, price .... 30 cts. Bound in boards, with cloth back .... 50 cts.

Parlor Tricks with Cards, containing Explanations of all the Tricks and Deceptions with Playing Cards ever invented, embracing Tricks with Cards performed by Sleight-of-hand; by the aid of Memory, Mental Calculation, and Arrangement of the Cards; by the aid of Confederacy, and Tricks Performed by the aid of Prepared Cards. The whole illustrated and made plain and easy, with seventy engravings. Paper covers, price.................................. 30 cts. Bound in boards with cloth back .... 50 cts.

The Book of Fireside Games. Containing an Explanation of the most Entertaining Games suited to the Family Circle as a Recreation, such as Games of Action, Games which merely require attention, Games which require memory, Catch Games, which have for their objects Tricks or Mystification, Games in which an opportunity is afforded to display Gallantry, Wit, or some slight knowledge of certain Sciences, Amusing Forfeits, Fireside Games for Winter Evening Amusement, etc. Paper covers, price............................... 30 cts. Bound in boards, with cloth back... 50 cts.

The Poet's Companion; *A Dictionary of all Allowable Rhymes in the English Language.* This is a Book to aid aspiring genius in the Composition of Rhymes, and in Poetical Effusions generally. It gives the Perfect, the Imperfect, and the Allowable Rhymes, and will enable you to ascertain, to a certainty, whether any word can be mated. It is invaluable to any one who desires to court the muses, and is used by some of the best writers in the country. Price .... 25 cts

Rarey & Knowlson's Complete Horse Tamer and Farrier, comprising the whole Theory of Taming or Breaking the Horse, by a New and Improved Method, as practiced with great success in the United States, and in all the Countries of Europe, by J. S. RAREY, containing Rules for selecting a good Horse, for Feeding Horses, etc. Also, THE COMPLETE FARRIER; or, *Horse Doctor;* a Guide for the Treatment of Horses in all Diseases to which that noble animal is liable, being the result of fifty years' extensive practice of the author, by JOHN C. KNOWLSON, during his life, an English Farrier of high popularity, containing the latest discoveries in the cure of Spavin. Illustrated with descriptive Engravings. Bound in boards, with cloth back.. 50 cts.

Send Cash Orders to **DICK & FITZGERALD, 18 Ann St., N. Y.**

Popular Books sent Free of Postage at the Prices annexed.

Live and Learn; A Guide for all who wish to Speak and Write correctly; particularly intended as a Book of Reference for the solution of difficulties connected with Grammar, Composition, Punctuation, &c., &c., with explanation of Latin and French words and phrases of frequent occurrence in newspapers, reviews, periodicals, and books in general, containing examples of one thousand mistakes, of daily occurrence, in speaking, writing, and pronunciation. 216 pages, cloth, 12mo. "Live and Learn" is a most useful book, designed as a guide to Grammar, Composition, and Punctuation. So few people speak or write really good grammar, and fewer still punctuate decently, that a book that informs them how to do so—and not only that indicates their faults, but shows them how they are to be corrected—cannot fail to be popular; there is not a person, indeed, who might not learn something from it. Price............75 cts.

Inquire Within, for anything you want to know. A book of Universal Knowledge, containing more than Three Thousand Facts for the People, and will give you correct information on every possible subject that you ever heard or thought of! Whether you may desire to make love to a pretty girl, or cook a dinner—to cure a sick friend or cut an acquaintance—to get up a dinner party or dine abroad—to play at cards, at chess, or any other popular game, or go to church—whether you wish to establish yourself in life according to the rules of etiquette, or live in a plain, genteel way—this is a book that tells how to do it. It is the most wonderful and valuable book ever printed. Price............................$1 50

The Secret Out; or, *One Thousand Tricks with Cards.* A Book which explains all the Tricks and Deceptions with Playing Cards ever known or invented, and gives, besides, a great many new and interesting ones—the whole being described so accurately and carefully, with Engravings to illustrate them, that anybody can easily learn how to practice these Tricks. This book contains, in addition to its numerous Card Tricks above described, full and easily understood explanations of some Two Hundred and Forty of the most curious, amusing, and interesting Sleight-of-Hand and Legerdemain Tricks ever invented, and which are illustrated by Engravings to make each Trick understood with ease. Illustrated by about 300 Engravings, and bound in a handsome gilt binding. It contains about four hundred pages. Price.................$1 50

Laughing Gas. An Encyclopædia of Wit, Wisdom, and Wind. By SAM SLICK, Jr. Comically illustrated with 100 original and laughable engravings, and nearly 500 side-extending Jokes, and other things to get fat on; and the best of it is, that everything about the book is new and fresh—all new—new designs, new stories, new type—no comic-almanac stuff. It will be found a complete antidote to "hard times." Price..............................25 cts.

Charley White's Joke Book. Being a perfect Casket of Fun, the first and only work of the kind ever published. Containing a full expose of all the most laughable Jokes, Witticisms, &c., as told by the celebrated Ethiopian Comedian, CHARLES WHITE. 94 pages. Price...................12 cts.

Black Wit and Darkey Conversations. By CHARLES WHITE. Containing a large collection of laughable Anecdotes, Jokes, Stories, Witticisms, and Darkey Conversations. Price..............12 cts.

Chips from Uncle Sam's Jack-Knife. Illustrated with over one hundred Comical Engravings, and comprising a collection of over five hundred laughable Stories, Funny Adventures, Comic Poetry, Queer Conundrums, Terrific Puns, Witty Sayings, Sublime Jokes, and Sentimental Sentences. The whole being a most perfect portfolio for those who love to laugh. Large octavo. Price...25 cts.

Fox's Ethiopian Comicalities. Containing Strange Sayings, Eccentric Doings, Burlesque Speeches, Laughable Drolleries, Funny Stories, interspersed with Refined Wit, Broad Humor, and Cutting Sarcasm, copied verbatim, as recited by the celebrated Ethiopian Comedian. With several Comic Illustrations. Price..12 cts.

Send Cash Orders to DICK & FITZGERALD, 18 Ann St., N. Y.

Popular Books sent Free of Postage at the Prices annexed.

That's It; or, *Plain Teaching.* By the author of "Inquire Within," "The Reason Why," "The Corner Cupboard," "Live and Learn," "The Biblical Reason Why," &c. Illustrated with over 1,200 Wood Cuts. 12mo, cloth, gilt side and back. We commend to the attention of parents, teachers, and friends of popular improvement, the recommendations which "That's It; or, Plain Teaching," has received from gentlemen well qualified to pronounce judgment upon the soundness of its moral tone, and the accuracy of the varied information contained in its pages. Every illustration is employed for a purpose, or a number of purposes, and is made, by numerous references, explanatory of things which, without such assistance, could only be imperfectly conceived. The work contains nearly 400 pages, and over 1,200 wood engravings, and forms one of the cheapest and most interesting books of elementary instruction ever published. Price..$1 50

Narratives and Adventures of Travelers in Africa. Illustrated with numerous fine Engravings, and containing a Map of Africa, on which the routes of Dr. Livingstone and Dr. Barth are accurately traced. Large 12mo, gilt back. An intense interest has recently been awakened, and widely extended, in regard to South Africa. Questions are, in consequence, frequently arising as to the character of its surface, its diversified tribes, its plants, and its animals; and the remarkable circumstances under which, after long concealment, they have been gradually disclosed to our view. The object of the present volume is to meet such inquiries by proper details, on the highest authority, abundantly interspersed with *true* stories of chivalric enterprise and heart-thrilling adventure. It respectfully solicits, therefore, the acceptance of all ranks, and of all ages. Price...$2 00

Duncan's Masonic Ritual and Monitor; *or, Guide to the Three Symbolic Degrees of the Ancient York Rite;* and to the Degrees of Mark Master, Past Master, Most Excellent Master, and the Royal Arch. By MALCOLM C. DUNCAN. Explained and interpreted by copious notes and numerous engravings. Although this work is a complete Ritual of the Symbolic and Chapter Degrees, and is also profusely illustrated with engravings of the Secret Signs and Grips, it is not so much the design of the author to gratify the curiosity of the uninitiated, as to furnish a guide to the younger members of the order, by means of which their progress from grade to grade may be facilitated. The " work " laid down in this book differs from any thing heretofore published. No Mason should be without it. Bound in Cloth. Price...$2 50
Leather tucks (Pocket-Book Style) with gilt edges..........................$3 00

The Lady's Manual of Fancy Work. A Complete Instructor in every variety of Ornamental Needle-Work, with a list of materials and hints for their selection; advice on making up and trimming. The whole being a complete Lexicon of Fancy Needle-Work. By Mrs. PULLAN, Editor of the London and Paris Gazette of Fashion, and Director of the Work-table of Frank Leslie's Magazine, Illustrated Magazine, &c., &c. Illustrated with over 300 Engravings, by the best artists, with eight large pattern plates, elegantly printed in colors, on tinted paper. Large octavo, beautifully bound in fine cloth, with gilt side and back stamp. There is no imaginable species of Fancy Needle-Work, Knotting, Knitting, Netting, Lace-Work, Embroidery, Crochet, &c., &c., which may not be found fully illustrated in this volume; and here are complete instructions for the inexperienced, from the pen of one of the ablest of needle-women of the present age. Price..$2 00

Anecdotes of Love. Being a true account of the most remarkable events connected with the History of Love in all Ages and among all Nations. By LOLA MONTEZ, Countess of Landsfeldt. Large 12mo, cloth. These romantic and surprising anecdotes really contain all of the most tragic and comic events connected with the history of the tender passion among all Nations and in all Ages of the World. It is precisely the kind of book which a man will find it impossible to relinquish until he has read it through from the first to the last chapter. And besides the exciting love histories embraced in this volume, it really contains a great deal of valuable historic lore, which is not to be found except by reading through interminable volumes. Price....................$1 50

Send Cash Orders to DICK & FITZGERALD, 18 Ann St., N. Y.

www.ingramcontent.com/pod-product-compliance
Lightning Source LLC
Chambersburg PA
CBHW051849300426
44117CB00006B/329